TERROR
OUT OF
ZION

TERROR OUT OF ZION

Irgun Zvai Leumi, LEHI, and the Palestine Underground, 1929–1949

by
J. Bowyer Bell

St. Martin's Press, New York

This book was written under the auspices of the Institute of War and Peace Studies, Columbia University

Copyright © 1977 by J. Bowyer Bell
All rights reserved.
For information, write:
  St. Martin's Press
  175 Fifth Avenue
  New York, N.Y. 10010
Manufactured in the United States of America
Library of Congress Catalog Card Number:
ISBN: 312-79205-0

Library of Congress Cataloging in Publication Data

Bell, J. Bowyer, 1931-
  Terror out of Zion.

  Bibliography: p.
  Includes index.
  1. Jewish–Arab relations—1917–1949. 2. Irgun
Zvai Leumi. 3. Lohame herut Yisrael. 4. Israel-Arab
War, 1948–1949. I. Title.
DS119.7.B382   956.94'04   75-26172

Published simultaneously in U.K. by St. James Press
For information, write:
  St. James Press Ltd.
  3 Percy Street
  London WIP 9FA

Unless otherwise indicated, all photos are courtesy of the Jabotinsky Archives and Library

For Virginia Oliver Bell, 1892–1972, who had a mother's misguided optimism that eventually I would settle down to something substantial. While Jewish revolutionaries are probably not what she had in mind, I hope that when this comes to her attention it will be regarded as substantial, in size if nothing more.

CONTENTS

FOREWORD

What now seems a very long time ago, I became quite innocently involved in Middle East matters while pursuing quite conventional spoors in military history. It then seemed to me, on most limited evidence, that the Irgun Zvai Leumi, the militant Zionist underground army, had a disproportionate effect on Palestinian events, so much so that I considered at some later date focusing on that one small aspect of Middle Eastern history. When, however, the opportunity arose, I discovered that there had been very little disinterested investigation of the Irgun. Many of the available conventional sources were in Hebrew, and most of the former members—clearly the most fruitful source—lived, naturally, in Israel. Since I did not really want to learn Hebrew or live for an extended period in Israel, I turned my attention to another set of contemporary revolutionaries, the Irish Republican Army, who spoke a relatively comprehensible variant of English and lived somewhat nearer to hand.

In Ireland I discovered similarities in the experience of the IRA and the Irgun sufficient to warrant an extensive research proposal. Under the auspices of the Harvard Center for International Affairs, with the aid and comfort of Tom Schelling, in 1968 I began to investigate all those who revolted against the British from 1944 until the end of empire at Aden. Later a further chapter had to be added on Ulster, where my Irish friends resurfaced as has been their wont for generations. Thus I finally arrived in Israel to interview the old members of Irgun and LEHI, the Stern Group. Many of them were hospitable and charming. I developed a special interest in the Palestine underground, for they were also articulate and had been most efficient. This had seldom been the case with the underground, where the articulate are often irrelevant, and, more often than not, incompetence is all but institutionalized. The result was that I spent too much time on the Irgun and in Israel over the next year or so. And when the time came to write one case study of many, it was only with great anguish and a cruel hand that I cut down the chapter on the Irgun. All those splendid adventures, amusing old war stories, and the horror and terror of the underground which had no real part in academic analysis ended on the cutting room floor. I noted to my indefatigable agent, Ollie Swan, that I would only have to double the chapter to have a book—not that I had time for an Irgun book. Soon thereafter Tom Dunne of St. Martin's Press agreed that it might, indeed, make a book, even if I had to postpone beginning it until after my annual tour of small wars, coups, and basement bombs. So the book, like Topsy, just growed—far longer and in far greater detail than I had blithely assumed during the course of a quite splendid editorial lunch.

What evolved out of the extended series of interviews in Israel, England and elsewhere was an authoritative but hardly definitive work on a most neglected aspect of Zionism—at least in English. All the old views, personal vendettas, frozen postures and outraged indignation collected over generations of political feuding have tended to obscure the role of the Revisionist Zionists. The orthodox version of David Ben-Gurion, the Jewish Agency, Haganah and others has largely dominated the written word, especially in the diaspora, where the dissidents are relegated to a minor role as terrorists and the unsavory and unproductive policies of the orthodox hidden away. It appears that Irgun-LEHI were considerably more important than common wisdom would allow. Their analysis was often far more accurate than that of the recognized institutions, and their relative present obscurity—not to mention their deserved reputation as a terrorist group—has been a conscious rewrite of history. The orthodox view of Irgun-LEHI has only begun to erode under disinterested scholarly attack and the shifting tides of Israeli political fortunes. Thus, as an account of the adventures of the underground, this book is in a small way revisionist history—with a small "r" of course, since as an innocent Episcopalian with slightly liberal leanings and a bias in favor of efficiency, I have no niche in the jungle of Zionist politics.

Many who have been kind and helpful will be disappointed that I have strayed from a reality they took such pains to reveal. Memory is selective; and, over a generation, a careful, if often unconscious, filtering process goes on by necessity, since those dimming adventures have great present import. The Middle East abounds in myths, and they are often not too distant from reality. Even today what happened at Deir Yassin—massacre or military operation, or at the King David Hotel—intentional murder or no, has a considerable importance to people not then born. In the heel of the hunt, I have written my way, and hence take all the blame for error and misrepresentation, for following too readily the devices and desires of my own heart rather than the testimony of the witnesses to the real deeds.

I would like to thank all those witnesses whose names are hidden away at the end of the book, thus separating them as far as possible from any responsibility. In a few cases special thanks are warranted: to Sir John and Lady Shaw—after its years in gestation I suspect Sir John doubts the existence of this work; to Dr. Ely Tavin, who seemingly commutes from Israel to New York, thus making himself readily available for consultation and query; to Dr. Yehuda Ben-Ari of the Jabotinsky Institute in Tel Aviv, whose patient and scholarly advice has been most welcome, as has the assistance of the Institute secretary, Edna Zamir; to Lee Winograd, who on my last trip to Israel was more than kind; and finally to Jerachmiel Romm. Several individuals have over the years been kind enough to send me written comments: Sir John Shaw, David Niv, Eliahu Lankin, Yehuda Ben-Ari, Samuel Katz, Nathan Yellin-Mor, Yisrael Eldad, and Menachem Begin. Tavin and Yellin-Mor visited me at Harvard, where the former was involved in a seminar that included an Irish counterpart.

Finally, in New York, my work on a variety of revolutionary topics has been made possible by a grant from the Ford Foundation, where Craufurd Goodwin and Alessandro Silj have always been more than helpful. The Institute of War and Peace Studies has been a warm and effective base. Its director, William T. R. Fox, is genial, concerned and ever on call; Anna Houri is a paragon of charm and efficiency, and everyone is delighted that I like to do my own typing. Tom Dunne of St. Martin's has been an ideal editor, although he may have destroyed my liver in efforts to be supportive.

J.B.B.

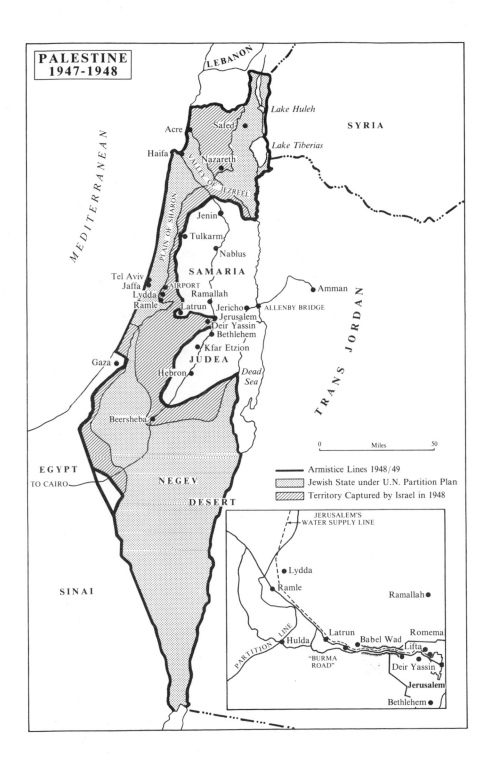

PALESTINE
1947-1948

LEBANON

SYRIA

Lake Huleh

Acre   Safed

Lake Tiberias

Haifa   Nazareth

MEDITERRANEAN

VALLEY OF JEZREEL

Jenin

Tulkarm

Nablus

PLAIN OF SHARON

SAMARIA

Tel Aviv
Jaffa   AIRPORT   Ramallah   Amman
Lydda   Jericho
Ramle   Latrun   ALLENBY BRIDGE
                        Jerusalem
                        Deir Yassin
                        Bethlehem

TRANS JORDAN

Kfar Etzion

Gaza   JUDEA

        Hebron   *Dead
                      Sea*

Beersheba

0   Miles   50

EGYPT
TO CAIRO   NEGEV

DESERT

SINAI

——— Armistice Lines 1948/49

▦ Jewish State under U.N. Partition Plan

▨ Territory Captured by Israel in 1948

JERUSALEM'S
WATER SUPPLY LINE

Lydda

Ramle   Ramallah

PARTITION LINE

                              Romema
        Latrun   Babel Wad   Lifta
Hulda   Deir Yassin
"BURMA
ROAD"   **Jerusalem**

                    Bethlehem

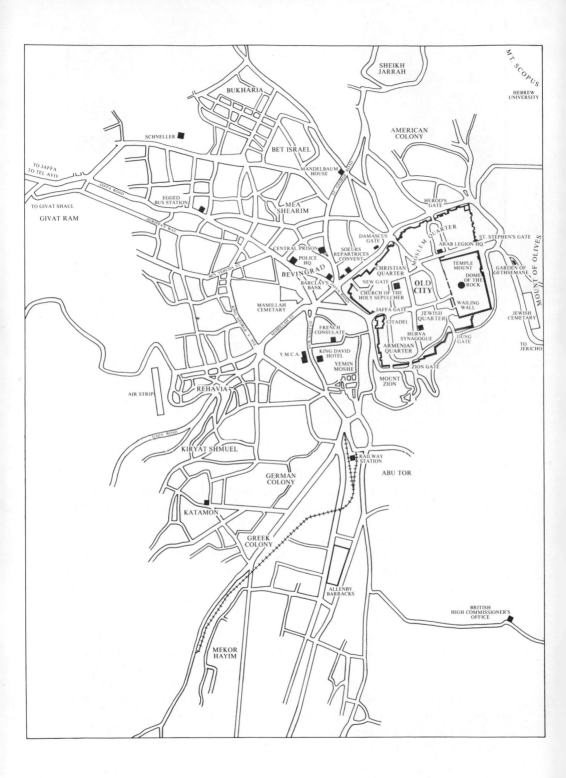

PROLOGUE:
The Massacres of 1929

Be'dam va'esh Yehuda nafla!
Be'dam va'esh Yehuda takum!

In blood and fire Judea fell!
In blood and fire Judea will arise!

On Saturday afternoon, at three o'clock, August 17, 1929, a group of small boys were in the midst of a scratch football match at the Maccabi grounds near Mea Shearim in the New City of Jerusalem. The field lay between the headquarters of the British police and the Bukharian quarter next to an Arab garden. The football bounced free, over the boundary line and into an Arab tomato garden. One of the players, a young Sephardic Jew named Abraham Mizrachi, dashed off to retrieve the ball. None of the boys paid close attention to Mizrachi. Suddenly, an Arab was near him, one no different from the others, and then he was gone. Mizrachi lay bleeding among the tomato plants, stabbed by the mysterious Arab apparently without warning, without a word. At eight-thirty the following Tuesday evening, Mizrachi died at the Government hospital. The Arab disappeared, never to be found, but his motive was obvious—Mizrachi was a Jew and vulnerable. In mid-August 1929, in Jerusalem, that was sufficient for many Arabs.

After the several quiet years following Arab attacks on Jews in 1920 and 1921, there had been a growing intercommunal tension. In 1928 a particularly abstruse wrangle occurred over the right of Jews to introduce a screen separating men and women during Yom Kippur services at the Wailing Wall. The British police had intervened and removed the screen during the services. This outraged the religious Jews, who resented the sacrilege, as well as the militant Zionists, who were certain that the Mandate Authorities were increasingly evading the commitment to encourage a Jewish Homeland in Palestine. Religious scuffles over minute points of privilege and arcane practices had long troubled Palestine. The quarrels over control of bits and pieces of the Church of the Holy Sepulcher were legendary—with repairs prohibited the very existence of the Church was endangered. The Wailing Wall incident engendered rumor and willful provocation within the Arab community. Tales were spread that the Jews

1

were out to seize the wall—al-Buraq al-Sharif in Arabic—which formed part of the base of the Dome of the Rock and Aqsa Mosque. As time and imagination combined to exaggerate Jewish intentions, many Arabs believed that the Jews intended to seize these holy places. There was little doubt among Jews that various Arab nationalist leaders, in particular Haj Amin al-Husseini, the mufti of Jerusalem and chairman of the Arab National Committee, were the source of the rumors and that the British intended to tolerate the situation.

As a result, two days before the stabbing in the tomato patch, on the Jewish fast of Tisha b'Av, members of Betar, the militant Zionist youth group, had demonstrated. The day of mourning for the destruction of the Temple was used as an opportunity to display Zionist pride and resentment. The blue and white flag was flown, nationalist songs were sung, and, not unexpectedly, the Arabs were provoked. All during the winter of 1928–1929 the Arabs had been inflamed by rumors, passionate speeches given in the mosques, and a growing conviction that the Jews were determined to destroy their holy places and that Al daula Maana—"the government is with us." On August 16, there was an influx of aroused Arabs into Jerusalem, where many were further excited by a speech of Hassan Abou Seoud, sheik of the Aqsa Mosque. Many Jews feared that matters would not end at the edge of the tomato patch. After the boy died on August 20, difficulties arose concerning the funeral route: the British security forces did not want another incident. On the morning of the funeral, when the Betarim attempted to force their way through the police cordon along the Jaffa Road, the police charged the procession, batoned both mourners and Betarim, and injured twenty-four Jews, one seriously. The Arabs, hearing of the police charge, the bloodied Jews and the coffin abandoned in the street now *knew* that Al daula Maana.

On August 22 the Arab newspaper *Falastine* said there was, indeed, more to come.

> In Jerusalem there is great excitement. The atmosphere is tense, and it is apprehended that tomorrow when many fellaheen assemble for prayers in Jerusalem a substantial answer will be given to these incidents.[1]

The day this veiled warning appeared, thousands of fellaheen (villagers) began drifting into Arab Jerusalem, ostensibly for the Moslem holiday the next day. Most were armed with a motley collection of archaic weapons, ancient swords, elaborate daggers, wooden staves, fighting clubs and even a few guns. On the next day in the Old City, the mosques were jammed as the devout heard further exhortations to defend the faith against the Jewish threat: the enemy was at the gates. At 12:30 P.M. on Friday, August 23, the first mob poured out of the Jaffa Gate in search of Jews. Thus began a cycle of violence that soon spread across Palestine.

All day Friday the Arab mobs attacked the Jewish quarters. In the surrounding hills they attacked isolated Jewish settlements. Whole Arab villages turned on their Jewish neighbors, looting, burning and killing. The Jews felt that British protection, even in Jerusalem, was grudgingly given, slow to arrive and often ineffective. They also thought that if the underground Jewish militia Haganah, organized into self-defense patrols, had not rushed from one crisis point to the other, the slaughter would have been far greater. As it was, they claimed, too many Jews had been murdered and maimed because of British caution.

The garbled news of the fighting spread beyond Jerusalem across Palestine, creating deep apprehension among the Jews, who had been uneasily watching the growing signs of hysteria and unease in their Arab neighbors. They were afraid that the British would not protect them until too late, that if they were isolated or helpless such protection would be an invitation for the mobs to swarm down on them, shouting al-Daula maana.

Few Jewish settlements were as isolated, as vulnerable, and as tempting as Hebron. There had been Jews in the town for hundreds of years, a deeply religious Haluka community focusing on an ancient Hebraic past and a distant messianic future rather than on the immediate Zionist present. They had not bought and transformed Arab lands nor displaced Arab labor. For centuries their routine had changed little. Bilingual, largely Sephardic, the six hundred Jews lived mainly in an ancient ghetto behind heavy walls, usually in harmony with their thousands of Arab neighbors, whom they closely resembled. During the troubles in 1920 and 1921, there had been no violence in Hebron, although everyone knew that some Arabs had been tempted by the Jews' isolation and the prospect of looting. Still, restraint prevailed, and Hebron had remained calm.

In 1928 and 1929 the intercommunal tension was obvious. Even the most devout Jews perceived the level of Arab hostility. There were rumors, hints, strange glances, far-off ripples made by the Mufti and his friends. On the Thursday before the fighting in Jerusalem, Aref el-Aref, the Arab governor of Beersheba, had spoken in the mosque at Hebron. The Jews heard that he had insisted the government was with the Arabs. The otherworldly Jews of Hebron reluctantly had to accept the real world, the barely muted excitement in the town, the danger of a pogrom. Still, as before, Hebron might be spared. Then, Friday morning, villagers armed with swords and staves began appearing in the streets. Arab friends told the Jews of armed gangs. The rumor was that the men intended to go up to Jerusalem, but Jewish anxiety would not be stilled. A delegation led by Rabbi Jacob Joseph Slonim and Rabbi Frank, representing both the Ashkenazi and Sephardic communities, sought out the Arab governor for reassurance. Abdullah Kardos told them, "There is no fear of anything happening. The British government knows what it has to do."[2] While cheered by this news, the Jews also knew that in Hebron "the British government" consisted of R. O. Cafferata, assistant district superintendent of police, plus a few Arab constables and medical officers.

On their return the delegation found that not all of the Arabs had gone to Jerusalem as rumored. The streets were still filled with young men brandishing sticks and sabers. Most Jews stayed behind closed shutters to wait out the troubles. The Arab mob, enraged by a rumor from Jerusalem that Jews were killing Arabs, began to stone the Yeshiva school. Inside Knesset Yeshiva Israel two young men were deeply engaged in their own studies, still largely unaware of the ugly temper of the town. One of the young men, Samuel Rosenholtz, heard the tumult and rushed out the front door. The mob surged forward, struggling to get to him. He was stabbed, his blood pouring over the steps, and died almost immediately. Elsewhere, Dr. Kitayon of the Hadassah hospital was stoned by another group of Arabs and rescued by two public health officers. At about the same time another young man named Axelrod was stabbed and wounded. Most of the Jews did not know what was happening except that a pogrom seemed in progress. In their anxiety many crowded into Rabbi Slonim's house, where there was an atmosphere of hysteria. Suddenly Rabbi Slonim and his daughter rushed into the street and began running back and forth between his house on the Beersheba Road and his son's house on the Jerusalem Road. The surprised and scattered Arab mob began howling and throwing stones as the couple twisted and turned. The few constables who had rushed up were hard put to keep off the Arabs and persuade Slonim to go back in his house. Instead, clutching his daughter, he harangued the constable in charge and remained the target of a continuing shower of stones until he was escorted to safety. Grudgingly, the Arab crowd straggled off to learn the news from other parts of the town. Friday ended with no more violence. Superintendent Cafferata felt that Hebron had weathered the storm: the boil had burst, the volatile mob dispersed. He again reassured the Jews that the worst was over, but they could only hope this was true.

The next day, August 24, the Hebron Jews were now thoroughly alarmed and stayed indoors, peering out as clumps of armed Arabs again gathered in the streets. Soon after 7:30 A.M. they were again joined by fellaheen intent on going to Jerusalem but willing to wait in Hebron. At 8:15 a mob began stoning an isolated Jewish house on the Russian Building Road at the north end of town. Cafferata had been wrong, and his few constables and officers were armed only with staves. With the Arabs simultaneously assaulting Jewish houses all over town, the small force protecting the Jewish ghetto was a fragile defense. In the meantime, the mob arrived at the Heichel house and began stoning the windows and door.

The police arrived, but not in time. Foolishly, in a hysterical panic, two young men came out the front door, shrieking and waving their hands. They ran directly into the mob, and were repeatedly stabbed. A few police managed to disperse the Arabs, who, inflamed by the two murders, repeatedly risked the batons of the six constables. All over town the Arabs were attempting to break into Jewish houses with crowbars, sledgehammers and battering-rams. Though driven back twice, on the third attempt a mob broke down the back door of Rabbi Epstein's house and rushed into the courtyard. They found one old man in a bathroom and stabbed him to death.

Another mob began sacking the shops, Arab as well as Jewish, in the suq. Finally, Cafferata armed the police. He ordered the crowd to disperse, and when they did not he fired into them. In front of the Mizrachi Hotel and on the Jerusalem Road, police fire at last dispersed the mob, clearing the streets. By then, however, those who had sacked the suq were storming the ghetto, slashing and stabbing as they went. The police rushed after them. Stumbling up a narrow tunnel passage, Cafferata discovered an Arab cutting off a child's head with a sword. His arm was lifted for the second cut when he saw the superintendent and tried to run. Cafferata shot him in the groin, then continued deeper into the ghetto. He suddenly saw Constable Issa Sherrif from Jaffa in mufti standing over a woman who was covered with blood. Issa Sherrif had a dagger in his hand and appeared stunned at the unexpected sight of Cafferata. He ran into a nearby room and tried to bolt the door, explaining in Arabic, "Your Honor, I am a policeman." Cafferata shot and mortally wounded him before he could bolt himself in. Fifteen minutes later the ghetto was clear. It was 10:30. There were several more attacks on Jewish homes, easily dispersed by the police firing into the crowd, but for two hours the Arabs had been able to slaughter freely. Sixty-four Jews were hacked to death and another fifty-four wounded. Women, children, and old men were stabbed and slashed, often repeatedly. Cafferata and the police had killed eight Arabs and wounded ten others. Soon after noon, reinforcements arrived from Jerusalem, and an hour later the entire Jewish community was moved either to the police barracks or the hospital.

Some Jews had been overlooked. A number were hustled away from the edges of the mob by police or medical officers. Many were saved by Arab friends. One woman found room for seventeen Jews. The families of Moshe Masha, Borowsky, Schnauirsohn and Rabbi Slonim were saved by their neighbors. Nassar Eldine tried but failed to protect the Jews in his house. The 484 refugees in the police barracks and the public health department hardly knew what had happened.

Our condition in the police house was ghastly. . . . There was no water. One Englishman took pity on us and brought us a can of water. There was no toilet . . . We begged to be allowed to telephone or telegraph to Jerusalem. We were not permitted. We said, "We will telegraph only that we are well." But the governor only wanted us to wire, "Hebron all right."[3]

Hebron was not all right. The survivors believed the Jews had been butchered because for two hours the police refused to fire on the mobs. As Rabbi Slonim noted, he lived because he had been saved first by God and then by his neighbor the Arab landlord. Most felt the same. The Jews of Hebron had been betrayed by the British, by Cafferata, who had waited too long to fire on murderers. If Arab violence had spent itself in Hebron, this was not true elsewhere; if Hebron provided evidence of British collusion in murder, there would be more to come.

On August 24 there was also trouble with Arab gangs from Nablus and Beisan. All during the next week, Arab irregulars and Bedouin brigands attempted to overrun isolated Jewish settlements in north and south. On Sunday, August 25, fighting and sniping spread along the ill-defined boundary between Jaffa and Tel Aviv. The Jewish suburbs of Jerusalem continued to come under attack, and the police always seemed slow to respond. As soon as the British withdrew, the Arabs returned. Finally, the security forces insisted that these vulnerable Jewish districts be evacuated. To the Jews it seemed that the innocent were being punished. On August 24, 25, and 26, there was serious fighting in Haifa, and on August 27 near Acre. Most incredible of all, on August 29, the butchery of Hebron was repeated in Safed. After six days of rioting and slaughter throughout Palestine, after the arrival from Malta and Egypt of British reinforcements, after repeated requests by the local British commander for reinforcements, troops were finally dispatched too late to prevent another massacre and the destruction of a substantial part of the Jewish quarter. Perhaps Cafferata had been foolishly sanguine; perhaps he had been honestly cautious in firing into the mob—the Jews of Hebron did not believe this, but there could be no British excuse for Safed.

The British authorities were distressed and indignant that the Jews could not realize their difficulties in maintaining order, the necessity for care and caution, the reality of British honesty and good faith. Sir Walter Shaw came to the Mandate and fashioned one of what was to be a long and futile series of command papers. He concluded that the violence had been "neither provoked, premeditated, nor directed against the British administration. It was from the beginning an attack by Arabs on Jews for which no excuse in the form of earlier murders by Jews was established." Finally, the root cause of the violence was the Arabs' disappointment of their political and national aspirations and fear for their economic future.[4] The British authorities could hardly be to blame. Everyone had done his best. Cafferata was recommended for a decoration. The memorial of the Hebron survivors, refugees in Jerusalem, presented matters in a somewhat different light.

The Government . . . did not fulfill its duty and provide protection for its peaceful and defenseless charges. The governor, Abdullah Kardos, and Commander Cafferata . . . deprived us of the means of appealing for help and defense, betrayed us with empty promises, and gave the murderers and robbers their opportunity. The police . . . did not fulfill its duty, and behaved with contemptible baseness.[5]

The massacres of 1929, costing the lives of 133 Jews and 116 Arabs, cast a long shadow. There had been trouble in Palestine before, but the events of 1929 confirmed certain trends within Zionism, engendered certain new directions, and produced dreadful evidence for those whose faith in Britain had begun to erode. The fanatical Arab mobs, composed of illiterate and simple peasants stirred up by evil men, were not seen as the major factor in the massacres even if they had looted, burned, and murdered. Behind the Arab mobs in Hebron and Safed and the 133 dead, lurked the interests of imperial Britain, publicly committed to Zionist aspirations but demonstrably pursuing other policies for other purposes. British perfidy aside, the long August week had demonstrated the woeful lack of Zionist preparation for a military defense. If Jews were not again to be vulnerable to mobs and brigands, there would have to be changes. The more militant Jews of Palestine began to regard the traditional Zionist policy of havlaga—self defense—with skepticism, began to doubt the traditional British connection, and started to seek other forms and directions more appropriate for the new Jew, who had come to Palestine to build a nation. Out of this appraisal would arise a new underground military organization, Irgun Zvai Leumi.

NOTES

1. Maurice Samuel, *What Happened in Palestine* (Boston: Stratford, 1929), p. 64.

2. Ibid., p. 118.

3. Ibid., p. 121

4. Great Britain, Colonial Office, Palestine Commission, *The Disturbances of August 1929*, vols. 1-3 (London: H.M.S.O., 1930).

5. Samuel, p. 121–122.

PART 1

THE RISE AND DECAY OF THE IRGUN:
The Jabotinsky Years

Betar—
From the pit of decay and dust
Through blood and sweat
A generation will arise to us,
Proud, generous, and fierce.

—Vladimir Jabotinsky

There had always been Jews in Jerusalem and Palestine, almost, perhaps, from the time of Abraham and Isaac. But for over a millennium, they were men of prayer, mystics, immigrants who came to die in the Holy Land, biblical scholars living in the narrow ghettos of Hebron, Safed, Tiberias, and the Old City of Jerusalem. Through the long centuries of Turkish suzerainty they maintained a Jewish presence, but their Arab neighbors rarely felt either provoked or endangered.

At the beginning of the nineteenth century, much began to change in the Middle East. In March 1799, Napoleon called upon the Jews to "rally under their flag and restore Jerusalem of old."[1] It was not until a half-century had passed that Napoleon's seed took root, for most Jews in western Europe anticipated their assimilation in the new nation states as Germans or Englishmen of the Hebrew persuasion, while the millions trapped in the pales of eastern Europe sought only to survive. The uncertain currents of Jewish nationalism thickened and spread as a result of the disappointments of the western Jews and the fears of the eastern. In 1840 the Damascus Blood Libel occurred when seven Jews were arrested and tortured with the obvious connivance of French Franciscans—an atavistic return to the medieval persecutions. In eastern Europe, particularly in Russia, conditions worsened. There was a pogrom in Odessa in 1871; and ten years later, after the assassination of Alexander II, another wave of pogroms swept across Russia. Finally, the Dreyfus case in 1894 and 1895 revealed deep-seated anti-Semitism in a supposedly rational French society. Captain Dreyfus was condemned on trumped-up evidence, and for many Jews France was condemned as well. The alternative to assimilation or forbearance was found by some in Napoleon's almost forgotten appeal.

Zionism—a term not coined until 1886 by the Austrian journalist Nathan Birnbaum—coalesced around several complementary ideas. One was the revival of Hebrew as a living language, not simply a tongue of ritual. Men like Chaim Nachman Bialik and Eliezer Ben-Yehuda produced not only a contemporary literature but a contemporary language adapted to everyday use. There would be a Hebrew language for a Hebrew state. Then the idea of a return to Palestine arose. Joseph Salvador suggested in France in 1853, "A new state will be founded on the shores of Galilee and in ancient Canaan. The Jews will return through the combined forces of historical memory, persecution in various countries, and the puritan sympathy of biblical England."[2] The idea of a return took on a practical, pragmatic garb. The political obstacles eventually could be surmounted by establishing agricultural colonies. The Jews would truly return to the land. Leon Pinsker thus fashioned a concept of "practical Zionism": "The Jews must become a nation once more, a people with its own land."[3] And so the first immigrants arrived in a parched and barren land, where malaria was endemic, the swamps undrained, the land eroded, and the 250,000 Arabs miserable. Some came with faint hope of a distant state, but all came possessed of a vision.

The Arabs soon realized that the new Jews were different. They had come not to pray but to work, not at the end of their lives but at the beginning. They wanted to farm the land, to transform it. The early settlers of the first Aliya (wave) faced dreadful obstacles between 1882 and 1903. They toiled and often died in malarial swamps or on the edge of the sand dunes. To the Arabs these Jews were the "children of death". They watched their sacrifice without understanding and with limited sympathy. Gradually, as a result of grinding labor, the contributions of sympathizers, especially Baron Edmond de Rothschild, and a will to persist, the Jews fashioned a few groves, some green fields, a scattered presence, and engendered the hostility of the Arabs. In 1891 an Arab delegation of notables petitioned the Turkish sultan—the first protest against the Zionist presence. It was a presence still fragile, closely wedded to the soil, dependent on foreign support, a tiny base for the grand dreams of the new Jews. The Arabs saw their swamps turned into groves and their desert into vineyards. Their land had been purchased and transformed; their labor and virtues ignored; their country infested. When they contemplated the Arabs at all, the Zionist settlers could find no clash in aspirations, no cause for anguish or protest. They neither understood the Arabs nor realized their anxiety about the tiny Jewish presence.

The distant forces that would soon enlarge the small Jewish community were at work far away, beyond Arab vision and in most cases beyond Zionist control. In Russia the pogroms began again; those bloody attacks on innocent and defenseless Jews became all but institutionalized. While many Russian Jews sought salvation in one or another variant of the new revolutionary philosophies—anarchism, Marxism, populism, or syndicalism—others were attracted by the Zionist option. The Dreyfus affair revealed that anti-Semitism was prevalent everywhere; it was simply more virulent in Russia. Covering the trial for his Viennese newspaper, Theodor Herzl found his life transformed, and, as a result, Zionism was as well. Herzl accepted the need for a Jewish state, and in *Der Judenstaat* argued that the problem was national and the solution political. He sought such a solution not by linguistic revivals, promises of redemption, or new agricultural settlements, but by diplomatic initiatives. When these aborted, he regrouped in August 1897 and created a new organisation. Over two-hundred delegates to the Zionist Congress met in Basel for three days and established the World Zionist Organization. Herzl felt that the first great, practical step had been taken.

> If I had to sum up what happened at the Congress of Basel, I would say that I founded the Jewish state. This would provoke universal laughter today. But perhaps in twenty years and certainly in fifty, it will be there for all the world to see.[4]

Despite the evolution and maturation of the World Zionist Organization and the establishment of further institutions to strengthen immigration to Palestine, Herzl's life became an endless, futile, hectic trip back and forth across Europe, as one grand scheme after another collapsed. The Turks listened to his offers to trade gold for the scrap of desert called Palestine and did not reply. The British considered Cyprus, then Egyptian Sinai, and finally Uganda as a site for Jewish colonization. That some Zionists also considered these at least as a way station to Palestine indicates the vast differences in aspirations, ideals, and programs contained within the new World Zionist Organization. Herzl saw all of the powerful who would receive him, from the hated Russian Interior Minister von Plehve to the pope. He met opposition, sympathy, or polite boredom in his endless interviews with the powerful, but he could never discover the right combination of national interest, the magic formula that would permit the creation of what to him was an obvious necessity. On July 3, 1904, after eight years of unrelenting activity, he died.

The Zionists soldiered on, torn by the arguments of the practical and the political, divided into a left, Poalei Zion, and a religious right, Mizrachi, on either side of the general Zionists in the center. Outside, in the diaspora, the concept of Zionism was under heavy attack from the left—the Bund or the Yiddish Unions—and by the comfortable, who felt their assimilated status threatened by the many eastern Jews agitated by Zionist ideas. Some contributed to the practical Zionists who planted new fields but drew back before the uncertain complications that political Zionism would introduce. And political Zionism had already added a new and contradictory factor to European politics. Everyone knew that the Zionists were anti-Russian, since the movement was illegal there and many of its leaders were avidly sought by the tsarist police; many also assumed they were pro-German. The Turks, even the Young Turks, who were aided in their revolt in 1908 by the Jews of Salonika, had little sympathy for Zionist maneuvers. In fact, in each capital, including Berlin, there were those who saw Zionists simply as agents of their enemies. At the beginning of the twentieth century, Europe was increasingly frozen into blocs, a maze of alliances and alignments, and it was impossible to be friends with everyone. Increasingly, the Zionists suspected they might become the enemy of all. While the investment of the practical Zionists had produced visible results, for the political Zionists this was insufficient to transform reality. It was impossible to create a state orange grove by orange grove.

In Palestine the small but steady immigration of the second Aliya, largely from eastern Europe, by 1914 reached a total of eighty-five thousand Jews: the Yishuv were 12.5 percent of the population of Palestine, in forty-three rural settlements. The first kibbutz, Degania, was founded in 1909 and became the model for others. On the dunes to the north, beyond Jaffa, a new all-Jewish city was established. Tel Aviv was growing fast, and soon the names of the founding Zionist fathers appeared on the new street signs: Ben-Yehuda Street, Rothschild Boulevard, Pinsker Street. The children of death had become a pioneer memory, but the prospects of transforming the Jewish presence into a Jewish state still seemed dim.

In fact, in the decade after Herzl's death and even beyond, those Zionists who actively sought a state were undoubtedly in a minority. Even in Palestine only half the Jews were Zionists, and many of these had only the most narrow and parochial interest in the land—it was a site of an agricultural colony, not a basis for a nation state. In a real sense they missed the logic of Zionism, the power of their slowly expanding presence. They ignored both the local Arabs, who knew the Zionists better than they knew themselves, and the political dreamers. After 1908 the Young Turks' grip on "southern Syria" began to loosen. Palestinian Arabs began to protest the presence of the new Jews. The old they had tolerated and detested, but the new bought land and displaced Arab workers. The Jews had come to work, not to be landlords, and defended their new groves with vigor. The anti-Zionist newspaper *Al-Karmel* was established in Haifa—the way of the intellectual; but the raids on Jewish settlements escalated—the way of the brigand. Usually the Jews paid no attention to the editorials of *Al-Karmel*, defended their settlements with the Hashomer home guard (founded in 1917), and ignored the Arabs. The belief remained general that there need be no clash of destinies if an accommodation, perhaps even an alliance, could be fashioned. So the practical Zionist continued to build roads, dig canals, and establish schools, while in Europe the advocates of a political strategy sought a great-power patron.

Certainly the day of the Turk was drawing to a close. For a century the Ottoman Empire had been in decay, its vital signs fading. Egypt had gone, and Greece, the Balkans, and Cyprus. The two Balkan wars in 1912 and 1913 revealed the decay of Turkish vitality. To many, collapse seemed but a matter of time. If there were to be such serious and extensive changes, the problem for the Zionists was to find an ally who would support a Jewish state. The Turks' old enemy, Russia, was obviously a hopeless case; and despite Herzl's hopes, the idea of any Turkish regime, weak or strong, abetting Zionism seemed now to most a nonstarter. A favorite of some was Great Britain. There was long-standing British interest in Zionism, and under the influence of Chaim Weizmann it had remained keen. Britain obviously had highly significant imperial concerns in the eastern Mediterranean—a Jewish ally might not be unattractive and was certainly romantic. Then too, if there were to be a general war, it seemed likely that the Triple Entente—Britain, France, and Russia—would be opposed by an increasingly pro-German Turkey. If there were to be change, a tacit alliance with one of the powers capable of imposing change became highly desirable. This became Weizmann's and many others' central purpose. They were, however, in a minority in their choice of allies. Too many Jews hated Russia—any enemy of the tsar was a friend of the Jews.

The opening of the war in August 1914 created chaos in Zionism. The vast majority of the members saw Russia as the great oppressor, dreamed of a tsarist defeat, insisted on support for the Central powers. Two key Zionists, however, persisted in their different vision which insisted that an Allied victory would bring in its train a Jewish state. In England Chaim Weizmann sought with mixed results in the early war years to interest the government in issuing some tangible evidence of British support for Zionist aspirations. His ally was Vladimir Jabotinsky, one of the most remarkable and charismatic figures produced by Zionism.

Jabotinsky, born in Odessa, was a most atypical eastern European Jew. He was poet, orator, and linguist, fluent in Russian, German, Italian, French, Spanish, English, Polish, Yiddish, and Hebrew. He wrote originally in all, translating from each, slipping from one to the other. He had studied first in Switzerland and then in Italy. In Rome he had read law, studied the Risorgimento and political theory, and learned the local dialect. He began to write poetry in Italian. He sent his impressions in Russian to an Odessa newspaper under the byline Altalena. On his return to Russia, the new pogroms of 1903 and 1904 thrust him into politics. With Meier Dizengoff he formed a self-defense movement in Odessa. His conversion to Zionism brought to the movement a man of startling talents, an orator with the gift of tongues, a prolific writer, a man of searching and unconventional vision who soon attracted devout disciples and—given the nature of Zionist politics—adamant opponents. The pragmatic Zionists suspected his elegant ideas, his vast generalizations, his politics, and his charismatic appeal: they preferred specific programs to mere personality. No one could deny, however, that after he became a committed

Zionist the movement was never again quite the same—some argued that this was not necessarily a virtue. Thus Jabotinsky's pleas for an Allied victory that would bring with it a triumph for the hated tsar appalled his Zionist colleagues in Russia but did not altogether surprise them.

Like Weizmann in England, Jabotinsky's first attempt to acquire leverage for Zionism was a project to gain some sort of charter from the French premier, who showed minimal interest. Since Weizmann was at least having some success in Great Britain, Jabotinsky proposed the formation of a Jewish Legion within the British Army. The idea obviously had multiple attractions: if the Zionists were the allies of the victors, a place, however small, might be found for them at the peace table; and for the first time since A.D. 135, there would be a Jewish army, a certain asset in the uncertain future. There was some encouragement and considerable opposition from anti-Zionist Jews, from Jewish emigrants from Russia, and from certain quarters within the British establishment. The British did agree to a Zion Mule Corps; but Jabotinsky all but a traitor in the eyes of eastern Jewry, insisted on a real legion and persisted in his arguments. Eventually, in February 1918, Jabotinsky's persistence was rewarded, and the Jewish Legion—the 39th Regiment of the Royal Fusiliers—paraded in London on the way to the Middle East and the conquest of Palestine. An enthusiastic Jabotinsky served first as a noncommissioned officer and later as a lieutenant, but his propaganda and the legion's military success were overshadowed by Weizmann's diplomatic triumph.

On November 2, 1917, in the form of a letter to Lord Rothschild from the British Foreign Office, signed by Arthur James Lord Balfour, the Zionists at last had a public commitment to a Jewish homeland by a great power.

Foreign Office
November 2nd, 1917

Dear Lord Rothschild,

I have much pleasure in conveying to you, on behalf of His Majesty's government, the following declarations of sympathy with Jewish Zionist aspirations which has been submitted to, and approved by, the cabinet.

"His Majesty's government view with favour the establishment in Palestine of a national home for the Jewish people, and will use their best endeavors to facilitate the achievement of this object, it being clearly understood that nothing shall be done which may prejudice the civil and religious rights of existing non-Jewish communities in Palestine, or the rights and political status enjoyed by Jews in any other country."

I should be grateful if you would bring this declaration to the knowledge of the Zionist Federation.

Yours sincerely,

ARTHUR JAMES BALFOUR[5]

This was a curious British mix of self-interest: gratitude for Weizmann's crucial development of a process for making the acetone needed by the munitions industry; imperial consideration; hope for Jewish support of the war, particularly in America; post-war imperial consideration; biblical romanticism; and the complex interplay of personal interests and ambitions of those in power—all coalesced to produced the Balfour Declaration. The future of Palestine, however, was far from determined. Not only was the war still to be won—the Turks with German aid had not proven as feeble as expected—but also there existed other less public agreements on the future of the Middle East. In 1915 and 1916, in the Sykes-Picot Agreement, the British and French had sketched out spheres of interest. On October 24, 1915, Sir Henry McMahon, British high commissioner in Cairo, had also promised help to Hussein Ibn-Ali, sherif of Mecca, in his bid to restore the caliphate in return for his aiding the British war effort. The McMahon Letter and the Sykes-Picot Agreement were sufficiently vague so the British could deny that they contradicted the Balfour Declaration. As the war progressed and such secret diplomacy became less secret (the new Bolshevik regime in Russia published choice selections from the tsarist diplomatic archives), the Zionists accepted the Balfour Declaration as a beginning.

During 1918 there was a Zionist scramble to build up assets for the ultimate peace conference. President Woodrow Wilson's concern with small nationalities seemed to be a net gain. Jabotinsky's legion and the Zion Mule Corps were a positive contribution to the British war effort, even if the spectacular although militarily marginal campaign of Lawrence of Arabia got the headlines. British victories in the Middle East were made far easier with the creation by Aaron Aronsohn of a Jewish intelligence network, Nili, in Palestine. In 1916 Aaronsohn was brought to London where he, too, influenced prominent British figures. In certain quarters in London, the existence of a Jewish homeland as a British client in the Middle East seemed to be of imperial advantage, as the variously ambitious powers maneuvered for gain before the peace conference. There were, of course, Zionist liabilities as well. Many Britons, particularly the forces in the Middle East, favored the Arabs over the Jews. The French had an interest in southern Syria, and even the Italians wanted something as a reward for their participation in the war. In any case, the Zionists came out of the peace negotiations with what they wanted, what the British seemed to want, what the French permitted, and—most surprising of all—what the Arabs apparently felt did not deny their interests. In the last case Emir Feisal, son of Hussein, exchanged letters with Weizmann and Felix Frankfurter advocating Arab-Jewish collaboration.

The form of postwar Palestine was defined in a League of Nations Mandate to Britain, accepted at the San Remo Conference in April 1920, confirmed by the League Council on July 24, 1922, and effected in September 1923. The Mandate reflected the commitment made by Balfour:

> Whereas the Principal Allied Powers have also agreed that the Mandatory should be responsible for putting into effect the declaration originally made on November 2nd, 1917, by the said Powers, in favour of the establishment in Palestine of a national home for the Jewish people, it being clearly understood that nothing should be done which might prejudice the civil and religious rights of existing non-Jewish communities in Palestine, or the rights and political status enjoyed by Jews in any other country; and
>
> Whereas recognition has thereby been given to the historical connection of the Jewish People with Palestine and to the grounds for reconstituting their national home in that country . . .[6]

Long before the British control shifted from military occupation, often enforcing Turkish law, to the Mandatory Authority, it had become abundantly clear that matters could not be sifted out as neatly as some optimistic Zionists had hoped. In the first place, the language of the Balfour Declaration and the League Mandate was vague—what exactly was a national home, and what was the responsibility of the British to encourage it? Much more to the point, the Palestinian Arabs had demonstrated a belief that the Jewish presence in Palestine did indeed prejudice their rights.

Arabs everywhere in the Middle East were disturbed at the Anglo-French maneuvers that limited their independence, established mandates or vassal states, and prevented a unified Arab nation. In Palestine the Arabs made known their displeasure by attacks on Jewish settlements. To Jabotinsky's dismay his legion had been swiftly disbanded by the British, so that in 1919 he had to reorganize a Jewish defense from scratch. In the meantime, the settlements had to depend on their own resources to repulse the brigands and local raiders. In upper Galilee four Jewish villages came under heavy Arab attack in February 1920. One of the most notable of the new militant Zionists, Joseph Trumpeldor, who had lost an arm during the Russo-Japanese war and had fought at Gallipoli with the Zion Mule Corps, was killed at Tel Hai village. At Passover the Arabs rioted in Jerusalem, but the Haganah managed to hold off all Arab forays into the New City. The toll for the Passover pogrom was five Jews dead and two hundred wounded. More incredible in Jewish eyes, Jabotinsky was then arrested for violating Article 58 of the Ottoman code, which forbade arming the inhabitants of the empire with the intention of provoking rape, pillage, devastation, and assassination. He received a fifteen-year sentence and was imprisoned in the Acre crusader fortress. Although the sentence was appealed, along with ninteen others, and overturned ten weeks later, considerable damage was done to British credibility. The Arab nationalists whom the Jews thought responsible for the riots, Haj Amin al-Husseini and Aref, had been swiftly pardoned.

Matters hardly improved the following year. The new civilian high commissioner, Sir Samuel Herbert, a Jew, named Haj Amin al-Husseini as the new mufti of Jerusalem. The mufti was not tamed by the honor, and continued to agitate against the Jews. In May 1921, there were severe riots in Jaffa and further raids on Jewish settlements. This time 47 Jews were killed and 146 wounded, while the police and British military killed 48 Arabs and wounded 73. The subsequent investigation by Sir Thomas Haycraft, chief justice of Palestine, concluded that the Arabs reacted spontaneously out of their fear of mass immigration, and, if blame were to be placed, it must fall on various Zionist statements and the arrogance of the young Jewish settlers. The innocent victims apparently brought their ills upon their own heads. Worse, the British government in London presented firm evidence that such Arab violence paid off.

In June 1922, a new "Statement of British Policy in Palestine" was issued by the colonial secretary, Winston Churchill. It appeared to be the first step backward from the Balfour Declaration—a redemption in depreciated currency. Then on September 16, the British gave the land across the Jordon to Emir Abdullah to compensate him for his inability to snatch a more satisfactory prize during the various postwar maneuvers. This unilateral revision, accepted by the League but not by the more militant Zionists, reduced the Palestine Mandate to ten thousand square miles—nearly half of it desert. Still, most of the rich land was on the West Bank, and after the 1921 pogroms the practical Zionists set to work once more to build a Jewish national home. There was much to be done since the war years had been hard on the Yishuv. Immigration had dwindled to a trickle and then stopped. The Jewish population declined. The Turks treated the Zionists as potential enemies, disbanded the Hashomer watchmen and harassed the Jews. The practical Zionists, as usual, felt that the primary task in the face of both Turkish and Arab violence and British reneging was to continue as before creating Zionist facts.

For Jabotinsky and his friends such Zionist facts would be insufficient. Much was needed: a real Jewish army, not the illegal Haganah that had fallen under control of the Histadrut labor organization; real immigration in great numbers—forty thousand a year for twenty-five years— instead of the drift out of the Mandate that was not even being replaced by new arrivals—in 1927 two thousand new immigrants arrived and five thousand Jews left; and there must be a state, a Jewish commonwealth, on both sides of the Jordan. Basically he wanted more; he wanted it swiftly; he had no time for caution, dogmatic revolutionary theories, or the anguish of advocates of assimilation in the diaspora. Once out of Acre, where he spent his time planning, reading, and writing poetry (including a hymn to the slain Trumpeldor), Jabotinsky began to organize for that future. In 1921 he founded the Union of Revisionist Zionists. He crisscrossed the eastern European diaspora, rounding up support. In 1923 in Riga, he formed the first unit of a new youth movement, Betar, the name a Hebrew anagram for Trumpeldor, Hero of Tel Hai. In March 1924, the Revisionist Zionists opened a small office in Berlin, and by September there were over fifty new groups throughout the diaspora.

Over the next decade Jabotinsky created an alternative Zionism, a current viewed with great suspicion by the Zionist left; for his new Revisionist movement appeared to be garbed in the clothes of European fascism and dedicated to principles of the antirevolutionary right. In point of fact, the ideology and program of Revisionism were much less important than its posture. Jabotinsky created an atmosphere, an attitude, rather than a new ideology.

As a young man, Jabotinsky had favored nationalization of the means of production and the inevitable class struggle, but gradually he drifted away from the socialists and communists whose internationalism he found inimical to Zionism. His aide in Austria, Robert Stricker, focused Jabotinsky's attention on the works of the Viennese writer Josef Popper-Lynkeus, who had suggested that there need not be total equalitarianism in a future society, but only a guaranteed minimum—beyond that individual initiative would be rewarded. Jabotinsky took the idea and translated it into Hebrew as a welfare state but not an equalitarian society. Popper-Lynkeus thus made his only significant convert. The Zionist left attacked Jabotinsky not, however, because of these rather conventional proposals but because he advocated national compulsory arbitration of labor disputes and opposed the use of trade unions as political instruments. The Zionist left, of course, really did not need to seek out such specifics, for they distrusted the whole direction of Revisionism.

Jabotinsky proposed to create a Jew who would not fit easily, if at all, into the doctrinaire categories of the left, now committed to international socialism adapted for Zionist purposes to Palestinian conditions. Jabotinsky proposed first Monism, the single ideal of the Jewish state—as yet none of the orthodox and official Zionists had called specifically for a state; second Legyon, military training; third Giyus, national service in the homeland; and fourth and most important Hadar, the transformation of the ghetto Jew, the Jew of the Pale, into an aristocrat. Of all the forms and programs initiated by Jabotinsky, the Betar most nearly reflected these ideas in action.

Spreading out from Riga, Betar filled a previously unarticulated need for many young eastern European Jews. They entered a world of solemn processions, parades, banners and flags, rituals, patriotic poetry, uniforms, and training camps. They came from homes reeking of fatalism and suffering; they came, like the goyim, handled weapons, fired on rifle ranges, learned to fly, march and sail. Betar training camps were dotted throughout Europe. A naval training station was established in Cittavechia in Italy. Young men came to Palestine to work without wages, to build as well as to defend, to serve and to sacrifice. Their elders might place major emphasis on diplomacy and the shifts of great powers, but the Betarim foresaw Zion redeemed through a blood sacrifice. Hence the ideas of Abba Achimeir, leader of the visionary Brit Habiryonim, found favor; he stressed not action but purpose—the amount of blood shed was the sole criterion of a revolution's validity. The poems of Uri Zvi Greenberg, filled with death and sacrifice, became immensely popular, as did Jabotinsky's hymn to Trumpeldor and especially his "Shir Betar", the Hymn of Betar.

Betar—

From the pit of decay and dust
Through blood and sweat
A generation will arise to us,
Proud, generous, and fierce.
Captured Betar
Yodefet and Masada
Will arise in strength and majesty.

Hadar—

A Jew even in poverty is a prince
Though a slave or a tramp.
You were created the son of a king,
Crowned with David's crown,
The crown of pride and strife.

Tagar—

Despite every beseiger and enemy
Whether you rise or fall
With the torch of revolt
Carry a fire to kindle: "No matter."
Because silence is filth
Give up blood and soul
For the sake of the hidden beauty
To die or to conquer the mount.

Yodefet, Masada, Betar

Obviously, this poetry of blood sacrifice, the uniforms and monster parades, the endless speeches of the dramatic and charismatic Jabotinsky looked very much like fascism to the Zionist left. To a degree they were right: such ideas molded in such forms had become vastly popular throughout Europe and beyond. The Blueshirts in Ireland, Silvershirts in Brazil, the Bund in New York, and the Iron Guard in Rumania—these movements attracted men as diverse and as talented as Mosley in Britain, Ezra Pound in Italy, and Count de la Rocque in France. Much of fascism was, of course, tainted with anti-Semitism, but this was not invariable. More to the point, Jabotinsky's group differed profoundly in that he had modeled Betar on the mass, democratic movements of national liberation like the Czech Zokol; and he had no time for the lurid fantasies, perverted myths, and obsessional and xenophobic conspiracy theories of so many fascist movements. While the Betar could hardly be likened to the Boys' Brigade or the Sea Scouts, the movement did have much of the idealism of those far more apolitical groups. However defined, there could be no denying that Betar had a tremendous attraction, and, placed under Jabotinsky's control, it was a most powerful instrument.

Exactly how the instrument was to be used in conjunction with the more conventional Revisionist political party, which still participated in the World Zionist Organization, was less clear. Although Jabotinsky differed considerably with the orthodox—or was seen to do so—on the future structure of the Jewish national home, his strategic interpretation was not that great. Certainly he placed less stress on planting orange groves, although the Betarim on arrival in Palestine were to be pelugot, farmers and laborers, during their two-year period of service. Basically Jabotinsky, like the others, believed that the British government was fundamentally in favor of Zionism, had both a moral and political commitment to the Jewish national home as well as imperial interests complementary to Zionism. There was really no alternative to the British connection, but Jabotinsky was willing to recognize that London might have to be pressured. Even after the apparent British security lapses in 1920 and 1921, the massacres in 1929, the shift away from full support, he was still Anglocentric in forecasting the future of Zionism. After 1929, however, he and many others in the Revisionist movement began, ever so gingerly, to shift their ground.

In the meantime, despite the apparent collusion of the British authorities in the massacres of 1929, Jabotinsky, if not all the Revisionists, remained focused on the British connection, thereby ignoring the Arabs. Ignoring or at least discounting them was easy because Arab society and politics in Palestine appeared to the more sophisticated Jews as alien and also primitive. This was surely true: Arab alliances and alignments were based on blood ties, old feuds, the capacity to reward and punish, the demands of pride, and the fear of shame. There were no real political parties in Western terms, only shifting coteries of men linked by common enemies. The major political division was between the Husseini and the Nashashibi, not between left and right, or even past and future. For decades there had been no unions, clubs, or front groups, and most of all no trace of contemporary ideologies, even in debased form. Most of the Arabs lived hard and parochial lives, tied to village and land. They sought a protector or an intermediary, had only a dim grasp of the ideas of the world beyond the furrow. Even in the urban warrens of the Old City or Jaffa, most Arabs were innocent of all but inherited prejudice. The Arab masses proved apathetic until roused to hysteria. Then they could be moved to brief, frenzied action, only to collapse once more into lethargy. They formed the stuff of mobs, not political parties.

The educated Arabs, if conservative, were concerned with the Koran; if not, it would be poetry and the law. There was little of the Levantine stimulation of Beirut, the cosmopolitan atmosphere of Alexandria and Cairo, or even the nationalist ferment of Damascus. For over a century southern Syria had been a backwater within the Turkish empire. There was, of course, a scattering of intellectuals, lawyers, doctors, and merchants who had been to Baghdad or had treated with the Turks, students attracted by the ideas of the West, and the conventionally and conservatively educated Islamic leadership. In Zionist eyes, however, Arab leaders, if noticed at all, were primitive fanatics without ideas, filled with ambition and venom, manipulated by more sophisticated players. This was demonstrably not the case, but certainly comforting to the Zionists, who preferred a British conspiracy to an Arab antagonist. Their prime antagonist, the mufti of Jerusalem, made cunning use in 1929 of what appeared to be Arab weakness: the limits of the mob, the paucity of any but orthodox ideas and prejudices, the power and accomplishment of the Zionists, and the bias of the British. The fellaheen might not grasp the subtler points of Marx or Locke, but they would defend the holy places from the infidel, would strike out in jealousy and despair at the Jewish usurper, and were told that the government was with them. And so the mufti made his point, bloody but effective, traditional and primitive—the Jews could discount it at their own risk. Yet the Zionists believed the British were at fault, the Arabs were manipulated, the Jews were murdered by proxy against the real imperial interest of Britain.

In subsequent years, when the Arab-Israel conflict had become one of the most intractable and dangerous aspects of the contemporary world, it would be difficult to grasp just how little presentiment the Zionists had showed. Certainly up to the Balfour Declaration and somewhat beyond, there seemed to be a feeling that Palestine, however defined, was largely empty, that the Arabs who were there—miserable, ill fitted for the modern world, diseased, and dirty—would either benefit by the Zionist presence or would leave to find a niche elsewhere in the vast Arab lands. Remedial steps were taken to reduce the potential for violence among the landless fellaheen, who were sold out by the effendis and displaced by the concentration of land in fewer hands (including Zionist), and the rising anti-Zionism in Palestine was minimized. The orthodox Zionist view that accommodation was possible had been confirmed by the Weizmann-Feisal and Feisal-Frankfurter letters. If that opportunity had slipped away, another would sooner or later reappear. Only Jabotinsky's circle doubted an Arab accommodation. The orthodox Zionists knew that the future could not be built on injustice. David Ben-Gurion, a dedicated and talented leader of the Zionist left, for example, insisted in 1918 that there would never be a population transfer and in 1925 that there must be a real effort "to find the way to the hearts of the Arab people."[7] Thus, certain of their own intentions, they could not see where Zionism would lead. They could explain away the protests of the notables, the editorials in newspapers, the brigands and snipers, the riots, the troubles of 1920 and 1921, the massacres of 1929, the agitation in the Arab capitals, the anger all about them. The trouble resulted from outside agitation, the fanaticism of the misguided, the manipulation by certain British Arabists, the residue of Islamic xenophobia, and perhaps the tactical errors of the Zionist presence that could with good will be erased.

No matter the weight of blame and the degree of responsibility to be allotted, there could be no denying that the Haganah were quite unprepared for the 1929 massacres. They were stretched to the limit in both Jerusalem and Tel Aviv, where the Jewish quarters had to be defended by volunteers armed only with staves. The settlements, too, had to depend either upon their own resources, often insufficient, or the arrival of the British, usually delayed. There was no coherent plan of defense, few readily available trained men, a lack of arms. Many, including many of the Haganah commanders, felt that changes had to be made to prevent a similar disaster. The Haganah was neither Jabotinsky's overt force nor a covert defense militia drawn from the Yishuv, but the armed wing of the Zionist left. The Haganah had become an integral part of the Histadrut—an ineffectual part according to many, especially the Revisionists. As a result discussion began among many Haganah commanders that led to the formation of a second Haganah, Haganah-bet, (also called Irgun Yemini or Irgun-bet) under the command of Avraham Tehomi, former commander of Jerusalem, open to all except members of the Communist party. Although all varieties of political opinion were reflected in the membership, members of Betar, General Zionists and the national religious Mizrachi party were especially attracted. Tehomi was known for his militancy as well as for his feud with the more conventional Zionists, who feared he planned a Haganah takeover. He soon recruited new members, especially from among the graduates of the Betar military school who had fought outside Haganah control in 1929.

At first, however, Haganah-bet was tiny: three hundred members and a handful of old arms. There was a central committee, Merkaz, that oversaw the staff, enlistments, supplies, and finances, and a three-man staff responsible to Tehomi. One of the first steps of the new commanders was to seek additional arms in Europe. Tehomi later even undertook this mission personally, traveling to Finland to purchase Suomi machine guns. Other arms were smuggled into the Mandate in odd lots; some were purchased or stolen locally. Many of the new volunteers were asked to supply their own pistols. In three years there was a remarkable change: the three hundred members increased to three thousand; there were training schools in Jerusalem, Tel Aviv and Haifa. There were naturally political problems as well as military ones for the Revisionists, and Jabotinsky became increasingly concerned that the Betarim volunteers gave first loyalty to Haganah-bet. Ultimately and reluctantly, in December 1936, Tehomi signed an agreement that Haganah-bet would not be used against Revisionist interests. This satisfied Jabotinsky, if not Tehomi. By then events beyond the question of Haganah-bet loyalty were increasingly occupying the attention of the Zionists.

Zionist relations with Great Britain continued to decay. In 1931 a new white paper, based on the reports of the Shaw Commission and Sir John Hope Simpson, was published by the colonial secretary, Lord Passfield (Sidney Webb). The Zionists and their British allies were stunned to discover that the report urged that immigration and land purchase be restricted. The atrocities at Hebron and Safed were rewarded. Denunciation of the Passfield Report was so bitter and widespread that the Labour prime minister, Ramsay MacDonald, already beset with political and economic problems, hurriedly dispatched a letter to Weizmann on February 13, 1931, assuring him that the terms of the Mandate would be fulfilled. For the Arabs this became the Black Letter, and their triumph turned to ashes. For the Jews the exchange only gave rise to renewed suspicion of British motives, British intent, and British justice. The Labour cabinet managed to alienate everyone, a maneuver that their Conservative opponents would in time repeat. Increasingly Palestine, like Ireland, seemed to destroy British political reputations without subsequent British advantage.

When the seventeenth World Zionist Congress met in Basel in 1931, the Revisionists had 21 percent of the delegates, a very considerable showing after only six years of organizational work, often in the face of the most bitter opposition. To a degree the Revisionists benefited from a rising wave of militancy, both in Palestine and the diaspora. In 1931 for the first time in seventeen years, Moshe Segal of the Betar blew the shofar before the Wailing Wall, violating a British restriction which sought to soothe Arab sensibilities at such an intrusion beneath their holy places. Also in 1931, to protest the Passfield report, hundreds of Jews refused to be counted in the census, and went to jail instead. And for the first time, a Jew, Avraham Selman, denied the validity of the British courts: Britain, he said, was an alien occupier. Selman stood alone, however, and was imprisoned for five months for what the cautious saw as a foolish gesture. In Basel, too, the Congress took no dramatic steps, forged no new path as Jabotinsky urged, although there was a vote for a resolution calling for "intensive colonization"—Article 6 of the Mandate. Jabotinsky insisted on more. He felt that Britain had taken the wrong road, that a parting of the ways might be at hand. In a speech delivered in Yiddish at Warsaw on December 28, 1931, he pointed out the grave dangers for all concerned if Britain persisted.

> England is no longer inspired by her old lust for building and leading. And what we ask of the English is, indeed, this lust and resolution, the capacity for more courageous, more creative action, which is the indispensable prerequisite for the establishment of a colonization regime with the object of carrying the Mandate into reality. . . . If conditions remain as they are, there will come into being, in Zionism, a new form of movement which will take all things into account. The effect of this situation will, no doubt, be that it will become as uncomfortable for England to rule Palestine as it is for the Jews of Palestine to be ruled by her. All this is liable to cost our people a great deal of further suffering; but I am afraid we will have to pay for England's action in Palestine. That action threatens to drive the Jewish masses . . . along a dangerous road. English agencies now seem to be engaged [in the] systematic galvanization of pan-Islamic fanaticism in its most medieval and reactionary forms . . . threatening not only for Jewish settlers in Palestine, but also the whole of Europe's colonial system. . . . England may soon have to render an account for this shortsighted and dangerous gamble with the world's security, conducted under her aegis.[8]

It was not a particularly auspicious moment for such a program. The world was slipping deeper into depression, and a combination of factors, including the exchange regulations of most central European countries, began to dry up immigration to Palestine. In 1929 5,269 Jews arrived in the Mandate, in 1930 4,994, and in 1931 only 4,075. Then, just as the founding fathers of Zionism had foreseen, the Jews, without a land of their own, were everywhere vulnerable. Anti-Semitism, endemic in eastern Europe, arrived in Germany in a particularly virulent form with the advent of Hitler as chancellor. Although there would be many twists and turns before Nazi Germany decided on a final solution, the *Endlösung,* to the "Jewish problem," world Jewry was all too familiar with Hitler's views. No one could foresee extermination, and for years a large number of German Jews could not accept the thought of emigration. From the very first, however, a steady stream of them began to immigrate to Palestine. Many were not Zionists and some expected to return; they had no interest in Hebrew and little in the Jewish national home. German policy soon encouraged Jewish emigration by legal harassment—taxes, expropriation, professional restrictions—and by condoned intimidation. Although many of the Jews driven from Germany did not come to Palestine, others did. In 1932 immigration was 9,553, double that of the previous year, and after that the flood came, the fifth *Aliyah*: 30,327 in 1933, 42,359 in 1934, 61,859 in 1935. Jabotinsky had his massive immigration, but also new problems as well as some familiar ones.

In 1933 the mufti once more organized demonstrations against the tide of Jewish immigration. The mosques became seats of incitement, and unsavory propaganda once more circulated in the bazaars. This time, however, the disturbances were directed against the British administration, condemned for the retreat from the Passfield Report and blamed for the sudden surge in Jewish immigration. For the Revisionists 1933 marked their split with the World Zionist Organization, the recognized institutions of the Yishuv, and Weizmann and Ben-Gurion. The crisis came most unexpectedly when the brilliant Zionist organizer Chaim Arlosoroff was murdered on a lonely beach near Tel Aviv. Arlosoroff was chief of the political department of the Jewish Agency and an articulate opponent of the ideas of the Revisionists, even though some of his less public predictions—ultimate armed struggle—differed little from those of Jabotinsky. As he lay dying, Arlosoroff said his assassins were not Jews; Captain Harry Rice, deputy inspector general of the Palestine Police, nevertheless arrested four Betarim. Each was identified by Mrs. Arlosoroff: Avraham Stavsky, Zvi Rosenblatt, Yehuda Mintz, and Abba Achimer. At once a wave of indignation swept Palestine. The guilt of the four was assumed by the orthodox Zionists, and a campaign of vilification was undertaken in the press and on street corners. Revisionists became pariahs. At the trial of Achimer, there was evident collusion between witnesses and the police, and some of the evidence was faked. At Mintz's trial Mrs. Arlosoroff was caught in a contradiction and accused of lying by the court. The case was dismissed. Rosenblatt, branded by Mrs. Arlosoroff as the actual killer, was found to have been addressing a meeting in a different part of Tel Aviv at the time of the murder and was acquitted. Avraham Stavsky who Mrs. Arlosoroff said had held the flashlight for Rosenblatt, was convicted and sentenced to death on June 10, 1934. The trial had so many apparent irregularities that the Palestine appeals court overturned the verdict and set Stavsky free. By then the Arlosoroff case was a cause célébre: it polarized Zionist opinion within and without Palestine and assured the expulsion of the Revisionists.

Clearly, the depth and fervor of the orthodox Zionists' reaction—the bitter indignation they husbanded for decades, refusing even after the establishment of the state of Israel to reopen the matter, despite new and conclusive evidence of Stavsky's innocence—cannot be explained simply by the facts of the case. The Zionists, especially the Zionist left, wanted to believe the worst, hated and feared the Revisionists with a passion they could no longer conceal. Jabotinsky to them was little better than a cryptofascist, the Betarim his militaristic bodyguard. The first Betarim parade in Jerusalem on October 13, 1928 had marched between crowds howling insults. Jabotinsky did not always suffer fools gladly; his ideas were often more lucid than many of the old revolutionary dogmas imported from eastern Europe; he had often been proven right by events—these facts grated on orthodox sensibilities. They wanted to believe the Revisionists guilty. They seized on the murder as welcome provocation for a witch hunt. Thus at the World Zionist Congress in Prague in 1934 the 52 Revisionist delegates were practically put in quarantine, vastly outnumbered by the 138 socialists out of the total 318. Righteous indignation became the watchword. When the trials in Palestine revealed the fragile foundation for such indignation, the opponents of Revisionism simply became more righteous.[9] Not all Jabotinsky's political enemies were swept away in the tide of hysteria. Many, like Ben-Gurion, felt that the reaction to Arlosoroff's death had been excessive and misguided, that the Revisionists had a part to play in Zionism. In October 1934, Jabotinsky and Ben-Gurion met in London to seek a modus vivendi that might lead to accommodation. The Revisionists would agree to end their boycott of the various Zionist institutions, which in turn would again issue immigration certificates to Betarim. Both sides would end their attacks and insults. Both men saw the agreement as a means to reunite Zionism, but both underestimated the residue of bitterness. In March 1935, the Histadrut voted against accepting the agreement already ratified by the Revisionists. In April 1935, the Revisionist executive formally decided to form an independent worldwide Zionist movement. In June a plebiscite supported the decision, 167,000 to 3,000. On September 7, 1935, 318 delegates elected by 713,000 Revisionists from 32 countries met in Vienna and formed the New Zionist Organization (NZO). As always, Jabotinsky went his own way.

Increasingly, he felt a driving sense of urgency. Time appeared to be running out for European Jewry, particularly those in Germany and eastern Europe. He wrote of "dark clouds that are gathering over the heads of the Jews of Europe."[10] He spoke before huge Revisionist crowds to the horror of the more conventional Jews, who felt his prophecies might prove self-fulfilling. Even though anti-Semitism was institutional in Poland and Germany, and virulent, fascist racism was everywhere, many Jews refused to accept Jabotinsky's slogan, "If you will not liquidate the diaspora, the diaspora will liquidate you."[11] How to liquidate the diaspora baffled all concerned. The Nazi government in Berlin often expelled German Jews; but unlike the Jews of Poland and the Balkans, the German Jews often managed to acquire entry visas, husbanded some small resources, and to a degree controlled their destiny. The many who remained in Germany assumed that this too would pass in time. In Poland only a very few Jews could plan ahead; millions of others could only wait; and the waiting was growing more painful. They feared that their misery would not pass but would become unbearable.

The worldwide depression had particularly baneful effects on the Polish Jews. Over a million were unemployed and unemployable, without land, effective skills, or the opportunity to use their talents. Dependent on charity, crowded into miserable and decaying slums, they existed on the edge of starvation, a drain on Poland's declining assets. Even those more fortunate Jews with money, talent, or friends increasingly found informal anti-Semitism defined as a policy of the state. Jews at the university increasingly faced public humiliation, physical harassment, and the constant, adamant expression of Polish hatred. Those in professional or commercial positions were driven into penury. In 1937 university students were segregated, a special Jewish ghetto of benches created. Even the more responsible and thoughtful Polish leaders could not hold back the rising tide of anti-Semitism. Those more opportunistic or prejudiced did not want to do so, but the very size of the Jewish community—3,500,000—compounded the Polish problem. What was to be done with the millions of superfluous Jews? The problem existed elsewhere in Europe but was particularly acute in Poland. Jabotinsky recognized that "We have got to save millions, many *millions*. I do not know whether it is a question of rehousing one third of the Jewish race, half of the Jewish race, or a quarter of the Jewish race; but it is a question of millions."[12] Talking in millions in 1936 was, to the conventional, dealing in fantasy.

The Poles listened. A man who advocated smashing in the gates of Palestine with a million immigrants might well be a man who could aid in solving Poland's Jewish problem. To get rid of a million Jews, or even a great many Jews, would strengthen the country, mute the dangerous anti-Semitic plague, and ease social tensions—a net gain. Early in 1937 Jabotinsky came to a Warsaw dinner arranged by Meir Kahan with two dozen Polish officials, members of the secret service, army officers, and Count Lubinsky of the Foreign Office. Subsequently, there were constant contacts between Kahan and Polish officials, between various NZO representative and the Polish government. What gradually evolved by 1938 was an unofficial alliance. The Poles would train and supply a military expedition composed largely of Polish Betarim and some Palestinian officers. Palestinians would be trained in Poland and sent back to the Mandate. Polish arms were turned over to NZO representatives to be smuggled into Palestine. Illegal immigration into Palestine under NZO auspices was encouraged. Since both the Poles and the NZO felt that a Jewish commonwealth in Palestine would be to British advantage, even if established by force, neither felt they were being particularly disloyal to their British alignment. The Poles, then, would continue the NZO alliance even while depending on British protection in an increasingly hostile world of German expansion. In any case, the date for the proposed descent on Palestine was April 1940. Given the relatively small British military presence in the Mandate in 1936, the project was hardly as far-fetched as might be assumed. At worst, the NZO would get arms, training, and aid in illegal immigration, and the Poles would reduce the number of unwanted Jews.

Jabotinsky and the NZO had no intention of waiting until April 1940 to open the gates of Palestine. In 1936 the NZO began to organize immigration into Palestine on a considerable scale. New British quotas began cutting into the monthly totals just as conditions in Europe worsened. The direction of illegal immigration—Aliyah Bet—after 1936 became a vital part of the NZO's program. Jabotinsky's son, Eri, commander of the Palestine Betar, took over the receiving end, while in Europe NZO representatives negotiated the purchase of ships, devised appropriate documents, made necessary friends, collected the emigrants, and hoped that the small tramp steamers or ancient coasters would not only get all the way to Palestine but also slip past any British patrols. Although the Histadrut in 1934 had organized an illegal attempt with the ship *Velos*, not until 1938 was a second attempt make with the establishment of the Immigration Bureau, Mosad, under Shaul Avigur. During 1936 and 1937 the NZO was alone. Even after 1938 there were many who opposed this provocative evacuation that endangered the lives and health of the Jews crammed into leaky old boats. The Revisionists persisted and were often joined by private parties, at times operating for profit, so that three streams of illegals ran into Palestine after 1938. With no central accounting and the need for secrecy, the total of Aliyah Bet between 1936 and 1939 may have been as high as forty thousand. Certainly thousands arrived in Palestine, slipped ashore, and disappeared into the Yishuv. They were not the millions that Jabotinsky wanted, but they did arrive.

Their arrival and more especially the huge German influx of the fifth Aliyah raised once again for the Arabs, the British, and the Zionists the questions about the nature of the Jewish national home. Jabotinsky spoke of millions and the Arabs of minority rights for Jews in an Arab state. Some Zionists contemplated partition or federalism, but none wanted a limit on immigration. The British, as always, shifted between the two poles, contemplating concessions that the Arabs would find contemptible and the Jews a betrayal. In 1937, in a statement submitted to one more royal commission, Jabotinsky defined the maximalist position.

The idea is that Palestine on both sides of the Jordon should hold the Arabs, their progeny, *and* many millions of Jews. What I do not deny is that in that process the Arabs of Palestine will necessarily become a minority in the country of Palestine. What I do deny is that *that* is a hardship. It is quite understandable that the Arabs of Palestine would also prefer Palestine to be the Arab state No. 4, No. 5, or No. 6—that I quite understand; but when the Arab claim is confronted with our Jewish demand to be saved, it is like the claims of appetite versus the claims of starvation.[13]

It was also understandable that the Arabs of Palestine, watching the rising tide of Jewish immigrants, did not accept Jabotinsky's logic. They saw only that they were denied justice and their land was lost because of disturbances far off in Europe, not of their making. Why should the Arabs suffer in silence to exculpate others? They would not.

In 1936 Arab sufferance of European hegemony in the Middle East seemed at an end. In Cairo negotiations over a new relationship that led in time to the Anglo-Egyptian Treaty revealed a new militancy. What the Egyptians really wanted was absolute rather than formal independence. In January 1936, there was serious rioting in Syria, followed by a general strike. In March France announced a willingness to negotiate Syrian independence, an initiative that would lead to another Arab state and increased agitation for a similar concession in Lebanon. Across the Jordon, Abdullah had been ruling a technically independent state since 1938, although Britain retained military and financial control. Thus there was movement toward ultimate Arab suzerainty nearly everywhere but in Palestine. Conditions in the Mandate for the Arabs continued to deteriorate: the widespread and increased unemployment, the highly visible and expanding Jewish presence, and the news from abroad, especially the rioting in Damascus. Equally effective was the anti-British propaganda of the Italians, whose victories in East Africa indicated the decay of British imperial vitality. There was as always the constant stream of rumors: the Jews were plotting; the British were in collusion with the Zionists; the Jews were arming. The Arabs knew that the Jews *were* arming. At Jaffa in October 1935, a barrel of cement broke open while being unloaded to reveal smuggled arms. No one could prove anything, but the Arabs were certain the Revisionists were responsible. A one-day general strike was held, but the matter hardly ended there. The Arabs felt something must be done—all the Arabs, the conservative Nashashibi as well as the "fanatical" Husseini.

On November 25, five Arab Palestinian parties presented a petition to the Mandate authorities demanding representative government, an end to land sales, and an end to the Jewish immigration. In December the high commissioner proposed a council scheme that was immediately rejected by the Jews, so the Arabs did not have to take a position. Beyond this, there was no sign of British concession or Zionist moderation. In 1935 61,854 Jews immigrated to Palestine. Few left. The Jewish brithrate apparently surpassed the Arab. Unless something were done in a very few years, the Arabs would be a minority in their own country.

On April 15, 1936, two Jews were killed by Arab bandits near the Tulkarm-Nablus highway, a center of both Arab nationalism and endemic brigandage. On the following day two Arabs were killed near Petva Tikva. On April 17, there were demonstrations in Tel Aviv at the funeral of the murdered Jews, and several Arabs were attacked on the streets. Tension rose in Tel Aviv and Jaffa. In March the citrus had been shipped out of Jaffa, and the workers, the hauranis, traditionally volatile, were at loose ends, open to incitement and eager for trouble.

Jaffa had long been disorderly, a breeding ground for agitation. Spilling down from the small hill overlooking the harbor in a warren of narrow lanes and obscure tunnels, the old city behind the clock square existed largely beyond the law, a haven for the wanted. It was rarely patrolled, with only the Franciscan monastery on the hillside as a sign of the outside world. The new city had been built toward the north and Tel Aviv, pocked with the modern concrete CID station and dominated by the Hassan Bek Mosque. The mean streets of the Manshiya quarter abutted Jewish Tel Aviv. There had been a long history of friction along this blurred line, and few were surprised when on Sunday, April 29, the fragile order in Jaffa collapsed. There were several thousand Jews within or close to Jaffa, all hostages to fate when Arabs began attacking in the streets. Nine Jews were killed, and a huge Arab street mob began to march on Tel Aviv. The police were slow to act, and the situation slipped out of control. To prevent the mob from breaking through into Tel Aviv, the British had to open fire. The mob reluctantly dispersed. At midday an RAF armored car squadron dispatched from Ramele arrived in Tel Aviv; and by midafternoon order was fully restored—too late for the nine dead Jews, and, as it soon developed, too late to keep the cork on the bottle of Arab nationalism.

While disorders continued in Jaffa, Arab leaders met the following day at Nablus, organized the Arab Higher Committee, including representatives of both the Husseini and the Nashashibi, and called for a general strike on April 22. The Arab revolt had begun, hardly to the surprise of many within the Palestinian Mandate administration, who felt the Arab demands were just and the Colonial Office in London obtuse in failing to produce adequate concessions and guarantees. In fact many Jews, especially the Revisionists, believed that once again the Arabs were justified in their cries of Al duala Maana, for there was abundant evidence that if the government was not actually supporting the revolt, many within the government were not opposed to such an expression of legitimate Arab grievance. Certainly, as order began to decay, British security precautions left much to be desired. Arab brigands in the north burnt trees, destroyed crops, and fired into settlements. The situation in Jaffa again deteriorated; instead of imposing order and curbing the Arabs, the British chose to evacuate the three thousand Jews to Tel Aviv. Barred from the Jaffa port, the Jews built their own at Tel Aviv, thereby increasing Arab unemployment and anger. Elsewhere in the Mandate, the Arabs regularly shot at Jewish traffic, fired at isolated farms or settlements, tossed bombs from passing trains into Jewish quarters. This time the scale of the violence resulted in regular clashes with British security forces. The nature of the irregular fighting, where the Arab could do what came naturally, and the general strike, where no action was required because many Arabs were already unemployed, meant that the Arab Higher Committee could direct a continuing confrontation rather than incite a single wave of pogroms, as had been done in 1920, 1921, and 1929. The result was that the Mandate slipped toward anarchy: in the first six months of the revolt, eighty-nine Jews killed and over three hundred wounded. In May British reinforcements began to arrive, but the security response still appeared at best languid and at worst collusive. On May 18, the high commissioner announced that no extra immigrant certificates would be approved for the next six months, and that another commission to investigate conditions would be appointed once the general strike had ended. Once more Arab violence, condoned by the British, had produced concessions.

The Arab Higher Committee was no longer content with reduced immigration or the promise of yet another commission. Concessions were not enough; the Arabs wanted the country. And they thought they could get it, or at least see that the Jews did not. For almost the first time in Palestinian history, old feuds and parochial loyalties were put aside by the Arabs, and there was solid support for the general strike. Those who might have dissented recognized the dangers of retaliation. Everywhere the Jews and the British were on the defensive. The Arab nations were enthusiastic. Italian money proved forthcoming. By summer opportunistic brigands from isolated areas or from across the borders operated freely. More formally, an irregular army of mujehadeen was formed under the command of Fawzi el-Dine el-Kwakji, an Iraqi officer and Syrian rebel who had advised ibn-Saud of Saudi Arabia. The force was funded through the mufti's control of Moslem funds, by Arab donations, and with Italian subsidies. Along with the mujehadeen, who at times would fight openly against the British security forces, were the fedayeen, irregulars who sniped, burned, and looted when the opportunity arose. The representative of the Arab Higher Committee in London, Djamal al-Husseini, a relative of the mufti, explained that the conditions to end the general strike were simply no more Jewish immigration, no further Jewish land purchases, and the establishment of an Arab national government in Palestine.

In September the British army under Lieutenant General Dill took over control of security from the RAF. Before Dill there had been no general officer in the Mandate. The British went on the offensive, scattering the ill-disciplined Arab bands and moving up into the hills. There was no indication that London would accept Arab demands or offer further substantive concessions. Then, too, the élan and determination of the spring had begun to fade. The general strike had little effect on the Jews, who lived inside their own economy, and the British Empire could clearly stand the loss of Arab tax money. Worse, if the strike lasted into November, it would be impossible to pick, transport, and ship crops: the Arab segment of the economy would be bankrupt. Everything became more difficult. Both the Haganah and Haganah-bet took serious steps to improve Jewish defenses, to create elite striking groups, and to take positive though still defensive actions against Arab harassment. Vulnerable convoys turned out to be decoys; tempting settlements proved to be traps; Arab bands ran into night ambushes outside their own villages. In June 1936, the British decided to establish a Jewish supernumerary police force. In July some twenty-two thousand of these special police, Notrim, were appointed to act as a protective militia for the Jewish settlements and quarters. The force soon became a legal cover for the Haganah and an increasingly effective shield against Arab forays. On September 29, the British declared martial law, but did not impose it.

The Arab Higher Committee decided that before the general strike collapsed of its own weight and the mujehadeen and fedayeen went home, something had to be salvaged from the sacrifices. This the British were quite willing to stage manage. On October 10, Emir Abdullah of Transjordan and ibn-Saud of Saudi Arabia appealed to the Arab Higher Committee to call off the strike. The committee promptly complied: a most remarkable maneuver, where the heads of Arab states acted as self-appointed mediators. Everyone knew why the Arab Higher Committee was so compromising, the British so conciliatory, and the two monarchs so inventive. The Palestinian Arabs could save face and await the new commission with some equanimity, since leaks and rumors indicated that the British at last recognized the error of their ways. Once more, violence seemed to have succeeded for the Arabs, although the somewhat limited concession had proved more costly than anticipated: officially 195 Arabs were killed and 804 wounded, 89 Jews killed and over 300 wounded, with 16 police and 21 military killed, and 102 police and 104 military wounded. Unofficially, at least several hundred more Arabs were killed. The Arab economy was severely damaged, especially in Jaffa, where the port would never return since the Jews continued to use their own new facitities at Tel Aviv. Still, with the new commission on the way and the assurance that this time surely the government was with them, the Arabs had great hopes.

Balancing Arab hopes with Jewish fears during the previous six months was a severe trauma for the Yishuv. A great many illusions, rewoven in the six years since the 1929 pogroms, were shredded. The militants and the militarists were proven right, and the necessity not only to contemplate violence but also to organize a response to it convulsed the Yishuv. There was no gainsaying the fact that a Jewish national homeland could not be built on a foundation of ruined vineyards, burned groves, mutilated cattle, and murdered kibbutzniks. An army was necessary, a strategy essential. Much of the Zionist left viewed the events of 1936 with despair, for they kept believing that an accommodation with the Arabs was both possible and desirable. To respond to Arab violence with Jewish violence would only postpone such an accommodation and might, indeed, prevent it for the foreseeable future. Yet to stand idly by guaranteed that the long sacrifices of practical Zionism, the groves and settlements, would be destroyed, Jews would be killed, and the most fanatical Arabs encouraged to further violence. Any decision on fundamental matters within the Yishuv evolved out of an incredibly complicated series of compromises, special formulas, trade-offs, and often pragmatic evasions of the end result. This in effect happened in 1936. The moral principle of havlaga, self-defense, became the key to action. There would be no offensive military actions, no resort to counter-terror; the Jews would ward off violence, not initiate it. In principle, if not always in detail, havlaga was accepted by all the agencies and parties of the Yishuv from Ben-Gurion to Jabotinsky. Those responsible for the application of havlaga in the field were somewhat more flexible. During the summer of 1936, the Haganah, under a democratically elected command that often had little control over those who did the defending, began the creation of special groups, which after various transformations would ultimately become the Palmach, a mobile striking force. In the meantime various Haganah units interpreted havlaga as permitting preventive ambushes, decoys, and night fighting on the edge of Arab villages. There were many, especially those in Haganah-bet, who felt this was insufficient. Other Haganah-bet commanders believed that, havlaga or no, in dangerous times there was no need for two Haganahs. The militants disagreed, for they considered the other Haganah as a pawn of the left, hampered by socialist dogma that prevented an effective defense of the Yishuv.

A group within Haganah-bet led by Gundar "Arieh" Yitzhaki, Arieh Ben-Eliezer, Benjamin Zeroni, Ben-Zion Shoshani, Charnoch Kalay, and Aaron Haichman not only distrusted the other Haganah but also wanted to discard havlaga. In fact, various members of Haganah-bet wanted to initiate reprisal operations in hopes of intimidating Arab attacks. In July 1936, an Arab tossed a bomb from a train as it passed Herzl Street in Tel

Aviv. Several Jews were wounded. In response Haganah-bet fired on a trainload of Arabs. For the more conventional within Haganah-bet, the call for retaliation had been disturbing. They felt such attacks would be ineffectual and potentially provocative, both in Arab and British eyes. The major disagreement, however, continued to be on the separate existence of Haganah-bet. Long discussions began in August 1936, and intensified after the end of the first period of violence in October 1936. Some commanders, especially Moshe Rosenberg in Tel Aviv, suspected Tehomi would make a secret deal with the Haganah commander, Eliyahu Golomb. By the spring of 1937, negotiations had reached the point where most of the Haganah-bet senior commanders felt sufficiently united to cable Jabotinsky for permission to effect a reunion. Jabotinsky refused, as always doubtful of the militancy and intention of the other Haganah. Avraham Tehomi and his colleagues felt that they could not accept Jabotinsky's position. Tehomi, many of the senior commanders, and perhaps a quarter of the three thousand members, mostly Mizrachists and General Zionists, withdrew in April and rejoined the Haganah. Others, as is always the case in a split, simply resigned. The remainder, largely the Betarim, adopted a name that had once been used instead of Haganah-bet, Irgun Zvai Leumi (National Military Organization), and became in effect the military arm in Palestine of the NZO.

The first commander was Colonel Robert Bitker, formerly the Betar commander in Shanghai. Bitker was neither diplomat nor conspirator but a soldier, new to Palestine and ignorant of Hebrew. The problem was not so much Bitker's qualifications as the general uncertainty about the future direction of the Irgun. Jabotinsky still accepted havlaga and in any case the Arabs remained quiescent, awaiting the Peel Commission's report. For the moment Bitker concentrated on reorganizing. His chief-of-staff was Moshe Rosenberg, formerly second in command in Tel Aviv, and the regional commanders were David Raziel in Jerusalem with Avraham Stern as his number two; the secretary of the high command, Charnoch Kalay in Haifa, and Aaron Haichman in Tel Aviv, where the greatest Irgun strength could be found. There were also Betarim units in the various NZO settlements. Total strength was approximately eighteen hundred; but the split resulted in a loss of arms, and finances were fragile at best, so replacement and intensified training would be difficult. Still, the need for action had been great, despite the problems, even before the split. On March 14, for example, Arieh Yitzhaki and Benjamin Zeroni, in retaliation for Arab sniping, tossed a bomb into the Azur coffee house outside Tel Aviv. Arieh was dismissed for the time being, but there were many in the new Irgun who had lost all patience with havlaga.

The time for such a serious strategic reversal had not yet arrived, for all during the spring attention was focused on the deliberations of the Peel

Commission. The Yishuv still largely assumed that the destiny of Palestine would be decided elsewhere by others. In July 1937, the commission produced its report: the desire for independence and the fear of Zionism had driven the Arabs to revolt. Consequently there was no possibility of making the Mandate work—the only solution was partition. The Zionist reaction was anguished. Jabotinsky, of course, was adamantly opposed to partition. The statelet would be a tiny canton with a dim economic future and indefensible borders. He did note, however, that at least the British now officially foresaw the existence of a Jewish state of some sort. The orthodox Zionists were deeply divided, although the World Zionist Congress at Zurich in August accepted partition. The Arabs saw no reason why the imperialist occupier had any right to give away part of their homeland. They rejected the idea without qualifications. The British thus came no closer to an accommodation, although they were now on record that the aspirations of the Jews and Arabs in the Mandate could not be accommodated. "An irrepressible conflict has arisen between two national communities within the narrow bounds of one small country."[14]

The leadership of both the NZO and the Irgun assumed that this irrepressible conflict was about to enter a new and more deadly stage, that the long pause from the end of the general strike to the Peel Report was about to come to an end. In Palestine the Irgun commanders felt that if the sniping, arson, and murder began again, the most effective defense would be retaliation. Increasingly during 1937 there was strain between the Irgun—an independent military force still only lightly tied to NZO control—and the political leadership of Revisionism, many of whom saw the Betarim move into the Irgun out of their control. Still the core of the movement remained Jabotinsky, ceaselessly traveling through the diaspora; if there were to be a change in military policy, clearly Jabotinsky would have to approve. In July in Alexandria, Jabotinsky met with Bitker and Rosenthal, and agreed to a policy of retaliation. In point of fact, Jabotinsky did not believe in indiscriminate retaliation, but was willing to listen to the Irgun military commanders' explanations of the real difficulties in limiting operations to the "guilty." The militant among the Irgun—not all the organization—increasingly began to feel the distance between the politicians, including Jabotinsky, and what they saw as Palestinian reality. Many in the Irgun felt the only way to the state was armed struggle. As Stern had told the Polish Betarim in 1937, the time for parades had passed. The slowly widening division was actually encouraged by the NZO politicians, who wanted to maintain a distance from any future violent military policy. Jabotinsky indicated he did not want to know certain things; soon he was not told certain things. Soon the division would be complete—ain gesher, ain kesher (no bridge, no connection)—and cause serious command conflicts, but in August 1937, there were other and more immediate problems.

For the Irgun the major difficulty was that Bitker did not work out as a commander. Not all was his fault, for the exact mission and form of the Irgun remained uncertain. Some, including Jabotinsky, foresaw a real army accepted or tolerated by the British authorities. Others began to talk about going underground. Many were eager for action, and Bitker had no clear direction to offer, no missions to assign, no operations to plan. His staff work was hampered by personality clashes. He did not solve his financial problems. In fact in attempting to do so, he compounded his difficulties. Arrangements were made with three former members of the old Brit Habiryonim to rob a bank messenger. The attempt collapsed; three men were arrested, although a fourth, Avraham Selman, the man who had refused to recognize the British presence in Palestine, escaped. It was clear that Bitker was in some way involved. Then the bound body of a young Irgun man, Zvi Frankel, was found floating in the Yarkon River. He had killed an Arab in Jaffa and become the focus of a wide police search which had swept up his mother. The Irgun high command asked money from the head of the Revisionist organization, Dr. Arieh Altman, in order to spirit Frankel out of the country. Some of the money was apparently used during the messenger robbery, and there was the suspicion that no serious effort would be made to help Frankel flee. Some assumed he had been eliminated to prevent his talking. In any case, the matter was quite sordid, and as the man at the top, Bitker received the blame. He resigned and left Palestine for the United States. Moshe Rosenberg took over, and several of the younger militants moved into prominence, especially David Raziel, commanding officer in Jerusalem, and Avraham Stern, secretary of the high command.

Stern was an archetypal revolutionary intellectual, handsome, intense, a linguist, a man not for the easy life, uncomfortable with moderation and delay. Raziel was quite different, calm, thoughtful, a taciturn military man with deep religious convictions. He did not have Stern's sophistication and cosmopolitan elegance, but he still exerted a magnetic effect within the Irgun. The two had collaborated on a training manual in Hebrew, *Haedaach* (Pistol), and worked intimately within the high command. Both for different reasons distrusted politics; both had become impatient with the hesitant and cautious military policy of Bitker and Rosenthal. The new commander, mindful of the dreadful losses suffered by the enthusiastic during the First World War, did not want to commit the Irgun to open insurrection or full retaliation risking British oppression until the last possible moment. Stern, Raziel, and the others consequently pushed for real action, something more than an occasional reprisal raid. They recognized that the Mandate was slipping from British control.

On September 27, the seriousness of the Palestine situation became evident. L. Y. Andrews, district commissioner in Galilee, and his police escort were all murdered by Arab fedayeen. Beginning with the publication of the Peel Report, the Arab operations once again escalated. This time the mufti was better prepared for an irregular war, and by late September Fawzi el-Kaukji's fedayeen controlled much of the countryside; road and rail traffic was imperiled, and the Arab urban warrens were beyond effective police control. On October 1, the Mandate administration declared the Arab Higher Committee an illegal organization, warrants were issued for the arrest and deportation of its known leaders, and hundreds of suspects were picked up and interned. Security forces arrested four members of the Arab Higher Committee, who were exiled to the Seychelles, and prohibited the entry of two others then abroad. Two escaped the net, as did the mufti, who went underground for two months and then slipped way by ship from Jaffa to Syria. By then British control of the Mandate was seriously challenged. Late in December near Tiberias, Arab irregulars and fifteen hundred British troops clashed in a three-day battle. Although only eleven rebels and two soldiers were killed, the scale of the revolt was revealed. In December the appointment of a new high commissioner was announced: Sir Harold MacMichael, an Arabist and former member of the elegant Sudanese Political Service; but many in Palestine, especially in the Irgun, wanted additional evidence that the British truly intended to crush the revolt. Once again it appeared, to most Revisionists that the British Arabists intended to manipulate rebel violence to imperial advantage. Already, at the September 1937 meeting of the League of Nations Council, the British had backed away from imposing the partition suggested by Peel. Now as the months of rebellion passed, there were no decisive results from British security operations. There were fifteen thousand armed rebels, three times the number in the field in 1936; and the Mandate authorities still showed no inclination to treat the rebellion as more serious than high-level banditry. Not until October 1938 was suppression of the rebels turned over to the military.

Despite Jewish doubts the British security forces did pursue a more effective counterinsurgency policy by the spring of 1938. Efforts were made to clear and improve the roads in rebel-held territory, especially to the west of Jenin, a seat of dissidence. A barbed-wire fence was erected along the Syrian border, making infiltration more difficult. Sir Charles Tegart also undertook construction of heavy stone police towers at strategic points—Tegart fortresses. The British were also eventually aided by growing Arab divisions as the universal support present during the autumn of 1937 began to decay. The mufti concentrated on eliminating his enemies, almost entirely Arabs, and the more conservative and prudent middle-class nationalists sought a means of accommodation with the British. In turn British authorities hoped that carefully orchestrated concessions would further erode Arab unity, isolate the mufti, and permit a reimposition of order. On March 15, 1938, new immigration quotas were announced that would permit only three thousand Jewish immigrants over the next six months, contrasted to eight thousand the previous year. In 1935 there were sixty-two thousand Jewish immigrants; in 1938 only ten thousand. Then in June a crude British maneuver further eroded British credibility within the Yishuv and further complicated the already difficult security situation.

Although in August 1937, Jabotinsky gave Rosenthal permission to undertake reprisal operations, the Irgun for the most part had been remarkably restrained, given the level of the Arab revolt. While there were regular incidents, sniping, bombing, and attacks on settlements during 1937 and early 1938, the major confrontation was between the Arab fedayeen and the British security forces. In early September the Irgun responded to the murder of three Jews with a counterattack that killed thirteen Arabs. On November 14, there was an open and, in orthodox eyes, a blatant violation of the principle of havlaga. On Black Sunday around Jerusalem, David Raziel organized a series of offensive retaliatory operations against notorious centers of Arab brigandage. Ten Arabs were killed and many wounded. The Jewish Agency was outraged and accused the Revisionists of "marring the moral record of Palestine Jewry, hampering the political struggle and undermining security." Even within the NZO in Palestine and the diaspora, a sense of unease existed. The result was a tacit Irgun return to havlaga and no further indiscriminate or offensive retaliation. This restraint on the part of the high command was tenuous. Rosenthal had trouble reining in the militants, and further Arab provocation was almost certain to play into their hands. What happened was a British provocation.

All during the spring the village Arabs in Galilee had been firing on Jewish traffic, particularly on the Acre-Safed road. There was a particularly unsavory incident when a taxi was ambushed. The driver stalled the cab. In a panic all five Jews leaped out and took cover in a roadside ditch. The Arabs rushed in with swords, slashing and stabbing. They raped a young woman and mutilated her body. All five Jews were hacked to death. There were no security people about, and the murderers disappeared back into the hills and into their villages.

The Jews of Galilee were horrified and largely helpless. No one knew which Arabs had been responsible, and both the Haganah and the Irgun still avoided indiscriminate retaliation. Three young Betarim from the nearby Rosh Pinah settlement felt that something must be done. One, Shlomo Ben-Yosef, who had come to Rosh Pinah from Poland for his pelugot service, had turned to Avraham Shein and Shalom Zurabin on hearing the news and demanded, "And what are we doing? We are sitting quietly doing nothing."[15] They scoured about and found a revolver and an old grenade, and planned to ambush the Safad-Tiberias bus on April 21.

On the way out of Safad their line of sight was blocked by a Jewish car, but on the return trip later in the day they had a second chance. Misjudging the speed of the bus going downhill, they missed with their shots. The grenade was a dud. All three were promptly arrested for what appeared a futile, bungled, and quite unimportant incident. The British administration, however, took a different view; for here was a clear case of Jewish terrorism that would require an evenhanded response: there needed to be an example of British impartiality to soothe Arab anxiety.

Although it was pointed out that the Arab provocation was great and continuing, that all three young men were of good character without records of any sort, had never been familiar with firearms, and had hurt no one, the court was not impressed. Counsel did persuade the court that Zurabin was "mentally unbalanced," so the case against him was dropped, but the other two were judged guilty. On June 5, both were condemned to death. Counsel managed to get Avraham Shein's sentence commuted because he was under eighteen, but the court would not relent on Ben-Yosef. Still there was hope, for in a similar case in Gaza an Arab youth of good character whose act had injured no one was reprieved. This time however the Palestine administration made it abundantly clear to the new GOC, Major General Haining, who had just taken over from Wavell, that it was the urgently expressed wish of those in authority that the sentence be confirmed. It was. Ben-Yosef would die.

It was so patent that the sentence related not to Ben-Yosef's crime but to the furtherance of British policy that outrage spread far beyond the Yishuv. Not only did various Palestine Jewish parties and individuals plead for clemency, but also did the Jews of the diaspora. In Ireland Robert Briscoe, former IRA leader and later a Jewish mayor of Dublin, contacted first Jabotinsky then Lord Nathan in London and sought a legal loophole to stay the execution. All were refused. Ben-Yosef's counsel was refused a stay. A plea for clemency by the Polish government in the name of Polish citizen Shlomo Tabachnik—who had made his way illegally from Poland into Palestine—was also ignored. It was obvious to everyone, including Ben-Yosef, that Britain was determined to set an example. On the eve of his execution, a group of journalists visited Ben-Yosef in his cell in the Acre fortress.

> Do not console me . . . I need no consolation. I am proud to be the first Jew to go to the gallows in Palestine. In dying I shall do my people a greater service than in my life. Let the world see that Jews are not afraid to face death.[16]

Chief Rabbi Herzog in Jerusalem asked that the date of execution, June 29, at the very least be postponed one day, since on Rosh Hodesh no rabbi could give him consolation. The request was denied.

On the morning of June 29, Ben-Yosef washed, brushed his teeth, drank a cup of tea, and waited. He was dressed in the traditional red burlap suit of the condemned man when he was taken from his mean, bare cell. As he walked the few yards down the corridor toward the gallows room, he began to sing the Song of Betar.

> From the pit of decay and dust
> Through blood and sweat
> A generation will arise to us,
> Proud, generous, and fierce.

He entered the small, high-ceilinged room at the end of the corridor. From the roof hung the heavy, corded rope, dangling from a steel beam. Before him was a crude, uneven wooden platform, set in the floor over the pit below, with the clumsy drop lever to one side. The walls were white, water stained, the plaster peeling and racked, the floor of rough tiles. It was a long way from Poland. As the noose was placed over his neck, he called out, "Long live the Jewish state! Long live Jabotinsky!" The noose was adjusted. The CID officer who had walked him to the gallows stepped back. There was a pause, then the lever was pulled. The trap opened with a heavy clunk and Ben-Yosef dropped into the pit, hanged by the neck until dead. On the wall of his cell he had scratched "To die or to conquer the height" and "Death compared with one's country is nothing." The Irgun had a martyr. The British had their example, and a great deal more trouble than they ever anticipated. Now that there was evidence that the government was with them again, the Arabs unleashed a series of terrorist attacks on the Yishuv, and the Irgun responded in kind.

Even before the Ben-Yosef case, the moderate center within the Irgun had been eroded. Moshe Rosenberg was too cautious for his colleagues. When he went to Cyprus on business, he received word from Raziel that the CID was on his trail, and that he should not return. Rosenthal felt he was being edged out. He stayed in Cyprus for a while and then went on to Warsaw to meet Jabotinsky. By then Raziel had taken over as commander, discarded havlaga, and taken much of the Irgun underground. To his colleagues Raziel was the ideal leader, a devout Jew who had studied at a Yeshiva school, majored in Talmudic studies at Hebrew University, and each morning put on his tefillin to pray. He seemed as much a biblical captain as an underground commander. His advancement in the Haganah, which he joined in 1929, and then in the Irgun had been rapid. First he was arms supervisor in Jerusalem and then in recognition of his talents, commander. Unlike many Irgun commanders he had never been in Betar, but like them he believed that freedom would come only with the sword. More to the point, he inspired deep loyalty and total confidence. His operational planning was painstaking, his leadership exemplary, his concerns predominantly military. Few but his wife, whom he married in April 1938, knew of his lighter side of songs and poetry. For others he was the grey wolf of the Irgun, lone, quiet, implacable, handsome, and deadly. In other times in other places, he might have become a rabbinical scholar, but in Mandated Palestine he accepted that there was no such possibility. He cut away nonessentials, kept his private life very private, and moved underground. Until his marriage he had a small room in the Keren Avraham section of Jerusalem, a tiny square with a bed, chair, desk, and lamp, the floor cluttered with piles of books. Under the desk was a special pile on the Irish revolution. (Raziel saw a Palestinian parallel with Ireland, but in 1938 the immediate threat remained the Arab fedayeen.) Ben-Yosef's death released the pent torrent, for, on the same day Rosenthal left for Cyprus and Raziel became acting commander. The Arabs would be treated as dreck (dirt). The time of parades had passed and the time of vengeance was come.

On July 4, the Irgun attacked Arab quarters, first in Jerusalem and then in Tel Aviv. Five were killed and twenty wounded. Two days later, an "Arab" porter carried milk cans into the Haifa fruit and vegetable market. As soon as he found an empty corner, he left his cans and disappeared into the crowd. A few minutes later the cans detonated with a huge roar, spewing fire and fragments into the milling crowd of shoppers. Twenty-three Arabs were killed and seventy-nine wounded. A similar attack in the Arab quarter of the Old City of Jerusalem on July 15 killed ten and wounded twenty-nine more Arabs. The biggest explosion of all came on July 25, again in Haifa, leaving thirty-nine dead and forty-six wounded. In three weeks seventy-six Arabs were killed, while forty-four Jews and twelve members of the security forces had died violently. If the butcher's bill counted, the tide had turned against the Arabs; but there was no visible reduction in the level of violence. The Mandate simply seemed to be drifting toward chaos, as the British now had another enemy creating a three-cornered war, one the British did not seem to be winning.

Everywhere the security situation deteriorated. The fedayeen still largely controlled the hills. Both in the Old City of Jerusalem and the mazes of Jaffa rebel control was firm during 1938. The Arab irregulars still fired at easy targets, tossed bombs from trains, sabotaged public facilities, and burned what they could. The Irgun continued to respond with counter-terror, a policy that had no immediate returns and often proved deadly for those involved. On July 26, for example, the day after the big bomb in Haifa, a similar attempt was planned in the Old City. Eighteen-year-old Yaacov Raz, dressed as an Arab, pushed a barrow of vegetables with a time bomb inside into the watermelon market. By this time every Arab had become acutely suspicious of unfamiliar bearers of cucumber casks or strange shoeshine boys. An Arab woman stared at him and suddenly shouted, "Yahud! Yahud!" (Jew, Jew). Someone else snatched Raz's basket and found the bomb under the vegetables. Realizing his danger, Raz turned and was rushing through the crowded market, hoping to disappear down an alley or into the crowd; but the alarm spread too quickly. Just as he was nearly away, an Arab leaned forward and shot him as he fled. He staggered on, bleeding profusely, until he collapsed at the edge of safety. The police and disguised members of the Irgun command rushed him to the Hadassah hospital, but the security forces soon arrived and moved him to the Government hospital as a suspected terrorist. There his condition worsened. He began to run a fever and slip in and out of consciousness. He feared that in his delirium he would babble information to his guards. When no one was watching he reached down and opened his own wounds. Within an hour Yaacov Raz had bled to death.

The Irgun attacks continued. One of the most active men was Gundar "Arieh" Yitzhaki, who had been dismissed for tossing the first retaliatory bomb into the Arab cafe in Yazur the previous year. Arieh became the Irgun's explosives expert, devising letter bombs to mail to Arabs in Jaffa, trapbombs that would detonate when the CID explosives experts tried to dismantle them, and disguised time bombs for the Arab markets. He used as well as made his bombs, throwing them into shops in Jaffa, cutting the railway lines, participating in operations against Arab buses on the Jaffa-Salameh road, and in an attack on the village of Salameh. Ultimately, he made the one fatal mistake never permitted those who live with explosives. On August 5, 1939, he was at work alone in the Irgun underground bomb factory, when there was an intense flash and a huge roar. Arieh was apparently holding the nearly completed bomb in his hands. The impact was awesome. One hand was gone completely, the other was in shreds. He was blind, his face torn and burned, and blood pumped from a deep wound in his chest. The room was splattered with blood and bits of burned flesh. The detonation almost immediately attracted a CID team, who knew what the crash meant. Rushing into the room, they found Arieh's shattered remains. Grossly mutilated but still alive, he had only time to answer one question: "Who are you?" "My name," he replied, "is death."

For the British in 1938, during the weary cycle of terror and counter-terror, there seemed no way out. Extensive arrests of Irgun and Betarim suspects did not seriously impede Raziel's campaign. On the other hand, the bombing campaign had little effect on Arab militancy, and at one point, when the Irgun in Haifa shot a Jew wearing Arab clothing, there was the possibility of a civil war with the Haganah. By 1938 the Haganah was far more militant, especially under the influence of Orde Wingate, who in 1936 organized special commando units. However the principal commander, Golomb, was opposed to the Irgun's counter-terror tactics. The Haifa incident led to no confrontation but to a Jabotinsky-Golomb meeting on July 10 in London to discuss a merger. Jabotinsky, too, disliked indiscriminate retaliation, and in a time of growing anxiety felt a single military organization might be desirable. Discussions throughout August led to an agreement on September 19, in the house of the mayor of Tel Aviv, for a separate-but-equal alliance. Many in the NZO and the Irgun still had grave doubts about the militancy of the political leadership of the orthodox Zionists and preferred some freedom of action. The members of the Haganah did not want to become entangled in Raziel's provocative terror operations. Both sides' military commanders were willing to enter such an agreement, but as usual political opposition from the left closed off this option. Even if Jabotinsky had agreed, there was opposition within the Irgun in Palestine. In fact Jabotinsky was increasingly isolated from military policy, even from the plans for the expedition out of Poland.

When originally proposed, the Polish expedition anticipated a Palestine denuded of significant military forces, the growth of the British military presence in response to the Arab revolt and Jewish reprisals did not seem an insurmountable obstacle. The Irgun was now an underground army and could be expanded well before the arrival of the expedition by the illicit shipment of arms and the opening of Polish training camps for Irgun cadres. If, as anticipated, five thousand armed and trained Polish Betarim could be brought to the Mandate to bolster the two-thousand-member Irgun, the British would be sorely pressed. This was particularly true since in 1938 Europe seemed to be drifting toward a war that would severely tax British resources. Britain might prefer a deal with the Zionists. Such a move might at once create a trained Jewish ally, a stable and orderly Palestine, and release men for other fronts. The Arabs would not be a problem: those who would not acquiesce to the inevitable could be intimidated.

In Poland the Irgun's emissaries, in particular Avraham Stern, had increasingly acted independently of NZO control, building up a network of dedicated militants like Menachem Begin, commander of Betar, Nathan Friedman-Yellin and Samuel Merlin, editors of *Die Tat*, and Dr. Israel Scheib, an almost mystical visionary rabbi, who edited *Der Moment* and dreamed of a Hebrew state. They maintained contact with the Poles. Arms were collected and in some cases shipped back to Palestine in washing machines, in vans of personal belongings, and in mislabeled crates. An officers' course was planned in the mountains of Zakofna in southwest Poland for members of the Palestinian Irgun. In a house on Yehuda Halevu Street in Tel Aviv, on February 25, 1939, Raziel addressed the first twenty volunteers—including some of the most promising Irgun people like Yaacov Meridor and Eliahu Lankin—who then left by ship for Bessarabia, on to Constanza, and after twenty-four hours on the train arrived in the Polish camp. There, under Polish officers, courses were offered in a wide variety of subjects: codes and secret communication, sabotage, partisan warfare, even conspiracy. When the course finished in May, Stern arrived to deliver a stirring graduation address. The men, with the exception of Meridor, then returned to Palestine. Meridor stayed back to oversee packing the arms—Polish and French rifles, Hotchkiss machine guns, revolvers, explosives, grenades—arms sufficient for the anticipated five thousand Betarim. All this activity in 1938 and 1939 went on without Jabotinsky's knowledge. This drift of the Irgun away from NZO control produced one more internal crisis.

In February 1939, Jabotinsky called an all-faction meeting to sort out the Irgun-NZO relationship, a conference that would include Raziel, who had never belonged to the NZO or Betar, and who was not known to many of the diaspora leadership except by his impressive reputation. Raziel went first to Warsaw to be briefed by leading NZO figures including Arieh Ben-Eliezer and then on to the meeting with Jabotinsky on Boulevard Victor Emmanuel III in Paris. There were representatives of the NZO and Betar, each of whom presented, often and at length, his special view of the best structure for the movement. As was his habit, Raziel kept his own counsel, said nothing, replied to questions with monosyllables, and greatly disturbed Jabotinsky, who could not comprehend the young man. Raziel's fame had already spread through the diaspora. Samuel Katz, a South African constantly traveling in and out of Palestine on NZO business, had written enthusiastically after first meeting the Irgun commander.

> Of the younger generation here, Raziel is the first who has impressed me as a leader. He is on quite a different plane from all the others I have met. He is the new type of Jew: a soldier. He is tough, he knows what he wants. He is full of "professional" knowledge and he is disseminating it.[17]

So here was the new type of Jew in Paris, who spoke Hebrew, prayed daily, wrote a manual on the pistol, read Clausewitz and the Talmud, engendered deep loyalty and widespread enthusiasm—and had nothing to say. His silence amid men who talked endlessly convinced Jabotinsky that the right man had come to the top of the Irgun. Raziel became Jabotinsky's man in Palestine. The arrangement made in Paris really changed nothing, but satisfied the NZO. The commander of the Irgun would be a member of the Betar command and commander of the Palestine Betar. Thus in Palestine the Betarim were in effect absorbed by the Irgun, and the Irgun now had a formal position within the Revisionist movement. Jabotinsky and the others were satisfied. Raziel appeared to be satisfied—he remained quiet.

On February 21, after another stop in Warsaw, Raziel flew to Lydda airport, arriving the next day. On February 23, he spoke to those about to leave for Poland, without Jabotinsky's knowledge. Little changed for the Irgun except that the pace of outside events quickened over the last months of 1938. In Palestine the British finally took serious steps to end the disorder. On October 18, the military took over the Jerusalem district. On October 24, all Mandate road traffic came under security control. Reinforcements arrived, made use of the improved roads, and began winkling the Arab fedayeen out of the hills. Infiltration across the Mandate borders trickled off and stopped. Freelance brigands went home, and el-Kaukji's bands began to dissolve. The early Arab enthusiasm was stopped by month after month of sacrifices. Arab unity collapsed in recrimination and quarrels; and the British kept up the military pressure, so that by 1939 the end of the revolt was in sight.

Despite the improvement in the Palestinian situation after October 1938, it was a trying and difficult year for the British authorities. The death toll for all concerned was much too high: 486 Arab civilians killed, 636 wounded; 1,138 rebels killed, 196 wounded; 292 Jews killed, 649 wounded; 12 others killed, 6 wounded. The British security forces lost 69 killed and 233 wounded and presumably killed a great many more rebels than officially listed. While it was true that the armed rising seemed to be ending, the bands breaking up, and their leaders quarreling, the British recognized that the basic Arab grievances remained. The year ended on a hopeful military note. Although the security situation had improved and order had increasingly been imposed, the political dilemma remained: the Mandate was unworkable, and the obvious alternative, partition, would be imposed on the Arabs and opposed by the Jews. One more commission—the Woodhead Commission, appointed on February 28, 1938— reported on November 9, suggesting a new partition model that was obviously a nonstarter. Simultaneously, there were a variety of informal proposals, all of which envisioned limitations on the Jewish national home and an Arab majority. These suggestions were not uncongenial to the British administration in Palestine, to British Arabists, or to many in London concerned with British imperial interests at a time of rising threats from Nazi Germany and Fascist Italy. Once the Arab rebels were crushed—reinforcements were brought into the Mandate after October to accomplish this—an accommodation might be fashioned that would placate the Arabs, if at Zionist expense. In August 1938, Malcolm MacDonald, the colonial secretary, came to Palestine to consult with High Commissioner MacMichael. On November 23, 1938, MacDonald announced a round table conference that would convene on February 7, 1939, to be attended by representatives of the Arabs and Jews. With the European situation critical, the time had come to finish with Palestine.

The St. James Conference was attended by envoys of the independent Arab states. Jamal al-Husseini was head of one Palestine delegation and members of the Nashashibi composed another, along with representatives of the Jewish Agency, Agudath Israel (orthodox Zionists), and dignitaries of British Jewry. The NZO was not represented because the Jewish Agency had refused to invite them. In London the Jewish representatives were understandably fearful that they would be asked to endorse a prepared British "solution" that would at best freeze the situation and at worst call a halt to the march of Zionism. From the first, MacDonald underlined the primacy of British imperial considerations if war came. British air and sea lifelines to India and the Pacific crisscrossed the Arab Middle East. The naval base at Alexandria was vital; Iraqi oil piped into Haifa was vital; Iranian oil had to move through the Persian Gulf, and the British navy through the Suez Canal. A tranquil Arab world was essential, for even Saudi irregulars or a renewal of irregular violence in Palestine could endanger crucial British interests. The arguments of Ben-Gurion, Weizmann, and the rest, the intervention of Orde Wingate stressing the potential Jewish military contribution in any war, and the old friends in high places were weighted in the balance by MacDonald and his military advisors and found wanting. The Arabs were more important; in a war against Nazi Germany, the archenemy of Jewry, all the Zionists would have to aid Britain. Although some within the British political establishment clung to the efficacy of Neville Chamberlain's appeasement policy, the St. James Conference indicated that others did not, that war loomed, and that the Arabs had to be placated. Not surprisingly, despite a welter of proposals and intense discussion, the conference produced no solution. The Jewish representatives simply could not concede as much as MacDonald required, nor were the Arabs willing to accept less than all. With conciliation and agreement impossible, the St. James Conference collapsed; and the British felt free to announce an imposed solution, in their own best interests if no one else's.

In Palestine the direction of British intentions, if not the details of negotiation, soon became apparent. Mobs taunted the Jews as "children born to die." The Irgun replied in kind. During the month of February, 113 people were killed and 153 wounded in the Mandate. It was a long and bloody month and underlined the need for the restoration of order. On March 15, the Germans occupied Prague. Chamberlain's dream of peace in his time had all but collapsed. Others might dream of further appeasement, but the pragmatists foresaw imminent war. On March 18, in a speech at Birmingham, Chamberlain announced the end of concessions. Two days before came Malcolm MacDonald's final proposals. There would be no Palestinian state for ten years and then only with a Jewish-Arab agreement. Over the next five years certificates for seventy-five thousand Jewish immigrants would be issued, but after that no more without Arab approval. Finally, there were limits placed on land sales to Jews. The Arabs felt cheated, the Jews betrayed, the British confident that they had acted as honest brokers. Efforts to prevent or delay the release of the proposals in a white paper failed; and on May 17 they were published. The Irgun blew up the Palestine Broadcasting Service the same day. Next day, May 18, spontaneous rioting took place at the Immigration Office. Zionist-British relations were transformed even within leftist Zionist circles. The Jewish Agency entered into an activist period—although immigration and settlement were stressed as the appropriate response to the white paper, a military alternative was developed as well. Yitzhak Sadeh began organizing a large field force, and a new unit, the Special Squads, was formed. The Special Squads were intended to punish Arab terrorists and Jewish informers, undertake anti-British operations, and train for illegal immigration—in this they paralleled the missions of the underground Irgun. The Irgun, however, had already existed as an underground force with no need to fight through the bureaucratic and ideological jungles that hampered the Haganah. While the operations of the Special Squads against Britain were erratic, occasionally independent, and often linked to the immigration struggle, the Irgun suffered from no such restraints. The high command remained of one mind, its actions tied only in theory to NZO decisions. And the Irgun commanders knew that the arms for five thousand men were already packaged for consignment—a real shift in the Palestine equation was imminent. In the meantime the Irgun undertook a series of anti-British operations and continued to push counterterror against the Arabs.

On May 23, in Jerusalem, the Irgun killed their first policeman, Arieh Polanski. On May 29, a bomb was detonated in an Arab movie theater in Jerusalem. In June there were bombs in telephone booths in Tel Aviv, Jerusalem, and Haifa. On June 12, the main post office was bombed. There were bombs in coffee houses, and there was sniping against Arab quarters. On July 30, the Jerusalem radio station was sabotaged. All of this had occured, however, without Raziel, who had been arrested in late May just before he could open further unity negotiation with Pinchas Ratenburg, head of the Vaad Leumi. He had been replaced by Kalay without any change of policy.

In August a trap mine was prepared for Ralph Cairns, commander of the Jewish department of the CID, who was accused of torturing Irgun prisoners. Both Cairns and another British officer, Barker, were killed in the explosion. The CID got their own back a few days later, when, on August 31, they swooped on a house in Aharonovitz Street in Tel Aviv and arrested Kalay, Stern, Dov Haichman, and two others. The entire high command had been lifted at one go, leaving the new man on the outside, Yaacov Meridor, an awesome reorganizing task. At this point the bombs and assassinations of the Irgun—a campaign waged almost in isolation of other considerations—became all but irrelevant. While Raziel and then Kalay were concentrating on their violent reply to the white paper, Europe had rushed down the road to the war that would change everything. After the German invasion of Poland and the subsequent British declaration of war, the assumptions of the white paper policy appeared vindicated: the Jews of Palestine could not oppose Hitler's enemies.

British Palestine policy has remained, even a generation later, a source of confusion and partisan contention. There are still heated advocates of various conspiracy theories, although the nature of the conspiracy differs from one exposition to another. The fatal flaw in each theory is the assumption that Britain ever had in Palestine a conscious, coherent policy that was an integral part of a grand design. British Palestine policy was more often than not a sometimes thing, a garment of rags sewn by various hands for various, often contradictory, purposes. Within Palestine, and within Zionist circles in the diaspora, Palestine was so crucial to the central interests of the Jews that all tended to assume that it was equally crucial to Britain. Surely the British knew what they wanted, what they intended. Surely Palestine was vital to imperial interest, a continuing factor in all British strategic concerns.

Alas, for those watching fearfully for every hint of movement in London or Jerusalem, this was not the case at all. Palestine seldom became important at a cabinet level except when there was real trouble. Then the inclination was to make it go away with a promise or a report or a shift in personnel, so that attention could be redirected to really important matters: the woeful state of the economy, great-power maneuvers, the prospect of war, the next election. Several other factors operated that further confused analysis. First, Britain faced a contradictory responsibility in terms of the Mandate; second, it compounded the administrative tasks in the Mandate with overlapping interests—the Colonial Office, the Foreign Office, and the General Staff; and third, Britain found Palestine a unique colonial experiment that engendered unexpected responses.

There is no doubt that at various levels, from the cabinet down to the clerks in the administration, many people tried to make the Mandate work, did not see that there was a contradiction between a Jewish national home and the aspirations of the Arabs. The land could not be twice promised without causing endless anguish and ultimately a resolution based on force. The British—the CID inspector or the colonial secretary or chief of the General Staff—had to lean either one way or the other in interpreting the scope of the Jewish national home. And there were those people who simply wanted to see the taxes collected, malaria eradicated, the brigands arrested or the roads repaired. Others higher up, with more responsibility, often simply wanted to do the bidding of the cabinet and thus found their power purposeless when the cabinet appeared to have no clear course but the evasion of decision.

The peculiar nature of Palestine meant that previous British imperial experience was inapplicable. Ordinarily, at the edge of empire, the wilderness was tamed, order imposed, the rule of law established, and the natives taught to play the game. Since the British game was often so obviously superior to what had previously existed, a great many natives chose to play. Order was maintained not so much by laws as by mirrors: a few British policemen, a local constabulary, and the acceptance of the population. In time the natives felt that they no longer needed a British coach to play the game and agitated for self-determination, a process that might, in the more primitive areas, be a prolonged procedure, in others somewhat swifter. In Palestine this model simply did not fit. The Arabs did not want to play the game. For most Arab nationalists this role was insufficient, a constant humiliation, acceptable only if other Arab rivals were more dangerous than the British protector was arrogant. In Palestine, then, from the first, the Arabs wanted independence; lacking the conventional skills and capacities of Western societies, they resorted to their primitive virtues—brigandage, religious fanaticism, riot. In time the British might have reached an accommodation, as the French did in Syria, kept a restricted imperial presence, adapted to independence (as they would do in Egypt), but Zionism hindered any such conventional solution. No one could quite find a satisfactory way to define out of existence the Balfour Declaration.

When it became imperative to do so in preparation for the onset of war, the Yishuv had become for both Arabs and British too great a factor simply to brush under the carpet. The Jews of Palestine were too numerous to be ignored, even though they themselves often felt powerless. And this Jewish presence constantly grated on British imperial sensitivities. Like the Arabs, the Jews had no interest in the British game, needed no introduction to the law. The Yishuv also from the first entered into an adversary position with the administration. The Jews sought change, the administration—like any administration—the easy life. While anti-Semitism may have played a part in individual cases, British distaste was inspired by the attitudes and actions of these new Jews, whose aspirations contradicted British imperial interests. It was always too simple to see British policy as slowly tilting to an Arab accommodation, cunningly eroding the Jewish national home for special advantage. Rather, the contradictions in the Balfour Declaration remained, thereby imposing contradictions on British policy. Hence no one could ever be exactly sure of British intentions, since there was ample evidence to prove they would stay or go, opt for partition or oppose it, abet Arab rebellion or crush it.

If there was one period of coherence where even the usual fig leaf of hypocrisy was eschewed, that occurred from December 1938 until well into the war. British policy in Palestine was based on an analysis of British needs in the event of a European war, the relative strategic assets of Arabs and Zionists, and the impact of such a course elsewhere. Once that course had been undertaken, dissent at all levels was for some time minimal, and from policeman to high commissioner the administration in the Mandate followed the London Arabist line, sometimes with compassion for the anguish of the Yishuv, often without. The outbreak of the war against Hitler assured that the Jews would have to accept their present white-paper position, persisting until a better day. Thus, unlike previous tilts, the new British posture did not guarantee a violent attempt to redress the balance. Even the Irgun felt it mad to oppose Hitler's most effective enemy, and it would be two years before a few followers of Avraham Stern would undertake armed action against the alien occupier.

Jabotinsky announced full NZO support for the British war effort on September 5, 1939. Raziel, in the Sarafand camp, endorsed the decision by letter the following day. On September 9, an Irgun broadsheet to that effect was distributed. As the only Zionist commander free in Palestine, Zeroni refused to accept Raziel's instructions. Deeply committed to the campaign against the white paper, Zeroni feared that an Irgun alliance with Britain would destroy the organization, transform it into an imperialist tool. He was almost alone. Meridor returned from Poland and assumed command, with his first priority a prison break to free Raziel and as much of the leadership as possible. Although Meridor managed to smuggle himself into Sarafand camp disguised as a laborer, the escape plan aborted. Meanwhile, inside the camp, there was an intensive debate over the immediate future. Stern preferred an equal truce to a unilateral cease-fire, but there was as yet little dissent from the Jabotinsky-Raziel position. Outside, the NZO leader, Dr. Altman, who had been under house arrest, opened efforts to have the prisoners freed now that the Revisionists backed the British war effort, an effort so far less than promising.

Although Britain had entered the war to protect the Poles, within a month Poland had been overrun, first by the Germans and then by the Russians. While the speed and skill of the German blitzkrieg—the Russians had rolled in from the east as a scavenger army—stunned and disheartened the Anglo-French allies, all for them was not lost. Some in London and Paris felt an accommodation with Hitler was still possible, even crucial, now that the eastern front had disappeared. In any case, as weeks passed with only limited fighting, the impact of the initial German triumph ebbed, but not in Palestine. For the Revisionists, the disappearance of Poland, and with it the Polish Betarim, ended the dream both of a 1940 expedition as well as the support, funds, and enthusiasm of the strongest and most militant segment of the diaspora. No one, of course, foresaw the holocaust, although Jabotinsky's oratory had certainly indicated such a possibility, but everyone recognized that for the foreseeable future the Polish Jews were lost to Zionism. As the war progressed, with one German victory after another, Zionist disarray was compounded; the Baltic states of Latvia, Lithuania, and Estonia fell to the Soviets, and with them many Betarim disappeared; Czechoslovakia had already been occupied; the Balkan states rapidly became hostile to Jews in general and Zionists in particular, and eventually, except for Yugoslavia, they allied themselves to Germany and the *Endlösung*. That, however, in the autumn of 1939, was part of an unimaginable future. All the Irgun knew was that at a severe moment of crisis, with the entire high command arrested, the news from Europe was appallingly bleak. In time it became clear that a few of the more resourceful or fortunate Polish Revisionists had evaded arrest or internment and reached Palestine. Somehow, in some way, the core of the militants dribbled into the Mandate over the next few years: Menachem Begin, Natziv of the Polish Betar, after a series of adventures as a Russian prisoner of war and a member of General Wladyslaw Anders's pro-Allied Polish army; Rabbi Scheib; Yellin-Mor, and Stern's other contacts smuggled out and then smuggled in. One complete Betar unit arrived intact. In October 1939, however, all was chaos at the Irgun center: the commanders in prison, the members out of touch.

During the last week of October, chained hand and foot, Raziel was removed from Sarafand camp and taken to the King David Hotel in Jerusalem. There he was released as a result of the intervention not of Altman but Ruttenberg. Why the Jewish Agency wanted Raziel alone freed, why the British agreed, and why Raziel accepted the offer remain moot questions. Certainly the remaining Irgun commanders in Sarafand were embittered. Even without policy differences, those inside and those outside of prison, limited to covert communications, holding different priorities, and with vastly differing schedules, often exaggerated misunderstandings into bitter divisions. The process began with Raziel's release, leaving the others to nurse their grievances in an atmosphere of growing distrust.

Once free, Raziel found that there was little that he could do. The cease-fire meant the end of the underground mission of the Irgun. Although some NZO leaders called for enlistment in the British army, the Irgun's position remained unclear. Some Revisionists wanted an entirely separate Jewish army. The NZO representative in London, Hillel Kook, left for the United States as "Peter Bergson" to form the committee for a

Jewish Army, plus a host of front and support groups. Other Revisionists would have been satisfied with Weizmann's request for a Jewish division within the British Army. The Irgun, however, dithered and only much later encouraged selective enlistment. In June 1940, the British released the remaining members of the high command, and the recriminations began. Raziel resigned, to the horror of Dr. Altman. "How can you," Altman asked, "who have seen so much warfare and blood, back down at such a critical time?"[18] For a month the acrimony and confusion continued. Increasingly, most of the commanders backed Stern as an alternative to Raziel, but at Altman's request, Jabotinsky cabled his reappointment of Raziel. Jabotinsky had grave doubts about Stern's practicality and regarded his dream of an armed uprising as premature. At the end of 1938, when Stern was in Poland, Jabotinsky had personally rejected the idea. Jabotinsky had decided in February 1939 that Raziel was his man.

Then on August 4, six days after Raziel's reappointment, Jabotinsky died while on a mission to the United States. By then two attempts to heal the split between Stern and Raziel had failed. With the movement split, with Poland under Russo-German occupation, with the strength of Betar in eastern Europe lost forever, with Jabotinsky dead, with no mission in Palestine, the Irgun had no apparent purpose.

It continued to drift. Some members left to enlist in the British army; but others preferred to stay in Palestine as the Axis victories became more threatening. Only once or twice did an occasion occur that permitted real action. During 1940, as conditions for European Jewry worsened, the erratic and illegal immigration into Palestine became a crucial matter for the Yishuv. Jews fortunate enough to reach ports in Rumania and Bulgaria were crammed into tiny, unsanitary, barely seaworthy hulks that had been scavenged or bought by agents of the Haganah or the Irgun or by private individuals. In November 1940, two of the ships reached Palestinian waters, and the British interned the newly arrived "illegals." On November 20, the Mandate authorities announced that the immigrants would be expelled to the island of Mauritius. The illegals were transferred to the *Patria* in Haifa harbor preparatory to expulsion. The Haganah and Irgun put a protest bomb on the *Patria*. Meir Mardor of the Haganah smuggled the explosives on board, but no one had calculated just how fragile the *Patria* would prove. The explosion on November 25, instead of being a symbolic display, tore out the side of the ship, which sank almost immediately. Over 250 lives were lost. Even then, only the intervention from London prevented the surviors of the explosion from being expelled. Nothing saved the illegals of the *Atlantic*, who were sent to Mauritius and, according to High Commissioner MacMichael, would never be permitted to return. At best the Irgun tried to maintain some momentum, scavenge arms, collect funds, although the Mandate authorities warned in the summer of 1941 that further "extortion" would not be permitted—the Irgun fund raisers were not inclined to take no for an answer.

There was, of course, the possibility of a real alliance with the British that would permit the Irgun to act as a military unit. The Irgun intelligence officer, Yoseph Dukler, who had briefly been commander during a crisis, had already established informal contacts with the British during the efforts to free the prisoners. In the meantime Raziel reconstructed a high command which included Meridor, Moshe Segal, Nissim Cohen, and Dov Rubinstein as chief of staff. Stern and the others went their own way, determined to organize an armed struggle no matter what. Raziel then sounded out Keitling, commander of the Jewish department of the CID, but without results. Finally, Arieh Possak and Yitzchak Berman, who in June 1940 offered Irgun help to the British, received some signs of official interest. In January 1941, Berman went to Cairo, and it became clear that the British were indeed interested in organizing special operations using Palestinians. In March and April the first sabotage group was trained for a mission in North Africa. It failed. On May 13, Berman was asked by Colonel Simpson if the Irgun would undertake a special operation in Iraq.

By mid-1941 the British position in the Middle East had been transformed. The Germans were threatening Cairo. France had fallen, and the collaborationist Vichy government had grown lax in maintaining neutrality in Lebanon and Syria. The Irgun had made contact with the Free French, foreseeing a Middle East alliance based on mutual interest. In April a pro-German coup brought a new man, Rashid Ali, to power in Iraq. The mufti arrived in Baghdad to plot once again against the British, who seemed isolated and on the point of collapse. With German bombers nightly over the home island, with the sea lanes interdicted by German U-boats, without allies or military prospects, Britain was *in extremis*. The mufti was delighted with Rashid Ali's advent and the German connection. Hitler had not only shown himself a great commander, but also his views on Jewry appeared identical with those of the mufti. In fact, as early as November 1937, the mufti had dispatched Dr. Said Iman to Berlin, where he met Goebbels and von Ribbentrop. In September 1940, the mufti's private secretary, Osman Kemal Haddad, had been sent on another mission to Berlin to propose a formal German-Arab alliance, again without specific results. German intentions in the Middle East were complex and often contradictory. Berlin's policy was in the hands of various competing bureaucracies with shifting priorities. The mufti had some difficulty in understanding why a firm agreement was not possible since the Arabs and Nazis had such bitter mutual enemies and so few differences. The Germans at last showed serious interest in Rashid Ali's fate. By then Rommel's panzers threatened Egypt, and in June 1941 Operation Barbarossa was launched against Russia—trouble in the British rear to the south of Russia offered immediate charms. To the British it was a clear danger. In May 1940, German support planes began landing at Syrian airbases on the way to Iraq. With only limited resources the British had to strike swiftly before Rashid Ali could be fully reinforced.

The British decided to use members of the Irgun for a penetration sabotage raid against an oil refinery in the Baghdad area. This attack was supposed to cause confusion at the center and thus distract Iraqi attention from other British maneuvers. Although such an agreement would mean that the British officially recognized the Irgun—the operation was authorized by Wavell, commander in chief of the Middle East—the Irgun high command wanted more: the opportunity to capture or eliminate the mufti in Baghdad and the right to operate independently. The second condition was readily accepted, but the British balked at the mufti. The reply was, "No mufti, no action." The British commanders felt that the Irgun raid might be crucial, since Rashid Ali had rounded up all British citizens in Baghdad and threatened to kill them if bombed—the sabotage operation would be a proxy air raid with no risk to the civilians. Still they were reluctant to become involved with the mufti, so they indicated that as long as nothing officially was known nothing could be done officially to limit the Irgun's operation. Raziel was delighted and chose the three-man team of Meridor, Yaacov "Sika" Amrami, and Yaacov Tarazi. Raziel as "Ben-Moshe" would lead the operation. When the four men flew into Habbaniya, the only British territory in Iraq, they found that the oil-sabotage job had been canceled and were asked instead to undertake an intelligence mission toward Pluga to discover the extent of Iraqi defenses. On May 17, accompanied by a British major and his aide, the four were driven beyond British lines until they arrived at an area that had been flooded by the Germans. Raziel decided that Meridor and Amrami would commandeer a small boat and see what they could discover, while the others returned to base. The car started back.

Tarazi took out a package of cigarettes. Raziel asked if he could have one. Tarazi tapped out another, but

> before I could take out the matches the whole world blew up. A bomb exploded on the roof of the car. I sat next to Raziel and saw his face dripping blood. I was in shock. I raised his head and this stopped the blood. I didn't know if I was coming or going. Where the major had been sitting was a mound of flesh. His head was gone and the sergeant's legs were removed. On the roof of the car was a big hole.[19]

A German scout plane poking about just beyond British lines had spotted the military car, drifted down unnoticed by the occupants, and dropped a single bomb. The major was killed instantly; the wound on the right side of Raziel's head was fatal; Somehow the sergeant lived. Tarazi, splattered with others' blood, had not been touched. When Meridor and Amrami returned to find that Raziel had been lost, they were shattered.[20] Jabotinsky and Raziel both dead, Stern and the old high command gone, the Betarim of the diaspora gone. It seemed like the last blow for the Irgun.

After carrying out a sabotage raid on a bridge southwest of Baghdad, Meridor returned to Palestine to assume command of the nearly defunct Irgun. His most important associates were Arieh Possack and Israel Pritzker, his intelligence officers—intelligence accumulation seemed the only remaining mission. Even Raziel's last high command faded away. Moshe Segal joined the Haganah, Dov Rubinstein died, and Nissim Cohen was arrested. Dukler's colleague in making the British connection, Yitzchak Berman, continued to work for their intelligence. He was assigned to Turkey and disappeared out of the Irgun net. Other less important members simply went into the British army. Only Pritzker seemed to have a mission, and his contacts with the CID became intimate. The British security forces increasingly saw underground Palestine through Irgun eyes. Their reports used Irgun terminology, and their estimates were based on Irgun information. There were those in the Irgun who suspected that this influence was not a one-way street, that Pritzker was being controlled by those he thought he manipulated. The Sternists, now intently sought by the British security forces as they began their bank raids and gunbattles, believed that Pritzker was in league with the CID. There was little secret made that the Haganah and the Jewish Agency adamantly opposed the Sternists and had given information to the CID when necessary; but there was no firm evidence of this as far as the Irgun was concerned. The rumors and growing lack of trust, however, had an effect, and Pritzker was eased from the center of the scene. Henceforth, no matter how valuable British contact appeared, Meridor and the others decided against such a course.

Meridor did not pretend that the Irgun had an immeditate vital function: his was a caretaking responsibility. He again reorganized the high command to include Raziel's sister Esther, but the high command became a revolving door. With Jabotinsky's control gone there were constant difficulties with the NZO as well. The NZO-Irgun agreement defining the various responsibilities and limits did not work particularly well. There were sporadic distributions of pamphlets and broadsheets, and an occasional clandestine radio broadcast. Some arms were lifted from the British, but little could be hidden. Various sabotage devices and operations suggested by Meridor to the British and Russians were declined.

One of the few positive notes was the arrival in Palestine of Menachem Begin in early May 1942. He had been appointed commander of the

Polish Betar in 1938, captured by the Russian army in 1939, and sentenced to hard labor until 1948. He had enthusiastically volunteered for General Anders's Free Polish Army and arrived in Palestine with them—a backdoor entry to the Promised Land. Begin's presence did not ease Meridor's command problems, the squabbling and feuds, the drift and resignations, the suspicions about the CID connection, but at least his advice was a net asset. Meridor in fact began to suspect that his own usefulness as commander had nearly come to an end.

Meridor felt the time had come for action, at best a real revolt but at least a significant operation. At the beginning of 1943, however, the prospects for any revolt remained dim. The strength of the Irgun had eroded; there were few arms, few safe houses, few armories, little equipment, less money. Meridor decided on a single spectacular operation. He intended to kidnap the high commissioner. Such a deed would in no way harm the British war effort, still an important consideration, but would punish MacMichael, the symbol of the closed gates. Increasingly, during 1941, those closed gates became of paramount importance to the Yishuv as rumor piled on rumor that European Jewry was undergoing unprecedented suffering. In April 1942, the mass deportation of the *Endlösung* had begun, and by the time the World Zionist Organization met on May 9–11, 1942, in New York, news from occupied Europe indicated that only 25 percent of the endangered Jews might survive. In Palestine, on July 18, *Davar* first published the probable fate of European Jewry. On December 17, the Big Three announced the transportation of the Jews "in conditions of appalling horror and brutality" to eastern Europe.

> None of those taken away are ever heard of again. The able-bodied are slowly worked to death in labour camps. The infirm are left to die of exposure and starvation, or are deliberately massacred in mass executions. . . . The number of victims of these bloody cruelties is reckoned in many hundreds of thousands.[21]

No one could think yet in the millions, but in Palestine Meridor had lost patience. MacMichael would be kidnapped and then secretly shipped to "exile" in Cyprus. The British would be humiliated and the cruelty of the closed gates revealed to the world. Alas, like so many other Irgun operations and expectations during the bitter years of drift, the MacMichael kidnapping aborted, and hope of a revolt again faded. Meridor felt that he had done all that he could. He approached Menachem Begin and suggested that the Irgun needed a new commander, that he had exhausted his own possibilities, that a new direction under a new man was needed. At the same time, Arieh Ben-Eliezer, who had spent the early war years in the United States, arrived in Palestine with firm word concerning the fate of European Jewry and an intense sense of urgency. Something must be done, and he agreed with Meridor that Begin was the man to do it. The long drifting twilight of the Irgun must end. Somehow, some way, they must strike the first blow. There must be a revolt not only against the British, but also against history as written by the holocaust, and against two thousand years of persecution. To do less would be to damn Jewry, in Palestine and out, and tolerate a collusion in genocide little different from that of the British. Begin seemed to be the man to lead these few frantic men, driven by history and despair, into the underground, against an empire, against all odds, in what might be no more than a blood sacrifice. By the end of 1943, the black despair that had driven Stern to arms had grown darker.

NOTES

1. Jacques Soustelle, *The Long March of Israel* (New York: American Heritage Press, 1969), p. 16. see also F. Pietri, *Napoléon et less Israelites* (Paris: Berger-Levrault, 1965).

2. Soustelle, p. 16.

3. Ibid, p. 17.

4. Theodor Herzl, *The Complete Diaries*, New York and London, Herzl Press and Yoseloff, 1960, vol 2, p. 581.

5. Walter Laqueur, ed., *The Israel-Arab Reader* (New York: Bantam, 1969), p. 18.

6. Ibid., p. 34.

7. Walter Laqueur, *A History of Zionism* (New York: Holt, Rinehart and Winston, 1972), p. 220.

8. Jabotinsky's Warsaw speech translated and supplied by the Jabotinsky Institute, Tel Aviv.

9. Even after the state of Israel was proclaimed, the attempts to organize a disinterested investigation of the Arlosoroff affair was rejected by the government. Eventually, in 1955, a Jewish policeman, Yehuda Tannenbaum-Arazi, proved that Arlosoroff, as the Revisionists claimed, had been killed by Arabs.

10. Laqueur, *History of Zionism*, p. 322.

11. Jabotinsky coined this slogan in 1936 included in a letter to Dr. Yehuda Ben Ari, December 24, 1970.

12. Laqueur, *Israel-Arab Reader*, p. 60.

13. Ibid., p. 61.

14. Ibid., p. 57.

15. Elazar Pedazur, *The History of the Irgun Zvai Leumi*, vol. 1 (Shilton Betar: Israeli Department of Education, September 1959), p. 42.

16. Samuel Katz, *Days of Fire* (London: W. H. Allen, 1968), p. 26.

17.   Ibid., pp. 16–17.

18.   Daniel Levine, "David Raziel: The Man and His Times," (Doctor of Hebrew Letters diss., Yeshiva University, 1969), p. 296.

19.   Ibid., p. 312.

20.   It was in a similar operation against Fort Gouraud in Syria that Moshe Dayan lost his eye.

21.   Great Britain, *Parliamentary Dates*, Commons, vol. 385, col. 2083.

PART II

THE NIGHTS
OF DESPAIR:
Avraham Stern and the
Men Without Names

We are the men without names, without kin,
Who forever face terror and death . . .
In the days that are red with carnage and blood,
In the nights that are black with despair.

— *Stern*

Stern never had time for prudence. Orthodoxies and conventions offended him. Brilliant, at ease in Greek and Hebrew, politically erratic, handsome and charismatic, his colleagues often despaired of making conventional use of his undeniable talents. When the split came in the summer of 1940, few were surprised. It had been obvious for years that Stern would not wait on events, could not compose his soul, and sought a means to act. He attracted about him impatient, driven, desperate men who also mistrusted politics and believed in deeds. After September 1939, as the Irgun drifted in the doldrums without a mission, its leadership shuttled in and out of prison at British convenience, Stern's need for action became overpowering. His disagreements with Jabotinsky, now in distant exile, cut off from Palestinian reality, and with Raziel, who as the quiet, grey wolf of the Irgun felt no compulsion to blood sacrifice, were as much a matter of style as substance. Stern differed on specifics, of course, but what made him different was his vision, so luminous that his followers were blinded to the obstacles that Raziel, Meridor, and the rest could so clearly see. The Sternists went their own way, on a path leading for most to prison or an early grave. Yet they walked into harm's way with a driving sense of purpose, a mission that would become messianic as the dark nights of despair began to close in about them.

First organized as the Irgun Zvai Leumi-be-Israel, they hoped that most of the organization would follow them. In fact, most of the high command did follow Stern. Despite some initial recruiting success, it was soon clear that a new form would be necessary. The result was Lohamey Heruth Israel (Fighters for the Freedom of Israel) or LEHI, directed by a high command but dominated by Stern, now known by his underground alias "Yair" (Illuminator).[1] Some solid Irgun men like Yehoshua Zelter and Zeroni had come along, as did many of the converts Stern had made in Poland. An important volunteer was Israel Scheib who joined after escaping Poland and arriving in Palestine. LEHI was still relatively small, ill-equipped, and poorly funded, without any significant political support either in the Mandate or abroad. Consequently, in order to act on events, to have an impact on the future, Stern and LEHI had to fashion strategy and tactics that recognized this unpleasant reality. Unlike the Irgun, an underground army, or the Haganah, an underground militia, LEHI would be a revolutionary organization employing the traditional weapons of the weak. All were familiar with their eastern European revolutionary ancestors, the anarchist assassins, syndicalist gunmen, the Black Hand, and the People's Will, and all knew the fate of tsars, kings, and some bourgeois politicians.

Recourse to revolutionary terror was neither alien nor unpalatable; it caused Stern and LEHI no moral qualms; the only concern was how effective it would be. Even then, Stern's strategy was not simply terror, or terror as a last option: in his analysis of the reality of 1940, violence would play only one part in the approaching drama. As the years passed, however, that part dominated the script. LEHI as the Stern Gang evolved in conventional eyes into the most violent and unrestrained terrorist organization of the modern era. To many people, the Stern Gang remains the epitome of terrorist vocation, a tiny group of men without restraint, driven by dreams and fantasies, rebels beyond compromise, demented gunmen in pursuit of the impossible.

The reality of LEHI, certainly to those early converts, was quite different. Certainly Stern—Yair—was a charismatic, compelling leader; certainly there were dreams and a distaste for cant and compromise. But Zionism was a dream, and each year the realization of the state came closer. This, as much as anything, caused anxiety within LEHI; for these men, all true believers, suspected that the tides of history were about to be reversed. Someone must make the Yishuv realize that Britain had sold out Zionism in the name of expediency, that a homeland was never given but won, that the time to act had come. Stern remained convinced that Britain, as foreign occupier, was the main target. The Anglocentric strategy and assumptions of Weizmann and the Jewish Agency had been a snare and illusion from the beginning. The Jews who believed in a community of Zionist and British interests and in a British moral commitment to the Jewish Homeland were the dreamers, not LEHI. Year after year, orthodox Zionists explained away British policies, the slow shift, the commissions that whittled away at Zionist privilege, the concessions to the Arabs, the restrictions on the Jews.

On a grander scale the Conservative government had time and again appeased the archenemy Hitler and sacrificed old friends. Yet, even in the ranks of the Revisionists and Betar, not until the white paper of May 1939 did the growing suspicions receive confirmation. There were still some who explained away even this betrayal as a momentary British aberration, but not Stern and LEHI. They trusted none but the pure, their own, never princes, pacts, and promises. They realized that Britain had deceived them and they had deceived themselves. Mattiyahu Shmulevitz, who under sentence of death had a natural interest in the procedure of judicial hanging, said, "The noose, whose presence we had only previously suspected, tightened, and we dropped into a bottomless pit."[2] Stern recognized the pit, but the rest of the Irgun, after the outbreak of war in September, remained trapped between their abhorrence of Hitler and their suspicions of British intentions. And the Irgun had collapsed. Despite orders, some had gone into the British Army to fight Hitler and gain military experience. Some, like Raziel and Meridor, had cooperated with the British in the Middle East. Others simply waited. Once out of prison, Stern refused to wait. He saw Shmulevitz's bottomless pit and a way out in LEHI's recourse to terror.

While personal terror was the key ingredient in Stern's strategy, he recognized that there was no need to limit his operations to revolutionary violence against the British authorities in the Mandate, for those authorities had many enemies who might be LEHI allies. Stern and his colleagues believed there was no fundamental clash in the aspirations of Arab nationalists and Zionists: the Arabs had been misled in their recent attacks on Jews. There were regular LEHI attempts to make contact, to establish an anti-imperialist front. The only result was a few tenuous discussions, often in prison, and no effective cooperation. More promising, if less ideologically attractive, were Britain's declared enemies, first Germany and then, in June 1940, Italy. No matter that these potential allies might be the enemies of Zionism and were demonstrably anti-Semitic in posture and policy—Mussolini had initiated anti-Semitic measures to cement his Pact of Steel with Hitler. If the Axis won the war, which did not seem unlikely after the collapse of France, only LEHI would have earned sufficient credit as a collaborator to negotiate with the victors. If the Axis lost, only the tiny LEHI splinter would be contaminated by collaboration, and the other Zionist institutions could deny them with ease. In 1940 and 1941, such an analysis was easier in the Mandate than subsequently. Palestine was, by distance, by the interruption of conventional travel, by wartime censorship, and most of all by the results of Axis victories, quite isolated from European events. LEHI lived in a pre-1939 world. The evolving nature of Germany's anti-Semitism remained unknown until 1943: the holocaust was in 1940 quite beyond belief; even with the mounting evidence in 1943, there were many who refused to believe it. Little was known of Mussolini's sudden conversion to anti-Semitism. Stern had long been impressed with Italians, if not with the fascists, and they seemed unlikely converts to racism. In any case, even if Nazi Germany were anti-Semitic, so was Poland; but this had not prevented the Irgun-Polish alliance—indeed, anti-Semitism had been the foundation of that alliance since an easing of Polish prejudice in the 1930's would not have been to the advantage of the Irgun and Betar. To Stern the Axis, and especially Italy, appeared to be a potential ally of great worth, more so than the undisciplined and erratic Arab nationalists. Naftali Lubentschik was dispatched to Beirut to make contact with the Italians and sound out German sentiments. Later Nathan Friedman-Yellin was sent on a similar mission to Syria. Nothing came of Stern's diplomatic maneuvers except the arrest of his envoys when they returned to the Mandate.

Thus LEHI had to depend on its own resources, and materially they were scant indeed. Spiritually, however, the men of LEHI felt that in undertaking a revolt a major step had been taken beyond the old Zionist positions. Zionist politics, even within the Revisionist movement, involved endless quibbles and distinctions, the constant clash of strong men thwarting each other in a dozen languages. Movement was difficult through thickets of spite, in the face of old grievances, leftover programs from other days, the claims of obscure theologians and café revolutionaries from Riga or Vienna, arguments stale from endless ideological dissection. As much as anyone could, Jabotinsky opened a door to action, to the creation of new forms that filled a deep need in eastern Europe. For the first time within Zionism, men had marched. The new converts of Betar looked not to old dogmas but to the aspirations of dignity, strength, and power. The flight schools, military camps, and uniforms lifted the Betarim from a future of spring planting and sick cows. These young men had wanted to be soldiers, just pelugot, not farmers. In a very special way, Stern attracted these pure idealists, stripped away the political priorities of Revisionism and, in Jabotinsky's quip, became Weizmann in reverse, offering not politics but deeds, not programs but purpose. The willingness to sacrifice for the dream by undertaking a campaign of personal terror without real allies, arms, money, or popular support, and most of all without an end in sight, remained the one great LEHI asset. And on this single, simple base, Stern and his followers built their revolt.

Stern, of course, while a singular man, was by no means simple-minded, nor was his armed campaign a romantic plunge into frenetic and foolish action. One could not conduct a campaign of limited terror, no matter how determined and bold, without organization, funds, an armory, and the most crucial of all revolutionary tools, a printing press. Almost from the moment of the split, Stern faced serious and unexpected problems. As is often the case after a revolutionary schism, both sides lost more than anticipated. Former members refused to take sides. Arms dumps disappeared and were forgotten, or were moved and lost. There was a scramble for the known caches—the Sternists hurriedly swooped down on an arms dump in a village north of Tel Aviv that the Irgun people had assumed was theirs. A safe house might no longer be safe. The suspicion of informers tainted past loyalties. At the very first there were encouraging signs: perhaps a thousand Irgun members followed Stern's lead, but within months the early converts fell away, and no one appeared to replace them. The strong LEHI centers in Tel Aviv and Haifa became considerably less strong; elsewhere cells simply disappeared. By autumn Stern was left with a few hundred loyalists, a like number of sympathizers, and very little else. There was still no money. One of the first operations was a raid on the Anglo-Palestine Bank in Tel Aviv in September 1940, which netted £5,000. A raid against an Arab bank in Jerusalem failed. Much more to the activists' liking, however, was the bombing on December 19 of the government immigration office at Haifa to protest the deportation of the illegal immigrants to Mauritius. For the British to close the gates to the Promised Land appalled every Jew; to deport those who had come so far produced widespread anguish and frustration. The Haifa bomb seemed to mark a real beginning.

Arms continued to be scavenged and stolen, an elderly Belgian revolver here, an old World War I Parabellum there. It was an armory without order, often without ammunition, repeatedly depleted by raids, unavoidable losses, and the inroads of old age. The most valuable asset was the radio. Then a means to print the internal newspaper *Bamachteret* (In the Underground) was found, and Stern could set forth his principles. Money was collected from friends, from each other, from the doubtful, and from the grudging. When this was not enough (and it never was), LEHI turned to robbery and then extortion. Efforts to explain the revolutionary purpose and principles behind theft, extortion, abduction, and murder convinced very few, not even the militants within the Irgun, who increasingly felt LEHI's policies insane. Despite opposition and indignation, LEHI pursued the means to act, but almost all the energies of the movement during 1941 had to be dedicated solely to creating and maintaining the organization. Even then there was no real growth, but rather a slow erosion of activists and the collapse of the remaining vestiges of popular support. Larger events elsewhere during 1941 had transformed everyone's priorities except, apparently, LEHI's.

During the arguments within prison and after Stern's release, the key point had been the Irgun's response to British belligerence, but all the analysis had been completely within a Palestinian context—the war was a long way off. The first impact of the surrender of Poland and the disappearance of the Betar base had thrown the Irgun even further back into parochial concerns; for now there would be no Project Altalena and, as Jabotinsky and Raziel agreed, no further action against the British. Stern's intentions did not seem a serious matter, particularly since in prison he could not fashion the means to strike at the Mandate authorities. In May and June, when the German panzers struck through the Allied front and into France, the distant European war began to come closer. With France out of the war and the Battle of Britain underway, the possibility of a German invasion of England transformed the prospects of the Yishuv. A German victory in Europe would almost certainly mean the collapse of British control in the Middle East, perhaps even a German occupation of the Mandate. In September, when the Luftwaffe switched attacks from the RAF fighter and radar installations to London, the implications were not clear in Palestine; but as September crept into October without a cross-channel invasion, observers realized that Britain had gained a breathing space. The blitz gutted British cities; the U-boats gnawed at British lifelines, but the end was not yet in sight.

There were, in fact, encouraging signs. On October 28, the Italians invaded Greece, but the Greeks resisted fiercely and in a winter campaign drove the Italians back into Albania. Then, on December 9, General Archibald Wavell launched an offensive against the Italian positions in Libya. The Italian front collapsed and the Allied army pushed on to Bengasi. Meanwhile, to the south, the British attacked Italy's East African empire along several axes. By February 1941, the key Italian position at Keren in Eritrea had fallen, and the prospect of continued Italian resistance became slight. In May the British entered Addis Ababa. By then, however, the rest of the military picture had changed once more to British disadvantage.

In February and March the German army moved into Hungary, Bulgaria, and Rumania without meeting any resistance by the governments, which were co-opted into the Axis. In the case of Yugoslavia, an unexpected coup nullified such a surrender, and the Germans launched an invasion. Simultaneously, panzer columns also invaded Greece. Yugoslavian resistance crumbled, leaving only a few guerrillas in the mountains. The Greeks hung on during April, aided by a British expeditionary force diverted from Egypt. This occurred at the very time that Wavell's Libyan triumphs had given way to a series of sharp reverses administered by General Rommel, who arrived in Tripolitania in February. The Italo-German attack on March 31 scattered the British force, isolated some units in Tobruk, and by April 4 drove the rest across the Egyptian border. To the north the British were forced to withdraw to Crete on May 1, and lost even that toehold by the end of the month after a German parachute drop. The British position throughout the entire Middle East appeared very fragile indeed, and it seemed that at every hand a plot was underway to take advantage of Britain's impending defeat. The bazaars seethed with rumor; German and Italian agents were said to be plotting everywhere; and the drawing rooms were crowded with Anglophobes.

In Egypt the pro-British ministers had been replaced in September 1940 by neutralists, and King Farouk was secretly encouraging pro-fascist politicians. Britain over the years had built up a considerable store of Egyptian resentment, damaged pride, and ill-hidden frustration. With Rommel at the gates, there were many who saw the opportunity to rid Egypt of the British, once arrogant, now *in extremis*. On May 16, 1941, the British managed to arrest Ali al-Masri, the former Egyptian chief of staff just before his plane was to take off secretly for Vichy-controlled Beirut. The British were perfectly aware that he was not the only Egyptian plotter; in fact, eventually, the British had to call up their tanks and impose a satisfactory government on Farouk.

In Iraq the plots of Arab nationalists had already forced British intervention. Rashid Ali, head of a pro-Nazi military clique, the Golden Square, had been installed in power in March 1940 and then eased out for a less provocative leader in January 1941. The pro-British cabinet of Taher al-Hashimi stumbled along until April 2, when Rashid Ali took over again in a bloodless coup. Again the British felt compelled to act, and Churchill ordered an invasion from India. On April 29, British troops landed at Basra. On May 2, the British attacked at Habbaniya in western Iraq and defeated a substantially larger Iraqi force. It was during these operations that Raziel was killed, during a deep-penetration raid. On May 30, the British captured Baghdad; and, for the time being, Iraq was pacified.

By then the situation in Vichy-controlled Syria and Lebanon was acute. During 1941 Italian and German agents and officers became increasingly active. On May 12, the first German planes arrived on their way to help Rashid Ali. The French governor of Syria and Lebanon, General Henri Dentz, had orders from Vichy not to interfere with the airlift. On May 14 and 15, the RAF bombed airfields in Syria. By June 4, 120 German planes had landed in Syria. Dentz, recognizing that the British had been provoked beyond measure and aware that the Free French representative, George Catroux, wanted an invasion, managed to get the German airplanes taken out on June 4, but he was too late. On June 8, the Allies invaded and occupied both Syria and Lebanon.

On a map it would have appeared that by the time Hitler launched Operation Barbarossa against Russia in June 1941 the British had shored up their Mideast position. Egyptian conspirators had been arrested, Rashid Ali crushed, and Iraq, Syria, and Lebanon occupied. Off the map, everyone recognized that these had been desperate operations made necessary by the growing Arab confidence in a British defeat. Rommel had moved further into Egypt, and there was very little between his panzers and Cairo. The expeditions into Iraq and Syria had been small, improvised affairs of odd units, bits and pieces, woefully outnumbered and outgunned by opponents who collapsed on contact. In point of fact, the British grip on the Middle East was all but a confidence trick, managed with mirrors and good luck. With the daily report of fresh German victories in Russia, where dozens of columns raced eastward, occasionally looping about to scoop in whole Soviet armies, the collapse of all coherent resistance seemed a matter of time. In a few months the panzers would be poking south through the Caucasus. Rommel might already have reached Cairo and moved on Palestine from the southwest.

During the bleak months of 1941, the war had come to dominate the thinking of the Yishuv. It was no longer a question of distant campaigns but a clear and present danger. The Palestinian Arabs made no secret of their glee at the British plight and Jewish vulnerability. Their fedayeen gangs began to operate again. Palestinian Jews serving in various units in Egypt or Syria sent back little cheerful news. Even the British willingness to take convicted felons like David Raziel and Moshe Dayan out of prison to use as commandos showed the seriousness of the problem. Everyone feared the worst. The Irgun made contact with the Free French to plan a resistance movement if Palestine were overrun. Others moved into the hills to inspect possible last lines of defense. Even the optimists feared that time was running out.

In the midst of this gloom and anxiety, Stern and LEHI continued on their course. In January 1941, the LEHI proposal, delivered by Lubentschik in Beirut to the local German intelligence agent Roser, and to Otto von Hentig of the German Foreign Office, was transmitted to the German consulate in Beirut. Beirut was a city engrossed with rumors, a gossip mill without secrets, alive with fantasies. Even if the LEHI contact had been elsewhere, it was likely that by 1941 there would have been leaks in Palestine. In 1941 almost no Jew had any sympathy for Stern's mad plans and flawed strategy. Just to tolerate LEHI, to pay money, to look the other way, now seemed a betrayal of the British defender and the future of any Jewish Homeland. Stern seemed not a prophet without honor but a man out of time and place. Even the Irgun was alienated. In fact, LEHI people assumed that Irgun intelligence, in particular the mysterious Israel Pritzker, had tipped the British security forces off to Lubentschik. Consequently, he ended up in Acre prison. No matter, if the Yishuv did not yet know that LEHI had contacts with the Nazis, the British did, and responded accordingly.

In 1940 Stern sought a grand role and embarked on a revolutionary adventure, but by 1941 he was responsible for bank jobs and extortion. None of the LEHI operations—arms thefts, bank robberies, shots in the night, gunbattles with the CID, posters on the walls—inspired the dedicated to act or educated the frightened to defiance. Years before Stern's poems had sung of blood and sacrifice, had foreseen the long nights of the underground. He always seemed to have a romantic longing for death. Now, his refusal to recognize the reality of a world war, the implications of Rommel's panzers and Rashid Ali's plots all but guaranteed his end. His alternative to orthodox Zionism had narrowed to a gang of men on the run. There was no longer hope of triumph, only the prospect of humiliation, disaster, prison, or death. Stern's operations only endangered the existence of the Yishuv.

During the summer of 1941, LEHI radio broadcasts confirmed no change in their attitudes or tactics. The "revolutionary" robberies continued. On December 26, 1941, LEHI pulled off two daring daylight hold-ups in Jerusalem. The next operation was a disaster. On January 9, 1942, a raid on a Histadrut bank in Tel Aviv collapsed in gunfire when the employees refused to give up the money. Two Jewish bank employees were shot dead. No underground radio could explain away dead Jews, men who were not in the police or the British army but simply had been protecting Jewish property. The Yishuv were horrified. The British, too, were adamant that such outrages must be brought to an end; viewed simply as a criminal gang, LEHI was a dangerously disruptive force in the Mandate. In the ensuing searches and interrogations, the CID arrested two prime LEHI suspects, Yehoshive Becker and Nissim Reuven. Deputy Superintendent Schiff, in charge of the Tel Aviv police, and his principal deputy, Inspector N. Goldman, felt confident that they would be able to testify to excellent effect when the two men came to trial—and so did LEHI. All during 1941 British security forces had grown more effective and more determined, particularly since there was an increasing number of Jews, appalled by LEHI's operations, who were willing to give information. In Tel Aviv High Commissioner MacMichael noted that Schiff had been "particularly assiduous in his pursuit"[3] of LEHI people. He now appeared to have scooped up two men guilty of a most unsavory killing. The revolutionary tactics of Stern, now a man on the run with a thousand-pound price on his head, had come down simply to the murder of Jews during commission of a robbery. Schiff, a Jew, hoped that the arrest of Becker and Reuven would be the beginning of the end, and in a way it was.

LEHI naturally did not see the raid on the Histadrut bank as simple robbery, or the two dead Jews as martyrs. Consequently, the immediate necessity was to protect Becker and Reuven, which meant that Schiff and Goldman were prime targets. The operational LEHI people in Tel Aviv, familiar with CID habits, devised a two-step plot. They hoped to trap the entire leadership of the CID. At a little after 9:00 A.M. on January 20, a premature explosion apparently wrecked a LEHI bomb factory at 8 Yael Street. As always, Schiff, accompanied by his CID team of inspectors and constables, rushed to the site to sift the ruins. As soon as Schiff and the others burst into the upstairs room at 9:20, a second bomb detonated. Schiff was killed instantly, Goldman fatally wounded, and two British officers, E. T. Turton and Z. Dichter, were seriously injured. Only Constable Schlewen escaped with minor wounds. The core of the anti-LEHI

CID group in Tel Aviv—four Jews among them—was wiped out; the witnesses against Becker and Reuven would not appear. The British authorities were seriously alarmed. LEHI was delighted, particularly at catching Turton, who had accompanied Ben-Yosef to the gallows in 1938, but disappointed that the other British CID people had avoided Yael Street. MacMichael, less delighted, cabled London that the "criminal activities of a pseudo-political terrorist gang known as the Stern group seriously unsettled Tel Aviv."[4] The trapbomb seriously unsettled the police, who determined to wreak vengeance. It was open season on LEHI.

Consequently, by February it was very difficult for LEHI. Two wireless sets were lost, a bomb factory discovered, more members arrested. British searches, sweeps, and road blocks eroded LEHI ranks; worse, the few remaining supporters outside the movement lost heart. There were no safe houses for those on the run, no place to turn, always the prospect of betrayal and the news of more arrests. Then came a further and nearly fatal blow. A LEHI headquarters in Tel Aviv at 30 Dizengoff Street was raided, obviously the result of a tip-off. The CID team was led by Inspector Geoffrey J. Morton, whom LEHI had missed with the Yael Street trapbomb, and Constable J. T. Wilkin, a keen young officer with perfect Hebrew, who was obviously destined to go far in antiunderground work. Morton, Wilkin, and the CID found that they had made a clean sweep, not only a bomb factory but the central leadership of LEHI: Avraham Amper; two recent escapees, Zelig Jacques and Moshe Svorai; and the director of the LEHI technical department, Yaakov Labshtein. All four surrendered but Morton, who, claiming he feared they might set off a bomb, opened fire anyway. Amper and Jacques were mortally wounded, and died later in the hospital. Both Svorai and Labshtein were severly injured. The CID had not forgotten Yael Street. Within the remaining core of LEHI, police brutality, basement tortures, and murder of suspects became incorporated into a new movement mythology. Despite Stern's plea that they deny themselves personal vengeance, few wanted more than an opportunity to strike back. In February, however, there was very little opportunity to do more than keep ahead of the police.

Even Stern could find no place to stay. A few of the less timorous finally agreed to hide him, but only if he gave up his campaign. The Revisionists could find a place. The Haganah could find a place. Sanctuary was offered by a kibbutz if he would suspend his activities. He refused. Times and men had changed, but not Stern. It was clear to him that the end of the road was near. The search for him was intense. His picture was on every wall. Every newspaper in Palestine, including the Revisionist press, published the wanted photographs of the LEHI leaders. Each day, accompanied by one or two LEHI girls as cover, he crept around Tel Aviv. At night, during the blackout, there was no peace. British patrols stopped passersby and flicked on torches. Stern had to get off the streets at night. The frightened few who would take him in dwindled. He carried a small suitcase containing a collapsible cot and a few clothes. And he still carried the dream. Finally, the short list of old friends was finished. He could not risk his cot in the shelters. The only place left was Tova Svorai's attic flat at 8 Mizrachi B Street in the Florentine quarter of south Tel Aviv. It was hardly going to be a safehouse, since Moshe Svorai had been shot and arrested during the raid on 30 Dizengoff Street less than two weeks before; but it was literally the only place.

Stern arrived with his scuffed suitcase and his folding cot. At least he did not have to use the cot, for there was the Svorai sofa. He stayed inside and kept in touch by smuggling letters out. On the morning of February 12 he sent out instructions to decline a last offer of sanctuary.

> Thank him on my behalf. My response is obviously negative: I am not one of those who surrender themselves voluntarily to the police or to those who serve it and do its will from either the left or the right. (Even the left is ready to take care of me if I would hand myself over to it.)[5]

A few hours later, at 10:30 in the morning, there was a pounding of heavy boots up the narrow stairs. The CID decided it was time to move on Tova Svorai's flat, for they suspected she was hiding someone. Led by Wilkin, the police pushed into the apartment, bringing with them two downstairs neighbors, Mrs. Wiesel and Mrs. Goldberg, as witnesses. There was no sign of Stern, but there had been no chance for anyone to get away. The police persisted, and almost immediately Stern was pulled out of a wardrobe, handcuffed, and pushed down on the sofa. Tova Svorai was ordered to dress, then bundled downstairs and into a patrol car.

Wilkin was tense with triumph, for he knew whom he had. In fact all the police were tense—there had been so much shooting. While two officers kept their pistols on Stern, Wilkin ordered Constable Yeracmiel Lustig to telephone Morton. When he arrived, the two witnesses were sent downstairs, the police guards in the room removed, and Morton was left only with Constable Tennant and Stern. Wilkin immediately left Mizrachi Street, hoping that he could put some distance between himself and what he knew Morton intended. As soon as the other officers had left the room, Morton walked over to Stern and jerked him to his feet. Neither had spoken. Stern had said nothing since being pulled from the wardrobe. Morton then pushed him toward the window. As Stern passed him, Morton lifted his revolver and shot him in the head. After Stern collapsed on the floor, Morton leaned over and shot him in the chest. He turned to Tennant and said, "You saw that he tried to escape."[6] Stern lay in a widening pool of blood until a party of British soldiers arrived and wrapped him in a blanket. He was carried down the narrow stairs, still bleeding. A small crowd had gathered in front of the door, but all they could see was a bundle, with black shoes poking out at one end, and a few last drops of blood. Suddenly, from further up the street, Tova Svorai began shouting, "Jews, they are killing Stern! Jews, they are killing Stern!" They had killed him. Stern bled to death in the gutter of Mizrachi B Street, a condemned man from the moment Morton closed the door behind him, perhaps a doomed man from the very start, certain sooner or later to be shot down "while trying to escape." For LEHI it was the night of blackest despair, but not the end of the dream. For Stern's death was not an end, but a beginning.

The first priority, really the only priority, for LEHI became vengeance. To protect himself, Wilkin had rushed to Yitzhak Berman and told what had happened. Stern had been murdered; the CID must pay. Vengeance, however, proved difficult. Key LEHI leaders were regularly arrested. The new acting commander surrendered in despair. With Stern gone, his death still a blow beyond absorption, with every hand turned against them, with repeated losses of the tiny store of explosives and arms, the remnants of LEHI took weeks to piece together an operation, which soaked up practically all existing resources. Morton proved elusive, but there were others. On April 22, at 8:15 A.M., the official car of M. J. McConnell, assistant inspector general of police, waited outside his door as usual. Two minutes later, an Arab servant wandered by and, noting the waiting limousine, seized the opportunity to curry favor. The moment Inspector McConnel emerged, he swept open the door with a grand gesture. A small package tumbled in front of him. As the Arab innocently leaned over, the package detonated with a roar, killing him instantly. The shaken McConnell was left standing over his shattered corpse. Matters might have been even worse: LEHI had carefully mined the road to the cemetery in order to catch the inspector's funeral cortege—many of McConnell's colleagues would have followed him to the grave. Unfortunately for LEHI, the Arab servant was not buried in the same cemetery, and the mine had to be dismantled.

Once more LEHI had to begin at the beginning. This time the prime target was Morton, stationed in Lydda. Not only the murderer of Stern and the others, Morton had a reputation with LEHI as a man who enjoyed killing. At 8:15 A.M. on May 1, just as his car passed from his house in Sarona to police headquarters in Jaffa, an electronically detonated bomb blasted across the road—and missed. It was the last bomb for a long time. By mid-May LEHI had almost collapsed. Most of the members were in Mizra internment camp, in various prisons, or deep underground in hiding. Since the trapbomb in January, twenty important members had been captured, three killed "resisting arrest," and over 150 were imprisoned.

The radios were gone, the newspapers defunct, the arms dumps lost. Two vengeance bombs had failed. There seemed no way to continue. Zettler was still on the loose, but reduced to sleeping on park benches; and a young volunteer Joshua Cohen retreated into the groves outside Tel Aviv. There were only a few isolated men on the run.

The summer of 1942 was a cruel time; but it was also the beginning of the effort to recreate LEHI without Stern, a task undertaken simultaneously and independently inside prison, in Cohen's hideout, and through the efforts of the few still free. One of the few LEHI people on the outside, Anshuel Spilman, who had arrived with Israel Scheib and the other Polish Sternists in June 1940, began to contact those on the run or hiding out. He found that Tel Aviv was reasonably sound with fifty members, but Haifa was down to twenty actives, and when he arrived in Jerusalem he could turn up only a single follower. There were a few others abroad serving in the Allied forces, and a few more scattered about Palestine—a grand total of eighty. Still, eighty was a beginning. Spilman remained in Tel Aviv while "Elisha"—Yerachmiel Aaronson—took command of Haifa. Zwi Prunim began at the beginning in Jerusalem. Joshua Cohen, the eighteen-year-old activist who, after the last bomb attack on Morton, had withdrawn to the orange grove, existing for some time on food packages smuggled in by his girl friend until contact was made with the new web. Cohen then turned his refuge into an arms training center as a tiny stream of new recruits, attracted by the Stern legend, began making their way to him. Some, like Eliahu Hakim, who originally joined LEHI in 1940 at sixteen but was forced out by his horrified family, came back as soon as the chance was offered. A few LEHI people managed to break out of prison—two escaped from Jerusalem central prison in December 1942—but the real hope was that some of the high command could be sprung. Inside prison and out, the key man was Yitzhak Yzertinsky, who had already demonstrated vast organizational talent. If anyone could put LEHI back together it would be Yzertinsky, a sound, taciturn man of deep beliefs; but he was out of circulation in Mizra detention camp near Acre.

By the beginning of 1943, the British security forces saw the situation as easing in Palestine. The United States had entered the war, and in both the Pacific and Africa the worst seemed over. Victory might be a long way off; but Russia had not collapsed, the Germans had not reached Cairo— the Axis tide had begun to ebb. The Irgun had remained quiescent, and LEHI, to all intents and purposes, did not exist. For the authorities there were matters far more serious than the foolish aspirations of a tiny handful of fanatics. It soon turned out that the fanatics had not been entirely eliminated. As with all political prisoners, covert communication in and out of prison swiftly became a fine art. Messages could often be turned around within a day, so that even in the most difficult times there could be regular contact into Mizra. While those on the outside concentrated on staying outside, the LEHI people inside pursued parallel courses: one to get out—an escape—and two to analyze what had gone wrong. The second, they believed was as important as the first, for if Yzertinsky and the others could be freed it must be to good purpose. The result was an almost continuous LEHI prison seminar in strategy and tactics—the Mizra university.

They felt that the Irgun might never take arms in a real revolt, might be willing to press the British but not to fight them. Thus LEHI had to assume the entire responsibility for opposing the British, still the foreign occupier, the obvious target. Whatever the direction of the war, there could never be a compromise with Britain. In this matter the Jewish Agency was obviously still clinging to old illusions despite the closed gates, the refusal to create another Jewish Legion, the 1939 white paper. Even the Irgun could not break free of Jabotinsky's decision not to oppose the British during the anti-Hitler war. In this matter the events of 1941 and 1942 had changed no one's mind: Britain was the enemy, patently anti-Zionist and pro-Arab. Until the Irgun recognized this, if they ever recognized this, LEHI would go it alone. Thus the basic strategy was to strike as soon as possible in any manner that would hurt. While all the LEHI people in Mizra knew of the other famous undergrounds—Russian, Chinese, Irish—and had considered their tactics and techniques, the Palestine problem appeared unique. Within the Mandate the Jews were a minority, politically the Revisionists were a minority of Jews, and the LEHI was smaller yet. Worse, the overwhelming preponderance of Jewish opinion opposed LEHI. To wage any kind of campaign would be grievously difficult, yet it must be done. Thus Stern's basic premise was accepted; the obvious difficulties of 1941 and 1942 were recognized, and questions of organization and tactics began to dominate the seminars.

One of the basic tactical mistakes of the 1940-1942 period was that the underground was not deep enough. The long previous period of relatively open activity, the political involvement with the Revisionist party, the Irgun-CID link of Pritzker, and the leaks through old friends, family, and former associates had left few secrets when the CID began looking in earnest for LEHI people. LEHI suspected also that the Irgun, the Haganah, and the Jewish Agency had collaborated with the CID to cripple their militant rival, and that such collaboration was LEHI's own careless fault. This time all such connections would be broken: there would be absolutely safe houses or, if this proved impossible, bunkers would be constructed in deserted areas—an option already independently adopted by Cohen. Legal identities, physical disguises, and conventional occupations would hide the LEHI from everyone but a trusted inner circle. This time they would really be men without names, without kin.

Along with the tactical problems of creating an organizational under-ground that could contemplate a revolt, there was, as might be expected within any Zionist organization, endless theoretical analysis of all aspects of Sternist ideology—philosophical and theological questions of looming import. Despite the time devoted to such issues, the real cement holding LEHI to a revolutionary course was the general desire for action, to turn the dream into reality through deeds. There were those, like Friedman-Yellin, disproportionately concerned with political issues—fashioning a common anti-imperialist front, the importance of Russia in the postwar world, the need to contact Arab nationalist movements. Others wanted to take a position on specific issues, such as opposition to strikebreaking. At the other end of the spectrum, Scheib articulated a mystical belief in a greater Israel, a Hebrew state that was the foreordained child of history, a biblical gift. Most important, all the LEHI people in Mizra *knew* the fu-ture could be shaped, knew the purpose and direction of thousands of years of history, grasped their own role, and were frantic to act it. As the weeks dragged into months, they were condemned to the deadening rou-tine of camp life: roll call, mess line, volleyball, exercise in circles, semi-nars, discussions, endless chess games. Their world ended at the strung wire, the glinting Mediterranean in the distance, and mud and dust before them.

Mizra was divided into four separate camps: Jews, Arabs, enemy aliens and prisoners of war. Since by and large only the Jews had any seri-ous interest in breaking out, the British had placed the Jews' compound near the center of the camp. Mizra was far from escape-proof, even with a military training camp and an antiaircraft unit blocking the south side; but there was no point in getting people out if LEHI could not take care of them on the outside. What was needed instead of a mass break was to slip two key people out in such a way that they would have time to reach friends to the south in Haifa before the British knew they had gone. Once in Haifa, Spilman could pass them along, and LEHI on the outside could absorb them. After considerable contemplation, the prisoners devised the Italian-bridge-game gambit.

The Jewish compound nearest the sea had eight huts, a kitchen, showers, WC, a parade ground for exercise, and a shifting population of some 100 to 160 prisoners. As early as April 1941, there had been 150 de-tainees in Mizra, and the figure remained pretty much the same until the internees were shifted elsewhere. Each of the other three compounds was exactly the same—huts, kitchens, showers, WCs, parade grounds for ex-ercise, though their populations were more stable. Outside the four com-pounds was a central office bloc, barracks for the guards, and several warehouses, all within an outer fence of wire that was only loosely guard-ed. Security, in fact, was not the problem with the war drifting further

away and escape pointless. Where would an Italian POW or a German to-
bacco buyer go—where would a LEHI revolutionary go? The LEHI problem was to get out with time to reach Haifa. The plot, then, concentrated
on creating artificial roll calls that would give two men twenty-four hours
to get clear.

Yzertinsky would be one and the second choice was Eliahu Gil Adi.
He was very intelligent, maddeningly brave without fear or hesitation,
and perhaps the best and most dedicated of all LEHI gunmen. Adi had
lived so long on his nerves he no longer seemed to have any. On one January morning, the two, along with several others, were released from the
Jewish inner compound by the guards, as was the custom, to pick up food
from the commissary, which was located outside the inner compounds
but inside the outer wire. They simply slipped around the commissary and
into a storage shed to wait for night. In the meantime the rest of the prisoners came back with the food, along with two Italians from the alien's
camp who had been for some time in the habit of playing bridge with two
Jewish prisoners. The guards counted everyone back into the compound.
There were now the right number of Jews, but the aliens were two short.
The switch had been timed after the aliens' count and before the Jews', so
the guards were no wiser. After the bridge game, and after the guards had
changed, the Italians left the Jewish compound. They explained their
presence to the new guards, who were familiar with the long-running
bridge tournament, and returned to the aliens' compound. The aliens now
had the proper number for the evening roll call, but the Jews were again
two short. This particular evening, the Jewish volleyball game inexplica-
bly ran quite late. The players had to rush first to the showers and then to
their proper huts. The guards had to hold up counting until each hut was
sorted out and everyone was back from the showers. The result was a
sporadic count that took some time to complete. Finally, the three huts in
the second row had been finished and the guards reached the last hut,
which was going to be two short. Just as they stepped up to the door, a
prisoner who had "forgotten" rushed out to get water for the night. The
guards waited at the door for his return, for, according to regulations, everyone had to be inside before the count could begin. Suddenly, out of
sight on the side of hut three, a window popped open. A prisoner leaped
out and threw a blanket over the wire separating the Jewish compound
from the next cage, so that if anyone glanced up they would notice nothing but "laundry." Quickly two already counted prisoners dropped out,
rushed over to the last hut, the guards and prisoners were still clumped
around the door, grumbling about the returning water carrier slopping his
way across the compound. On his return, the count was, as expected,
quite proper. The guards locked up for the night. In the meantime Yzertinsky and Gil Adi slipped up to the outer wire, cut through the bottom

strand with wire clippers, slipped under, and then began the long trudge to Haifa. There Yzertinsky was outfitted with a Polish uniform by Spilman, and presently made his way first to Tel Aviv, then to the orange groves. The waiting had ended.

During much of 1943, Yzertinsky, Spilman, Cohen and the others rewove LEHI's web. It was very difficult. There were still arrests, and all the problems of creating an organization from an orange grove. There could be only the odd operation, a robbery or an arms theft, a bit of sabotage, and the wall posters. Much of the public, and even the British security forces, overlooked these efforts as simply part of the general criminal background, or the work of a few isolated fanatics. At least the CID was right about the numbers; for although LEHI still had a short list of particular targets—Morton, Wilkin, and the others concerned with Stern's murder—they could only strike once.

On September 3, LEHI assassins shot and killed Pritzker. There was no doubt that his contacts with the CID had been impressive, permitting the Irgun to maintain a watching brief on the police and on the Haganah; but in 1941 and 1942 Pritzker was judged to have collaborated by tipping LEHI people. LEHI in fact had long suspected, although the Irgun people contacted adamantly denied it, that Pritzker's connections at some point had become too good, that he was not manipulating the police but rather the reverse. By 1943 the efforts by Meridor to bring in Menachem Begin as the new Irgun commander meant that Pritzker was eased away from the center, his plots and maneuvers no longer relevant, and the CID connection of dubious worth. He was vulnerable. LEHI snatched at the opportunity, ignored the Irgun's contrary advice, and shot Pritzker as a British double agent. Such an operation, very much in the 1942 tradition of vengeance mixed with personal terror, gave no indication that the new LEHI would be in any way different or more effective than the old organization. There appeared every likelihood that there again would be gunfights on Dizengoff Street and men killed "attempting to escape." What happened instead was a most spectacular escape, sufficiently daring and effective so that for the first time in years there was some popular sympathy for LEHI.

By early 1943 the major concentration of LEHI prisoners was at the Latrun detention camp southeast of Tel Aviv, about halfway to Jerusalem. Latrun, a clutch of dull barracks separated by wire fences and outside wire nets overlooked by watchtowers, could have been the archetype for twentieth-century detention camps—Long Kesh or the Curragh in Ireland might be wetter, Machava in Mozambique hotter, and the Greek islands more isolated—but generations of prisoners would have felt at home. As in all internment camps, life was inbred, organized without privacy, and conducive to feuds, ideological splits, pointless wrangles. There were, as always, the programs: the political seminars, Swedish exercises, volleyball, language lessons, lectures on revolutionary tactics or Zionist history, cards, dice, and the long hours of pacing in circles. The hours were regular, one day like the next under the searing Palestine sun in the summer, when the parade ground turned into baked earth; in the winter miserable, dank, and cold, a sea of mud. Food was adequate but monotonous, gossip and rumor rife, the future uncertain. Unlike prison, where a formal sentence, five years or fifteen, imposes a form and order to life, a past, a present, and a promised future, detention kills the spirit. No one knows how long his term will be. Even democratic governments under threat tend to adjust their judicial practice with emergency legislation or invent new interpretations so that suspects—the Japanese in California, the Irish Republicans in Ulster, African nationalists in South Africa—can be locked up at the convenience of the security forces. With political prisoners, particularly those interned during an armed campaign, the prospect of release can only come when their comrades outside falter. Freedom is the child of defeat. As a result, every revolutionary organization makes a concerted effort to engage the prisoner in active and productive tasks that will serve the revolt. The struggle simply evolves in a different form when an activist is interned, and tactics are so adjusted: riots, hunger strikes, harassment of guards, insistence on special rights and privileges, a militant prison organization with appropriate ranks and committees; and escape is always the first duty.

At Latrun the problem of escape, even during the quiet year of 1943, proved formidable simply because of severe physical obstacles. The LEHI people were caged in open view. Their huts were regularly inspected. The site spread out flat in all directions. A tunnel would have to be very long, would produce vast quantities of dirt, and absorb wood and wiring. And, of course, the project would take months of excruciating labor. From the moment the first LEHI internees arrived, the tunnel was a first priority.

At Latrun, the major problem was the tunnel entrance. The Jewish compound had the usual rows of huts, but only one, number four, near the corner by the first wire fence, could be a base because it was closest to the outside wire. Consequently, the prisoners in number four were the only ones who could contemplate a tunnel. The hut, a shoddy, oblong barracks twenty meters long, with a stone floor, held twenty narrow cots. There were a few nails driven into the wooden walls for clothes, and in one corner a pile of empty suitcases. There was no way to hide the tunnel opening; and even if there were, the formal inspections every three days would have immediately revealed an attempt to chip away at the stone floor. So for weeks the twenty men chewed over how to open a tunnel when there was no cover, when guards might walk in at any time and when they were certain to do so every three days.

At three in the morning, approximately the same time the LEHI at

Mizra had completed their Italian-bridge-player gambit, the answer came
at Latrun. Suddenly, with a whoop, Yehuda Ben-David leaped up, dashed
across the narrow aisle, thudded on Mattiyahu Shmulevitz to announce in
a piercing whisper that he had it. After breakfast roll call the next morning, the twenty men dashed about collecting odd boards. They borrowed
nails and a few tools, to be carefully returned to the appropriate authorities. There was soon a great banging and hammering, with people stumbling over each other, as a large wooden wardrobe took shape in the corner of the hut. At last, everyone told everyone else, we can hang up our
clothes properly, keep the suitcases out of sight, clean the hut properly.
The next morning at eleven, the superintendent of prisons arrived for his
regular before-luncheon inspection. All twenty men lined up to await his
reaction to the new addition. "What's this?" he grumbled. There was a
babble and then the hut leader explained the wonders of such a wardrobe.
Number four would be neat and tidy, look better, and be far easier to
clean, all virtues in any well-run institution, including and especially prisons. The superintendent was absolutely delighted, thought it was a splendid show, a jolly good idea. He immediately ordered all the rest of the
Jewish hut leaders to be brought on the run to see what real initiative
could do.

   Jewish initiative soon devised a tunnel entrance under the wardrobe.
At its base the stone floor was chipped away to create a square entrance
to the dirt below. A new floor was created, composed of two stone triangles. One of the triangles was firm and would be propped from below, but
the other was the tunnel lid, solid stone with the edges hidden by false cement. Two tiny open ears were cemented into this triangle so that a wood-
en handle could be slipped across to lift the trap. The next great obstacle
to a tunnel—where to put the dirt—was solved as well. Number four
showed a sudden and quite unexpected interest in gardening, an interest
that would flower as more appropriate weather permitted a real growing
season; in the meantime, early work on the flower beds permitted scattering the first dirt from the tunnel shaft. The prisoners stitched up special
underclothes with drawstrings. They would waddle out to the far muddy
corners of the yard, tug on the drawstring, the bottom of a bag would
open, and a train of fresh dirt and pebbles would drop out unnoticed. By
early February progress was quite heartening: the shaft was under way,
the dirt moving out without problems, and the camp authorities did not
seem unduly worried about the early gardening. Soon the horizontal tunnel could begin.

   First, however, the LEHI people decided that certain security precautions were necessary. February 12, 1943, the first anniversary of
Stern's death, was approaching. It seemed likely that the British would be
prepared for some sort of demonstration and might lay on a special

search. It was decided to seal the tunnel trap door with real concrete, and wait until after February 12 to dig further. Right on cue, at four in the morning on February 12, the military and police barged into the Jewish compound and woke everyone up. In number four the prisoners were lined up by their cots, and the security forces began to poke and pry. Nothing was found, but one clever police superintendent began scratching about the floor at the base of the wardrobe. After all there were only so many places in the largely bare hut to hide anything. He stooped over and began picking at the cement. Standing right next to the wardrobe by his cot was a LEHI man who had been arrested by the superintendent a few months before. He desperately tried to make conversation to take the superintendent's mind off tunnels and loose cement and the floor of the wardrobe. He received little more than grunts and monosyllables in reply, despite lavishing great praise on the improved Hebrew of the superintendent, displayed only in an occasional "lo" or "ken" (no or yes). He scratched some more around the wardrobe, and finally began thumping the tunnel trapdoor. All twenty men, fretting in assumed boredom, could plainly hear the solid thuds on the supported triangle change to the hollow echo of the lid. Apparently the superintendent could not, for he quit thumping and got down on his knees, felt around, and grasped the two wire ears, gave a tug or two, stood up, and announced that the inspection was at an end. No one could believe that he had missed the implications of the wire ears or had not heard the hollow echo. On the other hand, there had been no sign of elation, no glee, just a stolid, policeman-like plodding away into the dark February morning. There was a possibility that he had found the tunnel and kept his delight hidden, so that months later, when the LEHI people emerged from their "secret" tunnel, they could be shot "attempting to escape." No one had any doubt that the police had neither forgiven nor forgotten the gunbattles and trapbombs of the previous year.

After two weeks of debate, while the tunnel remained sealed, they decided to go on; no one could face endless detention without any hope of escape. The digging pushed on horizontally, toward the first line of wire and the road on the other side, six or seven meters away. The tunnel pilings came from the hut's bed slats, so that as the length of the tunnel increased the sleepers began to sag in the middle. Once out of slats—to use more would have put the beds on the floor—bits of wall were used, parts of tables, empty huts were gutted, and there was always a need for more. An electrical system was installed, bleeding off the camp supply with a hidden tap. The wire had been stolen; the insulation was stolen; and various fixtures were adapted from stolen bits and pieces. The electrical system contained an alarm as well. The lookout in the WC hut outside number four could switch the tunnel lights on and off whenever guards moved toward the gate. For a while this worked ideally; but it was obvious that, as the tunnel advanced, the digging crew would not have time to scramble back down the shaft and into the hut. In the meantime, there seemed no serious problems. The amount of discarded dirt grew until the whole compound seemed to have risen. Some of the new gardens refused to flourish in the tunnel dirt, so there had to be constant replanting to keep the entire garden project abloom and bright. The diggers were fortunate that no substantial rocks blocked their path, although it was regularly necessary to smash up those too large to dribble out through the special underclothes. Again they were lucky, for the rocks were limestone or chalk that could be broken up with their homemade tools. In fact everyone was quite cheered, until the tunnel depth had to be increased to drop below the road.

Working on the tunnel face, all had noticed that as they went deeper the air became fouler. During one shift, Shmulevitz noticed that his shortness of breath was giving way to blinding headache. The next shift crawled back, vomiting and gasping. No sooner would a digger reach the tunnel face than he began retching, unable to dig, barely able to crawl back out. Without air, no one could work. First an air-conditioning system was attempted, constructed from stolen oddments and with great ingenuity. A hose was run down into the tunnel and an air-pump activated. The system worked splendidly, except that by the time the air reached the tunnel face there was nothing left of it. There were too many leaks and a limit to what the men could steal or build. Ultimately, five or six of the men discovered after painful trial and error that they could work on the tunnel face for a fifteen-minute shift. It then took forty-eight hours to recover from the splitting headaches and the vomiting. There was no alternative, because the tunnel had to go under the road and there was no way to put in an airshaft, which the guards would spot. Finally, the low place was passed, as winter and the wet and sticky mud ended. This was crucial; for now that the tunnel was closer to the surface and beyond the road, air holes to the surface were possible.

During the summer the progress was impressive, but now the diggers were potential hostages who could be trapped underground if there were a flash search. Luck became the dominant factor. The tunnel crept past the second wire fence and on toward the distant outer perimeter. Every so often a wee white flag popped out of the ground so that directional adjustments could be made. The plan was that the tunnel exit would open in a wadi, the one blind spot between the machine gun towers' searchlights. It was hardly likely, in any case, that the British guards would think to turn their backs on the Jewish compound and look some seventy-odd meters to the outside wire—and if they did the tunnel opening would be hidden down below in the wadi. Finally, early in October, the tunnel—seventy-two meters, soundly butressed, well-lit—reached the side wall of the wadi. Word was sent out to the LEHI command that the twenty, along with Friedman-Yellin, a member of the high command, who was in an adjacent hut, were ready to come out.

Everything on the outside was not quite as ready, for if the twenty-one came out of the tunnel and LEHI had no place to put them, the exercise would have been in vain. LEHI was hard pressed to move them to safety and find them a decent refuge—despite Yzertinsky's efforts there was still little popular support, and hardly any safe place but the orange groves. Word was smuggled back into the compound that the breakout must be held off until the end of the month. On the outside a bunker was constructed in the sand dunes near Bat Yam. The twenty-one would come out of one tunnel only to go into another. The entire escape would be a truly underground operation. In the meantime, the delay caused considerable confusion within the hut. After digging for eight months, producing a long and elegant tunnel, the men found it difficult to suffer through weeks of anguished waiting, fearful that at any moment their luck might break and the British would discover the tunnel. It was all too much for one man, Adam, who had recently had his sentence extended by six months "in accordance with emergency regulations"—the sixth such extension.

Adam felt that Yzertinsky might not realize the risks of the delay. Innocent of just how limited were the resources of LEHI on the outside, he decided upon a solo escape in order to convince Yzertinsky to move. Obviously, any escape from Latrun would put the tunnel in even greater risk, so Adam decided to arrange his own transfer. He made his way, painfully, to the mustafa, the camp infirmary, and there collapsed, writhing in pain. Neither morphine nor ice helped, he lay groaning on the floor clutching an old scar. In time an ambulance arrived from Jerusalem so that the poor man could be rushed to a specialist, since the mystified Latrun staff could not locate the trouble and were reluctant to let him die on the floor. Just as he was being loaded into the ambulance, along with two policemen, each armed with a submachine gun, a wadded note was stuffed in his pocket by the camp grievance committee chairman. He was a hut-four man, and had been summoned to watch Britain's exemplary treatment of the sick. Written in the elegant calligraphic script of Friedman-Yellin, the note authorized Adam to escape if he could; for Friedman-Yellin quite obviously recognized that Adam's seizure had a hidden motive. In Jerusalem, less than a week later, after several examinations (the specialists were equally puzzled) a liquid diet, and nights of stifled moans, the anguished patient stumbled, doubled up, into the bathroom. A minute later a tall, erect gentleman in khaki shorts and a white shirt, smoking a pipe, strode out and marched off down the hall, through the front door of the hospital. Adam was out.

On the evening of October 31, Adam and two colleagues slipped under the outer perimeter wire and crept down the wadi to the tunnel exit. The side of the wadi crumbled as, one after another, like LEHI rabbits, the men of number four popped out, nineteen of them along with Friedman-Yellin. They moved down the wadi, below a bridge, and under the break in the perimeter wire. On November 1, at Latrun, there was no breakfast roll call for hut four, only vast chagrin on the part of the camp authorities. There was vast enthusiasm within LEHI at the arrival of the twenty accompanied by Adam. The only sour note was the death of Siman-Tov, shot November 3, in the Plain of Sharon during a British security sweep. Most of the other escapees had by then been moved to the bunker in the dunes near Bat Yam. The new LEHI was almost ready to act.

The new LEHI that arose from the groves, the dunes of Bat Yam, and the mean back-street rooms of Tel Aviv and Haifa, would be fashioned in the image of Yair by three remarkable and disparate men. Yitzhak Yzertinsky, the first on the scene after his escape from Mizra in January 1943, known in the underground as Michael, became the organizer, a man of no doubts and few words. He let his hair grow and evolved into the mysterious Rabbi Shamir, with a long black beard and appropriate mien.[7] Until his arrest and internment in Eritrea, Shamir controlled operations. His colleague, Dr. Israel Scheib, sounded like the spirit of terrorists past. A small, stooped man with a halo of greying hair, Scheib was literally possessed of a revolutionary vision. With a doctorate from the University of Vienna, an expert of Schopenhauer, Scheib in Palestine as Eldad was the dreamer-turned-activist, the scholar engagé, who could see what others could not, would advocate personal terror when others would not. If Shamir were the body, Eldad was the spirit of LEHI. Yet, personally, he was a mild and charming man, witty in conversation, and quite incapable of violence himself. When he was whisked from a prison hospital in a spectacular escape in May 1945, he refused the offer of a revolver with horror: "What would I do with that!" But he knew what others must do with it; and he could tell them why, just as Shamir told them how. The third member of the triumvirate, Nathan Friedman-Yellin (Yellin-Mor), Gera in the underground, was a thin, tall young man with gold-rimmed spectacles, an ideal candidate for a café table, a glass of tea, and an endless dialogue on the tactics of Zionist ideology. He was not, however, the mild-mannered former Polish school teacher he seemed, but a shrewd and dedicated revolutionary publicist, constantly sharpening LEHI tactics, fashioning political positions, explaining correct action and appropriate responses, ever mindful of the big picture. He had neither the transcendental, luminous vision of Eldad nor the organizational competence and operational control of Shamir; but he balanced the leadership, provided political direction, was the mind to Eldad's spirit. So Yair had not one heir but three.

Shamir, Eldad, and Yellin-Mor led an equally diverse organization of all sorts and conditions. Yet those of LEHI "were like the strings of a harp, tuned to a single melody. And perhaps the reason we harmonized so well was that each string remained true to itself."[8] The melody had been written years before by Stern.

> In days that are red with carnage and blood,
> In nights that are black with despair.

This tune, whistled briefly in a minor key as the underground LEHI radio began to broadcast, became an anthem in cellars and alleyways, in cheap rented rooms, in the bunker under the dunes, and in upstairs bedrooms above unsuspecting parents. It was the melody of men and women on the run, without names or prospects, under the orders of Shamir, caught up in the dreams of Eldad, acting for the purposes of Yellin-Mor, always in memory of Yair. There had never been a revolutionary-army organization quite like LEHI. A tiny group of strange men and women, desperate beyond measure, on the far edge of history, despised by their opponents, abhorred by the orthodox, denied by their own, hunted and shot down in the streets; they lived briefly, during those dark years of despair, on nerve rather than hope, always on the run in that bitter underground world of blood and despair, but more excruciatingly alive than they would ever be again.

> We are the men without names, without kin,
> Who forever face terror and death.
> We serve our cause for the length of our lives,
> A service which ends with our breath.

Everyone who came to LEHI entered into a mysical bond. All were dedicated to the destruction of the alien occupier and the creation of a Jewish state—they were a few hundred against an empire. Among the members were Sephardim, Yemeni dervishes, communists, dropouts from the Irgun, new immigrants who knew neither Hebrew nor Palestine, and sabras. Each had somehow been fired by the example of Stern, a man few had met but all felt they knew. LEHI created a haven for those dedicated to the absolutes, those without restraint, for those who could feel in each other the dream at work. Two millennia of dark and bloody history sat on their shoulders. Some might take special interest in Yellin-Mor's politics and programs, others in the biblical vision of Eldad, but few had come to LEHI to discuss an anti-imperialist front or the biblical basis of the state. Rather they answered an ecstatic call within themselves to participate in a violent redemption. Not only power and the state would come from the barrel of a gun, but also their own salvation.

We will wrestle with God and with death,
We will welcome the Redeemer of Zion.
We will welcome him. Let our blood
Be a red carpet in the streets,
And on this carpet our brains
Will be like white lilies.

This they took from Yair, the Illuminator. Theirs would be the revolution that he sought, a man who could not conform, who would not wait.

LEHI reflected Stern, and became almost an extension of his personality and his vision. His strategic analysis, his political program, his assumptions and judgments were all accepted, all admired, but had played only a part in the conversion of his first followers. Certainly, he had personal charisma. He could speak across cultures and backgrounds in secret thoughts that touched on special hidden longing, unleashed an intense commitment to act. The intellectuals accepted his analysis, the youth his dedication, the stolid his singular vision; but most important of all, those who had come with Stern, and those who came after him, were touched by his dream. After his death, the true believers still came, as intense as those who had known him in life. In the often dreary rounds of dull revolutionary tasks, during the intricate discussions of tactics and techniques, in squalid rooms and prison cells, behind the various rebel façades, burned Yair's vision of blood and sacrifice, death and transfiguration. Many who touched the flame died in the street gunbattles, in military operations to gain and preserve the state, in prison, or at the end of a rope. All were marked, no matter what their subsequent paths. None ever forgot Yair's melody; none ever really retired from LEHI—it was "a service which ends with our breath." Little wonder that the British in 1942 found them unreasonable fanatics, deadly dreamers. They would find them so again.

During the autumn of 1943, LEHI was approached by members of the Irgun to explore the possibility of a new united front resistance movement, Am Lohem, that would even include some of the more militant members of the Haganah. LEHI, however, while encouraged that the Irgun seemed determined to go over to armed struggle, had grave doubts about compromising its members by collaboration with the Haganah. The Irgun, particularly if Begin took over as commander, was a known quantity, and cooperation would be possible; but no one had much faith in any of the orthodox Zionist agencies or leaders. In January 1944, however, when the Irgun under Begin did open their revolt, the early contacts between Shamir and Begin evolved into a tacit alliance. On the night of February 12, incendiary bombs went off almost simultaneously in the offices of the Department of Migration in Jerusalem, Tel Aviv, and Haifa. On February 27, income tax offices in the same three cities were bombed.

Then on March 23, the CID offices were attacked by Irgun commandos with casualties on both sides. Even with their self-imposed rule not to attack British military targets until Hitler had been defeated, it was obvious that the Irgun meant business. And LEHI was delighted.

On February 14, two LEHI men were pasting up wall posters in Haifa. Suddenly, around the corner came Inspector R. D. Green and Constable H. E. Ewer. When they tried to make an arrest, both were shot down, mortally wounded. LEHI insisted that every member be armed at all times and resist arrest. It soon became as dangerous for the police to stumble on the poster people as to ignore them. Even the Irgun protected their posters; and a few weeks later on March 2, when Constable D. V. Maynard came upon two Irgun poster poeple, a third man emptied his magazine into his back—eleven perforations, and he lived. Once more Palestine was the scene of cyclical gunbattles. On February 18, three days after the two constables had been shot in Haifa, a British CID patrol shot and killed an innocent Jew who had not replied swiftly enough to its challenge. On February 24, Inspector Morton escaped another bomb attempt. His car was demolished but he was only slightly injured. A second bomb wounded four CID men riding in another car. On March 13, in Ramat Gan, Zev Flesch of the CID was shot five times and killed by LEHI. On March 19, a LEHI man was shot and killed while resisting arrest by the CID in Tel Aviv. LEHI responded with another attack on the CID in Tel Aviv, killing two and wounding one. On April 1, Constable Polany was killed and Inspector Coles wounded. The open season on the police appalled and frightened much of the Jewish population. Chaim Weizmann personally cabled Constable Maynard after he had been shot.

> Allow me to express my horror at the hideous crime of the attempt against your life. I rejoice in your escape . . . My ardent wish is that the evildoers should be speedily discovered and the responsibility fixed upon the guilty.[9]

LEHI, on the other hand, felt that the CID was waging a terror campaign. In Tel Aviv Yerachmiel "Elisha" Aaronson, LEHI commander in Haifa, was resisting arrest while unarmed. Shmulevitz was Elisha's armed escort until just before they arrived at the secret LEHI press. There he stopped, since he did not want to know the exact location of the press, and let Elisha go on around the corner and out of sight. A few seconds later came a flurry of shots and the next day the official announcement was made that a terrorist had fired on the police and was killed resisting arrest. The next day, with ten LEHI vengeance squads on the street, the British security forces stayed in their barracks and the police in the stations.

They soon came out again, and the fire fights continued. On April 5, Shmulevitz's luck ran out. For some weeks he had been using the Hasmonim School in Tel Aviv, during the afternoons when it was officially closed, as an interview site for potential recruits. On the afternoon of April 5, the closed classroom was suffocating, so between interviews he slipped out for a cold drink. A cruising patrol car pulled up alongside him and a voice requested him to come to the car. Shmulevitz decided that the request might not be arbitrary, since he was high on the wanted list, particularly after the Latrun escape. He turned and began running toward the corner. The police piled out of the car and began chasing after him. By then he had his revolver out. He turned and fired into Constable Dumbleton's face. Dumbleton collapsed against the car. The police scattered but began to return fire. They were almost too late, for Shmulevitz had nearly reached the corner, where he intended to drop a grenade and whip down an alley and away. Instead, another police patrol car appeared. There were more shots, and Shmulevitz, hit in the legs, surrendered. He was rushed off to prison. On June 26, 1944, he was condemned to death by the military tribunal in Jerusalem, still defiant; for he had known when he came out of the Latrun tunnel that he would "re-enter a yet deeper tunnel and continue underground the struggle for Israel's freedom."[10] Only the commutation of his sentence—Dumbleton did not die—kept the second tunnel from being his grave; but at least CID could feel they had him safely locked up in the Jerusalem central prison, far more escape-proof than Latrun detention camp.

On the day after Shmulevitz's capture, April 6, the CID had an even more impressive coup. The cycle of shootings had so alarmed the people in the Jewish Agency political department that a determined effort was made to cooperate with the Mandate authorities. Consequently, as soon as word came in about those responsible for the shooting of Polany and Coles on April 1, the information was passed to the police. The British then surrounded the LEHI safe house in the Jewish colony of Yavniel near Tiberias. They opened up heavy machine gun fire on the house, mortally wounding one of the three men trapped inside. The other two, Menachem Luntz and Zwi Grose, held out until their ammunition was exhausted and then shot themselves rather than surrender. Three days later a bomb in the Northern police station in Tel Aviv wounded three policemen. The next day an attempt on the life of the inspector of the Tel Aviv police failed.

At Passover Begin met with Shamir, in part to express his concern over the cycle of shootings. He noted that it was quite possible to evade arrest with appropriate papers, while an armed man risked death or capture at every roadblock or random search. And such unplanned incidents in effect gave the CID the initiative. Worse, the British had vastly complicated Irgun operations by bringing down police raids at the most delicate moments. Although LEHI was never inclined to take advice easily, in time the high command decided on "internal disarmament," initially opposed by those who assumed that no surrender was an unchangeable law, unique to the organization. In any case the LEHI high command was inclined to agree that something more was needed than the continuation of the CID vendetta: vengeance was not going to change history. Yet the organization still had at most only a few hundred people and very limited resources. LEHI could not pretend to undertake a conventional underground guerrilla campaign, such as Begin and the Irgun planned, nor would collaboration with the Irgun satisfy the high command. Under the growing black shadow of the holocaust, they sought instead a mission that would have a dramatic effect on events. Instead of police inspectors and Jewish constables, the high command wanted a victim whose death would, in Shamir's words, "change history." In 1944 the choice was obvious: High Commissioner Sir Harold MacMichael, the man who closed the Palestine gates, condemning thousands of Jews to Hitler's ovens.

MacMichael might be the chosen victim of LEHI, but the target of such a deed was broader. The leadership of LEHI accepted that murder simply for the sweetness of vengeance, no matter how notable the victim, would achieve little in the long run or not enough. By the deed LEHI wanted to educate the British to the dangers and costs of their white paper policy, and the Jewish population to the folly of acquiescense, to the advantages of the gun, and to the reality the Yishuv preferred to avoid as His Majesty's *Schützjuden*—protected Jews. Simply by his office MacMichael would have been a likely victim, but for LEHI Sir Harold had other unpleasant qualities. An Arabist and an austere, cool man with no interest in public relations or comforting explanations, as high commissioner he had displayed little interest in Jewish sensibilities. LEHI was certain that he was pro-Arab and anti-Zionist. When Joel Brand came out of Hungary to discuss a deal whereby the Nazis would release Jews in exchange for trucks, MacMichael had him arrested and deported to Cairo. This was in direct violation of his promise to Moshe Shertok of the Jewish Agency that Brand would be allowed to return to Hungary. MacMichael's only explanation was that "there was a war on." The British might, for imperial purposes in the midst of a war, placate the Arabs (although few Jews in Palestine saw the necessity of doing so), but for them to sit idly by, whether or not for imperial purposes, while the Jews of Europe were trundled into the ovens was quite unforgivable. And the British had evinced no sense of urgency. On July 6, 1944, Shertok personally asked the British foreign minister, Anthony Eden, to have Allied air strikes on the railways and concentration camps in Hungary. Not until September 1 did the Foreign Office reply, and by then the majority of the Hungarian Jews had been moved over those very railways into the camps and exterminated. For LEHI, long before September 1944, the guilt of the British in general and MacMichael in particular was manifest.

Despite what, to LEHI and the Irgun, seemed overwhelming evidence of British collusion in genocide, the orthodox leadership of the Yishuv still contended that Britain had both a pragmatic interest in favor of Zionism and a moral commitment to the Jewish homeland. Despite the white paper, the arms searches, the disproportionate sentences of Jews in 1943, despite Brand, despite all, Ben-Gurion, Weizmann, and company still placed their hopes in British promises. It was obvious to LEHI and the Irgun that petition politics could have no effect on Britain, could only gloss over Palestine reality with foolish optimism, thus immobilizing the Yishuv until it was too late. Something dramatic was needed. Once LEHI had struck at MacMichael, the deed, as Stern and his revolutionary ancestors long ago suggested, would educate. Just as Begin and the Irgun believed that their campaign would convert the timorous Jews to the possibilities of a revolt, so LEHI assumed that MacMichael's death would begin the transformation of the *Schützjuden*. Again and again the high command met in grimy upstairs rooms, refining and fashioning their revolutionary strategy of personal terror. They agreed that such a deed must be morally just and effective, otherwise it was only simple, criminal murder. "A man who goes forth to take the life of another whom he does not know must believe one thing only—that by his act he will change the course of history."[11] LEHI so determined and authorized the deed.

Authorization proved simpler than accomplishment. Even for such an assassination operation, LEHI still had limited resources. Despite the obstacles, MacMichael's movements were watched, the possibilities shifted, and the operation undertaken. The first attempt failed. So did the second, and the third. MacMichael led a charmed life. Despite his repeated public appearances, his motorcade visits, his regular pattern of movements, each time something went wrong at the last moment. His plans changed, innocent bystanders appeared, there was a slip or a misunderstanding. As weeks stretched into months, LEHI frustration grew. Finally, in early August LEHI intelligence discovered that MacMichael would drive from Jerusalem to Jaffa. This would be the sixth and last chance, for the high commissioner was about to leave the Mandate at the end of his tour of duty.

On August 8, 1944, MacMichael's limousine left Jerusalem for a reception in his honor at the Union Club in Jaffa. In the party were the high commissioner, his wife, his ADC Major Nicholl, and two police constables in the front seat. Just before four in the afternoon, the car passed through the fringe of Jewish Jerusalem, moving smoothly along the Jaffa Road at an even forty miles an hour. At kilometer four near the kibbutz Givat Shaul, the road bends under a steep cliff and on the other side the ground falls away into a steep ravine. Suddenly, from the cliff a single petrol bomb twisted down and smashed on the road ten yards in front of the car. The road was immediately covered with flames and LEHI opened fire with a submachine gun. Major Nicholl was shot through the lung, the driver was hit in the neck and thigh. Bullets continued to smash into the front of the car. The other constable, Hill, who had been shooting blindly out his side window from the moment the bomb detonated, managed to reach over and grab the wheel. The driver slumped down, his foot off the gas pedal, enabling Hill to run the riddled car into a roadside bank. By then the LEHI squad, who had watched the road covered with flames and their 9 mm. fire splattered all over the ambush site, began to withdraw toward Givat Shaul. This time, at last, the high commissioner's luck had run out. But it had not: he sat in the riddled car, amid the shattered glass and blood, with a slight wound to one hand. His wife was unhurt. LEHI had missed again.

MacMichael's luck was even better than he suspected, for LEHI was not alone in its plots against him. In 1943 even before the Irgun had opened the revolt, Meridor had been after him, first to kidnap him as a symbol; then in 1944 the high command had more deadly intentions. For a while there was an Irgun "painter" complete with easel, sketching scenes near Mikve Israel on the Jaffa Road, checking out an ideal site for a bomb to interrupt the high commissioner's scheduled trip. The painter even managed to pass a security check when a patrol stopped to investigate his presence—the officers felt he had a nice picture under way, and drove off down the road. That night the bomb was moved into place, ready to be electrically detonated as the limousine passed by on the way to Jaffa. MacMichael never did pass, of course, for the LEHI got to him first. It was the Irgun's last try as well, and the bomb had to be dismantled.

Well before the LEHI ambush, there was growing British concern that matters were getting out of hand in Palestine. On July 28, Mac-Michael informed the Colonial Office that "available information indicates that the security position may be deteriorating, and the outlook is not encouraging."[12] The attempt on his life simply underlined that deterioration. After the attempt MacMichael again reported on the "gangster virus" and the "vicious spiral of violence"—terrorism, he warned, is an infectious disease.[13] The disease spread. On September 27, the Irgun again attacked police stations in four separate operations, deploying, by British estimate, 150 men. Palestine was in a state close to open rebellion, no matter what criteria were used. LEHI people did their part; for on the day after the Irgun attacks, after thirty-one months, they finally caught up with Wilkin, promoted to assistant superintendent and moved to Jerusalem. He was shot and killed on the street, his assassins disappearing around the corner.

The British decided to move on two fronts. First, the detainees, a constant source of worry, were to be moved from the Mandate to Eritrea in East Africa, a maneuver certain to upset Jewish opinion. Second, pressure was to be put on the official Zionist institutions to ensure their cooperation with the British authorities in ending the violence. The Jewish Agency, already seriously concerned about the Irgun revolt, still hesitated to cooperate completely with the security forces, especially after the exile of 251 Jews from Palestine on October 18. Of course, the British continued security operations, sweeping up suspects. All this made it both easier and harder for LEHI to operate amid the rising turmoil.

After MacMichael's August escape, LEHI had to begin again planning a truly significant operation. Other proposals were considered, including an attempt on John Shaw, chief secretary of the Mandate administration, and the most influential force on local British policy. Then there was the distant but imposing figure of Lord Moyne, British minister of state in Cairo, an even more attractive potential victim than MacMichael. LEHI, however, decided to wait on Moyne until MacMichael had been dispatched. After MacMichael's departure and the appointment of the moderate Lord Gort, a man without any notable past anti-Zionist sins, the attraction of Moyne again increased. He had all of MacMichael's disagreeable faults and was more important to boot. The technical difficulties, however, were very serious. LEHI had a cell of sorts in Cairo, eight men and four women, who might be able to give aid and comfort, but they could not do the job themselves. Up to the autumn of 1944, they had been distributing pamphlets and looking for weapons, both with only marginal success. The assassins would have to be slipped out of Palestine and into Egypt to make their way to Cairo with a minimum of help. It was difficult enough to operate in Palestine—Joshua Cohen of the orange groves was finally arrested on September 29—and might prove even worse in Cairo. If, however, satisfactory cover could be arranged, matters might prove easier than anticipated. The British would hardly be prepared for violence at such a distance. The men selected to perform the deed would have to work out the details when they arrived in Cairo. The high command could thus do little more than ask for volunteers and wait for results.

There was little trouble attracting volunteers. Moyne was a *bête noire* to the underground. Even more than MacMichael, he had the gift of the hard word. Reputedly he had thwarted Brand's plan to rescue the Hungarian Jews with the retort, "What would I do with a million Jews?" He was an Arabist who, as colonial secretary, had followed a consistently anti-Zionist line. An ideal victim, then: because of his title, his cabinet rank, his connections in Britain, his friendship with the prime minister, it would be noticed when he was killed. Such a spectacular deed would elevate the purely tactical advantages of striking at an enemy of Zionism into a strategic victory. The British would recognize that Palestine would not be an issue to be settled as London chose. Moyne's death would internationalize the problem, and prevent the British from treating the Mandate as an internal matter. An operation in the heart of Cairo would reveal to the Arabs, whose destiny, according to LEHI, need not clash with that of the Jews, the advantages of an anti-imperialist policy, the possibility of armed resistance, and the frailty of the British lion. There were tremendous attractions to killing Moyne—the opportunity to change history. Two young men all but forced their services on the high command.

The first, Eliahu Hakim, a twenty-year-old Sephardic Jew, was born in Beirut. His family immigrated to Palestine, and he was brought up in comfortable circumstances in Haifa. His interest in politics was abruptly awakened when, during a demonstration, a British policeman lashed him on the back with a riot whip—a psychic scar that he carried with him to Cairo. "A British policeman made me decide to join LEHI."[14] In 1942, while still in school, he joined LEHI and later underwent training under Joshua Cohen. His family was appalled, and pressured him to quit. Instead he drifted. He worked briefly at a military camp at Bat Galim, but was restless and unsettled, and soon was fired. Family pressure to change his ways increased. They knew all too well the fate of many of Eliahu's older colleagues. At last they persuaded him to accept conscription into the British Army. He was shipped off by the army to Cairo where, unknown to parents, he continued his LEHI activities, mainly acquiring arms and aiding in smuggling them into Palestine. It was a small-time operation, but at least he was doing something. When he was ordered back to Palestine, he deserted and went underground full time. He became one of the small group of activists involved in the long string of abortive attacks on MacMichael, including the final ambush on the Jaffa Road. The high command recognized that Eliahu Hakim, with his dedication, military training, and Cairo experience, was an ideal candidate.

The other volunteer was less obvious. In fact, Eliahu Bet-Zouri was really self-selected, having convinced the high command that he *must* undertake the mission. At twenty-three he was three years older than Hakim and, too, had long been involved in politics. Born in Tel Aviv, a sabra, he attended Balfour High School until expelled for political activity. After the *Struma* incident, he and two friends planned a private attack on the high commissioner. When that misfired, he joined the Am Lochem movement. When that collapsed, although he remained in his position in the government survey department, he came to LEHI. Seething with indignation, he wanted action. His dedication and determination, it was felt, would compensate for his lack of operational experience.

Autumn 1944 was golden in Cairo. The searing heat of the summer had faded. The Nile, still red with the topsoil of the Ethiopian highlands, ebbed swiftly. The nights were cool, the breezes not filled with desert grit. The ever-present crowds would thicken at sundown. The narrow lanes and dilapidated squares of the old city became a mass of swirling jellabas, turbans, sheep, and lost camels, even the odd clerk in a three-piece suit and a red fez. The more affluent, in summer suits and dinner frocks, sat on restaurant boats moored along the river, or in garden cafés, and ate grilled pigeon and tehina salads late into the night. The poor had to make do with *ful* sandwiches and black tea at the edge of the Azbakiya Gardens. The rich filled Shepheard's Hotel and the French restaurants; the clubs were always full. All through the night people were buying and selling—orange juice from the tiny carts, American cigarettes from British soldiers, or each other. The city never slept, teemed with life—camels to one side, Land Rovers to the other, goats at the traffic crossing. The taxis circled endlessly about the Place de l'Opéra, honking and hooting at the old lorries held together with bailing wire and the Bren gun carriers filled with cheerful drunks.

In many ways, despite the wartime shortages and problems, 1944 was for Cairo a special moment, a brief year of respite. The politics of violence, the endless wars, Nasser, Palestine, the coups and the conspiracies lay ahead; the exciting days of the desert war with Rommel at the gate were in the past. Cairo enjoyed the pause. The bars, clubs, and bordellos were full of people celebrating their distance from the wars or their triumph over the bureaucracy. There were all sorts and conditions of clerks and soldiers and authorized personnel. Out of sight, the pashas and the court, fully corrupt, venal without charm, lived in their own lush Carine society, far beyond the economies of clerks or the ken of drunken Anzacs, staggering through the dim streets. Theirs was a vastly international city of Greek merchants, Coptic importers, Albanian planters, Italian bankers, Armenians, Turks, Jews, all floating on the misery of the Egyptian poor. The rich were largely ignorant of the dreams of the newly ambitious bank tellers and officer cadets—the heirs to the future. The British ruled all this with arrogance and few qualms, manipulating the politicians when necessary, dismissing them if need be, largely uninterested in the muttering of Egyptian nationalists—"little men," mustached, whispering on the sly in French. For the British generals and administrators, Cairo, even wartime Cairo, remained simply an imperial bastion. Most of them loathed the vacuous and venal froth of Farouk's Cairo, knew little of its wretchedness, and found their pleasures and friends among their own. In the autumn of 1944, this huge sprawling city, filthy and various, absorbed one more exotic, Eliahu Hakim, a prospective assassin.

For Hakim that Cairo autumn was a strange, unreal time, stretched between his Palestine past, his friends in the dingy rooms of the underground, and the awesome, looming deed that would change history. On arrival he began the traditional rituals of the assassin. The misleadingly aimless wandering about on the victim's trail, seeking patterns and rumors. Where does he eat? When does he leave the office? Where does his limousine park? Who is always at home? Who guards him? Who visits him? There was the strange, eerie dislocation of moving among a crowd of real people, rushing about their real business. They dash past with their vital briefcase or their tray of black tea or their blank mind. All the while, a thin young man with a dark mustache in a blue shirt, walking beside a pretty, dark-haired girl called Yaffa, loiters near the Nile Cornice, not far from the British Embassy. He is aware that he and she, unlike the others, are not real people, but instruments of fate.

From his previous visit Hakim was familiar with the world of LEHI in the city, the strange aliases, the safe rooms, the tiny circle of the trusted, the double and triple life of the underground; but in the autumn of 1944, the British did not even know he was in the city. Palestine and its troubles were a long way off; one deserter more or less did not matter. Hakim could wander freely. He went dancing, ate in restaurants, walked with Yaffa along the river, and each night returned to his small room at 4 Sharia Gheit el-Noubi in the Mouski district, far from the elegant embassies and gardens along the Nile. He could have been anyone. He certainly attracted little attention. And by the end of October, he knew Moyne's patterns, and chose his moment. Bet-Zouri arrived. Hakim's drifting was over. On November 2, Hakim walked passed Moyne's residence once more. The bicycles were hired, the pistols loaded. The deed that had seemed so unreal when the two young men accepted the mission had come down to a matter of timing and distance.

Monday, November 6, 1944, was pleasant as usual for the time of year. The warm, clear skies and bright sun of Cairo were a far cry from the fogs and drizzles of wartime Britain.[15] The trimmed lawns and gardens of the diplomatic quarter in Garden City, the elaborate Italianate palaces, the long, black limousine of generals and ambassadors, created an oasis along the Nile. This quarter de luxe was as isolated from the great winter battles along the Rhine as it was from the teeming, chaotic bazaars of central Cairo—except perhaps for the Bren gun carriers in the streets. The aura was of quiet and confident elegance, in an imperial world of ease and deserved comfort. In his office at 10 Sharia Tolumbat, at 12:50 in the afternoon, the Right Honorable Walter Edward Guiness, first Baron Moyne, had all but finished his morning's work as British minister of state in Cairo. Beyond his window, the steady din of the city reached faintly into the cool and shaded lawns. Down further on the Nile Cornice, great lateen-rigged boats drifted past date palms. It looked like a picture-postcard world; but Moyne, at the center of the web, ran a real world of British Mideast imperial matters. The war might have moved on but Moyne, and Churchill, remained acutely aware of future British influence in the area. For Moyne it was a splendid posting, a serious responsibility, a sign of esteem. He was competent, ambitious, talented, and Cairo had so far been good for him.

At 1:00, accompanied by Dorothy S. Osmond, his personal secretary, and his ADC, Captain A. G. Hughes-Onslow, Moyne left the building to be driven across Cairo for lunch. It was a quick ten-minute run and a welcome break from the office routine. His black Packard Saloon, driven by Lance Corporal A. Fuller, soon edged through the impossible traffic and crossed over the Nile bridge into Gezira. At 4 Sharia Gabaliya, Fuller turned the car into the walled yard, drove on past the underground garage, and pulled up before the three steps leading to the front door. Hughes-Onslow popped out of the right front seat and ran up the steps, reaching in his pocket for the key. Fuller opened his door and got out. There was a single moment of quiet just as Hughes-Onslow stopped before the door. Fuller snapped shut the front door of the Packard and started around the back so he could open the door for Moyne. From over the walls drifted the faint sound of traffic and the endless din of Cairo. There was the slight crinkle of cooling metal from the Packard. The garden was bright with the full afternoon light; a mass of color nodded in the flower pots at Hughes-Onslow's feet. It was 1:10; lunch would be on time.

Hughes-Onslow was about to take the key out of his pocket when he heard someone say in English, "Don't move. Stay where you are. Don't move." Hakim and Bet-Zouri were on time as well. Fuller had reached the rear of the Packard. He stopped. Bet-Zouri raised his revolver and fired directly into Fuller's chest. The slugs tore through his body, severing his right internal iliac artery, then smashed against the far garden wall. Fuller collapsed in the driveway, sprawled on his back. With massive intra-abdominal hemorrhages, he bled to death within minutes. Inside the car, Dorothy Osmond leaned forward at the sound of the shots. She heard Fuller groan but could not understand what was happening. There was a young man of medium height, about thirty, wearing grey trousers and a lighter jacket and tie. He was standing back from the car, holding a revolver. Another man, taller and darker, moved away from Hughes-Onslow on the stoop and up to the Packard's rear window next to Moyne. He looked once at Dorothy Osmond and said again in English, "Don't move." Moyne started to open the door and began to turn toward the young man. Hakim, pulling open the door, thrust his revolver toward Moyne, and began firing into him, slowly and deliberately. The first slug hit Moyne in the neck on the right side, just above the clavicle, jerking his head around. The second ripped into his abdomen near the twelfth rib, becoming embedded to the right of the second lumbar vertebra. Before Hakim fired again, Moyne raised his right hand to ward off the shots. The third slug only ripped across his four fingers and tore in and out of his chest in a superficial wound. Hakim stepped back. Moyne managed to cry, "Oh, they've shot us!" Blood was spurting out of his neck. Hakim drew further back and moved away from the car. Moyne slumped forward, unconscious. By the time Dorothy Osmond, sitting stunned next to Moyne, and Hughes-Onslow, still standing on the stoop, could grasp what had happened, Hakim and Bet-Zouri had run out of the yard.

Once out of the grounds, both jumped on their rented bicycles and began pedaling madly down Sharia Gabaliya toward the Zamalek Bridge. Once across and into the traffic, they could simply disappear in the mob. Chasing after them, Hughes-Onslow was only forty yards back, because he had cut through the back of the house. He rushed out the gate and stopped at the sentry box—Hakim and Bet-Zouri might have a forty-yard lead, but the alarm was given. Hearing the hue and cry behind them, the two men turned off into a side road, Sharia Bahres Amer, and then turned again by the residence of King George of Greece—they were very nearly away. Suddenly, just at the bridge, El-Amin Mahomed Abdullah, a member of the Ministerial Protection Squad, appeared on his motorcycle. He ignored a volley of warning shots fired into the air—Hakim and Bet-Zouri were determined not to injure any Egyptians in their operation—and pushed on. Others rushed up. There were more shots, and no place for the two men to go. They were captured.

In the meantime Dorothy Osmond ran into the house and telephoned for help. She asked the duty clerk to send for the police. As soon as Hughes-Onslow gave the alarm, he ran into the nearby Gezira police station and phone to the Fifteenth Scottish Hospital, to arrange for a doctor and ambulance. By the time he returned to the yard, Major H. W. Forester, alerted by Osmond's telephone call, had already arrived from the ministerial resident's office. It was just 1:15. Air Vice-Marshall Nutting and Major Woodford appeared. Forester walked over to Fuller, who was lying on his back in a pool of blood, obviously dead. The rear door of the Packard was open, the window down, and Moyne, hunched over in the seat, was covered with blood, apparently dead as well. It was very quiet. Three or four Egyptians huddled, terrified, at the gate. Two house suffragii stood in front of the steps gaping. No one said anything. The three British officers stood appalled, until suddenly Major Woodford noticed that Moyne's hand had moved.

When they rushed over to him, he regained consciousness but seemed confused. He asked Forester if he could be moved to his room, since he was feeling rather uncomfortable. Soothing him, Forester suggested that they wait until the doctor arrived. Moyne asked several times in a low voice when would the doctor come. In a very few minutes the doctor and an ambulance appeared. Moyne was driven straight to the hospital and admitted at 1:40, just forty minutes after he had left his office. At the hospital it was at once clear that his condition was critical. He had lost a great deal of blood through gross hemorrhaging and was still bleeding. His pulse was imperceptible; he was in shock. At 1:45 he had the first of three transfusions. His condition improved markedly; his pulse was 120 and his color was better. He could talk and began to complain of a burning pain down his right leg and an inability to move the leg. X-rays revealed an injury to the right side of his first dorsal vertebra. Later in the afternoon, his right arm became paralyzed as a result of the severe trauma around the neck wound. The doctors were reluctant to operate until his condition improved. At 5:30 a lumbar puncture revealed a blood stain. The time had come to operate. He was given another transfusion while the bullet was removed from beside the second lumbar vertebra. It was discovered that the bullet had punctured both the colon and large intestine, causing gross internal bleeding. The doctors cleaned the neck wound and the minor damage to his fingers and chest: all told, there were eight wounds. The prognosis remained poor. Despite the quick treatment and the surgeons' skill, there was little hope that Moyne would weather the shock and the loss of blood. Soon after he was wheeled out of the operating room, his condition began to deteriorate. His vital signs steadily weakened. The doctors could not reverse the decline. At 8:40 that evening he died.

Even before his death British security forces and Egyptian political circles had been thrown into chaos. No one had expected assassins in Cairo. No one knew who the two men were, who had sent them, or what they represented. All that was known were the names they gave: Saltzman and Cohen. The authorities remained confused: was it Saltzman or Zalzman? Anyway, the British did not believe these were their real names. During the afternoon and evening of November 6, the authorities continued to interrogate the two men.

The Egyptian government reacted to the news of the assassination with deep horror and immediate panic. In 1926, when an Egyptian assassinated Sir Lee Stack Pasha, British governor of the Sudan and commander in chief of the Egyptian Army, the reaction by London had been swift and far reaching—the Egyptians were expelled from the Sudan, Britain took sole control there, and demanded a large Egyptian indemnity as well. One mad moment in 1926 had lost the Egyptian monarchy an empire to the south that might never be regained. Neither King Farouk nor his premier, Ahmed Mahir Pasha, wanted another such disaster in 1944. Farouk hurriedly sent his own physicians to the hospital. The premier, accompanied by the foreign minister, rushed first to the Gezira police station to get a detailed account, and then to the British Embassy to offer their condolences. Farouk personally sent Hassanein Pasha to Moyne's residence to express his dismay. Amid the confusion of the moment, the Egyptians finally learned the only good news of the day—the assassins were not Arabs. Beyond that, no one knew anything. The next day the newspapers were filled with horror and outrage.

The British soon decided that one of the young men, first identified as Moshe Cohen Itzak, might actually be Private Eliahu Hakim, who had deserted on February 9. The other, Saltzman or Zalzman, remained an unknown. Although both suspects admitted the deed, Saltzman to shooting Lance Corporal Fuller and Hakim to shooting Moyne, they were forthcoming with very little else. They wanted an opportunity for the LEHI people in Cairo to go underground. On Tuesday, November 7, after nearly twenty-four hours of questions, the two finally announced they were members of LEHI: "What we have done, we have done on the instructions of this organization."[15] The British then discovered that Saltzman had used the name Hanan Michael while at a Cairo hotel on October 20-21, and that Cohen had been in Cairo for two months as Private Samuel Bernstein. Even later, when the two told as much of their story as they intended, British security never quite managed to fill out completely the Cairo picture.

For weeks the security forces continued an intensive investigation of the trail left by the two. A vast search and sweep operation checked out all Palestinians in Egypt. Eventually, several LEHI suspects were arrested, including all four LEHI women. Hakim's "girlfriend" Yaffa ended up in the women's prison in Bethlehem. In the meantime British police had uncovered ample and grisly evidence of LEHI's involvement. Ballistics tests on the bullets from the two pistols were checked with files in Palestine. Bet-Zouri's 1916 Parabellum was used in the murder of Constable Zev Flesch in Ramat Gan in March 1944. The report on Hakim's Nagant 7.62 revolver was even more startling: the gun was used in the murder of Ibrahim Hassan el Karam in Rehavia, Jerusalem, on November 14, 1937; in the murder of another Arab, whose name and dates had disappeared from police files; the murder of Constable Caley on March 23, 1943; the murder of Inspector Green and Constable Ewer in Haifa on February 14, 1944; and the murder of another constable in Tel Aviv on May 10, 1944. As recently as September 26, the gun was used to murder Wilkin in Jerusalem. The macabre Nagant was an incredible artifact of LEHI terror.

The two men, however, did not act like terrorists nor fit into comfortable categories. They had not even killed to save their own lives. It was apparent that they realized the risks they had taken in not shooting El-Amin off his motorbike. They explained why: it would have been the death of a potential ally, and would have alienated Arab opinion. Moyne was guilty; El-Amin was not. So El-Amin was alive, and on January 10 the two men were in an Egyptian dock, charged with murder. Those in the crowded courtroom saw two rather conventional-appearing young men, Hakim the taller in a jacket, Bet-Zouri in an open-necked shirt. Both stood calmly manacled between a group of Egyptian guards with red fezzes. They were placed behind an iron grill overlooking the courtroom. Both were, and had been since their capture, self-possessed, almost serene. They had, of course, no defense, only an explanation.

> Our deed stemmed from our motives, and our motives stemmed from our ideals, and if we prove our ideals were right and just, then our deed was right and just.

> We don't fight for the sake of a National Home. We fight for our freedom. In our country a foreign power rules . . . If we have turned to the gun, it is because we were forced to the gun.[16]

The court was not impressed. On January 11, both were condemned to death. Despite the almost universal horror in Cairo at Moyne's assassination, the bearing and presence of the men produced among many Egyptians a grudging respect. There was no doubt that both were idealists as well as fanatics; neither had hesitated to take the responsibility for the deed; neither seemed to fear death.

To the end both retained their composure. In his last letter Hakim insisted he was prepared for anything. "I am absolutely calm and my conscience settled because I have the feeling I have done my duty." The British had little sympathy with such idealists, or with the validity of such a duty. Lord Killean decided not to forward the final letters to the men's families. "I do not feel any consideration is due to these two self-confessed murderers."[17] Such men were beyond reason, compassion, or mercy. On February 24, Churchill, a personal friend of Moyne, said in Parliament, the execution of justice upon men should be swift and exemplary. Prime Minister Ahmed Mahir took the point.

On March 22, the eve of their execution, the Chief Rabbi of Egypt, Nissim Ochana, spent the last night with Hakim and Bet-Zouri. They remained calm. On March 23, they were dressed in the traditional, ill-fitting red-burlap suits of condemned men, marched barefoot to the gallows, were blindfolded at the scaffold, and hanged. They never anticipated any less. Hakim said just before he died, looking down at the red burlap, "This is the finest suit of clothes I have ever worn in my life."[18] For Hakim and Bet-Zouri it was a uniform of martyrdom and patriotism, not of shame. By the time the two put on the red suits, their deed had become part of the past, part of history. There was no longer any doubt that the situation in Palestine had become critical for LEHI, for the Irgun, for everyone. The assassination unleashed strange tides that threatened to swamp the Irgun revolt, and with it LEHI.

NOTES

1. Although it is the convention to refer to the Sternists as LEHI during much of 1940 and 1941, Irgun Zvai Leumi-be-Israel continued to be used by the members. Their opponents call them the Stern Gang, their friends the FFI.

2. J. Borisov, *Palestine Underground: The Story of the Jewish Resistance* (New York: Judaea Publishing Co., 1947), p. 21.

3. The High Commission to the Secretary of State for Colonies, 22 January 1942 (co. 732/439; no. 75156/151A, 4817).

4. *Yamin Velelot* (Supplement of *Maariv*), February 11, 1972, p. 56.

5. In 1955 Morton published his own account of the killing, contending that Stern had leaped toward the window. The inspector, fearful that he might set off an explosive device, was forced to shoot. There had not been a threat of such a device nor was there a thorough investigation of the incident. Morton's explanation contained internal contradictions. Years later, Sergeant Daniel Day, on behalf of the policeman Tennant, gave the account now generally accepted.

6. There is considerable difficulty with Hebrew underground names. First, they are transliterated into English with various spellings; second, many had a Polish name that was translated into Hebrew, then discarded for another alias that might be adopted ultimately as a postwar name.

7. Geula Cohen, *Woman of Violence: Memoirs of a Young Terrorist, 1943–1946* (London: Rupert Hart-Davis, 1966), p. 167.

8. Included in the open files of British state papers, (co. 733.457, no. 7515b/151D, 4819).

9. Borisov, p. 23.

10. Gerold Frank, *The Deed* (New York: Ballantine, 1963), p. 35.

11. The High Commissioner to the Secretary of State for Colonies, July 28, 1944 (fo. 371/40126, 5052).

12. High Commisioner to the Secretary of State for Colonies, August 8, 1944 (fa 371/40136, 5052).

13. Cohen, p. 166.

14. The events of November 6 were the subject of a detailed British inquiry. Various statements were taken in Cairo and dispatched to the Foreign Office on November 22, 1944 (no. 2436, fo. 371/41516).

15. *Ibid.*

16. Frank, p. 261.

17. The letters, in Hebrew, were never delivered. Copies can be found in recently opened British state papers, as well as Lord Killean's remarks.

18. Cohen, p. 62.

(above) The Arab riots in Jaffa, 1929. *(below)* British mounted police disperse crowd during Arab riots in Jaffa when 22 were killed, 130 injured, 1933.

(above) Arabs battle police in Jaffa's main square, 1936. (below)
Jewish refugees leave Old Town of Jerusalem during the 1936
riot.

(above) Jewish policemen at an outpost on Mt. Carmel, Haifa during 1936 riots. *(right)* During the Arab revolt, 1936–1939, British search Jews at Jaffa Gate, Jerusalem.

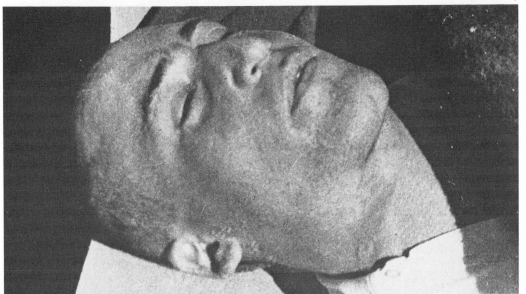

(above) Ben-Yosef after
being hanged in Acre
Military Fortress, 1938.
(left) Avraham Stern.

(right) No. 8 Mizrachi B Street in Tel Aviv where Stern was murdered. *(below)* The trial in Cairo of Eliahu Bet Zouri and Eliahu Hakim for the murder of Lord Moyne, 1944. *(bottom)* Hakim is on far left.

PART 3

THE REVOLT:
Menachem Begin:
"We Fight,
Therefore We Are"

History and our observation persuaded us that if we could succeed in destroying the government's prestige in Eretz Israel, the removal of its rule would follow automatically. Thenceforward we gave no peace to this weak spot. Throughout all the years of our uprising, we hit at the British government's prestige, deliberately, tirelessly, unceasingly.

-Begin

CHAPTER 1

The Impact of Insurrection, 1943-1945

We were not spared in order to live in slavery and oppression and to await some new Treblinka. We were spared in order to ensure life and freedom and honour for ourselves, for people, for our children, and our children's children . . . There is a life that is worse than death and a death greater than life.

-Meir Feinstein

While Stern had been driven to revolt by the compelling logic of his own vision, which transformed a few and was anathma to many, Menachem Begin entered the underground beneath the stark shadow of the holocaust, a unique catastrophe. Even without the certain knowledge of the fate of European Jewry that Ben-Eliezer brought with him when he returned to Palestine in the autumn of 1943, the urge to action was already intense. Even if the *Endlösung* still baffled the imagination, the worsening condition of the Jews of the European diaspora had been obvious from the moment of Hitler's advent: the Nuremberg laws, the camps and expulsions, the Crystal Night pogrom, confiscations, the tales of the refugees, first from Germany, then Austria, after the war from Eastern Europe, and the terrible rumors. Thus the British white paper policy from 1939 placed severe strains on even the most conventional and parochial within the Yishuv. Ben-Gurion's policy statement, "We shall fight the war against Hitler as if there were no white paper, and we shall fight the white paper as if there were no war"[1] proved scant comfort when the British closed the gates, exiling the wretched and desperate remnants that somehow reached the Promised Land.

Even if there had been no holocaust, no refugees, no war against Hitler, the British tilt toward an accommodation with the Arabs alarmed and angered even practical Zionists. From March 1939 until the end of 1943, however, the orthodox institutions had rarely countenanced violence. There were individual acts, unprovoked riots, strong resistance to

104

aims searches, and the occasional symbolic bomb; but, as with the Irgun, there was very little that anyone could *do*. Even the hard men in the Irgun felt that Stern's quixotic crusade was foolish and futile, so Meridor and the others remained trapped in their original dilemma. How could they open the gates without striking at Hitler's enemy? By late 1943 this distinction was eroded. Increasingly, they saw little difference between those who exterminated Jews and those who condoned that extermination by inaction. Even before Begin's command, the end of toleration had come within the Irgun. With Begin and his new strategy the dilemma could be evaded and the drive to action fashioned into a very special revolt.

To the romantic, Begin appeared a most unlikely underground leader. Unlike Stern, there was no aura of intense, burning, dangerous determination. Unlike Eldad, there were no visions. He was no gunman, no hard man on the run, no poet of revolution, no splendid figure ripe for legend. In fact he was not physically prepossessing and was described in the British *Jewish Terrorist Index* as having a long, hooked nose, bad teeth, and horn-rimmed spectacles. He closely resembled a small-town lawyer or a schoolteacher: middle sized, far from handsome, slender, immaculately dressed, with impeccable manners. In intimate conversation he was invariably kind and considerate. When he spoke in public (impossible in Palestine during the revolt), to some he was a great orator, to others a dangerous demagogue. He had a most remarkable presence in the underground, which created an atmosphere of contained power and moral authority, combined with a keen analytical mind cleared of the dense undergrowth of previous Zionist assumptions. All during the revolt his contacts were limited to his wife and child, a few couriers, and the few members of the high command. His influence and determination, however, spread out through the entire Irgun, his ideas and ideals constantly reinforced through the *Herut,* the news sheet written almost entirely by him. While in theory the high command determined policy, Begin's voice closed most arguments. His views, even when opposed to all others, inevitably won by dint of logic, by his grasp of the strategic options and consequences, and by his dominant presence. Not all in the Irgun favored Begin as commander, and at times not all commanders agreed with his policy—at one time no one did, but there never was a serious alternative. As Jabotinsky dominated the beginning of the Irgun, so did Begin the end, fashioning the fragments Meridor had managed to hold together into one of the most effective revolutionary organizations of the postwar era. Then, with the establishment of the state, he made sure his old gunmen went into retirement or into politics with the new Herut party.

In 1943 a state, a Herut party, even a revolt seemed a very long way off, except to Begin: he had not only vision and determination, but a plan.

Even with the Irgun's limited resources, it could bring down the imperial presence. Begin came out of the Polish diaspora; and after his arrival in Palestine in May 1942, he saw the British with new eyes. Although aware of the guerrilla strategy of the IRA and nonviolent disobedience in India, he devised a novel revolutionary strategy of leverage. He tested his approach during long conversations with Irgun leaders, especially during the autumn of 1943 when, under the name Ben-Zeev, he repeatedly met Ben-Eliezer in room 17 of the Savoy Hotel off Allenby Street in Tel Aviv. First, to clear up the problems of attacking Hitler's foe he suggested that no operations be mounted against military targets and that where possible no lives should be taken. He further proposed a series of spectacular underground operations that would humiliate the authorities, forcing them to resort to repressive measures that would antagonize the Yishuv, alienate Britain's anti-imperialist allies, Russia and the United States, and most important, deny the British support at home because of their recourse to counter-terror. The security forces would become involved in repression—internment, mass interrogation, martial law, executions—violating the British sense of justice. The army, police, courts, and administration would be damned if they reacted strongly, and damned if they permitted the Irgun free reign. Begin also assumed that the British would not run amok in Palestine, responding to provocation with German or Russian brutality. Palestine in the postwar world, with the impact of the holocaust, would be a glass house; and the Yishuv would be safe there, except for a few momentary "unofficial" lapses from British standards, lapses which would be exactly to the Irgun's purposes. In time the British choice would be between repression and withdrawal, and Begin was sure he would have history and logic on his side.

The tactical problem, then, was to create an underground to mount the operations to provoke this British response. The greatest potential obstacle was not the paucity of resources or the strength of the British Empire, but the reaction of the Yishuv. The Irgun did not need, and could not effectively deploy, a vast resistance organization; but even a small underground would need the toleration of the Yishuv. From the very first, Begin and the other members assumed that the authorized institutions of the Yishuv, the Jewish Agency and Vaad Leumi, the entire hierarchy of practical Zionism—the Histadrut, the Left, the Haganah, the new elite commando Palmach—would oppose any unauthorized separatist revolt. Whether this opposition could be translated into repression, whether the little people of the Yishuv would permit collusion with the British to repress the Irgun, were moot questions. The proper balance of official condemnation and public toleration would permit the Irgun to function. The longer the revolt lasted, the more obvious it would be that the original fears of the Yishuv concerning such provocation were groundless, and the more difficult for the authorized agencies to act against the Irgun with rigor.

One factor causing almost no concern was the Arab response. The reaction of the Yishuv was crucial, but that of the Arabs was ignored or minimized. "Of course the Arabs have rights, but our rights are far more important, our needs override theirs."[2] The Arabs would not oppose the revolt, and if they did, they could be intimidated. If the revolt were successful, the Arabs would manage to accommodate reality. So much for the Arabs—the major opponent was the British. Begin took a year's leave of absence from his army position of translator in the Jerusalem mayor's office in order to do "welfare work"—he did not approve of desertion.

As it became clear that the Irgun was going to launch a revolt under the direction of Begin, Meridor began to create an anti-British front, attracting those militants in the Palmach and Haganah who had lost patience. The new organization, Am Lohem, did indeed attract Palmach and Haganah members. There was a three-man command council, Meridor and Eliahu Lankin of the Irgun, and Aharon from the Haganah, and a series of policy discussions. Meridor's plan to kidnap High Commissioner MacMichael aroused more interest than proposals to attack CID stations or assassinate old police enemies like Wilkin. LEHI had always been more interested in hitting the CID, and LEHI declined to participate in Am Lohem. The kidnapping operation had to be postponed several times. There was waning enthusiasm and increasing difficulty. Then, one day, the Haganah people simply did not appear. On December 7, 1943, the Haganah general staff warned all its members that all Am Lohem activities must end within seventy-two hours. The Haganah felt that Am Lohem was only an Irgun stalking horse to involve their people in a separatist campaign, and they were quite right. After the collapse of Am Lohem, Meridor resigned as commander, and Begin took over. The Irgun would have to go it alone.

Begin's Irgun left much to be desired despite Meridor's efforts to hold the organization together. Years of inactivity had eroded the membership. By 1943, with Irgun permission, over a thousand members had volunteered for the British forces. Others did so without permission. The splits and particularly Stern's departure persuaded others to retire. The purposeless quarrels took their toll. Even with the rumor of action by December 1943, there were only six hundred activists left. The stores of arms and explosives were gone—lost, stolen, discovered, or forgotten— leaving a grand total of four submachine guns, thirty rifles, and sixty pistols of various and dubious makes. There was less than a ton of explosives and next to no chemical equipment. There was no decent printing press, no radio, no communications equipment or technological resources. Also, there was no money, the prime physical necessity for a revolt. There was, however, a core of dedicated and competent men, and there would be more from the training program directed by the Polish General Frabitze, who, like Begin, had come to Palestine with Anders's army.

Whenever new volunteers came to the Irgun, they did so for a variety of motives, not all acceptable to the command. The selection committee was often more concerned with weeding out the romantics and adventurers than increasing the membership. Usually, a candidate had to make contact with a known member, but the Mandate was small enough for the persistent to find their way to the appropriate contact. A meeting was then set up with the three-member selection committee. The candidate was interviewed at a safe house by these unseen interrogators. He would sit in a darkened room with a flashlight focused in his eyes, or be questioned from behind a screen. Once the basic informational questions—age, school, job, interests—had been answered, the interrogators focused on the candidate's ideological awareness. Why did the Irgun focus on an armed struggle? What were the issues at stake in Palestine? How does the Irgun differ from other groups? What is the Jews' historical claim to Eretz Israel? The same questions did not come up every time, but the committees easily eliminated those who had not contemplated the sacrifices— detention, expulsion from schools and jobs, even death—or answered in slogans with no grasp of the Irgun's purpose. Once selection had been made, the recruit had to attend four months of indoctrination seminars in groups of five to ten in which they were taught Irgun ideology and the iron rules of underground behavior. The ideological lectures were thought necessary in themselves, but those recruits of flawed purpose or excessive impatience could be weeded out during the seminars; and even after the final meeting any volunteer could still resign. Following the introductory courses, as the volunteer met more members, recognized safe houses, and became involved in military training, resignation was not so easy—a fact stressed by the instructors. Still, living above ground, since there were no more than forty full-time members, the new recruits continued regular two-hour classes, often in the evening, in arms handling and tactics. There was test firing by the sea or in the desert, and a volunteer might attend a camp training session over a weekend. Later, there were special heavy-weapons training camps, but in 1944 they had no such weapons. The most rigorous training was a year-long explosives course. The Irgun recognized the dangers, even to experienced people, in constructing bombs. Some revolutionary organizations, like the Provisional IRA, which were determined to raise the level of violence, have been willing to use relatively inexperienced people to handle explosives. The Irgun was not.

All the classes, camps, and training did not, of course, produce an army in any real military sense. In fact, as many of the recruits soon discovered to their disappointment, the purely military duties were cherished assignments open only to a few. To maintain the organization, to support the shock units, and especially to publicize the reasons behind the revolt, behind each operation, were almost as vital as fighting. Thus a young man who had joined an underground army to fight often found himself pasting copies of *Herut* on the walls of Ramat Gan or Haifa—an act that might result in years in jail or a bullet in the back.

Life in the underground was hardly romantic, except in subsequent recollection. There was the constant duplicity of hiding a secret life from parents, friends, or children—old friends had to be deceived or discarded, lovers lied to and often lost, a child's innocent comment feared. Begin, for example, had to decide whether to bring his family from Jerusalem and live openly or to go underground. He chose to live openly, first on the fringe of the Yemenite quarter of Petah Tikva, then, as Israel Halperin, in a house in the Hasidic quarter in Petah Tikva. Except for a few full time people, nearly everyone lived above ground, often in their own homes, under their own names, but always with another secret life. There was the daily round of quick meetings in dreary rooms with frightened hosts hovering at the door, tiny notes passed on street corners, rumors of disaster or arrests, or the headline in a paper that could not be acknowledged. There was never enough time or money. Everyone lived on nerves, coffee, and cigarettes.

Later, it seemed to the members that the months and years slipped by in a delirium of heightened reality. Neither the later open wars nor the postponed careers would ever have the drama of life underground. There was the pulse of knowledge when, walking down the dark streets of Tel Aviv, one heard through a strange window the whistled bar of the Betar song as the Irgun's illegal radio began to broadcast. There was the concealed joy when an operation went well and the hidden anguish when it did not—no one in the underground could cry in public, and few had time to laugh. Most members walked the streets above ground, paste on their fingers or cartridges in their pockets. Those on the run went through the motions of normality, tramped off to work each morning, hoping that old friends or enemies would not recognize them, and kept to their allotted underground rounds knowing that as the months passed their luck was dribbling away. No matter when their time came—a light in a detective's eye, a midnight knock on the door, troops at an unexpected roadblock, or the numbing thud of a bullet—there were others to fill their places, almost too many others as the revolt gained momentum.

The last of Begin's worries was a lack of courage. He had six hundred Irgunists, but weapons for fewer than a hundred. He could count on sympathizers in the NZO, even though in January 1944 he broke all formal connections with the Revisionist movement, and a few old friends. He could also count on the enmity and suspicion of the vast majority of the Yishuv and the dedicated opposition of his old Zionist enemies. There was a very small pool for his guerrillas to swim in freely—a tiny minority of another minority, taking on an empire, doing it on a shoestring. In 1944 the revolt cost between £1,000 and £1,500 a month— no small sum for the times—raised by sincere contributions, intimidation, and theft. There was almost no help from the diaspora, for even after the end of the war in Europe communication into the Mandate was difficult. By 1945 the monthly cost of rebellion had risen to £2,500 and continued to grow because of unexpected expenses: a special operation that could not be financed out of the monthly budget, a spectacular escape that might cost £3,000. Personal expenses could not be cut, since the full time people lived on a tiny expense stipend. Somehow the safe houses had to be maintained, arms purchased, bribes paid, cars rented, radio parts purchased. As a result little burglaries gave way in time to major "confiscations"—in 1945 well over £38,000 in diamonds was taken during a raid on post office parcel dispatchers, and £38,000 more was taken during a raid on a guarded train carrying the monthly pay of the Palestine railway workers. Later there was some help from the Revisionist movement in South Africa, but basically the Irgun, cut off in Palestine, had to depend on their own resources. Extortion, theft, and wary donations have always been revolutionary means, and the Irgun was no exception.

Much the same situation existed with the arms: some could be purchased illicitly from individual British soldiers; more could be stolen, either in odd lots or in a major raid on a British installation. Later the Irgun produced explosive grenades, Sten guns with wooden stocks, mortars, a variety of mines ignited by glass vials of acid, pressure, or electricity—these had more psychological than military impact. These hidden factories produced a whole spectrum of diabolical devices—a rocket weapon, a huge barrel bomb launched from a lorry—but the problem of conventional light arms was never satisfactorily solved, so that as late as November 1947, with an overall strength of two thousand, the Irgun had arms for only seven hundred. As LEHI had demonstrated in Cairo, even one pistol repeatedly used can have an impressive effect. Every weapon was treasured, a pistol protected as a jewel, and a machine gun was a major organizational asset. Years later, standing before shimmering Phantoms or long lines of main battle tanks, old Irgunist veterans remembering the cherished little pistol, the oiled cartridges, the pride of possession, often felt out of phase with time and reality. Then, so little had meant so much, while in a few minutes of fighting in 1973 or 1967 more arms were wasted than the Irgun had ever seen. There were, of course, virtues in privation: often a match is a guerrilla's best weapon. Those who must steal at risk cherish what they get, while those armed by aliens do not. In the underground, less is often more.

Certainly, when Begin took over in December 1943, there seemed little left of the Irgun. At the top was a small high command composed of Begin, Arieh Ben-Eliezer, who had helped fashion the strategy of revolt at the Savoy Hotel meetings, Eliahu Lankin, who had come from Harbin, China, and was the Jerusalem area commander, and Shlomo Levy, a sabra from Petah Tikva, who at nineteen had become chief of staff. A little later, despite some rumbling in certain quarters, Meridor returned to the meetings. During the course of the revolt, new men were added to fill vacancies caused by arrests or to take over expanded assignments—two, Jacob ("Eli") Tavin and Samuel Katz, served mostly abroad. Beneath the high command was a small general staff, divided into a support and a military section, never meeting jointly and maintaining liaison through the high command. The support staff was responsible for finance, intelligence, propaganda, and communications. The military staff was divided into operational units and support units—instruction, arms depots and manufacture, first aid, and planning.

Under the high command/general staff were six basic geographical commands: Southern, Sharon, Jerusalem, Haifa-Galilee, Tel Aviv, and Shomron, shifting in size and importance under the pressure of arrests and the efficiency of recruiting. Each had a commander, a small staff, and a core of members, but few were really strong, and several were often quite weak indeed. With only six hundred activists, there were never enough men to fill the slots on the organizational table, much less swell the ranks. The Irgun, for example, was supposedly divided into a reserve, shock units, assault forces and a propaganda force. There were never enough people to create either a reserve or a special shock force. In 1943 an ultrasecret red division, (Yehidot Mahatz-Yam) had been formed with a white squad and a black squad, the later combined members who knew Arabic and looked like Arabs for special activities in Arab areas. In 1944 the red division was dissolved and formed the basis for the Hok, the combat division. The secret division had produced problems within the ranks, not the least being the "resignation" of some of the best members of the Irgun in order to permit them to go into the red division, endangering the morale of those remaining. In reality, in 1944 the Irgun had only two varieties of volunteers, the fighters in Hok and the others who might move from other duties but seldom did.

Although the paper units of the organizational chart could never be activated, Begin still kept the old structure throughout the revolt, despite having too many pigeonholes for too few pigeons. Much of the time the skilled, cunning, or brave shifted from one job to the other, one operation to the next, one part of the Mandate to another. No one paid much attention to formalities, and the system worked remarkably well. Essentially, under whatever name, the Irgun was a small but elaborately structured revolutionary conspiracy, dependent on part-time operations and constantly reapportioned resources. Beginning with two hundred members in Hok and four hundred actives elsewhere, the Irgun could not even pass for a mini-army, even though Begin stressed that he led an army, not a party or a revolutionary organization. Because of the small size of the operational areas within the Mandate and their ability to move freely, the Irgun did not need too many more operational people. Only after the irregular Arab invasion in 1948 did the ranks swell, as the Irgun came partially out from underground, reaching perhaps ten thousand members by May 1948. To strike psychological-political blows by military means against the British presence, the Irgun had fashioned an ideal structure. Increasing the numbers involved risked an overload, enhanced the chances of repeated arrests and subsequent disorder. Men lost from a small organization could readily be replaced, often with a gain in efficiency, as combat-conspiracy experience was absorbed. A larger organization, with the inevitable dilution of talent and experience, would have been less efficient and far harder to maintain, would have demanded organizational efforts more profitably expended on operations. The entire Irgun, then, was a dedicated band of brothers with intimate loyalties.

By 1944 some of these brothers had lost all patience with the delay in mounting a revolt. On January 19, several young men broke into the garage of the British Steel Company in Haifa and sabotaged government cars with mines. When the police arrived they managed to capture one of those involved, Avtelion, who was tried and sentenced to ten years. By then the revolt was formally under way. Begin's Proclamation of Revolt appeared on February 1.

> There is no longer any armistice between the Jewish people and the British Administration in Eretz Israel which hands our brothers over to Hitler. Our people is at war with this regime—war to the end . . . This then is our demand: immediate transfer of power in Eretz Israel to a provisional Hebrew government. We shall fight, every Jew in the homeland will fight. The God of Israel, the Lord of Hosts, will aid us. There will be no retreat. Freedom—or death.[3]

Those who read the broadsheets or saw the proclamation pasted on a wall greeted the announcement with boredom or derision. Wilkin, promoted for his work against LEHI in 1942, announced to his superiors, "There's nothing to worry about."[4] He was proved quite wrong. By the end of the year, Wilkin had been shot down in broad daylight on a Jerusalem street by his old LEHI enemies. By then the Irgun's revolt was well and truly under way, and the Mandate was slipping into chaos.

In February, however, the common wisdom agreed with Wilkin. The first Irgun operation, against the offices of the Immigration Department in Jerusalem, Tel Aviv, and Haifa—symbols of the closed gates—were small-scale sabotage. They were cunningly planned with minimal resources. On the evening of February 12, a small group of the Irgun was asked to meet in Sharon Park on Hashmar Street in Tel Aviv. Not until the arrival of Ehud, the commander, did they learn that there was to be an operation and that a sack of explosives had been left in the bushes.

They moved out toward Kikar Hamoshavot, where the Immigration Department had second-floor offices. A key to the house next door had been made by a friendly locksmith, so that the four men carrying the explosives slipped in, climbed to the roof, stepped over to the next building, and broke in the roof door. The explosives were carried downstairs to the second floor; the office door was broken open, and the sack left. The four went out the way they came, past the two policemen guarding the building, who noticed nothing until the second floor blew into the street over their heads.

In Jerusalem a carefully planned spontaneous brawl on the street in front of the Immigration Department created such commotion—windows thrown up, loud complaints, howling and screaming from the beaten victim, "He's killing me!"—that the guard rushed over to separate the two combatants. His brief career as referee lasted just long enough for a man to pop around the corner and thrust a fused device through the barred but open windows. He slipped away, as did the chagrined gladiators. The policeman was still there when the offices blew up later that night.

The third operation in Haifa was an elegant exercise in deception. The Arab policeman made it a practice to stand stolid and unmoving at his post in the doorway of the building. On the evening of the twelfth, however, he noticed the arrival of a young Jewish couple in a doorway across from his post. In no time it became clear that the young man had serious erotic ambitions and the young woman no intention of resisting. There was scuffling and moaning in the doorway. The guard, eagle-eyed and alert, moved a bit closer to the couple in the shadows. There was no doubt in his mind that, unaware of his presence, they were making love. There were tempting glimpses in the dim light and small moans, as he edged forward another few feet to be on hand for the climax. Unaccountably, the two suddenly stopped and moved off down the street. The policeman reluctantly moved back to his post, but a minute before a bomb had been slipped into the doorway. When the device detonated, there were no casualties, although the policeman was reported in shock—perhaps more from the display in the doorway than from the explosion. Anyway, the Irgun was delighted with the first three operations. As expected, the orthodox Zionists were dismayed. Weizmann expressed his sympathy, shock, and wrath. The British were not especially concerned, for they had watched for years the rise of Jewish frustration.

As early as 1941, Oliver Lyttelton, minister of state in Cairo, in the midst of the most pressing military demands, had time and energy to spare for the Palestine problem.

> Our dealings with the Jewish Agency were uneasy and our general security in Palestine rested more upon military strength than upon any consent of the inhabitants to the existing regime.
> The great controversies about the extent and nature of the Zionist state were always hanging over us, though kept in the background.[5]

Then came the LEHI campaign of 1942, the continued illegal immigration, the World Zionist call for a Jewish commonwealth in the Biltmore Programme of 1942, the news of the holocaust, and the resistance to British arms searches.

> By January 1944 the attitude of the Jewish Agency towards the government had hardened to such an extent that any action conflicting with the policy of the Biltmore Programme or for enforcing the White Paper met with opposition and obstruction. The Jewish Agency was in some respects arrogating to itself the powers and status of an independent Jewish Government. It no longer attempted to deny the existence of arms caches, but claimed the right not only to hold arms for self-defense but to resist any attempt on the part of lawful authority to locate them. It was, in fact, defying the Government, and to that extent rebellion could be said to exist.[6]

If this were the case with the Jewish Agency, no one in the Mandate administration was greatly surprised that the Irgun set off bombs in government offices. No one liked it, of course, but there had been symbolic bombs before and probably would be again. In the meantime, the security forces soldiered on, the high commissioner kept to his allotted rounds, the shocked Arab policeman was released from the hospital, and the Irgun high command planned the next round.

On February 27, the income tax offices in Jerusalem, Tel Aviv, and Haifa were bombed. Orthodox Zionists were again dismayed. The Jewish Agency soon called for a day of fasting on March 23 in response to the holocaust. The Irgun knew that the British would be unmoved by the Yishuv not eating and decided to contrast the Irgun's position to the old havlaga mentality by attacking more serious targets: CID stations in Jerusalem, Jaffa, and Haifa. Although there would be no attempt to take lives following Begin's imposed limitations, bombing police stations was a far more serious matter than setting off a sack of explosives in an empty office.

The operation against the CID station at Haifa went off without a hitch. A large mine was placed next to the left wall and a warning called in to the police. Some hurriedly rushed out and down the street. Four others refused to be moved by terrorist threats. This proved a costly error; for the mine went off on a schedule, and the entire left section of the building crumbled in on top of those who remained. All were injured and three later died, Constables Allison, Mackie, and Harding.

The Jaffa operation, however, ran into difficulties even before starting time. LEHI, operating independently as always, had sent assassination squads into the streets of Tel Aviv to seek revenge for the death of one of their members shot on March 19. At 6:30 P.M., C. Brown, British chief clerk at the Tel Aviv district police headquarters, was shot and fatally wounded. Ten minutes later Constable Langtrey was shot and seriously wounded. At 7:30 Constable Caley, standing outside the magistrates' court, was shot and fatally wounded. The entire city was in turmoil, and a general military standby was ordered. After uniformed constables were taken off the streets, the army began armored patrols. All security installations were on full alert, and there were police blocks on the main roads. The Irgun, unaware of the commotion, became increasingly uneasy at the number of street patrols. The attack units' commander, Shimshon, decided to go ahead. Along with his three-man team, he took a taxi to the Shapiro district. There they paid off the taxi and moved ahead on foot to a safe house where they put on British uniforms and picked up rucksacks filled with thirty kilos of explosives. Where four rather harassed-looking young Jews had darted in the house, four very drunken British soldiers stumbled out and began to weave their way down the street. They hailed a taxi, clambered in, and directed the driver to Salame Street, which would put them just beyond the CID station. In the taxi the four began a round of loud, off-color soldier songs and the driver sped up, eager to be rid of the celebrants before they got sour or sick. The chaos in the back seat was obviously effective, because they were waved through police roadblocks, passed right by the station, they stopped the taxi fifty yards on the Jaffa side. They stumbled out in high glee; paid off the relieved driver; and began weaving their way back to the alley beside the station. Behind them, two worried Irgun cover parties had slipped through the patrols and taken up stations in the house opposite and at the top of the street toward Tel Aviv, to cover their retreat. Shimshon took his men straight to the alley, short of the police guard at the front door and opposite a single Arab watchman, who did indeed watch them walk down the alley and turn into the station's side door: so did the Arab policeman on duty at the door. They left their rucksacks after arranging the fuses, turned around, walked past the policeman at the door, past the watchman at the corner, past the police at the station front door, greeting all with great cheer. Once out of sight, they disappeared down the maze of alleys that led to the Maccabi quarter of Tel Aviv. Soon there was a shuddering explosion, but the cover parties did not get away as easily. Patrols ran into three suspicious men. A policeman foolishly flicked on his torch. Yitshak at once shot him. The other police opened up on the cover party and in exchange hit Ziv, who had to be taken to the hospital, where he was later arrested.

The Jerusalem operation proved even more difficult, despite careful planning by Eitan Livni, since early March high command operational officer, and the Jerusalem commander, Eliahu. Several days before March 24, a ladder was stolen, the Irgun in Jerusalem as usual having no funds, and carted through a house on the Jaffa Road into the courtyard of the Russian Building, where the CID headquarters were located. In the courtyard the ladder was carefully chained to the wall of the Jaffa Road house and left until it had become a normal part of the courtyard. On the night of March 23, the plan was to send an assault squad into the courtyard, where two "policemen" would tie up the night watchman and move the ladder against the rear of the Russian Building, while two "workmen" collected parcels of explosives previously left in the courtyard dustbins. Three men would pull the parcels up to the second floor balcony after the fuses were set. The assault group would be protected by two defense units, one forward and one in the rear. Once the explosives were placed, withdrawal would be made through the Jaffa Road house. The operation was timed to coincide with the cinema crowds, so that there would be lots of people in the area.

There were no early problems. Several "policemen" during the evening drifted into the courtyard and paused by the dustbins. Then two more appeared, walked up to the night watchman's shed, and bound and gagged him. They unlocked the Irgun ladder, moved it across the courtyard, and leaned it against the balcony. The other two assault members, dressed as workmen, trundled the packets from the dustbins to the base of the ladder. One waited at the base while the other three climbed up and lowered a rope. The first and nearly fatal complication occurred when one of the vials of acid for the fusing device broke and set a parcel on fire. The flames were quickly smothered before the parcel detonated and before the passing crowd outside the courtyard entrance noticed anything. The parcels began to be roped up. Then, obviously looking for a quiet corner, a British officer and a young girl wandered into the half-lit courtyard. They revealed a lack of curiosity about the workman, his pile of parcels and the ladder, and only apparent disappointment at his presence. They wandered out. The parcels started up again.

Time, however, had run out. A detective in plain clothes and a policeman near the entrance thought there was something bloody odd about a working party moving parcels up to the second floor of CID headquarters at 10:30 at night. There was a shout, and someone fired a shot. Immediately, the forward defense squad opened up. The operation fell apart. Police in the third floor of the building leaned out and fired at the three men on the balcony. The Irgun squad across the way riddled the third-floor windows. The courtyard was crisscrossed with gun flashes. Shattered glass sliced down in showers. The rear defense squad moved up to block the entrance to the headquarters and protect the line of retreat. By then Asher Ben-Ziman had been killed in the cross fire and Avraham Ben-Avraham badly wounded. The three units, however, withdrew into the house on the Jaffa Road, moved out among the crowds, and crossed over into the Nachlat-Shiva section before the police could circle around to the Jaffa Road. The "policemen" changed out of their uniforms in a Moslem cemetery and with the others slipped off to a meeting at the Menorah Club. Despite the efforts of two doctors, Avraham Ben-Avraham died just before dawn. Inspector Scott of the CID had also been killed. Since Avraham Ben-Avraham was buried without being identified with the operation, the British assumed that the score for March 23 was six CID killed and one Irgun, plus those lost earlier in the evening to LEHI gunmen and the dozens wounded in the course of the three operations.

The Irgun attacks, in part because of the serious CID losses, caused consternation in all segments of the Mandate. Bombs in empty government offices were one thing, but dead policemen and fire fights in downtown Jerusalem and Jaffa were quite another—a rebellion did exist. Three days later the British imposed a snap curfew on Tel Aviv, Jerusalem, and Haifa, rounded up likely suspects, and ran long identity parades. The death sentence, enacted in 1936 but since lapsed, was invoked for possessing arms and placing explosives. Inspector General Romer Jones of the Palestine police announced that the guilty were "youngsters who must be described as political gangsters."[7] Security forces would adopt a firm policy. The recognized Jewish institutions quite agreed. The Yishuv had suffered through Stern's gunbattles in 1942; and now in 1944 the madmen of the right were at it again. This time the provocation might well alienate the British, who ultimately would decide the fate of the Mandate, might alienate the other allies, who could urge a Zionist solution, and would in no way open the gates. Only Zionist logic, world opinion, and diplomatic pressure would persuade Britain to take action in the face of the holocaust. So the orthodox Zionists damned the gunmen once more. The Arabs, on the other hand, where any sentiment could be discovered, were surprised that the Jews had shot up three police stations and killed six British policemen, but were impressed perhaps more at British ineffectuality than at Jewish militancy. The Arabs, however, were leaderless, with the mufti in exile and the notables divided. They had no strong political institutions, no single spokesman, no real postwar strategy. If they planned for the future, they intended to wait and see what the British would do, what their friends in the Arab capitals would do, what others would do, for they felt increasingly isolated and confused. At least with the mufti, they knew whom to hate and how to strike; in 1944 they watched from the sidelines as the Irgun and LEHI took on the British.

For the high command, the fact that the Irgun could carry out the operations was not as important as the impact the revolt had within the Mandate and internationally. The response of the Yishuv was at first the most vital. An unending stream of Irgun proclamations, posters, pamphlets, and position papers were distributed so that the Jews would know what the revolt was, why it had been undertaken, and what its results would be. Isolated in his safe house, the mysterious Begin communicated with his people and with all in the Mandate from the pages of *Herut*. Endlessly writing, he produced a one-man newspaper. Distribution was difficult, and the pasters' vulnerability was high. At first *Herut* was printed in a little shop on the Tel Aviv-Jaffa border; but in August 1944, the Irgun got their own printing press. To make ends meet, the propaganda service even accepted commercial orders. A special underground printing bunker was prepared for the press, but before it could be completed an informer revealed its presence to the British. A second bunker was constructed, with a mechanical ventilator, in the second floor above a carpentry shop. The Irgun ran the shop, taking furniture orders, bringing in newsprint with the lumber and sending out *Herut* with the finished orders.

Crammmed into the bunker, the Irgun printers almost suffocated in the heat despite the ventilator; but they knew, and Begin insisted, their task was as vital as those in Hok. And they, too, had their martyrs. Ashor Tratner, a member of the eighth class at Haifa high school, was assigned as a paster. A police patrol caught him putting up a proclamation. He tried to get away and they opened fire, hitting him in the hip. Instead of taking him to the hospital or treating him, the police sent him around the bay to Acre prison where treatment was further delayed. Severe blood poisoning set in, and his leg had to be amputated. After weeks of suffering he died.

Even more effective than *Herut* was the clandestine radio. It usually broadcast for six minutes, leaving the announcer and engineer one minute to escape with the radio, for it was reputed that British tracking devices could home in within eight minutes. The first radio transmitter was built into a suitcase, and was lost on March 2 when a spot check on the street revealed that Yehuda Noah and his wife, Raziel's sister, were the underground radio team. They went to prison, and the Irgun was off the air. Another transmitter was found, and the six-minute broadcast began again, each introduced with the whistled notes of the Betar song. The LEHI, too, by 1944 was back in the propaganda business, producing *Ha-*

chazit (The Front), an internal newspaper *Bamachteret* (In the Under-ground), youth papers, endless pamphlets, the wall newspaper *Hama'ass* (Action), and whenever possible operated an underground radio. Coupled with what the Irgun produced, the Yishuv seemed to have explanations aplenty, but never enough for Begin, who knew the key to future opera-tions lay with the Yishuv.

> We disseminated the declaration of revolt through the length and breadth of the country, posting it up on the walls. . . . We published leaflets, appeals and communiques on military operations. At least once every two or three days, at times every day or every night, our message was proclaimed. We never tired of explaining.[8]

At best, the response of the Yishuv was ambiguous. As the high com-mand had anticipated, the average reader of the wall newspapers was not convinced that the British would not vengefully institute indiscriminate pogroms, indentifying all Jews with the terrorists. The immediate British reaction to the operations of February and March did not indicate such a policy, but there was as yet no firm proof that the Irgun was not risking the existence of the Yishuv. Nor was anyone certain that the Irgun and LEHI were not—proclamations and declarations aside—just carrying out a few symbolic strikes for political purposes. Thus the major response was consternation and anxiety in general, and bitter criticism by the official institutions in particular.

The first and predictable reaction of the Jewish Agency was that the legitimate democratic leadership of the Yishuv had been betrayed by men of narrow vision, dubious motives, and cold arrogance, who could only endanger the efforts to implement the Biltmore Programme that would win for the Jews their dearest aspirations. The first effort to persuade the Irgun to call off the revolt was an approach to the Revisionist party. Be-ginning on February 18, Dov Joseph for the Jewish Agency met with the Revisionists five times. Only during the last meeting on March 3 did he find out that they no longer controlled the Irgun. If the Jewish Agency wanted to negotiate they would have to deal directly with Begin. Instead, the Jewish Agency then sought to construct a program of oppositon. Something had to be done, for Begin's revolt was a direct challenge to their own authority. They assumed a fearful gamble with Zionist aspira-tions and the safety of the Yishuv. It was not mentioned publicly for the revolt might lead to defections of militants from the Haganah ranks. A few even favored cooperation with the British against the Irgun. Most were content with recourse to propaganda. On April 2, 1944, after long debate, an official policy of opposition was accepted: (1) efforts to stop extortion and terror, (2) increased propaganda, (3) isolation of the separa-tists. While still undecided on cooperation with the British, the program appeared on paper to be a very strong response. Most of the program remained on paper. Anti-Irgun propaganda was increased, and help was offered to those whose contributions had been extorted. Nothing else happened. The Irgun had passed the first hurdle—the recognized institutions and the Yishuv had not killed the asp in the egg.

On May 17, the Irgun carried out a successful operation against the central broadcasting station at Ramele to mark the fifth anniversary of the white paper. Although the Irgun had hoped to transmit from the station, their radio man could not work the equipment. While he was tinkering, the Hok team defended the station against attacks from the police of Tegart fortress, making use of their homemade mortar for the first time.

Coupled with the LEHI gunbattles, the spring was a difficult time for the British security forces. Between April 1 and May 6, eighty-one suspects were arrested; in a British coup on April 17, Ben-Eliezer was arrested in a hotel search. These searches and snap roadblocks became routine within the Mandate as the security forces geared up. Until 1944 the CID's Jewish section was less lively than the Arab or Axis sections (the Communist section was stagnant after 1941). Although many of the Revisionist party members were known, most of Begin's people were young and had never come to police notice. Still the arrests continued; heavy sentences were meted out, and determined searches made for the illegal radio transmitters and printing presses. On July 14, the Land Registry Office in Jerusalem was gutted and two Arab constables killed. On July 15, an explosives truck was seized and a British constable killed. On July 28, High Commissioner MacMichael reported to London, "Available information indicates that the security position may be deteriorated, and the outlook is not encouraging."[9] Ten days later the LEHI riddled his car on the Jerusalem-to-Jaffa road.

After the assassination attempt both the British and Jewish Agency's reactions to the continuing revolt hardened. The British intelligence files were of little use, filled with the names of "political" Revisionists and old-timers. There were few informers to open a way into the Irgun.[10] The underground cells were small and sealed; few knew more than a few. Conventional sweeps, intensive searches, and random arrests proved minimally productive. On August 16, for example, eighteen men and women were arrested at Tel Tzur. On August 23, there were Irgun arms raids on the CID barracks at Jaffa, Abu-Kabir, and Neve Shaanan. The Irgun announced that fourteen rifles were seized, hewing to their policy of telling the exact truth even when it was not very impressive. On September 5, the British mounted the first huge cordon–and–sweep operation in Petah Tikva and arrested forty-six people, but missed modest little Israel Halpern who, as Israel Sassover, moved out and into a new safe house on Bin-Nun Street. Meridor and the high command had for some time felt that

Begin's old house was dangerous. The British claimed, not without reason, that Petva Tikva was full of terrorists. On a Tel Aviv side street, the new house, halfway between the municipal abbatoir and the municipal dogs' home, would be more secure. There Israel Sassover grew a beard, adopted Roxy, the late owner's dog, and in time became a candidate for the post of second assistant to the third warden of Rabbi Simcha's synagogue down the street. There his first daughter Hasya was born, and illegally registered by Israel Epstein as his own child—Hasya Epstein. As Israel Sassover, Begin continued to write *Herut* and direct the revolt from the inside.

Obviously, the easiest solution for the British would be to let the Jewish Agency—the legitimate recognized authority—crush the revolt. In this case British and Agency interests ran parallel; in fact, the Irgun challenge was more dangerous for the Agency than for the British, since all the Yishuv might be punished for the acts of the few fanatics.

In an effort to find a compromise solution within the Yishuv, various contacts were set up that might lead to a Ben-Gurion–Begin meeting. The Irgun hoped that Begin's offer to continue the resistance under Ben-Gurion's leadership had a chance of being accepted. If Begin offered amalgamation, there would no longer be cause for suspicions about the Irgun's political ambitions. Ben-Gurion, however, saw only the challenge to the Agency's authority by men he never trusted. On their part the Agency leaders felt that Begin might be made to see that an end of violence had to come before the British were alienated and all the promised or prospective gains lost. In the end not Ben-Gurion but Dr. Moshe Sneh and Eliyahu Golomb of the Haganah met with Begin and Lankin on August 10. Sneh and Begin talked for some time without finding any common ground. Sneh was unable to convince Begin that the British intended to grant the Zionists "the biggest plum in the pudding." Begin felt sure it would in any case be a partition plum, and that nations were created not by accepting grants of plums, but by struggle. Essentially, Sneh and Begin talked at cross-purposes, for their basic assumptions differed. Sneh and Ben-Gurion wanted Begin to withdraw his challenge and let them go on with their work, while Begin felt their work should be revolt, not worrying about challenges. He assumed that the Yishuv had the potential to *force* the British to decide in Zionism's favor or be driven from the Mandate; Ben-Gurion did not. The negotiations thus ended after one meeting, and the Jewish Agency had to consider more stringent measures against the Irgun, for the revolt seemed to be gaining momentum.

On September 27, Begin devised a cunning two-level operation that guaranteed success no matter what the British response. For fourteen years the British, in the name of security, had forbidden sounding the

Shofar on the Day of Atonement at the Wailing Wall. The British insisted such an affront to Arab sensibilities might lead to another Hebron massacre. The Irgun began a Yom Kippur campaign of intimidation, threatening disaster if the British continued the prohibition. The walls were plastered with repeated threats. The Mandate authorities were obviously caught in a bind. If they maintained their old position in the name of order, they almost assured a situation in which the Irgun would feel justified in the use of violence that the ban was supposed to avoid. If they gave in to the Irgun threat, it would be a humiliating concession. As September 27 approached, the wall posters became specific.

> Any British policeman who on the Day of Atonement dares to burst into the area of the Wailing Wall and to disturb the traditional service—will be regarded as a criminal and will be punished accordingly.[11]

The Irgun was bluffing, since the high command had no intention of opening fire on anyone in the midst of the crowd of Jews crammed into the narrow alley in front of the Wailing Wall. What had been planned was a series of attacks on the Tegart fortresses to coincide with the Day of Atonement. The British would be unprepared for operations elsewhere, and on a high holiday to boot. More important, if the British did ban the Shofar, these attacks would be the Irgun's answer to them. The British kept away from the Wailing Wall. That night, the Irgun attacked the Tegart fortresses.

The attack in Haifa did not go well. The attack team could not penetrate beyond the first defense wall to put the second bomb against the door. The security forces sprayed a stream of machine gun fire back and forth in front of the attackers. There was nothing to do but pull back. The commander was hit in the hand, but given the volume of fire, the Irgun was lucky not to have taken more casualties. As it was, they nearly lost him after he was taken to the Rothschild Hospital where, after treating him, the chief surgeon called the police. By then the local Haifa Irgun commander had arrived, and the two escaped by jumping out a window before the police reached the hospital. At Beit Dragon near Jerusalem, there was also a fire fight; but the attack team broke into the courtyard and planted their mines near the door of the station. They could not actually get into the station after the explosion. At Katra, south of Rehovat, under a heavy cover fire, the Irgun broke into the station, killed two British soldiers and two police constables. Then they cleaned out the arms and ammunition, including a Bren machine gun, the very first heavy weapon the Irgun had managed to acquire. At Qalqilya, near Tulkarm, there was a twenty-minute delay in launching the attacks; so it was possible the police had heard of the other three assaults. In any case just before the five-man assault team reached the front door, a withering fire from inside the Tegart fortress hosed them down. Four were wounded, and, as the entire force attempted to withdraw, they came under fire from a train guard on top of a passing freight car. Even with that piece of bad luck, they managed to straggle back to their base near Petah Tikva. The British were stunned "at the deterioration of the situation in Palestine. The attack on the high commissioner is serious enough, but 150 men in four simultaneous assaults . . . "[12] Security forces estimated that the Irgun and LEHI had between five and seven thousand members. Serious steps had to be taken, including the deportation of detainees and pressure on the recognized Jewish institutions.

Up to September 27, the day of the Shofar, the Irgun had cost the British little but anxiety. Matters had not gone badly. The Jewish Agency pushed an anti-Irgun policy; the Yishuv was passive or hostile; the mini-raids had no real military importance. Lives were lost, of course, but not British credibility. But the British withdrawal in the face of Irgun coercion on Yom Kippur, coupled with the raids on the police fortresses, was a disaster for them, and a harbinger of others to come. Psychologically, it was a truly significant victory for the Irgun—the Wailing Wall was far more significant than the attacks. In these the British had simply been assaulted; in the case of the Shofar, however, they were intimidated into a humiliating withdrawal. The security forces preferred not to pay the Irgun's price at the Wailing Wall, and had thus, for whatever logical reasons, taken a step back. Equally important, even after the four attacks, the British did not seek revenge. Yom Kippur thus proved to the satisfaction of the Irgun that the British could be challenged successfully, and that, as anticipated, Britain would not pursue a policy of vengeance. All the professed fears of the Agency were groundless. Two days later the LEHI finally caught up with Wilkin. Lying dead in a pool of blood on a Jerusalem street, he was a mute witness to the changing times.

The Jewish Agency remained wedded to the proposition that the Irgun was a danger to the hopes of Jewry, that the campaign must somehow be stopped. The press stepped up their attacks on what *Davar* condemned as "this lunacy"—crimes that could bring calamity upon Jewish Palestine. At the very time the white paper logjam seemed to be breaking up, with hints of a new policy coming out of London, with open support in the platforms of both the Democratic and Republican parties in the United States, the separatists were shooting down policemen in the street. As far back as April the Labour party in Britain had renewed a position on Palestine more Zionist, if possible, than that of the Jewish Agency.

But there is surely neither hope nor meaning in a "Jewish National Home," unless we are prepared to let Jews, if they wish, enter this tiny land in such numbers as to become a majority. There was a strong case for this before the war. There is an irresistible case now . . . The Arabs must not claim to exclude the Jews from this small area of Palestine . . . We should re-examine the possiblity of extending the present Palestinian boundaries . . . We should seek to win the full sympathy and support of the American and Russian governments for the execution of this Palestine policy.[13]

Churchill, long sympathetic to Zionism, had privately indicated that the Yishuv would not be disappointed with a postwar settlement and that a good partition was under discussion. No matter who decided the future of the Mandate, either Labour or Conservative, there was increased sympathy in London. In September 1944, the war cabinet at last authorized a Jewish Brigade. All this might be lost if the separatists continued their murder campaign. Yet they seemed determined to continue.

On Thursday, October 5, the Irgun broke in the roof door of the office of Light Industry, a textile warehouse, on Nachlat Benjamin Street opposite Rothschild Boulevard in Tel Aviv. The next day, entering from the roof, the assault squad overpowered the few employees and unlocked the front door. A truck drove up, the driver leaped out and helped the other men load it with bolts of cloth. Then he climbed in and drove off. Another truck drove up, more bolts of cloth were carried out and tossed in. A small crowd began to gather, curious at the hasty loading of very odd trucks by strange men. Someone rang the police. The trucks continued to come and go. The crowd grew larger as the realization came that the Irgun was at work. They continued to loot the warehouse, hour after hour, until the Sabbath came at sundown, when piety limited the take, estimated at £100,000. Some of the textiles were distributed to needy families, some sold for weapons money, and some were recovered by the British, who were chagrined at the police's failure to take the telephone calls seriously. The Jewish Agency, unable to persuade Begin to stop, watched bitterly as the revolt gained momentum and sympathy. Stronger measures would be necessary.

The British were unsatisfied with the Agency's efforts. On October 10, came an official announcement calling for active collaboration with the forces of law and order. John Shaw, the chief secretary, recognized that in the long run only a radical political initiative would produce stability, but such a step should not be taken with undue haste. In the meantime the best strategy would be to isolate the Irgun within the Yishuv with the collaboration of the Jewish Agency. In the last two months alone, 118 Irgun suspects had been detained without noticable effect. Neither arrests nor high rewards—£8,000 on Begin—worked. By mid-October fifteen members of the Palestine police had been killed; and the Mandate authority indicated clearly that the Jewish Agency's continued inactivity would soon be viewed as disloyalty, guilt by association. Pressure grew within the Agency and Vaad Leumi to take effective steps to break the Irgun until the only point still at issue was the matter of overt cooperation with the British. This would be a risky tactic because Irgun intelligence could then denounce the Haganah leadership in reprisal. Early in October an informal decision was taken to coerce the Irgun by drying up their funds, protecting the contributors and seizing and holding as many Irgun militants as feasible. On October 20, the Haganah opened a training course for 170 men to wage the anti-Irgun campaign, called the Season. Golomb, who had returned from a trip to London, called for an end to terrorism and childish games in a press conference.

Then as the Jewish Agency decided on cooperation, at four in the morning of October 21, the British security forces removed 237 detainees from Latrun camp and 14 from Acre prison and deported all 251 to Eritrea. The Jewish Agency, deep in plans for the Season, publicly protested the exile of any Jew from Palestine, even terrorists. But it was too late to turn back. On October 25, the Inner Zionist Council announced that drastic steps would be taken to counter the terrorists. One last attempt was made to come to terms with the Irgun, when Golomb and Sneh met with Begin and Lankin on Allenby Street. In the name of Vaad Leumi, Golomb demainded the cessation of Irgun activities. Begin replied as expected. The only new factor was that Golomb now seemed to believe in the British Labour party, rather than in Churchill, as the best friend to Zionist aspirations. For Begin neither Sneh's Churchillian plum nor Golomb's Labour backing was anything more than the old delusion that "they" were going to give the Zionists "something." Finally, well after midnight, the street-corner conference broke up. Golomb warned Begin, "We shall step in and finish you."[14] The Haganah went back to preparing for the Season and the Irgun to preparing operations.

In undertaking the Season, the Haganah faced a difficult technical problem. The closing down of Irgun funds by protecting the contributors was really conventional police work, quite within the capacity of the organization. But to remove specific Irgun people from circulation without turning them over to the British or killing them was far more difficult. Obviously, informing on the Irgun would shift the practical work of arrest and detention to the British, already equipped with the physical necessities for coercion; however, the Agency had not yet felt this step necessary and feared that Irgun would also undertake a campaign of betrayal that could cripple the Haganah. The alternative was for the Haganah to seize and hold Irgun people in safe houses, a campaign of covert internment. It was not apparent at first that such a maneuver might prove only a stopgap. If the spirit and resilience of the Irgun could be broken swiftly, the tactics of internment might work; but if the Irgun persisted, the Haganah would shortly run out of safe houses. Then to back down by freeing the internees would be a disastrous loss of prestige, while to turn to executions would shake the whole moral position of the legitimate institutions. Unless the Irgun cracked quickly, the Jewish Agency would soon have to recognize that eliminating the Irgun meant a choice between the gun and collaboration with the British. The Jewish Agency, preferring half measures, did not want to face this choice.

Meanwhile, the Irgun was also having difficulties on the other flank with LEHI. Besides the old grieveances, both sides felt sharp differences in attitude, habits of mind, and particularly tactical considerations. Still, because of their heritage, their mutual enemy, their basic agreement on strategy, and their joint detractors within the legitimate institutions, a merger was an obvious course for both. Efforts during the summer of 1944 to affect a merger failed. The obvious advantage of an alliance was another matter, if only in order not to hamper each other's operations. This had happened during the Irgun attack on the Jaffa police station, just after LEHI assassination squads were in action. By the end of October, a working agreement was forged, an agreement that almost immediately revealed its shortcomings in practice.

On the evening of November 6, Begin and Meridor were sitting in the Irgun safe-house headquarters, waiting for Shamir and Yellin-Mor to arrive to work out joint operations. The radio was on, and the Irgun learned of the assassination of Lord Moyne in a news flash. They had no doubt who was responsible. On the following morning Moyne's assassination was universally condemned. The Egyptians feared they would be blamed. The Zionist institutions in Palestine and abroad were horrified at the "revolting crime." Weizmann, who two days before had met with Churchill, called at Downing Street to express his deep moral indignation and horror. The British were outraged at the senselessness of the deed. Few disinterested observers could understand why Jews would want to kill one of the leaders of Britain's war against Hitler. The Jewish Agency was appalled. The Mandate had already suggested that all Jews might be tarred by the terrorist brush, and now this seemed certain. Killing Palestine policemen was one thing, and bad enough, but it was quite another to kill a British minister of state, a personal friend of the prime minister.

Until November 6, the Agency felt that the tide of British official opinion had begun to turn away from the white-paper policy. On November 1, Lord Gort arrived, the successor to MacMichael, and he reportedly had an open mind. After Weizmann's lunch with Churchill on November 4, he came away convinced that the white paper was dead and that at worst the Zionists would get a good partition. Churchill had accepted as practical a proposal that 1,500,000 Jews should immigrate to Palestine over ten years and 100,000 to 150,000 orphans immediately. The prime minister had stated that if the Zionists could get all of Palestine, fine, and if not, partition was preferable to a continuation of the white-paper policy. The support in the British war cabinet for a good partition seemed to have jelled. If Labour should be in power at the moment of decision, Zionist propects would then only be more attractive. Then came the fateful blunder of Moyne's assassination. His death might indeed change history, but in a way hurtful to Zionism. Of this the Agency was certain. On November 17, Churchill, his voice choked with emotion, spoke before Commons.

> If our dreams for Zionism should be dissolved in the smoke of the revolvers of assassins and if our efforts for its future should provoke a new wave of banditry worthy of the Nazi Germans, many persons like myself will have to reconsider the position that we have maintained so firmly for such a long time. In order to hold out a possibility for future peace, these harmful activities must cease and those responsible for them must be radically destroyed and eliminated.[15]

On the elimination of the dissidents, the Agency and Churchill were of one mind. On November 20, the sixth Histadrut convention approved Ben-Gurion's four-part motion: expulsion of members of the separatist groups from their employment; denial to them of shelter and refuge; no submission to threats and extortion, and, most important, cooperation with the British to wipe out the terror. On November 22, Pinchas Lubianiker stressed their determination to eliminate the dissidents. "By fair means or foul, we must fight this thing as one united body. The fight against terrorism is primarily and fundamentally *our* fight. The business of liquidating the terror our *business*."[16] In Jerusalem Moshe Shertok noted that "Anyone who does not do everything in his power to uproot the evil abets it."[17] A few were not so adamant. Rabbi Fishman and Yitzchak Greenbaum opposed persecuting the underground and resigned. Others opposed collaborating with the British; but Ben-Gurion and the majority prevailed. After Weizmann's arrival in the Mandate on November 14, and Churchill's speech three days later, the majority felt that a policy of liquidation in cooperation with the British was essential.

Within the Haganah there were many who found such a policy congenial. Most of the significant Haganah members were men of the left, political opponents of the Revisionists, suspicious of the Irgun, and loyal to the established institutions. Many came from the rural kibbutzim, and saw the Irgun as a motley mix of recent immigrants, Yemenis, and misguided city youngsters led by dangerous and disloyal men. For them the Haganah was an inchoate army, the foundation not just of settlement defense but ultimately of a real army. Mostly, however, it was really an underground militia, with almost every unit tied to a settlement or a Jewish quarter, with a shifting strength of several thousand people and insufficient arms. For a decade various efforts had been made to construct an elite, striking mobile unit—the Palmach, but the Haganah's capacity to concentrate men in one place was not much greater than the Irgun's. This was mainly because the Irgun did not have to worry about settlement defense, for there were very few Irgun-Revisionist settlements. Still, the Haganah was a substantially large force, slightly better armed, and the covert arm of the recognized institutions. Unlike the Irgun's hankering for military form and protocol, the Haganah, and later the Palmach, scorned unnecessary regulations, formal guidelines, and the patina of an army in favor of equalitarian comradeship, a devout belief in spontaneity, daring, and individualism. Moshe Dayan was a typical product of this school—sabra, kibbutznik, son of a founder, future farmer, man of the left, daring, bold, and inventive—he was very different from the slight, bearded Israel Sassover, living in a Tel Aviv side street. It was not just background and style that caused friction between the Haganah and the Irgun, but the deeply held political beliefs of the Zionist left. Over the years Jabotinsky and all his creatures had become an abomination, in part because the answers of the orthodox left had been proven wrong. Now the Irgun was acting against the agreed consensus, the party line, the desires of the recognized institutions, and the interests of the Yishuv. The time had come to smash their pretentions.

Once the liquidation policy was accepted, the Haganah faced only one tactical decision: whether to operate against both LEHI and the Irgun. In the earlier operations of the Season, LEHI was ignored in order not to create a united separatist front; but logic insisted that the murderers of Moyne be included.The Season opened on LEHI. During this period regular discussions between Golomb and Yellin-Mor had found little common ground. After a LEHI man was kidnapped in Jerusalem and the LEHI archives on Arlosoroff Street in Haifa were seized, Yellin-Mor met once more with Golomb. What went on is uncertain. Yellin-Mor insists he made it clear to Golomb that, without the resources to begin counterkidnapping or the desire to cooperate with the British, LEHI could only retaliate against the leadership of the Haganah. Eldad and others insist that Yellin-Mor said LEHI would abandon operations in return for LEHI being excluded from the Season. What is certain is that the Haganah did not extend the Season to LEHI, and that there were no LEHI operations for six months. In any case the Season was open only on the Irgun.

The Season never really began on a single day, for almost as soon as the Irgun announced the revolt, on February 1, Haganah intelligence began to operate. On February 21, they kidnapped Yanovsky, in hopes of squeezing out information. Dressed as police, they snatched him in the street, shouting "Stop thief!" when he tried to break away. He was roughly treated during the interrogation, but the Haganah still got little of use. Increasingly during 1944, as the revolt gained momentum and the opposition of the Jewish Agency hardened, the Haganah and Irgun intelligence agents pitted wits. By October this silent war slipped over into something more serious. The Haganah knew that they had been setting up Irgunists either for arrest or kidnapping and suspected the same was true with their opposite numbers. When word of Haganah brutality began to leak out—beatings, cigarette burns, broken fingers—there was real fear that the Irgun would retaliate in kind. At this stage, much was still unknown to the Haganah. But those running the Season knew that next to Begin the key man on the other side was the intelligence officer, Yaacov Fershtei, whom they also thought was the number-two man in the Irgun.

Fershtei, soon to be better known as Ely Tavin, was well aware of the dangers he ran by operating during the early months of the Season. As the Irgun headquarters contact man with Sneh and the Haganah, he was well known to the hunters; and they were not hunting him simply to turn him over to the British, but to discover how the Irgun operated. In December 1944, they nearly got him. Tavin was running a zipper factory, a most innocent and non-revolutionary occupation. He traveled about the mandate, a slim young man with bushy hair and a winning smile, selling his zippers, buying raw materials, making friends, and performing all the simple rituals of a small businessman in troubled times. From time to time, he slipped away from his allotted rounds on Irgun business, delivering a message, carrying a small package, appearing late at night at a drop-spot. One of the contact points was a diamond factory near the main post office in Tel Aviv. Tavin had a key to the front door and no fear of the concierge, who happened to be an Irgun member. He had never had trouble there; but on this particular December night, as he talked to his contact, he heard someone move outside the front door. Men on the run, wanted, living on nerves, hope, and too much coffee gradually develop a feeling for their terrain, for the odd sound, the quick movement on the street behind them, a sudden stillness. Suddenly, without warning or visible clue, they will switch their routine, miss an appointment, turn into a strange shop Tavin had become very wary. At any moment, any time, climbing the steps of an apartment house, turning a corner, there could be an old friend turned informer. Tavin had no doubt that such a moment had come, for as he peered out into the darkenss he saw four dim figures loitering outside in the nearly deserted street. At least he knew they were there, and what he was going to do. They simply waited. Tavin had gone in; Tavin would come out.

Tavin and his contact both came out, slammed the front door, turned away from the four, and strode briskly toward the corner. As the four rushed to catch up with them, a bus drew up to the corner. Tavin and his contact swung aboard. At the very last second so did the four Haganah men. All fares were paid. The bus grumbled off toward Yarkon Street

along the seafront. Amid the old women out late with string shopping
bags, bored commuters, and tardy girls on the way to meet their boy
friends sat six very uneasy young men, living in a small world all their
own. There is seldom high or visible drama in the underground; men
speak on a street corner, read instructions from little fans of paper taken
from their cuff, and pass on. Or they sit on buses like anyone else. The
bus turned on Yarkon. A few passengers climbed off; a few climbed on.
The six remained seated. At the corner of Frishman Street, the hunted got
off, followed by the four Haganah men. Waiting on the other corner, the
area well lit and too crowded, they could do no more than watch. Tavin
sent his contact into a nightclub further down Frishman to Ben-Yehuda
Street. He swung onto the No. 4 bus. The two followed. He stayed on the
bus, a calm young man sitting nearly opposite two other slightly more
nervous young men. At the crowded bus station he bought a ticket for Rehovot. The two closed up behind to hear where he was going. They
bought two tickets to Rehovot and turned to find Tavin dashing to catch
the No. 5 bus back into central Tel Aviv. The ruse had been very cunning,
but the driver of the bus felt no great sense of urgency, idling the motor
and dawdling until the two last anxious passengers had a chance to climb
aboard. The bus made its way to Dizengoff Street, brightly lit, wall-to-
wall cafés, crowds moving slowly along to see and be seen. Tavin slipped
off the bus, and walked slowly past the tables filled with little old men
drinking tea from glasses and speaking Russian, berry-brown girls in from
the kibbutz, Jews that loked like Arabs, Arabs that were really Jews, pink
British policemen sipping iced beer—the whole strange Levantine mix of
wartime Tel Aviv. Dizengoff was the city's elegant artery. In a country
that was often shabby, where the exotic was mean, where golden buildings sat among slums, where raw concrete and stucco composed new
housing of little taste, Dizengoff was special. And especially hard to
leave, for each of the cross streets darkened within a few hundred feet
and became dangerous. The hunters could not strike on Dizengoff. They
could wait. But waiting in the pools of bright light was too dangerous for
Tavin.

   He stood uncertainly in front of the Esther Cinema. There was no
hope of ducking inside, since a popular film had produced a long line
snaking down the sidewalk. Suddenly a furtive man moved up beside him.
There was an uneasy moment, a queasy feeling, until Tavin realized that
he had been approached by a scalper not half as eager to sell a ticket as
Tavin was to buy. The deal was made; and Tavin shot past the line, gave
up his ticket, and disappeared into the Esther. For ten minutes he huddled
in the men's room. By then the two frantic hunters had rounded up their
own scalper, purchased a ticket, and split up. One went in the darkened
theater. The other waited. Tavin slipped out. The outside hunter moved a

little closer. Standing on the curb, Tavin waited until a special one-pas-
senger taxi passed, hailed it, popped in, and drove off. The hunter was left
frantically waving down full taxis going in the other direction. Tavin's
driver took him down to Allenby Street near the main post office, not far
from the start of the chase. There he switched taxis and drove on back to
the corner of Dizengoff Street. He got out and walked on cautiously to his
safe house, still on the loose and now very much a Haganah target.

He kept on the run for nearly two more months before his luck finally
ran out. On February 27, 1945, at four in the afternoon, he was slipping
toward an Irgun headquarters office in Tel Aviv when an officer of the
auxiliary police stopped him—just a few steps from headquarters at Ben
Yehuda and Jeremiah streets. The policeman informed Tavin, "My officer wants me to take you to the station." A taxi with two men in it pulled
up beside the auxiliary. It was all a little too neat for Tavin. He turned and
ran. This time the hunters were better prepared, and rushed after the fugi-
tive, shouting, "Stop thief!" Eager to cooperate, several pedestrians
closed up in front of Tavin. The police arrived and hustled him into the
taxi. As the driver turned the corner, Tavin was blindfolded and
handcuffed. He could not tell where he was taken, only that, as he sat and
waited for the hours to pass, people came in and out, asking questions.
He said nothing. Late in the evening he was informed that he was a traitor
working against Zionism. Tavin was all too aware of Haganah treatment
of other Irgun "traitors." The Haganah people insisted that all was not
lost, even if he could not have a military court (as Tavin insisted the Irgun
would have done), he could be forgiven if he would just repent and confess. The only man the Haganah really wanted was Begin, and despite Tavin's past operations they could thus afford to be generous. The interrogators could hardly have hoped the gambit would work, and it didn't. The
questioning went on and on, leading nowhere. The Haganah people grew
angrier, shouted and demanded. Finally they announced that there was no
more time, no more patience. If Tavin would not confess, he would die.

It was nearly two in the morning. He had been shifted to the watchman's hut in the orange groves of kibbutz Givat Hashlosha near Petah
Tikva, and the Haganah now made it clear that this was as far as he was
going. He was jerked to his feet, his arms handcuffed behind him. The last
thing he saw before the blindfold was a huge old Parabellum in his execu-
tioner's hand. He was shoved and manhandled out of the hut into the
grove. Standing in the cool night under the oranges with the wind on his
face, he had no doubt that the Haganah were serious. A voice told him he
had two minutes—were there any messages for relatives or final words.
Recognizing the accent, he cursed the voice in Russian, and said finally,
"You will have to pay for it." There was a long quiet moment. Then a
rasp, as the Parabellum was cocked. Then nothing. Tavin simply stood

waiting, as the seconds raced away. Still nothing. Then another voice: "You will get another two minutes." At first, Tavin had known he would be shot, but now he was not so sure. He replied that he hoped his friends would revenge his death, even if it were against policy. There was another long pause. The Parabellum was still cocked, the faint wind still blowing. Tavin was still standing under the oranges, as the seconds ticked away. There was a loud click. The hammer had been thumbed down. "I can see you want to think about it until morning." He was hustled back to the watchman's hut. He had been outside in the grove for less than ten minutes. Tavin had attended his own execution and lived to tell the tale. How long he had to live was not sure, but anything was better than standing under the gun, helpless to do more than wait.

Just before dawn on the next day, February 28, two more Haganah people showed up and announced that Tavin would be moved. He was still handcuffed. Stuffed in the back of a car between two guards, he was told that if they were stopped by a British patrol not to speak or they would kill him at once. Given the events of the night before, this had a certain charm. They drove for several hours. They did not meet a patrol. The car turned off the road and stopped. Tavin had no firm idea where he was, but the building was an old grain barn. In a corner there was an army cot, partitioned off from the rest by a piece of cloth. He was chained to the cot. The interrogation began again. He was less than helpful, and the Haganah became increasingly brutal. Questioned constantly by shifts that changed every two hours, he was allowed no sleep. When he refused to answer he was beaten, smashed in the face until he began to spit teeth onto the floor. He still would not talk. He was hung up on the wall, his hands tied behind his back, his arms stretched, so that after twenty-four hours he felt as if he would be ripped apart. He was beaten again. Days passed. He was never allowed to sleep. Most of the time he was kept chained to the bed, never permitted to use a toilet, lying in filth, mocked and beaten. His only weapon was the hunger strike—obviously the Haganah wanted information, not his death and gunbattles in the street. If he died, there would be more problems than if he lived. The Haganah relented after seventy-five hours, and brought in a physician to inspect the food he refused to eat. Lying in his own filth, covered with bruises, speaking through broken teeth, Tavin asked the doctor what sort of oath he had taken that he could tolerate conditions no different from those in a Nazi death camp. There was no answer—there could be none. There was no change in Tavin's condition, except that the beatings stopped. He remained chained in the dark. The Haganah explained that they were afraid to let him out to continue against them, afraid to kill him for fear of Irgun vengeance, afraid to turn him over to the British, since he might inform on them.

The endless dark hours crept by, one at a time. The first impossible week stretched into the second. The barn mice became tame and romped over his body. He began at the beginning and repeated slowly all that he had ever learned from A to Z, beginning with the alphabet and, as the third week crept into the fourth, culminating in Kant. His captors could not understand how he remained sane, and ultimately, after four weeks, they relented. They allowed him at last to wash, to have matzo for Passover, and to wear pajamas. But there were still the chains and darkness. There were still the mice. The Haganah exterminted the area with gas, but even then made him cover his face, kept him in the dark. From March 1 until May 7, there was never any light. Then he demanded the status of a prisoner of war. He had grown frail. The guards who stood duty around the clock ten meters away reported they were afraid he would die. His prisoner-of-war hunger strike lasted fifty-four hours. Since he refused to take water as well and had been very weak, huddled in chains dark day after dark day, the captors had to make up their minds quickly. Tavin became a prisoner of war, and was given light—a bulb burning twenty-four hours a day. There were no more mice, and he even received newspapers, with the political sections cut out. The papers were addressed to Ein-Haroe kibbutz, so after three months Tavin knew where he was: chained under a naked light bulb in the corner of an old barn in Ein-Haroe, waiting. June passed, then July. Finally, at the end of August, just two days before Rosh Hashanah, he was taken out of his tiny partitioned world of cot, orange box, and bare light bulb and put, still chained, into a Palmach ambulance. Begin had arranged his release. As a parting if unofficial touch, one of his guards beat him up once again—one for the road. It had been a long, squalid episode, begun in fear and ending in sadism. And it was only one story.

During the Season more than a thousand Irgun suspects were handed over to the British by the Haganah, including twenty-five ex-Irgun people serving in the British army in Egypt. Many were simply well-known Revisionists, politicals, out of touch with the underground. Others were retired or inactive. Some, however, were key people. One Friday, at the end of December, Lankin was out walking in the pouring rain, his first above-ground appearance in weeks. Two men suddenly began following him. He walked faster; so did they, catching up just as he crossed King George Street. When he reached Ben Yehuda, a taxi appeared with two more men. He was bundled inside and driven directly to Machaneh Yehuda police station, where he was met by CID Inspectors Curtis and Hamilton, along with a Haganah officer. The high command decided to send Shlomo Levy to take Lankin's place as commander in Jerusalem. He left Tel Aviv immediately. His car was stopped on the way by a police patrol, accompanied by two informers. A police raid directed by a Haganah man lifted Meridor in his house in Raanana on February 12. New men were brought onto the high command—Eitan Livni, Bezalel Amizur, Haim Landau, David Grossbard—there were never very many,[18] but the Irgun could barely continue operations. On February 1, there was the £38,000 daylight diamond theft, but after that, almost nothing. All the news for months was bad and brutal. The Haganah was not simply turning people in to the British but interrogationg them first: fingers broken in door hinges, regular beatings, burns, threats, more fake executions. The Season was cruel, often vicious, and clearly effective. As Golomb noted, "The organized Yishuv has brought terrorist activity to a standstill."[19] What Golomb and the others did not understand until too late was why the Irgun did not retaliate.

For the Irgun the two obvious options were violent resistance or surrender. In the high command there was no sympathy for surrender and near unanimity for hitting back. The Irgunist had warned the Haganah early on that their reaction to betrayal would be firm. The impact of accelerated kidnappings, physical beatings, expulsions from schools and jobs, the denunciations and deliveries to the British, created an atmosphere of absolute crisis within the Irgun and within the high command. Unless action were taken, the Irgun would be destroyed. The British had lists of hundreds of names, with more added daily from Haganah sources. They made daily roundups, arresting long-secret members, breaking into arms dumps and safe houses, even being led to a new V-3 rocket bomb by informers. The obvious step, the desirable step, the natural step, was to retaliate. The step was not taken because Begin imposed his will first on the high command, then on the Irgun.

> Not logic, but instinct said imperatively: "No; not civil war. Not that at any price." And who knows: perhaps instinct is the very heart of logic.[20]

Pragmatic logic was replaced with emotional logic, and, as Begin noted, the latter turned out to be more profitable in the long run. A policy of retaliation would have inevitably led to gun battles in the street, reminiscent of the LEHI shootouts of 1942, and could ultimately have had only one victor, the British. Given time and will, the Haganah would surely have won any extended underground war and broken the Irgun, but at the cost of undermining the legitimate authorities and the future capacity of the Haganah. Such a Haganah pogrom, however justifiable pragmatically as an authorized campaign, would only have appalled the Yishuv, already weighted down by the impact of the Holocaust. To rid Palestine of the separatists at the cost of a huge pool of Jewish blood would have given everyone pause. Certainly the prospect appalled Begin. He insisted that this time the Jews would not shed each other's blood as they had so often done in biblical days, that even at the cost of the Irgun and the revolt there would be no civil war. In any case, with luck, with persistence in the face of provocation, the time would surely come when the leaders of the Haganah would recognize that the Season was against their own interest, that it could only be distasteful to the Yishuv, placing them in the position of collaborators in an occupied country. In the meantime, the Irgun would burrow down, eschew revenge, and wait.

So the Season continued, month after month. The arrests and detentions continued. Sources of funds, voluntary and involuntary, dried up. Communications became difficult, training and operations impossible. Yet the Irgun remained in being. Despite the attrition of arrests, the basic strength remained the same; moreover, the new replacements were often unknown to the Haganah, the new commanders too young to have a reputation that would endanger them. Gradually, not unexpectedly, the enthusiasm of Haganah-Palmach began to erode. Many were shamed at the reports of torture, others at the necessity of informing. There were fewer volunteers for the Season, and growing defections. It began to appear as a collaborationist campaign. The rank and file began to express serious reservations. Even some of the previously righteous politicians of the left expressed doubts. Important as well was the shift in British relations with the Jewish Agency—the wonders that had seemed so certain were now no closer. In March 1945, a meeting of Season leaders held in Yagur heard Sneh and Golomb announce that activities against the separatists would cease. Until June, however, Haganah-Palmach intelligence pursued the Season and cooperated with the British, but with waning enthusiasm and diminishing returns. In May the Irgun was able to resume operations. In June the Season ended, except for Tavin chained under his naked light bulb. The Haganah were still afraid to admit that they had kidnapped him.

The Season was a disaster. In the spring of 1945, the Jewish Agency's alternatives of the previous November were still present: cooperate, tolerate, or destroy. Failure to destroy the Irgun in cooperation with the British was surely the worst possible policy. Six months of pressure had steeled the Irgun, improved its capacity to act under coercion, and, most important, had adorned the leadership with a mantle of national responsiblity. The Irgun, accepting the arrows of indignation, had prevented a civil war. The Irgun thus attracted the sympathy and understanding of many who abhorred their politics, suspected their motives, and even doubted their sanity. Their politics and their revolt might still be unpalatable, but their character was for many now above question, and their primary loyalty to Zionism and the Yishuv rather than to Revisionist interests undeniable. The Haganah's Season had maimed without killing, created sympthy where none had existed before, endowed the Irgun with a long-denied legitimacy, and when ended, assured Begin that the great divide had been safely if painfully passed: the revolt would have the toleration of the Yishuv. With the toleration, and perhaps soon with positive sympathy, the Irgun could persevere.

On Sunday, May 12, the British discovered a series of clockwork mortars buried about the mandate—in the King David Hotel, the government printing office, Bet-Dagun police station. Most had been deactivated by a heavy rain. On Tuesday, May 14, there was widespread sabotage. Over four hundred telegraph poles were destroyed by automatic explosive devices. An effort to place twenty charges in oil pipelines was foiled by the Haganah, still pursuing the Season. The Petah Tikva-Ras el-Ein road was reported mined. The next week more telegraph poles were exploded. The Season was sputtering to a close, as a mortar attack on the Haifa police station revealed. On May 17, *Davar* was still condemning the separatist terrorists, and would do so until July.

> If anyone again dares bring disgrace and danger upon the Yishuv, the Yishuv will again—and this time more vigorously—resort to all means at its disposal in order to incapacitate them.[21]

Nearly everyone else, especially the British, recognized that this was November rhetoric in May. Things had changed. The revolt was still on and the Season over. On May 8, the European war was over as well. Until the spring of 1945, British reaction to the revolt within the Palestine Mandate had been, both consciously and often unwittingly, most astute. With a little bit of luck, a degree of cunning, and more conscious leadership in London, the British might well have scraped through. By waving the carrot of a good partition and immediate immigration, the British had persuaded the Jewish Agency and Vaad Leumi to wield the Haganah-Palmach stick against the rebels. If the stick had been replaced by the gun, the Haganah would have simultaneously rid the Mandate of the terrorists and contaminated its own purity, not to mention security, by collaboration with the British. With any luck the divisions between the three covert military forces—Hagahah, Irgun, and LEHI—could have led to their mutual destruction and an orgy of recriminations. At the same time, if the cooperation of the Jewish Agency had been rewarded, even with promises, especially with promises, the long dependence on Anglo-centric strategy and the tactics of practical Zionism might have continued to hold attractions for the remaining leaders of the Yishuv. The long-awaited postwar solution could have been withdrawn further and further into the future, as the British held on to the plum for their own advantage. The refusal of the Irgunists to break discipline under provocation, and the end of the policy of collaboration by the Jewish Agency, meant that the desire to press rather than persuade the British was considerably attractive even to moderate Zionists.

To reverse the situation, Britain would have to depend on open coercion, which, unless swiftly successful, might well antagonize all of the Yishuv and simultaneously alienate Britain's prospective Arab clients because it was ineffectual. In May, however, the British authorities were sanguine about containing the Irgun in view of their remarkable success during the Season. They must have assumed, reading *Davar*, that the general distaste for Begin's revolt could still be exploited in practical ways. Then there was the obvious feebleness of the Irgun itself, reduced to blowing up telegraph posts. For the British to come down hard with the boot would be sufficient to maintain order, with or without further promises to the Jewish Agency. Clearly, just as Shaw had noted, ultimate stability depended on a radical political initiative, sensibly undertaken of course. In May 1945, it still seemed that the capacity of London to decide the fate of the Mandate to London's satisfaction, albeit with a *pro forma* bow to Washington, existed. In the meantime the essential point for the British authorities was to maintain law and order in the Mandate. The more astute realized, however, that London had already lost the best means of ending the revolt quietly and with clean hands, when the Season closed. With the end of the war in Europe, Britain had lost not only a Palestine collaborator but also invisibility. Henceforth there would be many eyes watching imperialist Britain through the glass walls of the Mandate.

Then, unexpectedly, the entire Middle Eastern kaleidoscope shifted. As the Jewish Agency waited with increasing impatience for a British initiative and the Irgun reorganized for operations, the London center was transformed. Flaunting the banner of victory, Churchill in May called for a general election, certain that his leadership would be rewarded at the polls. The result was quite the reverse. On July 27, the new Labour government, with Clement Attlee as prime minister and Ernest Bevin as foreign secretary, formally took office. As recently as April 25, the Labour executive committee had proclaimed the pro-Zionist intentions contained in a series of resolutions accepted since 1940. In May the Labour campaign conference reaffirmed the position. Whatever Churchill might or might not have done, the Labour party was on record. On May 22, the Jewish Agency sent a series of requests to the British government: (1) an immediate decision to establish a Jewish state, (2) the authority to be granted to the Jewish Agency to bring in Jews, (3) an international loan to transfer one million emigrants, (4) reparations from Germany, and (5) international cooperation to facilitate the emigration. Now the Labour party would act on these, unhampered by any imperialist, pro-Arab consideration. The full arsenal of Zionist pressure and persuasion was turned on the new Labour government. Zionist optimism ran rampant. Even the Irgun announced that they would hold off a few weeks to permit a satisfactory British initiative.

The newly vindicated Jewish Agency thought this Irgun decision simple sour grapes, a bitter, stubborn refusal to believe that the whole structure of Irgun strategy had been based on error and miscalculation, or to recognize that the collective wisdom of the legitimate authorites had, as always, proven more profound than the miasma of Revisionist-terrorist sand castles. Then a calm settled over Palestine while all eyes, Arab and Zionist, Agency and Irgun, focused on the seat of decision in London.

NOTES

1. David Ben-Gurion, *The Jews in Their Land* (London: 1966), p. 237.

2. *The Sentinel* (Jerusalem), vol. 1, no. 10, 7 April 1939.

3. Menachem Begin, *The Revolt: Story of the Irgun* (New York: Henry Schuman, 1951), pp. 42–43.

4. Ibid., p. 45.

5. Lord Chandos, *Memoirs* (London: Bodley Head, 1962), p. 222.

6. General Sir Harold Maitland Wilson, "Operations in the Middle East," Supplement to *London Gazette*, no. 37786, para. 323.

7. Elazar Pedazur, *The History of the Irgun Zvai Leumi,* vol. 2, (Shilton Betar: Israeli Department of Education, December 1969), p. 38.

8. Begin, p. 84.

9. Sir Harold MacMichael to the Secretary of State for Colonies, July 28, 1944 (fo. 371/40126, 5052).

10. Although before the revolt there had been several informers within the organization—and several shot, left on the roadside tagged "For the informer there is no hope"—after 1944 there were very few, almost always on a low level, except for one exception. H. Reinhold, a promising recruit and a potential leader, seemed trailed by a series of disasters and accidents until, on the evening of an important operation where he would be second in command, the penny dropped. He evaded Irgun vengeance in the Mandate and barely escaped being kidnapped later in Belgium, so his death sentence was never carried out. It was not elaborate internal security that protected the Irgun as much as the combination of the ethos of intimacy and dedication within a small conspiracy and the shadow of the holocaust that made treachery so very unattractive. Then, too, when the Season came, the British needed no informers within the Irgun.

11. Begin, p. 90.

12. War Cabinet, "Security in Palestine," October 7, 1944 (fo. 371/40127, 5063).

13. Jewish Agency, *Documents Relating to the Palestine Problem* (London, 1945), pp. 79–82.

14. Begin, p. 143.

15. Great Britain, *Parliamentary Debates*, Commons, vol. 404, col. 2242.

16. Pedazur, *Irgun* (Shilton Betar: May 1961), p. 3.

17. Ibid., p. 2.

18. During the course of the revolt the members of the high command were:

Menachem Begin (C in C)	David Grossbard (QMG)
Yaacov Meridor	Haim Landau
Arieh Ben-Eliezer	Amihai Paglin (Operations)
Eliahu Lankin (Operations)	Samuel Katz (Political)
Shlomo Levami (C/S)	Yaakov Amrami (Intelligence)
Eitan Livni (Operations)	David Tahori (Secretary)
Bezalel Amizur (Manpower)	Yaacov Ely Tavin (Diaspora)

19. Pedazur, *Irgun,* vol. 2, p. 25.

20. Begin, p. 152.

21. Pedazur, *Irgun, vol. 2, p. 27.*

CHAPTER 2

The United Resistance, 1945-1946

You have already accomplished an historic act, you have proved that it was possible to attack the British.

—Moshe Dayan

After the Labour victory at the polls, the Palestine Mandate slipped into an uneasy period of waiting. Newspaper reports appeared of terrorists arrested or killed, arms dumps discovered, and search operations undertaken. Most were inclined to agree with *Davar*: "The victory of the Labour party . . . is a clear victory for the demands of the Zionists in British public opinion."[1] For the Jewish Agency, it was a particularly rewarding victory; for it effectively destroyed the pretense and position of the Revisionists, who in May, with the end of the Season, had renewed sabotage operations and propaganda attacks on the authorized institutions.

> What is the reward that you, and our ailing nation, have received for your external restraint in relation to the enemy and your internal war against us? What more must happen to make you understand there is no way except direct war? Until when? How long?

> But this generation will not fail us. It will not disappoint us. We shall surely fight and prosper, for we have been forged into steel, each and every one of us carries on his lips and in his heart the song of revolt.[2]

Yet even the fighters of the Irgun announced a period of grace to give the Labour party time to act. The Agency needed no such deadlines, for sympathetic Labour initiatives were assured. The Labour party platform had already stated that more would be offered than had been asked. When in June the Irgun dispatched a request to 250 Jewish leaders in the Mandate asking for the establishment of a provisional government and a supreme national council, few felt it more than a gambit to bring the Revisionists under the negotiating umbrella before it was too late. No one in power had any intention of roiling the waters at such a promising stage with such foolish demands. Labour would act in good time. The weeks of anticipation passed. On July 26, Churchill departed, and the next day Attlee was in power. Soon Labour would act.

Instead of a Zionist decision from London, however, there were only disquieting rumors and vague postponements. The cabinet faced a massive array of problems; and the future of Palestine had a relatively low priority, however urgent matters seemed to the Jewish Agency. The real, crucial interest of most of the party and much of the cabinet, once the war in Asia was over, was the transformation of British society. Imperial interests had long been covered by well-meant and high-sounding resolutions, usually negative. Labour, anti-imperial by program and inclination, had seldom given long enough thought to the use of British power abroad or the advantages ensuing from such power. The party, isolationist and anti-militarist, welcomed the anti-fascist crusade in alliance with Soviet Russia and anti-imperialist America but did not foresee a postwar world shaped by narrow national interests or even British strategic interests. Thus the implications of a Zionist solution along the lines of the election platform had escaped most Labourites. The specialists in Whitehall pointed out to the new men that an outright Zionist solution imposed by Britain would surely alienate the Arab Middle East. British hegemony there would be threatened by disorder, subversion, and perhaps irregular war. More to the point, British economic interests would suffer. Thus, apart from the damage to British strategic interest and the Western alliance, such a move would erode the pay packets of the British worker and reduce the flow of capital needed to transform British society. Consequently, the complete alienation of the Arabs could not be contemplated without danger to policies and programs even more dear to Labour hearts than the triumph of Zionism.

In the bustle of constant crisis, there was not even time in London for a Labour reappraisal. The war in Asia was drawing to a close. There was the atomic bomb, the Big Three summit in Potsdam, all the awesome responsibilities of reordering the world after war. There were the endless hurdles facing the socialization of Britain. There was the unsteady economy, and the prospect of millions of returning veterans. Foreign Minister Bevin, beset by a multitude of decisions demanding instant resolution, seldom capable of quiet contemplation or extensive consultation with his colleagues, had to put together a Labour Palestine program that first and foremost protected British interests. He now saw many long-criticized imperial interests as vital to the future of the British worker, and hence to the new society his cabinet colleagues intended to fashion. The nature of Bevin's policy in substance, if not in detail, became increasingly clear to the Zionist advocates in London as the days passed. Instead of intimate consultation, they found closed doors. Instead of firm promises or even vague promises, they received only uncertain hints of some uncertain future policy. On August 25, the Colonial Office informed Weizmann that the immigrant quota of 1,500 would not be increased. Weizmann's Anglo-centric policy was devastated. In Palestine the hopes had been so high that this disappointment, which most accepted as a foretaste of worse, embittered all but the most unswerving Anglophiles.

The Jewish Agency had to reconsider future prospects. Bevin seemed immune to persuasion. Increasingly, the militants within the Haganah urged a policy of pressure, a demonstration to Bevin and the British that they could not continue to ignore Zionist demands. More distressing, there began to be leakage from the Haganah. *Herut* noted that twenty-five Palmach men had resigned to come over to the Irgun. August saw the intensification of Begin's revolt and the renewed plea by leftist newspapers to purge the dissidents. Purges and a renewed Season simply were not in the cards, rather the reverse. A truce with the Irgun was arranged, and Agency spokesmen suggested an amalgamation with the Haganah and a campaign to pressure the British into concessions. Such an agreement for the Jewish Agency would, at one stroke, remove a potential political rival, absorb a dissident military force, and end any further independent underground operations. The Irgun was not necessarily adverse to the closest possible cooperation with the Agency. Begin had already offered in 1944 to operate under Ben-Gurion. Grave doubts remained, however, about the timidity of Ben-Gurion's colleagues. Once absorbed and dispersed, the Irgun would be in no position to renew the revolt if the Jewish Agency and the Haganah lost their nerve or revised their strategy. There would in fact be no Irgun. The Irgun suggested instead a single strategic command of a united resistance that would in effect give the Agency a veto through the Haganah representative over all operations except arms raids. LEHI, somewhat more sympathetic to amalgamation, also accepted the idea of a united command. The result was Tenuat Hameri, the united resistance movement.

The movement was not, after all, very united. The partners were of unequal size, pursued differing strategies under diverse assumptions, and possessed varying capacities. At the top was a command composed of Sadeh for the Haganah, Yaakov Banai for LEHI, and first Livni and then the new operations officer, Amihai (Giddy) Paglin, for the Irgun. Below this small committee each organization remained in being, their operations usually coordinated but again for different purposes. Although the Haganah was largely satisfied with the new arrangements (the only concession Begin asked was the release of Tavin), the politicians were still reluctant to sign an alliance with Begin or authorize armed force. The Jewish Agency and many in the Haganah did not really contemplate a military campaign at all, preferring a limited doctrine of pressure. Sneh, who still saw Britain not as an enemy but rather as a bad partner, wanted to cause one serious incident,

> as a warning and an indication of much more serious incidents that would threaten the safety of all British interests in the country if the Government did not grant the Zionist requests.[3]

The Agency and Sneh, and especially the left, who still faced the end of havlaga with reluctance, also wanted any incident to be ideologically appropriate, related directly to the major grievance, the closed gates, and not integrated into any mad full-scale attack on British personnel and institutions. This, of course, was exactly what Irgun-LEHI did want: an expanded and escalated revolt incorporating the resources of the Haganah and recognized institutions. The idea of tying underground operations solely to the immigration problem seemed foolish and probably unworkable. The concept of incidents followed by pauses was viewed as little more than an elaboration of the old, familiar petition mentality, a misreading of British intentions and priorities. Still, Tenuat Hameri offered something for everyone. Irgun-LEHI would have the stamp of legitimacy: the revolt would be expanded; the Haganah could placate its eager militants and explore the limits of Sneh's incident strategy. Yet the Jewish Agency continued to delay—Zionist changes of mind are not made in a day nor without appropriate ideological editing.

Until the summer of 1945 the Revisionists, especially Jabotinsky and Begin, had been figures of scorn, mocked as fascist fanatics, militaristic maximalists, without a grasp of what was possible. Their analysis of reality was a cruel joke, their pretensions and plans ludicrous. The authorized institutions—Vaad Leumi, the Jewish Agency, and the rest—were thought responsible, sane, and respected. They possessed the appropriate vision, had fashioned the proper program, weighed the alternatives, chosen the future course. Then in August it became abundantly clear that something had gone wrong: the founding fathers had somehow erred. It was just as Begin had insisted: the British intended to cede nothing; just as Begin had predicted: the Yishuv had the capacity to lever the British out; just as the Irgun had always proclaimed: the state was not going to be created by founding kibbutzim, but by force. It is man's nature to see the mote in another's eye readily, in his own less readily. Few men had worked so hard, dreamed so well, created so much from so little, come so close to the vision as the generation of Zionists represented by Ben-Gurion and Weizmann. It was never their nature to question their own assumptions. They looked into the recent past and saw not Jabotinsky's prophecies but the fruitless counter-terror of the Irgun, not Begin's analysis of British capacity and intention but their own militant stand during the Biltmore Conference. They glided over the fact that a Jewish commonwealth is not a state, that they had once believed Britain would give them all, that the future of the Yishuv lay in the hands of others. They began to readjust history, to edit the Zionist vision, to shuffle the real world just a bit so the past would be the proper prologue. In all conviction and without great difficulty, they swiftly came to believe that such assumptions had always been accepted, but had been merely cloaked for tactical reasons. In effect, they stole the Revisionists' analytical clothes, then claimed that they, the righteous, had always been so garbed. Such a metamorphosis is not easily or swiftly made, was not in fact completed and frozen into the orthodox Zionist myth until much later. In September, however, the editing had begun, and as evidence the Haganah had treated with the Irgun.

While during September 1945 there was a rising tension in the Mandate, neither the Irgun nor the Haganah was prepared to launch major operations. The Haganah was still tethered by political caution and the Irgun by the ravages of the Season. Still the propaganda war continued, with a steady stream of pamphlets and wall newspapers. The Irgun had devised a pamphlet bomb that, deposited in the street, ticked away until detonation, then scattered news sheets over a wide and smoky area—a means of delivery difficult to ignore. On September 16, three such detonations in Jerusalem—one in the door of the Mea Shearim police station—injured nine potential readers. Other delivery systems had less serious side effects: a special favorite consisted of a teeter-totter placed on a roof, pamphlets on one end and a leaky bucket on the other, so that once enough water had dribbled away the pamphlets showered the street. The British sensed the darkening atmosphere, and kept up their searches and arrests: three terrorist suspects arrested, sixteen terrorist suspects detained at Latrun, twenty youths on arms charges at Haifa. The trials, inevitably producing guilty verdicts, were not always complete successes. On September 26, Izhak Ganzweich, who had fought in the Warsaw Ghetto and escaped to fight in Palestine, made a two-hour statement to the discomfort of the authorities. The authorities were, in addition, so uneasy at the reaction of the Jewish Agency, their recent ally and collaborator, that British reinforcements were dispatched to the Mandate. On September 28, the first units of the Sixth Airborne Division, diverted from the Eighth Army, began to arrive. On the next day a British constable was shot during a post office robbery attempt—the Troubles were under way again.

With the war over in Asia, just as Begin had predicted, Palestine became a glass house. Correspondents, attracted by the action, began to arrive. They were impressed by the security precautions and even more with the capacity of the underground. Richard Wyndham, the Middle East correspondent of the *News of the World*, reported that the Haganah had a strength of sixty- to eighty-thousand men and even armored cars, while the Irgun had five thousand well-armed men and the Stern Gang somewhat fewer. Two weeks later John Fisher of the *Daily Mail* was less impressionable, estimating Haganah strength at fifty thousand and the Irgun at fifteen hundred. He revealed that the Irgun was commanded by a thirty-eight-year-old humpbacked and hawk-nosed former law student at Warsaw University, who had been released from his translator's position in the mayor's office in Jerusalem for a year's leave of absence to do welfare work among Polish Jews in the Mandate, and who had instead gone underground. This was about the extent of British intelligence as well. The common wisdom was that the terrorists were evil, wicked men without restraint or morals, involved in wanton murder, extortion, and subversion. There was no support for them among the Yishuv, who were intimidated by their protection rackets, threats, and brutality. They were fanatics without a vestige of legitimacy. Somehow, they were also very effective, since the British could never grasp that their security forces faced only a small group of ill-armed above-ground rebels. Even though the Haganah was relatively large, most members were tied to settlement or neighborhood defense, and there was a severe shortage of arms. The mobile striking force, the Palmach, by the summer of 1945 consisted of only nineteen-hundred members, without heavy arms. In the autumn the total of potential underground fighters was something over three thousand. Concentrated in the habitable portion of the Mandate, protected by the Yishuv, and poorly armed, these would prove more than sufficient to create chaos.

The Haganah began to lose patience with the politicians who dithered on, fearful of chaos, of the British reaction, of the ideological dangers. On October 9, Kol Israel, the illegal Haganah radio station, began broadcasting. On October 10, the Haganah raided a clearance camp for immigrants at Athlit, south of Haifa, and released 208 Jews. This was an operation the hesitant could well accept, for the closed gates that kept the remnants of European Jewry trapped in displaced-persons' camps alienated everyone. On October 11, Kol Israel called for an active resistance movement to assist the immigration of Jews into Palestine. These were simply harbingers of Sneh's serious incident, which was planned for the night of October 31/November 1. Although the Tenuat Hameri agreement had still not been signed by the politicians, the Haganah agreed to coordinate operations for that night with an Irgun attack on the Lydda railway station and a LEHI attack on the Haifa oil refinery. The Haganah would concentrate on the Palestine railway and the Palmach on the coast guard. The coordination, extent, and effect of the joint operation destroyed the last shreds of British complacency.

The Palmach sunk two small police naval craft in Haifa and one in

Jaffa—symbols of the closed gates. The Haganah detonated over five hundred explosive charges all over the Mandate, producing 242 breaks in the railway lines. A bomb in Jerusalem damaged the stationmaster's office. The telephone installation at kilometer 61 on the Jerusalem-Lydda line was damaged. A petrol wagon was bombed in the Tel Aviv railway freight yard. The most serious single incident was the Irgun attack on the Lydda station. One locomotive was destroyed and six others damaged. The LEHI attempt against the Consolidated Refinery installation in Haifa aborted. For months, even before the formation of Tenuat Hameri, LEHI had planned to destroy the tank farm. LEHI people were hired as workers, nitroglycerin smuggled into the plant bit by bit and hidden. The night of the attack a small LEHI team broke into the installation. Moishele carried a suitcase filled with wired clocks and primed detonators, to be placed next to the smuggled nitroglycerin beside the tanks. As Moishele moved across the yard followed by Yehudai, there was a sudden flash and a huge roar. Moishele practically disappeared as the detonators went off spontaneously. Yehudai was badly injured. "My eye bled profusely. . . . It came out of the socket, and I took it in my hand with the blood and dirt and threw it away."[4] The police found Moishele's shattered body in the ruins. It was the last bloody act of a night of violence. The scope and intensity of the incident appalled the Palestinian authorities and outraged the government in London.

Speaking before the Commons, Colonial Secretary George Hall warned the underground of the dangers they ran in

> this wanton resort to force. Unless it is stopped and suppressed, the progress in relation to Palestine will be impossible, and the further steps we had in mind in our endeavour to settle this difficult problem will be brought to nought.[5]

Hall and London were quite out of touch with Palestine reality. They seemed to feel that the delay in the announcement of a future British policy in Palestine was the issue at point. As Attlee insisted on November 5, there was "No excuse for violence."[6] It would not pay. The next day more airborne units moved into Haifa. On November 8, Lieutenant General Sir Alan Cunningham arrived to replace the moderate Field Marshal Viscount Gort. There was every evidence that Britain had opted for the stick rather than the carrot. On November 13, Bevin presented his Palestine policy to the Commons. There were no plums, no promises. The monthly quotas would be continued, and Britain would consult with the Arabs concerning them. There would be consultation with everyone concerned about temporary arrangements before the final solution, which in the fullness of time would be presented to the United Nations, heir to the League of Nations Mandate system. In the meantime he could announce that the United States had accepted an invitation to join in an Anglo-American investigating committee. The immediate Jewish state, unlimited immigration, territorial expansion had all disappeared; what remained was only an extension of the white-paper policy, ill-disguised by the proposed Anglo-American committee. The gates would stay closed. The Arabs, newly united in the British-inspired Arab League, would be wooed, not the Jews. The Zionists had been led down the garden path by their old friends in the Labour party, only to find the gates were still closed, not simply to their political aspirations but to the destitute and desperate Jewish refugees of Europe.

A crown of scorn was thrust on Bevin's head. First he was pilloried as anti-Zionist, which soon proved to be the case; then he was unjustifiably slandered as anti-Semitic—an accusation often made with conviction against other dissenters from Zionism. Over the next three years, Bevin carried out, with hard words and a vigorous enthusiasm, the Palestine policy of the cabinet. It was not his own vendetta. There were Jews within the cabinet, and substantial Jewish representation within the Commons, which, unlike the Zionists, did not see Bevin as an unrepentant, overt anti-Semite, forcing on his party and cabinet colleagues a policy which, if they could only see clearly, would be rejected. In point of fact, Britain's Palestine policy was neither finely honed nor shrewdly fashioned. Bevin simply undertook to maintain a British presence in the Middle East that would be to Britain's advantage, first and foremost, that would involve America, thus muting transatlantic criticism, that would not alienate the Arabs and therefore, alas, would not placate the Zionists. To the Yishuv, British policy became what the Revisionists had always contended it was: one based solely on British interests, incompatible with Zionist ambitions. This was made abundantly clear when, in a press conference after his Commons speech, Bevin said that Britain had never undertaken to establish a Jewish state but rather a Jewish home. In November 1945, it was clear that such a British-built home would have few rooms, and those mean ones.

When the news arrived in Palestine, there was very serious day-long rioting in Tel Aviv. Three people were killed, thirty-three civilians and thirty-seven soldiers injured. The situation in the Mandate had almost slipped beyond British control. Knowledgeable people drew parallels with Dublin in 1920 or Athens in 1944. In the early spring of 1945, it might have been possible for Britain to have imposed a bad partition on the Jewish Agency, even one short of a state, by allowing relatively easy immigration to the new enclave, by withdrawing to secure military bases, and by letting the Arabs, preferably Emir Abdullah of Transjordan, have the remainder. In order to open the gates, the Jewish Agency might have mortgaged the future and reopened the Season. The Americans might have been satisfied with the magic figure of a hundred-thousand immigrants simultaneously urged by various Zionist groups. With the war still on and Russia still distant, the *fait accompli* might have eased Britain out. The prospect certainly worried the Irgun, who had little faith in the staying power of the Jewish Agency. But the British did not want to go, could not imagine that time was slipping away. A few months later, when Labour came to power, with Zionist opposition hardening, the war in Europe over, and the glass house too transparent for a *coup de main*, Britain might have tried the reverse, offering a relatively good partition, state included, hoping that the perpetual Arab disarray would prevent all but a momentary reaction. Syria and Lebanon, under French occupation, faced the same problem; Egypt was intent on a postwar British withdrawal; and Transjordan and Iraq were allied to London by treaty. Subsequent events suggest that neither course would have produced a solution tolerable to either side. The first option of both would probably have been violent opposition to any imposed restriction on their destinies. At least an attempt at an imposed solution would have been better than drift, and drift, compounded by muddle, became British policy. Bevin insisted that any future settlement must satisfy both the Arabs and the Jews—an impossible condition—and in the meantime Britain must soldier on, protecting all the inhabitants of the Mandate from each other.

There may have been those in London who still believed that Britain would be able to fulfill commitments to both Arabs and Zionists without loss of strategic advantage. Certainly it was comforting to believe it. In any case, up until the spring of 1945 things had gone largely Britain's way in the Mandate. After the autumn of 1945, nothing went Britain's way again. On every level, tactical and strategic, diplomatic and political, British policy floundered in a welter of errors. There was never any indication that anyone in authority had a reasoned policy or even a sense of the possible. The Mandate authorities were asked to impose order without a permanent British initiative. That was impossible to fashion because the demands of the Jews and Arabs were incompatible. At least this meant the British would stay, but despite an increasing amount of time and consideration invested by those concerned, no conclusion was reached on the value of the Mandate. All the options were considered. Whether to stay in Egypt or just the Suez Canal Zone. Perhaps Cyprus could be an alternative base, or Aden upgraded. To fall back to Kenya might be possible, or renegotiate the Arab-client treaties. London might even turn to private investment and aid, instead of hard bases and strict alliances.

Yet no decision as to what Britain's future interests in Palestine were and how they could best be achieved was ever really made. In the London power center were differing counsels. Many wanted to stay for strategic reasons; others to withdraw for political ones. Some insisted to the end that nothing could succeed unless both the Arabs and the Zionists could be satisfied, others had always believed such an accommodation impossible. Some wanted the Zionists placated for moral and historical reasons; many wanted the Arabs appeased on the same grounds. The arguments might as well have taken place in a vacuum. Nothing coalesced into a Middle Eastern strategy—Bevin seemed to want to freeze Palestine, hang on, and play the future by ear.

He found little time to listen to Palestine tunes. His cabinet colleagues could only attend to the most urgent dilemmas. The complexities of the social revolution absorbed much of the concern of the Labour party and cabinet. Abroad, Bevin had to tend with care relations with America and Russia, and the problem of Indian independence unleashed more serious forces than anyone had imagined. Western Europe seemed on the verge of collapse and penury, and Britain often appeared not far behind. The result was that, without firm central direction from London or a dramatic and effective initiative, those in the Mandate responsible for policy had to make do. Consequently, after 1945 a firm case could be made that British policy was following any one of several directions. Official statements, policy declarations at various levels, overt acts and rumors of plots were summoned as evidence that Britain intended to appease America by offering concessions to the Zionists, or intended to create a new Arab empire controlled through the puppet Arab League. There was undeniable proof that Britain intended to stay in the Mandate—why else continue to build elaborate military installations?—also that Britain intended to withdraw—why else organize the Anglo-American committee that could only suggest some form of Arab or Jewish independence? In London Labour spokesmen under attack in the Commons seemed to feel that the enumeration of British responsibilities, coupled with examples of past proposals, was the equivalent of a policy.

While many in Palestine sifted the uncertain evidence for the real intentions of perfidious Albion, the Irgun had no such worries. They continued to believe, and do to this day, that almost from the first the British imperial establishment intended to evade the terms of the Mandate concerning a Jewish national home, and that the entire direction of Palestine policy for well over a decade had been focused on that end. The only Zionist option was recourse to arms. So Begin and the rest busied themselves with operations, not British options. During November the Irgun's bare larder was considerably fleshed out by the purchase of Chilean nitrate from British Imperial Chemical Industries in Haifa. The appropriate documents were presented from the municipality of Hebron; the order was processed routinely, and a Jewish driver and municipal truck appeared and collected ninety-eight hundred-pound sacks. Nearly five tons of nitrate disappeared into the Irgun explosives factories; Imperial Chemical was left with an uncollectable bill, and the British security forces with the prospect of further trouble.[7]

The end of November proved a most troublesome time for the British. On November 23, two truck loads of arms were lifted from an RAF camp. Then, on November 25, the Haganah returned to action. An assault party hit the police station at Givat Olga, spraying the building with automatic weapons, wounding one British and three Arab policemen. That night an attack hit the coastal patrol station at Sydna-Ali near Herzlia. Again the building was sprayed with automatic fire, and explosives were tossed against the wall. Five British and five Arab policemen were wounded. Both stations were used as watch points for the detection of illegal immigrants, and were appropriate targets for the Haganah. The British by this time had little doubt that the Haganah was involved—letters and cables had been intercepted; there had been gossip and leaks. The authorities were also quite aware that the Haganah was not an independent underground organization, but an agency of the authorized Jewish institutions.

On November 26, British security forces, the Sixth Airborne, the Guards, the Police Mobile Force, and odds and ends, mounted a ten-thousand man cordon and search operation on the Plain of Sharon and in Samaria, near the coast. They wanted to comb out the terrorists and find the arms hidden in the settlements. Instead, they met violent resistance to the searches by the Jewish settlers. At the end of the day the toll was eight Jews dead and seventy-five wounded. The British reported sixty-five soldiers and sixteen policemen injured. They found few arms but arrested and detained 337 Jews and in the process, of course, alienated thousands more. On December 4, 140 detainees were released, innocent people picked up because something had to be done. On December 11, 120 more detainees were released from Latrun camp. Comb-outs and curfews that penalized many without turning up the guilty few only focused anger on the hunters, not the hunted, who were friends and neighbors. And such operations did not lower the level of violence. Throughout the Mandate were constantly increasing minor incidents—mines, shots in the dark, sabotage, arson, pamphlet bombs, unexplained explosions—punctuated by occasional large-scale simultaneous strikes.

The growing complaint of the Irgun was the Haganah's tendency to view the Tenuat Hameri campaign as a limited period of incidents separated by a pause for contemplation. Their focus was still on immigration, not insurrection. On Christmas day, for example, the *Hannah Senech* managed to evade the British naval patrols and hove to near Nahariya. All 252 illegal immigrants were brought ashore and moved to Haifa, where they disappeared. On the same day the Irgun, exploiting the holiday spirit, attempted to raid the Bet-Naballah army camp. The guards were offered bottled holiday spirits by several "soldiers" who had parked their vehicles near the main gate. The Irgun was unwilling to depend on the British guards having an inordinate thirst at their hardship post on Christmas, so the spirits were doctored with sleeping pills. The guards revealed a strong head for liquor and no interest in sleep. After a decent, if disappointing, interval, the "soldiers" drove off in their lorries—only to miss the almost immediate collapse of the entire guard. There was only slight disappointment, however, because, despairing of Haganah caution, the Irgun and LEHI decided on an independent operation outside the Tenuat Hameri umbrella. On the night of December 27, the Irgun and LEHI prepared a combined attack on the Jerusalem CID headquarters, on the Jaffa CID, and on the REME workshop at the Tel Aviv Exhibition grounds, where a large number of Thompson submachine guns were reportedly stored.

The Irgun, under the command of Eliahu Tamier, detonated a charge against the north wall of the Jaffa station. The assault team, loaded with additional explosives, rushed through, laid the charge, set the fuse, and withdrew through the hole. They were already well away when the second blast brought down part of the building. To the north, on the edge of Tel Aviv, a much larger operation was underway, commanded by Giddy Paglin, but the Irgun assault party on the armory found not the expected 250 Thompsons but only a few odds and ends. When a burst of fire hit the Irgun group, cutting down David Sternglass, Paglin led the men out and down to the nearby Yarkon River, where two escape boats waited. The boats moved off down the Yarkon to safety. In Jerusalem, the operation prepared by Livni was commanded by Shramkan. The main assault force moved on the CID on the Jaffa Road. At 7:15 they blew in the headquarters door and laid the second charge, which shattered the building, killing Constable G. F. Smith and four Basuto guards. Five other constables were wounded. Constable Nicholson and Superintendent Beard, along with four other policemen, rushed into the street where, standing isolated in the middle of Jaffa Road, they were sprayed with automatic fire by the Irgun covering party. Nicholson was killed at once and the others wounded. Further up, near the Zion Cinema, Constable Hyde was shot down and killed. The Irgun withdrawal was almost complete when Constable Flanagan leaned out and opened fire. A final burst of Irgun fire killed him as well.

The final toll of British security forces for the night of December 27 was ten dead and twelve wounded. For one British child, it was the second father lost to the underground. Mrs. Turton, whose husband had been killed by the trap bomb at 8 Yael Street in January 1942, had remarried G. F. Smith, who in turn was killed at the Jerusalem CID headquarters. The child, Ann, whose mother had died the previous March, also nearly lost her guardian, W. J. Howard Beard, who was wounded in Jaffa Road. Understandably, with twenty-two casualties, the British wanted swift action against those responsible. Even before Paglin and the rest had found their way to safe houses in Ramat Gan, the British army was mounting a huge cordon and search operation. Ben-Gurion and Moshe Shertok were brought to the high commissioner's office and lectured—this time they could honestly claim ignorance. In Jerusalem a 4:00 P.M. to 8:00 A.M. curfew was put into effect. Between 6:00 and 12:00 on Friday morning, the British Airborne and police in Ramat Gan questioned 682 males—38 were detained and a further 30 arrested for breaking curfew. Cages were set up in suspected zones, and all the males between sixteen and fifty were interrogated—1,455 in Jerusalem, with 59 detained at the first sweep, and a further 500 the second time around. No terrorists were discovered, even among the detained. No arms were found, except those left on the Exhibition grounds and in Jaffa Road—odds and ends, land mines and magazines. There was a minimum of Jewish remorse over the killings. Even the anti-terrorist *Davar*, whose editorial opposed the operation, found an explanation. As *Haaretz* noted, the real cause was the "stranglehold around Palestine."

For Palestine the new year, 1946, began as the old one had ended: cordon and search, patrol and detain. In Jerusalem there was a fifth continuous night of curfew, and more searches by the troops of the Highland Light Infantry, the King's Shropshire Infantry, and the Warwickshires. The old Montefiore quarter opposite the Citadel was cleared. British lorries convoyed the inhabitants to Talpiot detention barracks, while mine detectors when through the area. Four hundred suspects were detained briefly, thirty permanently. In Tel Aviv, a LEHI/Irgun bomb factory blew up at 86 Rehov Dizengoff, on the corner of Bar Kochba. Two suspects dashed out and down the street, under police fire. A five-hour search followed, producing two homemade bombs, an unserviceable revolver, and eight sets of British Army battle dress: a meager haul. The continuing curfew had almost become institutionalized—military patrols had rushed twenty-six women to hospitals, where they gave birth to curfew babies, twenty-four boys. On January 2, there was a big comb-out in Jerusalem along the Jaffa Road. At ten in the morning a police mobile force closed in, bugles blowing. Nine-hundred men were detained or questioned but only forty-five were kept. The Sudanese peanut vendors went untouched, unlikely candidates for Jewish terrorists. On January 3, there were dawn searches in Jerusalem. Finally, on January 5, the curfew was lifted. Over three thousand had been questioned and in the end fewer than fifty detained. They discovered a few more uniforms, nineteen cartridges in the bottom of a lorry used to move suspects, a little black powder, the odd gun, but no arsenal.

High Commissioner Cunningham had anticipated a better show by security forces. By December he had what should have been the means to impose order. All twenty-thousand men of the Sixth Airborne Division had been moved to the Mandate, and British troop strength continued to rise to eighty thousand. There were also the thousands of police, units of the Transjordan Arab Legion, and others attached to security duty. There were two cruisers, three destroyers, other naval units off the coast, and naval radar and communication bases on shore. The ratio of British security forces to the Jewish population was approximately one to five. By 1946 the Mandate was an armed camp, the countryside studded with the huge, concrete Tegart fortresses, British army camps, reinforced roadblocks, and observation points. The cities were constantly patrolled, and all government buildings protected by concertinas of barbed wire and sentry blocks. There were armed guards on the trains. For safety's sake, the British withdrew into wired and sandbagged compounds, self-imposed ghettos. The largest, in Jerusalem, was dubbed Bevingrad. Security regulations ran on for over fifty densely-printed paragraphs, including the death penalty for any member of a group whose other members had committed one of several crimes, including carrying inflammable material without first securing a license from a military officer. There were curfews, confiscations, searches in the streets, sweeps through the countryside, collective fines, detentions, and arrests for cause. Once the vast interrogation apparatus had filtered out the few hard cases, they were often exiled to camps in East Africa. The newspapers in the Mandate were censored, and travel was restricted. The mails were monitored, as was all overseas cable traffic. The Mandate became a garrison state under internal siege, and the garrison, despite its size, equipment, and determination, proved ineffectual and self-defeating.

To maintain law and order by emergency regulations guaranteed that neither would exist until the security forces managed to get on top of the situation. This they never did. Locked in their barbed-wire ghettos, with no adequate intelligence, the authorities faced a Jewish population alienated by growing British repression and its day-to-day indignities. Certainly, many Jews still disapproved of the terrorists, and were unaware of the existence of the Tenuat Hameri. On January 12, for example, seventy men of the underground stopped a train on a wooded curve near Benyamina with an explosive charge that wrecked the engine, knocked the first three freight cars off the track and left the next five telescoped in a zigzag muddle along the track. Three constables were injured and a £35,000 payroll taken. On January 15, *Mishmar*, a left-wing newspaper, responded with distaste and foreboding.

> If we allow the terrorists to run amok, they may gradually make headway among the Yishuv and eventually gain control. . . . It is not enough for us to dissociate ourselves from the terrorists or to condemn them: we must also act.

The British felt quite the same way, and unlike *Mishmar* had convincing evidence that the terrorists included the Haganah and had the blessing of the Jewish Agency. Despite the increasing British pressure, there was no evidence that terrorists of any variety had been damaged. On Saturday evening, January 19, a complex Irgun operation in Jerusalem that involved a prison break and an attempt to blow up the Palestine Broadcasting Service collapsed into gunfights. A few days later a mine was detonated in the coast guard station at Givat Olga, and there was an attempt on the RAF radar station on Mount Carmel—the Haganah's closed-gate campaign.

On Tuesday, January 29, the Irgun initiated still another arms-raid operation against the RAF base at Aqir near Gaza. Some weeks before, a Jewish civilian employee on the base (an Irgun member) had told his immediate underground superior that he had glimpsed lots of arms through the window of a hut. The information drifted up to Paglin at operations. It proved extremely difficult to get hard information from the man, who grew increasingly vague and uncertain. He could not draw a map or even read one very well. Paglin decided to snoop around outside the camp wire to see what he could discover. He knew the operation would be risky, since there had already been three raids on RAF camps. Security had been tightened up, and special instructions issued to all guards to ask for papers from everyone and check through to the day officer—no more saluting a carload of "British" officers. Paglin and two others began driving around the perimeter wire. He saw at once that he might get a truck in, but not out afterwards. He drove the old car further out along the wire, looking for an exit. Although he was far from any buildings, the British guards on full alert decided to investigate. They arrived with submachine guns and arrested all three—Paglin, Eliah Spector, and Livitah Horri—as suspicious. They were taken to the police station at Rehovot, where they tried to explain their innocence. Blundering and embarrassed, they finally admitted that they were beef scouts for a non-kosher concern. At that point Menachem Shiff, who was indeed in non-kosher meats, arrived outraged that his boys had been arrested for doing their duty. It all sounded kosher to the British, who released all three. Several days later the CID recalled that Livitah Horri was on the wanted list, and Shiff—or was it Steinhocken—had been kidnapped by the Haganah and turned over to the police as an Irgun man, hence he was at best a dubious character witness. They were a bit too late.

Paglin by then had found, on the way out of Aqir, an old, meandering road quite impassable because of cross-cutting ditches, low places, and eroded edges. At eight one morning a couple of Public Works Department trucks, neatly painted PWD, arrived; the workers, complete with cork hats, hopped down and began to work on the track. Ditches were filled in, low places raised and gravel added here and there. The end result was hardly more than a rough track, but it would do for one trip from the edge of the most distant runway over the fields to a firm secondary road. On January 29, after a rainy morning, a British jeep containing five RAF men, including Paglin as a pilot officer, drove confidently up to the gate on the east side, followed by a lorry convoying thirteen RAF's of other ranks. It was lunchtime, and the plan was to go through the east gate, drive to the firearms store, tie up the guard, load the arms, drive out down the runway and onto the sand track undetected. By the time the duty officer discovered that the men in the two vehicles had never appeared for lunch, they would be away free. Unfortunately, there was no east gate—the inside informant had confused east and west. Paglin ordered his driver Elizer Zimler, called "Jackson" because of his broad Scots accent, to drive down the road and stop. Josef Nahmeirs started up the lorry and followed. They both stopped by the side of the road while Paglin thought matters over. Suddenly two attractive women officers came into sight. As they came alongside the jeep, they slowed down, smiled, and stopped. Paglin was horrified—here he was, an elegant RAF pilot officer, who could only speak English with a most revealing accent. He poked "Jackson," who could now exploit his Scots accent. Zimler just hunched down in the driver's seat. One girl said something. Paglin poked Zimler again. He hunched down further. Paglin was wild. The girls stopped smiling. Obviously this RAF lot was atypical. They stalked off down the road, Paglin's romantic reputation in tatters but his disguise intact. It turned out that while Zimler had been in the RAF, stationed in Libya, there had been a hundred men and two-hundred women at the end of nowhere separated by a bit of desert. Most nights there was a rush of traffic between the two camps at lights out, and Zimler had known one of the girls very well indeed.

Paglin decided to go ahead and drive around the perimeter to the rear gate. There the Arab Legion guards saluted the RAF officer with enthusiasm, forgetting to ask for the proper papers or to check through with the duty officer. The jeep and lorry drove in and up beside the T-shaped armory, sited in the midst of the airstrips, a considerable distance from the main barracks. A Jewish worker was asked for the keys. When he refused he was knocked down and the door forced in. The "British" soldiers then held up the four RAF airmen in the hut, bound and gagged them, and coopted the five Arab civilians as loaders. Everyone was in a vast hurry to load the lorry, especially the Arabs, who were eager for the Irgun to make a swift and silent departure. In went twenty Brens, followed by hundreds of Stens. The heavy machine guns were left behind, because the RAF's 30-30 Browning was air cooled for planes and useless on the ground. The Arabs were exhausted, the real RAF airmen outraged.

There had been no alert. Even with the delay at the gate, the base was still eating lunch by the time the lorry moved away down the runway. The jeep followed. By the time the convoy turned off onto the sand track, a British sergeant returning from lunch found the squirming pile of bound and gagged men. The alarm went up. The guards closed down the gates and began searching in the obvious places, not glancing into the empty field at the end of the runway. The lorry plowed along undetected. Then it began to rain again, and the road, already wet, simply dissolved under the lorry. Overloaded with Stens and Brens, it wallowed to a stop. Nahmeirs reversed. The tires spun. All the men but Nahmeirs jumped off. It didn't make any difference; the lorry was in mud up to its hubcaps, and still settling into what had been the road. Everyone grabbed an armload of Stens—little more than a pipe, a folding hat-rack stock, a trigger, and a box magazine—and piled into the jeep. Within an hour a British search plane discovered the mired lorry, and the British got most of their weapons back, plus an Irgun Thompson gun. The jeep, previously stolen and regularly used, was returned to a hideout in a stable at Shanta Tikva, southeast of Tel Aviv.[8] The "British" RAF contingent dissolved and disappeared.

On January 31, it was announced that all Jewish drivers of RAF lorries had been dismissed. On February 3, and eight-man Irgun team, dressed in British uniforms, took a taxi—not a lorry—to an RAF medical unit on Jabotinsky Street in Tel Aviv. They overpowered two guards and three RAF men, bound and gagged them, and departed with two sacks of weapons: four Sten guns, eleven rifles, and three pistols.

All of this tactical flare, which made such good copy for the international press drawn to the expanding Anglo-Jewish "war," was most annoying to the British security forces but only a marginal matter as yet on the list of British postwar priorities. In narrow military terms the Tenuat Hameri campaign was a marginal if expensive matter for them. In human terms the cost was somewhat more onerous—on February 5, Nicholson, Hyde and Flanagan, killed on the Jaffa Road in December, were posthumously awarded the King's Police and Fire Service Medal for gallantry. On the same day there was an attack on the Safed police headquarters. On the next day an attack on a camp of the King's African Rifles, stationed in the Agrobank quarter of Holon, south of Jaffa, killed a British officer and an African soldier, and set off a riot. The African soldiers went berserk, rushed into a nearby Jewish settlement and, by the time order was restored, had killed two Jews and wounded four. The African troops were confined to quarters, but prospects of another ugly scene were very real. No one—the British, the Yishuv, or the Arabs—could see an end to the decay of order. No British policy had been offered save repression. The immigration quota was the same. The Anglo-American committee appeared to be more an evasion of responsibility than a fruitful initiative.

The British, of course, had their successes. On February 19, they captured LEHI's radio transmitter, sweeping up nineteen men, including Yellin-Mor, and one woman, Geula Cohen, the radio announcer, who had broken off the usual twenty-minute short-wave broadcast in mid-sentence. On the next day the Haganah hit RAF radar installations on Mount Carmel—eight RAF personnel were injured. On February 21, the Palmach attacked several police posts—Shefa Amir, twenty kilometers east of Haifa, Sarona, on the edge of Tel Aviv, and Kfar Vitkin, near Natanya. More impressive than one more incident was the aftermath of the Sarona attack, during which four Palmach men were killed. On the day of the funeral in Tel Aviv, fifty-thousand Jews marched with the coffins. Not only had the Jewish Agency opted for violence, but now also the Yishuv appeared willing to defy the British publicly. Such a demonstration had more profound implications for British security than even the most serious incident, and Palestine was once more on the eve of such an incident.

Early in February Livni, as operations officer, decided on a joint LEHI-Irgun move against RAF airdromes at Lydda, Kfar Sirkin, and Qastina. Paglin was put in charge of the Qastina operation with a two-week head start. All he knew was that an RAF airbase was in the vicinity, and, unlike previous operations, there was little opportunity for detailed planning. He managed one car trip that revealed where the planes—Halifax bombers—were parked, and where the perimeter wire ran. Since there was a 6:00 P.M. curfew on all road traffic, his major problem would be to get the attack party in place near the wire before that time. On the afternoon of February 25, two lorries filled with kibbutzniks, singing and dancing after a visit to Tel Aviv, rolled along the roads past British patrols. Approximately seven kilometers from Qastina, the two lorries turned off into a long-neglected camp. The two loads of kibbutzniks were swiftly transformed into two loads of Arabs riding on top of fodder. Under the fodder were a dozen sacks of ammunition and explosives, all carefully numbered, so that when unloaded inside the perimeter wire, each soldier would have his proper weapon or explosives charge. There were to be three explosives teams operating in three zones, and they were to begin operations simultaneously, and synchronized with the attacks on Lydda and Kfar Sirkin—too early, and all RAF facilities would be alerted; too late, and the British at Qastina would be waiting for them. As soon as it was dark, they pulled back out onto the highway and drove the seven kilometers to the perimeter wire. There were no British mobile patrols.

There was also no moon. When the two guides arrived at the wire they recognized nothing—they had never been there in the dark. One pointed off to the right, the other thought the Halifaxes were parked some ninety degrees to the left. The three zonal commanders began to squabble. The covering party had no idea where to go. At least the blocking units for the withdrawal route and the road to Tuvia, where a British armored unit was centered, could be put in place. When it was clear there was going to be no moon and no agreement between the two guides, Paglin had to decide. At the very last moment a British plane came in from the west with landing lights on. Paglin finally knew where his men were and moved the explosives teams up close to the parked Halifaxes. At exactly 8:40, one of the British guards noticed men near one of the planes and opened fire. Immediately there was a burst of automatic fire in return. The covering party began firing into the RAF barracks with submachine guns. Paglin had hoped to place his charges before discovery and feared that in the excitement uncoordinated detonations would catch some of his men withdrawing from advance posts. So under fire, he reassigned his explosives teams, while the cover party continued firing at the guards. At the very first explosion, as one Halifax flared up, colored flares in the burning fuselage began exploding. As one Halifax after another burst into flames, the entire sky over Qastina became a giant fireworks display—hundreds of flares, red, green, blue, white, yellow, bursting and flowering, rocketing in all directions. With difficulty Paglin persuaded his people to stop looking at the fireworks and withdraw through the wire. Even then some of the more enthusiastic spectators had to be prodded along.

There was no attempt to use the fodder lorries again, since the roads would be crawling with British patrols. Instead, Paglin intended to move on foot back through the fields and groves, slip across two main roads, and ultimately disappear beyond the closing rings of the British search. Although the RAF guards were still firing in the general direction of the withdrawal, there was suddenly a burst of fire, apparently from outside the fence, possibly from an Arab irregular attracted by the fireworks. The men sprayed the entire area with fire—ripping fruit off the trees, tearing up the paths, and pocking the fields. They lost one man killed, whose body had to be left behind. But after four or five minutes of concentrated fire, Paglin could move his column out. He was certain that the British knew he was in the general area and would throw out ambush rings. He recalled that his brother, who had been trained in night fighting by Orde Wingate, told him one gambit was for a convoy to drive along slowly, using only sidelights, and in any suspected area men would roll out of the trucks to set up ambushes while the convoy continued without stopping.[9] In forty minutes, when he reached the area of the first road, Paglin decided on great caution. The flares were still going up at Qastina, and as he and his two scouts moved closer to the road he saw several command cars moving slowly along with dim lights. He pulled back and moved his column five kilometers further along the road. Even then, when they slipped over, someone at an extreme distance opened up with automatic fire. It was the closest the pursuers came to the Irgun column.

The next day the British reported three Halifaxes burned out and eight damaged. The Irgun claimed twenty had been hit—Paglin remembered placing twenty-three charges. At Kfar Sirkin the Irgun claimed eight Spitfires destroyed and the British acknowledged seven, claiming one had been towed away under fire. At Lydda the Irgun claimed that grenades tossed into the aircraft dispersal area destroyed seven planes and damaged eight. The RAF admitted to two Ansons destroyed, along with three other light aircraft. The only Irgun loss had been in the burst of fire during the withdrawal from Qastina. A tremendous gain, unknown to the Irgun, was the impact of the Qastina operation. The British authorities were devastated. The aircraft that came in from the west was jammed with high-ranking British officers for a secret meeting in Jerusalem. The British were stunned to discover that the Irgun knew exactly when the plane would arrive and had so timed their operation. It was an appalling breach of security either in Jerusalem or Cairo. They assumed the operations in Lydda and Kfar Sirkin were merely diversions. The loss of an officially estimated £2,000,000 worth of aircraft was almost matched by the drop in British confidence.

Certainly, as the days passed and the operations continued, there was no reason for British confidence. On March 7, fourteen Irgun men dressed as Airborne soldiers raided the Sarafand army camp and drove off with a lorryload of arms. It was most depressing, even though security managed nine arrests, including two wounded men and two women. On March 10, it was announced that Lieutenant General Sir Evelyn Hugh Barker would replace Lieutenant General J.C. D'Arcy as general officer commanding. He had served during the previous Palestine disturbances with the Tenth Infantry Brigade and was thought to be a man with a firm hand. On March 8, the Anglo-American committee arrived in the Mandate, which showed at least some diplomatic movement. As usual, the Irgun paid no attention to political gestures and concentrated on the revolt.

On the evening of April 2, Livni directed a major operation against the Palestine railway system. Five bridges were blown along the twelve kilometers of track from Rehovot and Ashdod, where the station was destroyed. The railway between Haifa and Acre was cut. The Irgun attack force of over seventy-five men, divided into three teams, began to withdraw. Nearly a hundred active service people were involved, almost all of the Hok. There were a few casualties during the operation—one killed, Eliahu Lapidot hit in the right hand and arm—but the withdrawal proved a disaster. The British swiftly threw widespread ambush rings around the entire area south of Rehovot. One column did not reach Bat Yam until after eight o'clock, still inside the British ring. Within minutes paratroopers closed in on the men. There was a brief attempt at resistance—the paratroopers killed one and wounded several before the column surrendered. Two men managed to disappear in the dunes, one of them Dov Cohen

(Shimshon), commander of the unit; but thirty one, including Livni, could not slip away and were captured. It was a splendid welcome to Palestine for General Barker.

The losses at Bat Yam, serious as they were, did not stop the Irgun campaign in any way. Paglin replaced Livni on the high command as operations officer and at once began plans for an arms raid to make good the losses. Such raids, now a normal aspect of Mandate life, became increasingly more difficult after each try. The British filled in the chink in security, stopped up the new loophole, removed the incompetent, and rewarded the keen. Paglin had discovered, however, one more chink in the system at the Ramat Gan police station. Here there could be no frontal assault. The solid, two-story brown building was surrounded by concertinas of barbed wire, shutters sealed the windows, and the roof was guarded by sentries. Prospects for another lorryload of "British" troops with forged papers were dim. The police knew who should be going in and out the single gate. Even an attempt to force the gate rather than depend on guile would be dangerous, because an automatic alarm system connected all the rooms on the ground floor to other police stations and army security posts. All this Paglin knew from one of his contacts, Josef Zinger, a Jewish constable, who had "borrowed" a building plan. The guards, the gate and the alarm could all be neutralized if the Irgun could quickly get inside the ground floor. This Paglin believed could be managed. Arab petty criminals were often brought in by soldiers to be charged at the Ramat Gan station. It would need a three-minute performance by a "British" sergeant. Then the team would be in, the armory blown, and the whole lot back out into the lorry and away before anyone could be alerted: with a little luck a ten-minute job.

At noon on Tuesday, April 23, a lorry load of Arab prisoners stopped at the single main gate. The British sergeant climbed down from the cab and explained to the duty guard that he had brought in a lot of Arabs caught stealing. The guard motioned them in and ten Arabs, resplendent in scruffy robes and the odd turban, old sandals and a few plimsolls, each properly handcuffed, climbed down and followed the sergeant in to be booked. At the desk the police corporal opened his book, then his mouth. The sergeant had a huge Colt pointed at his nose. More distressing, the Arabs were throwing off their cardboard handcuffs, discarding their tattered robes, and revealing pistols and Stens. He and his two colleagues were bound and gagged. The station, still carefully guarded on its roof, was in Irgun hands—time elapsed, four minutes. A small charge blew in the armory door. Heavily laden, the former Arabs rushed back out to the lorry and tossed in thirty weapons and seven thousand rounds of ammunition. At this point a telephone operator managed to call through and alert the next police station. At the same time the guards on the roof tumbled to the fact that Arabs had gone in, and armed Jews had come out. They began firing into the yard. The police from Petva Tikva reached the first Irgun mined roadblock, and began to fire at the lorry. In the fire fight the Irgun lost two men killed. An Arab constable was hit and killed. Two more constables were shot. Another Irgun man was wounded just as he reached the lorry. He was dragged in. The driver was hit twice in the cheek, again in the arm. He managed to pull the lorry away from the police fire. As the lorry drove away, Major Donnelly shot the last Irgun man in the face. Hanging on the barbed wire, his face a blob of red, was Dov Gruner, a twenty-eight-year-old Hungarian immigrant. He had served five years in the Jewish Brigade of the British army and was wounded twice before. Ramat Gan was his first Irgun operation and his last. Nearly unconscious, he slumped, tore loose from the wire, and crumbled to the ground, face destroyed, breath bubbling through blood. He was carried into the station, where Donnelly and his wife tried to stop the bleeding with their six-year-old child's handkerchief. Somehow, despite his shattered jaw, Gruner managed to mumble, "Thanks." Gruner lived, and later, as a prisoner, caused the British far more concern than he did as a live gunman. That was in the future; but for the time being the Ramat Gan raid was simply one more incident, swiftly forgotten as worse followed.

On April 25, two days later, a LEHI operation absorbed all British attention. At 8:45 in the evening, an attack was opened on the Sixth Airborne car park opposite the Apak quarter police station on the Tel Aviv-Jaffa boundary. The paratroopers were caught unprepared and were badly mangled. Six were killed outright in the LEHI crossfire. A British police constable was wounded. A soldier stepped on one of the mines LEHI had scattered to block the flanks of the attack party. Another paratrooper was killed in the explosion, and three men were wounded. An immediate road curfew was ordered, and the usual extensive searches of the Samaria-Lydda district produced no terrorists. On April 27, two days later, the pipe major of the Sixth Gordon Highlanders played the dirge "Lochharbor No More" over the seven caskets. The paras were very bitter; none more so than Major General A.J.H. Cassels, their commander. He was horrified and disgusted—his men mowed down by fanatics, and no hand turned against the terrorists. He replied to the regrets of Acting Mayor Perelson of Tel Aviv with venom.

> I have received your message of regret but I have sent for you today to say how horrified and disgusted I am at the outrage committed by the Jews on the night of April 25, when seven British soldiers were willfully and brutally murdered by members of your community.
> As a result I have decided to impose certain restrictions on the Jewish

community as a whole. My decision to restrict the whole community has been made in order to maintain public security and because I hold the community to blame.

There is no doubt whatsoever in my mind that many members either knew of this project or could have given some warning before it happened.

Further, I am quite certain that if you, as representative of Tel Aviv, chose to do so you could produce sufficient information to lead to the arrest of the criminals.[10]

Cassel's righteous indignation was a tactical error. He was ignorant of the relation of LEHI to most of the Yishuv; and his tone and assumptions produced widespread resentment, a net gain for the underground. The British soldiers expressed their own indignation even more crudely. Their fellows had been victims of murder from a ditch. In Naynayah and Beer Tuveyah the troops rioted, smashed stores, and manhandled people on the streets. Within hours, anti-Semitic slogans appeared daubed on walls. Searches were cruder, insults freer, recourse to violence more regular—all was grist for the underground propaganda mills. This produced further British outrage; for the authorities felt that under the most outrageous provocation their troops were showing remarkable restraint. Somehow the victims were transformed into the culprits. And the *real* culprits, the terrorists, were permitted to operate without hindrance by the Yishuv. All Jews were thus equally guilty. And treated as guilty, many Jews began to regard British disgust and contempt as an honor, not a disgrace. Instead of nudging the opponents of LEHI toward renewed cooperation, reactions like Cassel's only isolated the British from the Yishuv, even those, and they were many, who abhorred LEHI.

On May 1, with Tel Aviv still under Cassels's curfew (finally lifted on May 12), the Anglo-American committee produced its report. They had pored over scholarly studies and endless government reports and proposals, traveled to displaced-persons' camps in Europe, visited Palestine, talked to experts, to the involved, to those in charge, to almost anyone. Their report tried to please everyone. The hundred-thousand Jewish immigrants that President Truman wanted would be permitted to enter the Mandate immediately. The trusteeship that Bevin wanted would be composed of a bi-national state, with one Jewish province and one Arab province, under a United Nations umbrella—a new British Mandate. There were more details and more tinkering with the existing structure. No one was satisfied. Truman doubted the political implications of the plan. Attlee refused to consider admitting the immigrants until the illegal Jewish underground was disbanded and the Jewish Agency aided in the suppression of terrorism. The Arabs wanted a Palestinian Arab state, not a mean slice of their own country with a British overlord. In June the council of the Arab League dispatched a memorandum to Washington denying the right of the United States to interfere in Palestine and one to London demanding immediate Anglo-Arab negotiations. The Jewish Agency contained some who were very tempted by the hundred-thousand immigrants, but insisted the binational trusteeship plan would not create the appropriate conditions for a Jewish national home. The end result of the Anglo-American gambit was nil. Britain would have to try something else or simply plod along and hope for the best.

London-watchers still could not discern what the British thought best. British troops were moving out of Syria and Lebanon—where would they go? Would Palestine be the core of the British Middle East presence? In Egypt Anglo-Egyptian talks concerning a new treaty relationship had stalled, but rumor indicated a reduced British presence there—was a shift to Palestine imminent? Would Haifa replace the Suez Canal Zone? Did Britain want a corridor through the Mandate? These were all big questions, which only marginally interested those in the Irgun and LEHI. Abroad, their advocates might become involved in the great issues, form committees and fronts, lobby ministers and senators, contemplate Soviet intentions or American strategic needs; but in Palestine, in the underground, the focus was operational. Those in LEHI and the Irgun could only act on the great issues by creating chaos in the Mandate, humiliating the British occupier, keeping up the pressure. The great events would thus take care of themselves. Life was more complicated than that inside the Jewish Agency. Ben-Gurion and the rest did not fully accept Irgun strategic assumptions, still contemplated Britain as a bad partner, and felt a responsibility to act in conjunction with Zionist initiatives and maneuvers abroad. Thus the Haganah's operations were still carefully limited, restricted to incidents timed politically or symbolically.

Lacking these problems, the Irgun and LEHI continued to mount operations. Some worked, some faltered. On Monday, May 20, three men held up the Nablus branch of Barclay's Bank. It took three trips to carry all the money out to the getaway car, while the patrons of the bank and people in the café across the street watched. Alas, of the £6,228 lifted £2,000 was found to be stamped with a huge "C" for nonnegotiable. The notes were on their way to be burned. Even more important than military operations, the Irgun exploited the trials of their arrested members. In June and July the high command devised leverage tactics to force the British one more step back into public humiliation.

From the beginning the Irgun had always considered the courts and prisons as battlegrounds. The courtroom was a public forum, the prison yard a base for confrontation and escape. Prisoners simply fought by other means—hunger strikes, defiance, arrogance, and ingenuity. No prisoner ever expected to serve a full sentence. Escape was a way of life, and no British warden or guard could forget the litany of the many successful breakouts. Even in the isolated deserts and bush of East Africa, tunnels were dug, wire clipped, and men broke free. In June and July in Palestine, however, the Irgun focused not on a major break, which would come later, but on coercing British justice.

On June 13, Joseph Shimshon and Itzhak Michael Ashbel, captured after the gunbattle in the Sarafand camp raid on March 6, had been tried on capital charges for discharging firearms, depositing a bomb on the parade ground of the Third King's Own Hussars, and removing a Browning automatic machine gun from the armory. They were found guilty and sentenced. General Barker confirmed the sentence. On June 18, the Irgun reacted. At 1:15 in the afternoon, an attack group armed with pistols and iron pipes entered the British Officer's Club, the Yarkon Hotel, on Hayarkon Street in Tel Aviv. The officers were herded into a corner. Two attempting to resist were clubbed. One, Captain D.T. Rea, was hauled out of the club unconscious, his hands bound, his mouth gagged with adhesive tape, and tipped into a wooden crate in the rear of a small green lorry, which drove off. Inside, Flight Lieutenant P.A.E. Russell tried to slip out of the dining room and through the back entrance. When he opened the back door two armed men forced him into a waiting taxi. His hands were bound and his service cap replaced with a white panama. He was driven away from Hayarkon across Ben Yehuda and straight on for a few minutes, until the cab drew up beside the small green lorry. Russell was tipped into the crate next to Rea, and the lid was replaced. The green lorry drove off.

Captains K.H. Spence and G.C. Warburton of the Fourth Paratroop Battalion, and A.E. Taylor of the Seventeenth Paratroop Battalion, also had their lunch at the club interrupted. They were picked out of the crowd by rank, hustled out to transport, and disappeared into Tel Aviv. At 6:30 that evening British communiqué no. 65 admitted that four British Army officers and one RAF officer had been abducted. All that could be found was one taxi, stolen earlier in the day and abandoned a few blocks away. By that time a twenty-hour curfew had been placed on Tel Aviv. All Jewish premises were declared out of bounds until the kidnapped officers were returned. The streets of Tel Aviv were flooded with security forces. British troops tore up the pavement, brought in sandbags, and created blocking barricades. Bren gun nests were set up in Mogen David Square, Herbert Samuel Quay, and elsewhere. There were constant cordon and search operations in various suspected areas. At Kfar Giladi, an eleven-hour search resulted in two Jews killed resisting and seven injured. No terrorists were discovered and no sign of the five officers.

On the next day, Major H.P. Chadwick, Jerusalem area security officer, had his routine interrupted. A taxi pulled up next to him on the street. Four armed Jews popped out and grabbed him. He was chloroformed on the spot. No one seemed to notice. His limp body was levered into the taxi, which then drove off toward the Bokhara quarter, northwest of the city. The score was now six-nil, and the entire Mandate was in an uproar. The Jewish Agency executive and Vaad Leumi, who had known nothing of the independent operation, issued a statement condemning the kidnappers: "Their act was insane."[11] In London to see Colonial Secretary George Hall, Ben-Gurion expressed his "distress and horror."[12] All feared that the Irgun had gone too far, and that the British reaction would be crushing. The Mandate had been slipping toward open war all the previous week, and the kidnappings were simply one affront too much.

The week before, on June 10, the Irgun had carried out still another extensive operation against the Palestine railway system, resulting in £100,000 in damage. Simultaneously at 6:45 P.M. three trains in the Lydda district were hit, ten coaches burned out, one engine blown up, and another derailed. A Jerusalem-to-Jaffa train was stopped and dynamited between Sarafand and Tel Aviv, and a Jaffa-to-Jerusalem train was hit three miles outside Tel Aviv. In one case the emergency cord was pulled. In Haifa a similar operation destroyed a locomotive.

Then, on June 16/17, combined LEHI-Irgun attacks destroyed eleven road and railway bridges in a twenty-one hour blitz. One operation proved a disaster for LEHI, more crushing even than Bat Yam had been for the Irgun. The LEHI escape truck ran into British Bren gun carriers and armored cars forming a block across the exit road. As soon as the lorry rumbled into range, British troops opened heavy fire. The windscreen shattered, the tires punctured and tore, the hood and radiator sieved. The LEHI people in the back of the lorry were in a heap; some were hit and groaning. A few managed to get out and answer the British fire. There were a few screams over the roar of British gunfire, the spark and clink of rounds hitting the lorry. Some in the muddle of bodies at the rear of the lorry were dead, many were wounded. The rest were covered in blood, hair matted, clothes soaked. The next day eleven LEHI people were buried in Haifa. This, followed by the kinappings in Tel Aviv and Jerusalem, created the crisis atmosphere.

As the days passed there was no sign of relaxation. One drama followed another. On June 20, Major Chadwick, who had been bound and gagged for nearly two days, discovered that the ropes were loose and his guard was napping. He squirmed free of the ropes, stood on the bed, and pulled himself up through a hole in the roof of the dilapidated house. As he jumped to the street, the Irgun guard came running out the front door with a pistol. Too late—Chadwick swung onto a passing No. 3 bus, which took him directly to military headquarters. A team of Argyll and Sutherland Highlanders rushed back to the Bokhara quarter, but unfortunately for them, Chadwick had been in too much of a hurry to leave to recall the exact location of the house. By then the Irgun had decamped.

The other five officers were still missing. The Irgun ignored the plea of the Jewish Agency to release them. At the same time there was chaos in the streets, as the Irgun made use of the courtroom to defy the British. On June 24, the thirty-one prisoners from the Bat Yam attack were put in the dock. Livni told Colonel Peel, the presiding judge, that Peel was "a representative of an occupying power, and we are Hebrew soldiers. As such, we deny you the right to judge us."[13] They took no part in the proceedings, answered no questions. All, however, used the opportunity to make a statement. Menachem Shiff, a twenty-two-year-old sabra who had joined the Irgun at sixteen, opened with a four-hour speech, concluding, "You cannot hold this country with bayonets."[14] He was interrupted repeatedly by the court, as were each of the others. Finally, with Livni finishing up the marathon, Peel insisted he sit down. He refused. Peel told the guards to force him down. Immediately the other thirty moved in a clump around him. In the midst of the confusion and tumult, Peel announced the session was at an end. On June 26, all were found guilty. On June 27, Benyamin Kaplan received a life sentence for firing on British forces, and each of the others got fifteen years. The crowded courtroom burst into song. Women screamed, cried, waved at the singing men, and once more the court collapsed into confusion.

The Irgun decided to release two of their hostages, Flight Lieutenant Russell and Captain Rea, along with a message that if the two men condemned for the Sarafand raid were executed, so would be the three remaining kidnapped officers. This was timed in part to affect the Bat Yam verdict, in part to reduce the internal housekeeping problems of two sets of hostages, but mostly to lend weight to the threat. Russell and Rea would come directly from within the Irgun, a more effective message than a wall newspaper. Both reported that they had been kept in a cellar, chained and guarded. Their contact was a man in a black mask, who brought them food and water, and on request a Bible and shaving equipment. They saw no one else until Saturday night at 10:45, when they were each given a pound note—for wear and tear—Rea a new shirt for his old bloodstained one, and all their possessions except Russell's ID card. Then dark goggles were put on them; they were guided to a car, and driven off with a woman and three guards. They were let off in Trumpeldor Street, not far from the Officer's Club. The Jewish Agency and Haganah announced that their intervention had been successful. The next day the Irgun denied this, insisting that the two released officers were messengers, the other three were hostages.

The curfew was still on, and there were continuous searches. On June 26, a large thirty-man raiding party stole nearly £40,000 in diamonds from a polishing plant. The end had come for British patience. They decided to come down with the boot.

British intelligence still did not know where to put the boot. They chose to hit the known and vulnerable Jews, members of the Agency or the other recognized institutions. The British had hard evidence that their protestations of innocence might be true in a few cases, but in reality the Haganah under Agency orders was as deep into insurrection as LEHI or the Irgun. Just before dawn on Saturday, June 29, a series of massive swoops began. The arrests and detentions were ordered personally by the British commander-in-chief, Middle East. The British lifted four Agency executive members: J. L. Fishman, the acting chairman of the Agency; Isaac Gruenbaum, picked up Shertok in a hotel in Tel Aviv, and Bernard Joseph, arrested in his house in Natanya. They missed Ben-Gurion, who was abroad, and a few others, but the arrests continued all day. A total curfew throughout all Jewish areas of the Mandate was announced. There was some resistance—three Jews were killed and a number injured—but the raid had largely been a surprise. By the end of the day, there were over a thousand arrests. The suspects were moved immediately out to Latrun camp. The searches of all offices, including those of the Jewish Agency, produced mounds of documents removed as evidence.

In Tel Aviv in July, the dragnet penned several thousand men in the streets, while detectives put them through a line-up. As the line stumbled by, a CID terrorist specialist, Sergeant T.G. Martin, scanned each man. The distinguished, black-bearded Rabbi Shamir finally reached the head of the line. Martin looked at Shamir for a very long time and gradually, behind the beard, the face of Yzernitsky of the LEHI high command took shape. Almost at once Shamir was on his way to East Africa. At least LEHI had managed to get Eldad out of prison. On May 26, a LEHI party had raided the Jerusalem hospital and carted him off, plaster back cast and all (he had shattered his spine in a previous attempt at escape). Not only did LEHI lose Shamir, but the arsenal in the Great Synagogue of Tel Aviv was discovered. In Jerusalem they were more cautious—the armory was too well hidden for the soldiers, who were reluctant to spark a religious incident.

As for Martin, the LEHI got their own back. He went on the blacklist. Two months later, on August 10, Martin was at one corner of a tennis court in Haifa, holding a ball and his racket. It was a quiet, sunny day, a long way from the Tel Aviv dragnet. He noticed two young men in white tennis costumes, carrying rackets and balls, moving alongside the court towards him. Martin suddenly realized that he had seen the two outside his house earlier that morning. He did not like coincidences, not in Palestine in 1946. He reached for his gun, never far away, but this time the bench was out of reach. The tennis players jerked out their revolvers and emptied them into Martin. They turned and walked out, rackets under their arms, revolvers out of sight. Martin's body lay crumbled on the foul line next to his two rackets and a white tennis ball that rolled slowly across the court to a stop.

The immediate response of LEHI and the Irgun to the Black Saturday swoop was not vengeance, but to keep out of sight until the pressure lowered. At first there was no sign of that. By July 1, the number of arrests rose to 2,718, four Jews killed and eighty injured. And the three abducted officers still had not been found. In the Commons debate on the arrests, it was insisted that no Jewish claims be considered while the officers were held. In Palestine the detentions continued. Latrun overflowed and some prisoners had to be sent south, to a camp at Rafa. On July 3, the sentences of the two Sarafand men reached High Commissioner Cunningham's desk. He commuted them, apparently accepting the Irgun threat as serious, and valuing his officers' lives more than those of Shimshon and Ashbel. At six on the afternoon of July 4, a lorry came to a stop on Rothschild Boulevard in the center of Tel Aviv. Two men pushed a large crate into the center of the street and drove off. Inside were the three captains. They staggered out, groggy from chloroform, with the same tale of guards, men in masks, and chains, each with his pound note for wear and tear.

The curfew was still on. The total of detainees in Rafa reached a thousand. The roadblocks were still set up. Black Saturday and its aftermath had deeply impressed the Jewish Agency of the dangers involved in further violent incidents. Ben-Gurion in Europe feared that the entire substructure of Jewish institutions in the Mandate was going to be dismantled. Until June he and the others had regarded Sneh's campaign as an effective means to pressure London, employ Palmach militants, and attract international interest and sympathy—all at acceptable cost. Now, since the British could not find those directly responsible for the military leadership, they had swept up the political leadership. A continuation of the Tenuat Hameri campaign might damage irreparably the basis of Jewish strength in the Mandate. Ben-Gurion must have known as well that if the campaign were discontinued for political reasons, the Irgun and LEHI would continue on their own way. He and the Agency would be left free to negotiate in the world arena with clean hands. The demand for action by the Palmach and Haganah could be satisfied by focusing on illegal immigration. In mid-July, these second thoughts and tentative considerations did not, quite yet, mean an end to the Tenuat Hameri, but the direction was clear.

In point of fact, in Palestine, far from Ben-Gurion's broodings, the Haganah representative to the Tenuat Hameri operations command had been urging a special attack almost from the time the British Army started carting off the files of the Jewish Agency on Black Saturday. Sneh and the Haganah command knew that, mixed in with the political chaff, was ample evidence about Tenuat Hameri, and important details and identities that would hamper future operations. Shortly before, on July 1, the joint command of Tenuat Hameri had already authorized the Irgun Operation Chick against the British Secretariat, housed in the southwest section of the King David Hotel. Simultaneously, LEHI was to mount a similar operation against the David Brothers Building. The King David component, however, was the key, for the building had become the hub of the British Administration under Sir John Shaw and High Commissioner Cunningham. An adjacent building was occupied by the British military police and the Special Investigations Branch. The entire hotel area was surrounded with heavy barbed-wire barricades. The security forces had erected elaborate nets to prevent terrorists from tossing grenades into the grounds . The Secretariat, the King David Hotel, and the police were all tied into a central alarm control, sited on Mamillah Road. At the first sign of anything suspicious, the alert would bring patrol cars, many tied into a radio net, to the King David. An incident of any kind would trigger a general alarm, the sounding of a loud terrorist siren, and a massive descent on the threatened area.

In the midst of all this martial display and security preparations, the remainder of the King David continued to function as a hotel, the social center of the Mandate, one of the great imperial establishments, like Shepheard's Hotel in Cairo or the Raffles in Singapore. Beyond the Argyll and Sutherland sentries, the Bren gun carriers, the endless rolls of wire, and the butterfly nets, cocktails were still served; Swiss cooks and Sudanese waiters plied their trades as in peacetime; elegant ladies in tea gowns chatted about their children's schools in England; sleek Syrian merchants with prayer beads could be found at the next table to empire builders, slightly moist in the July weather in their summer suits and regimental ties. The piles of scruffy paper taken from the Jewish Agency and piled in the Secretariat offices in the southwest wing seemed very far from the swirl and glamour of the hotel lobby. Paglin's operation had been repeatedly postponed, but the arrival of the agency papers meant that time was running out for the King David.

Once more Paglin had found a chink in British defenses. A variety of engineers, waiters, lobby dwellers, repairmen, and dawdling pedestrians had noticed that regular deliveries were made to the kitchen, which was not far from the basement area under the Secretariat. A cunningly placed charge in the basement would, on detonation drop the entire six-story wing in a heap. A first problem, even assuming entry, was that for the explosion to be effective it would have to be relatively large. The Irgun did not have the most sophisticated explosives and had to depend on volume. The material delivered to the hotel had to be heavy and bulky. Paglin decided that the King David kitchen would need milk, in substantial churns, but only two in the Hok assault party were told the target or tactics before they arrived at the assembly point.

At noon on July 22, there was a small explosion some fifty yards from the south end of the hotel grounds—a small swirl of dirty brown smoke. A few seconds later a second small explosion occurred in the lane, near the north end of the hotel, leading to the French Consulate. The drill would keep the King David area clear of pedestrians, but would not necessarily cause general alarm. In the meantime a commercial lorry turned into the sunken hotel drive from the north and rumbled on down to the basement entrance. The lorry stopped and fourteen people including a woman got out. Several men began unloading seven rather heavy milk churns, each stuffed with a TNT-gelignite mixture. The Arab kitchen staff was somewhat taken aback by the unexpected milk delivery, and began to protest. Johannides Constantine, a member of the hotel staff, noticed the lorry, the milk churns, and a strange Sudanese waiter in a tarboosh, who was pushing at the protesting kitchen staff. Constantine walked over to find out the trouble, only to discover that the kitchen staff had grown very quiet. The waiter had produced a submachine gun. Constantine also recognized an engineer he had seen loitering near the grounds. The other "Arabs" were manhandling the milk churns down a hall way outside the Regency Café. Constantine had not been the only one to notice something odd. Ahmad Abu Solob, a hotel porter, saw that two of the Arabs delivering milk were armed. He went to the nearest guard post and informed the police that someone was carrying milk churns into the Regency Café. He then made his way back to the kitchen and crept along the wall. Then he saw the staff under guard and the "Arabs" talking to each other in a strange language—not Arabic, Hebrew, English, German, or Italian, all of which Abu Solob recognized. He decided that discretion was the better part of valor, and popped into one of the pantry's large refrigerators. Each time he peeked out, the scene had not changed. One observer, however, opted for valor. A British officer strolling past noticed something curious. He spoke to the Sudanese waiter, demanding to know what was going on—he too found the answer, and began struggling with the waiter for the machine gun. Another Irgun man shot him, and he fell to the ground. Two military policemen at the entrance to the delivery road fired toward the kitchen. At 12:15 Inspector J. C. Taylor at the control center received word of some sort of alarm at the King David. He dispatched a police wireless patrol car. By then the seven milk churns, each carefully labeled "Mines—Do Not Touch," were in place around the central pillars under the southwest section of the hotel. Israel Levi connected the timing devices. The Irgun-Arabs ran back down the long corridor. The guards quickly released the frightened kitchen staff, who promptly fled to safety. So did the Irgun-Arabs, mingling with the staff. In front of the hotel drive a string of firecrackers went off to frighten away any pedestrians. Only eight minutes had passed since the operation began. The assault group was back on the lorry, and in a flurry of small-arms fire, the lorry drove away before Taylor issued a general alarm and dispatched his fleet of patrol cars. The terrorist siren began to blow.

The telephone operator at the hotel reported to the assistant manager that an anonymous woman had left a garbled message to evacuate the hotel because a bomb would go off in thirty minutes. A little later a similar call came into the *Palestine Post*, and another to the operator at the French Consulate, suggesting that the windows be opened. An army ambulance arrived outside the lane, drawn by the report that a British officer was wounded. At 12:31 Taylor at control center called off the general alert. K. P. Hadingham, superintendent of police, arrived at the entrance and was met by M. Hamburger, the hotel manager, who relayed what he knew. The alarm siren whined to a stop. Suddenly the frightened kitchen staff appeared, panting and disheveled, to blurt out their tale. Hadingham turned and began walking down the corridor towards the Regency. It was 12:35.

Upstairs, a world away, the scuffling and shots, the early warning explosions, the noise of the firecrackers, and the getaway fire all went unnoticed. No evacuation message was passed to the guests or the Secretariat employees. Sir John Shaw was quietly finishing up work in his office. Most of the civilian employees were preparing for lunch. The lobby of the hotel was filled with guests. In the lounge a mixed group, many in uniform, were deep in apéritifs. The bar was not too crowded. The staff had nearly finished the last touches for lunch. Charles Bayer had almost completed the last fruit bowls. It was all very normal, much like yesterday and tomorrow. At exactly 12:37 the milk churns detonated outside the Regency Café. Jerusalem was shaken by the huge explosion. Every electrical clock in the hotel stopped. The walls on the southwest corner of the hotel bulged outwards. A huge cloud of brown-grey smoke quickly mushroomed several-hundred feet above the hotel, turning the sunny day overcast. Then, under the thick smoke, the entire southwest wing began to crumble, one story crashing into the next with a roar of smashing masonry, collapsing woodwork, and the clank of bending iron girders. Over the din of the crumbling hotel could be heard the screams of those trapped and injured. With a final horrendous crash, the Secretariat became a huge pile of rubble. Just at the last, out of the chaos, a large iron safe arched out of the roiling brown smoke, turned over in the air, slowly once, and again, and smashed into a pedestrian walking on Julian's Way. The passengers of the No. 4 bus, which had drawn up just at 12:37, were all injured by the blast. Out of the smoking rubble clambered a few shaken soldiers and civilians. Covered in white dust and splattered with blood, they were stunned, unbelieving. Behind them in the smoking rubble were over a hundred employees of the Secretariat, British, Jews, Arabs, trapped, wounded, or dead.

A few had been lucky. Sir John Shaw's office was a short corridor length from the corner that was sheared off. He could take a few steps and look down at the ruins of the Secretariat and his staff. An office further down the corridor would have dumped him too in the smoking heap. Superintendent Hadingham was even more fortunate, for although badly injured by the explosion, he had not gone far enough down the corridor to reach the blast area or to be trapped by the falling building. Few others in the Secretariat were as lucky. In the hotel proper the blast blew out the entire end of the bar. Confused patrons had taken a sip of gin, been spun about by the shock, and turned to see the bar a shambles, the floor covered with shattered mirrors and broken bottles, the air filled with dust. The window panes were gone. Some sat stunned on bits of furniture, under torn curtains and broken light bulbs. In the lobby the first blast had lifted the marble floor in a giant wave, squirting sand up through the cracks that had for years escaped the cleaners' attention. As the floor sank back, the glass from the shattered windows sprayed across the room. In the lounge the apéritif drinkers were thrown to the floor, their glasses shattered, the air filled with plaster dust. Bayer's fruit salad was strewn in the glass shards and rubble, but he had not been hurt. Yet few people in the hotel proper had been injured. This was not the case in the Secretariat, sheared off and collapsed into a great pile of broken masonry under the brown smoke.

Within fifteen minutes the Argyll and Sutherland troops arrived with picks, shovels, acetylene blowtorches, and hand-operated winches. They were joined immediately by 260 Arab postal linemen. Searchlights were brought up, and more security people moved into rescue work. It was a grisly and prolonged task. Mingled in the shattered woodwork, under jackstraw girders, trapped between chunks of masonry, those alive were moaning. No one yet knew who was missing and who was not. The CID began operating out of the hotel dining room, the floor still littered with glass, fruit salad, and plaster. Lady Shaw set up a missing-persons office across the road in the YMCA. All night the digging went on. The papers the next morning reported forty-one confirmed dead and fifty-three injured. The figure for the missing was put at fifty-two, and those digging deeper into the ruin had little hope that many more would be alive: D. C. Thompson, an assistant secretary, was actually found alive thirty-one hours after the blast, but he was too badly injured to survive. The engineers moved in and continued to dig through the ruins day after day, but the search was for bodies, not survivors. On August 4 the final total was given as ninety-one killed and forty-five injured.

The official reaction evolved as expected. Attlee called the operation a brutal and murderous crime, noting that "The British Government have stated and stated again they will not be diverted by acts of violence in their search for a just and final solution to the Palestine problem."[15] The British insisted that no warning had been given, that the loss of life was a deliberate act of terror.[16] The Irgun insisted that there was ample warning, but the British had refused to evacuate the building. There could be no blinking the fact, however, that a great many innocent people were dead or maimed—bureaucrats, secretaries, women, and elderly civil servants. And there was no doubt that the Yishuv did not want to accept the blame. *Mishmar* reported "Treason and Murder," *Davar* "No Reason and No Atonement," *Haaretz* "A frightful blow to all the hopes of the Jewish people." In Paris Ben-Gurion told a reporter from *France Soir* that "The Irgun is the enemy of the Jewish people." The British were less than impressed with such disclaimers; and on July 24 a white paper was issued, detailing the Haganah's involvement in Tenuat Hameri and the ultimate responsibility of the Jewish Agency. Now Ben-Gurion and the Agency wanted out. The Haganah wanted their authorization of Operation Chick quietly buried. Israel Galili telephoned Begin and asked that the Irgun take sole responsibility. The Tenuat Hameri policy was a shambles, and the opportunity was clear for the British to begin to divide and rule.

The British failed to exploit their opportunity to divide the resistance and, worse, bungled again. The usual stringent curfew regulations went into force and large cordon and search operations were set in motion—a process continued until August 7. In Tel Aviv screening cages were set up in every Jewish quarter, and the army had orders to search every Jewish house. The night before the full curfew, Begin left his regular meeting with Yellin-Mor and Shamir of LEHI, and, with Landau, walked back to Bin-Nun Street. It was then too late to get out of Tel Aviv; so very early on the following morning, when the British troops moved into his back garden, he climbed into the tiny cubbyhole that Meridor had built into the house. His wife turned the radio up so that he could hear the progress of the search. And there he sat for two days and nights. There was no food, no water, no opportunity to move about, and no telling how long the British would stay in the garden. By the third day he was dizzy and could concentrate only on the lack of water. Not until four days had passed did the British pull out. Then Begin rushed from the cubbyhole and plunged his head into a basin of cold water, too thirsty even to drink. The search netted only one Irgun officer, but this was when Shamir with his long beard and rabbinical robe was arrested. It was not a very impressive gain, considering the size of the exercise.

By the summer of 1946, searches were normal operating procedure.

General Barker, going one step further, issued a secret order, vituperative in tone and language, to the British army, banning Anglo-Jewish fraternization and attacking in scathing terms the whole of the Yishuv.

> I am determined that they should be punished and made aware of our feelings of contempt and disgust at their behavior . . . I understand that these measures will create difficulties for the troops, but I am certain that if my reasons are explained to them, they will understand their duty and will punish the Jews in the manner this race dislikes the most: by hitting them in the pocket, which will demonstrate our disgust for them.[17]

Barker should have known that in Palestine his order would not be secret for long. In a week it was being pasted up by the Irgun and Barker labeled a confessed anti-Semite.

Nothing could put Tenuat Hameri back together again. All the worries and doubts engendered by the Black-Saturday arrests crystallized. Ben-Gurion made up his mind. Sneh flew to Paris to urge continued resistance. The answer was no, a relief to Galili and others who opposed the use of terror. The Haganah was permitted to carry out an operation at the end of the month and another two in August. On August 23, Tenuat Hameri was dissolved. Begin and the Irgun high command were disappointed at the withdrawal of the Haganah but hardly surprised, since little faith had been placed in the Jewish Agency's staying power. Begin also recognized that Ben-Gurion had maneuvered into a shrewd position. With clean hands, he could now hold firm as the British produced one unsatisfactory solution after another, confident that the Irgun would continue to engender chaos in the Mandate. The political benefits of the Irgun's military campaign would then fall into the lap of the Jewish Agency, fast becoming a state-in-waiting. There was little that Begin could do about this. The Irgun was cut off from any political base—the Revisionist party was simply a party, and could only aspire to a role of grumbling opposition in any future state, cut off from the events in the diplomatic world. Agents were dispatched—Ely Tavin, after he recovered, was sent off as a member of the high command in control of diaspora operations—but the only real focus remained operational within the Mandate, where there was no end in sight. The British were adamant they would not treat with terror. Begin was certain that in time they would recognize that with bayonets they could not impose a solution, they could not even maintain their position. They would soon go.

NOTES

1.   Lazar Pedazur, *The History of the Irgun Zvai Leumi*, (Israel), Shilton Betar, Department of Education, December 1960, vol. II, p. 34.

2. Ibid., pp. 28-29.

3. Great Britain, *Parliamentary Papers*, Cmd. 6873, "Palestine Statement of Information Relating to Acts of Violence," p. 4.

4. Geula Cohen, *Woman of Violence* (London: Rupert Hart-Davis, 1966), p. 104.

5. *Palestine Post*, 4 November 1945.

6. Ibid., 6 November 1945.

7. LEHI's explosives problem was greatly eased by Yaacov Heruti, appointed head of the engineering/technical department in 1945. Eliminating the most desirable varieties like TNT or nitrocellulose, which required complicated production lines, but retaining the essential requirements (combustible, shock resistant to bullets, transportable, and not effected by fire or weather), in two months he produced an alternative. Not as fast as TNT and still not weatherproof, the new explosive had to be primed with nitrocellulose cores in each block. The tremendous virtue for LEHI, however, was that production was simple and the materials involved legal. Heruti opened a paint factory, purchased the necessary machines and material, and hired a worker. His employee cheerfully turned out paint in two varieties—one that would explode and one that would go on walls. The new factory did not supply all needs, so LEHI, like Irgun, continued to steal from the military and civilian industry, buy from the innocent or corrupt, and devise new formulas for diabolical devices.

8. The faithful jeep, repeatedly used in operations, finally was lost when a wind blew off the shed roof.

9. Paglin's brother, a devout socialist unlike Giddy, disappeared without a trace when as a Haganah commando under a British officer he sailed on a commando raid against Vichy-controlled Lebanon.

10. Major R. D. Wilson, *Cordon and Search: With the Sixth Airborne in Palestine* (Aldershot: Gale and Polden, 1949), p. 47.

11. *Palestine Post*, 21 June 1946.

12. Ibid.

13. Jan Gitlin, *The Conquest of Acre Fortress* (Tel Aviv: Hadar, 1962), p. 21.

14. Ibid. p. 21.

15. *Palestine Post*, 24 July 1946.

16. The warning issue is still a live one. Indeed, Irgun propaganda at the time claimed that evacuation had been refused. "We are here to give orders, not take them," and that the three calls were all made. There may have been a fourth call to the Secretariat, but no survivor heard of it. The call into the King David Hotel switchboard might have been considered by the Irgun sufficient warning. Certainly it was not to Irgun advantage to be responsible for innocent lives, and it was their policy to warn targets—although false warnings were sent as well. The Irgun probably tried to get a warning through and either did not, which is almost certain, or were not taken seriously.

17. Jon Kimche, *Seven Fallen Pillars: The Middle East, 1945-1952* (New York: Prager, 1953), p. 42.

CHAPTER 3

A War of Attrition, 1946–1947

> How long does the Secretary of State for Colonies expect that this state of squalid warfare with all its bloodshed will go on, at a cost of £30,000,000 or £40,000,000 a year, keeping 100,000 Englishmen away with the military forces?
>
> Winston Churchill

At the end of July 1946, the House of Commons listened to an account of the Anglo-American committee's investigation. In Palestine General Barker's huge cordon and search exercise, Operation Shark, employing twenty-thousand troops, as usual came up with minnows, although Moshe Mizrachi, one of the guards of the kidnapped officers, was scooped up, and Stern's sister was arrested. At last there appeared to be moderation in the pace of violence: a few shots fired, a holdup in a café used by jewellers, and some bomb-hoax telephone calls. The authorities, furthermore, decided to take at least one stern measure that would show demonstrable results. On August 8, it was announced that there would be no surrender to violence, and even without United States involvement London would try to implement the Anglo-American plan. On August 13, it was revealed that there could be no more landing of unauthorized immigrants—all would subsequently be deported to Cyprus. On August 15, the refugee ship *Katriel Yaffee* was reported moved from Haifa harbor to Famagusta. The illegals were then transferred to the Karaolos detention camp. At the same time the British rushed the extension and completion of the security zones.

All told, August in the Mandate was relatively quiet. The only scandal arose with the trial of British Lieutenant Benjamin Woodworth, who had murdered Amran Rosenberg in Tel Aviv on June 19. He explained that Rosenberg's behavior was threatening: "I saw a British officer being jostled by those people, a thing which I had never seen in my life before."[1] He was eventually admitted to the mental ward of a military hospital, "suffering from a nervous breakdown." Other than the trial and an attack on the *Empire Rival* with limpet mines, life in the Mandate went on as usual. The British in London and Jerusalem might have felt a corner had been turned after the King David explosion: the Jewish Agency now opposed terror and knew that fostering illicit immigration would simply put refugees in camps in Cyprus instead of Germany. Obviously Operation Shark had driven the Irgun and LEHI deeper underground and out of the way, while further diplomatic maneuvers were undertaken.

In fact, for the first time in months, there really did seem to be some diplomatic action. After the collapse of the Anglo-American effort, a new British committee on July 31 produced the Morrison-Grady Plan, a proposal not unlike the 1943 cantonization scheme of the Colonial Office. There was to be a Jewish and an Arab province, two neutral zones, no final decision on the form of the ultimate state, and permission for the hundred-thousand Jews to enter Palestine. On August 5, the Jewish Agency turned down the Morrison-Grady Plan but suggested their own adjustments based on partition. On August 12, the Arab League, meeting in Alexandria, agreed to negotiate with Great Britain on the basis of the Morrison-Grady Plan, as long as the Jewish Agency and the United States government were not involved. Later in the month the revived Palestine Arab Higher Committee agreed to open discussions if Mufti Haj Amin were invited. At least everyone seemed willing to talk. On September 10, the British called a conference in London, attended by delegates only from the independent Arab states. The Arabs proposed a solution based on the 1929 white paper. Later in the month delegates from the Jewish Agency flew to London for talks that led to the usual impasse. It appeared that the British could either negotiate on Arab terms, alienating the United States and provoking full-scale resistance by the Yishuv, or abandon their Arab entente by permitting the establishment of a Jewish state, thus endangering the entire British Middle-Eastern position. There were still those seeking an accommodation between Jewish and Arab aspirations or at least a temporary formula that did not deny the future to either. The imperialists still felt a tilt toward the Arabs was vital, but the prospect of imposing any such course in the Mandate eroded daily. And there were still those in London who desired a Jewish state. The only option to evacuation and instant anarchy was to hold firm in the Mandate and urge concessions on the two sides.

For the optimistic there were shreds of evidence that firmness, detention, and the exile of illegals had a salutary effect on the Jewish Agency. As September brought an upswing in underground operations, the Jewish Agency condemned in the strongest possible terms the "gangsters" involved in the September 13 attacks on branches of the Ottoman Bank in Tel Aviv and Jaffa and the central police station in Jaffa. On September 24, however, the British indicated that this was insufficient, and no detainees were to be released given "present circumstances." By this they meant the escalating Irgun operations throughout the Mandate. There were still 394 detainees in Latrun and another 260 at the Rafa camp in Sinai; 25 women were in Bethlehem prison, over 300 men exiled to Eritrea, plus 230 prisoners found guilty in the courts. Most distressing of all for the Jewish Agency, there were some 5,100 refugees in Cyprus, a number that continued to grow. Finally, after the return of the Jewish-Agency delegation from London on October 29, the Inner Zionist Council condemned political terrorism. Even the optimistic had difficulty in noting a change of pace. From time to time, the Jewish Agency or Vaad Leumi condemned terrorism in general and spectacular operations in particular, and on occasion the Haganah cooperated with British security forces—one Haganah man was killed dismantling an Irgun bomb—but there was no return to the policies of the Season, and no narrowing the field of violence.

Actually, in the autumn of 1946, Palestinian violence bled over into Europe and Britain. At the end of August, newspapers reported that Scotland Yard had informed Monsieur André, head of the French Sûreté, that fourteen alleged terrorists were in Paris on their way to get Bevin. Stringent security measures were taken at the Hôtel George V, where the British delegation to the peace conference was staying. The French police reported no sign of any terrorists. The Chief of the Sûreté insisted it was "pure imagination." The newspapers would not be denied, and rumors of assassins along Pall Mall and the Champs-Élysées continued to circulate. There was actual substance to such rumors, but considerably less than the London papers imagined. In September 1945, the Irgun high command decided to send a mission to Europe to rescue refugees and bring them to Palestine, to recruit soldiers, procure arms, undertake sabotage operations against Britain, and finally to coordinate the activities of various sympathetic Zionist organizations. Ely Tavin, to be known as Pesach in Europe, was appointed to the high command in charge of diaspora operations, and left Palestine for Italy. In February 1946, Dr. Shmuel Ariel ("Elhanan") arrived in Paris as the Irgun representative. There was no representative sent to London.

When Tavin arrived in Rome, he had to build from scratch; but he had two immediate assets: first, the pool of Jewish refugees with their various skills and contacts, all eager to help; second, nearly as important, a vast pool of sympathy, particularly intense among those who had participated in the resistance against the fascists. Tavin began to set up a network of cells throughout the country. Arms courses were taught, and soon special commando programs opened at Triscasa and Ladispoli. The graduates moved back to their various cells to teach the new skills. An organization of partisans and ghetto fighters, Balahav, was created. The

Yiddish newspaper *Lanitzahon* and the *Irgunpress*, in English, French, German, and Italian, began publication. Handbills were distributed in the refugee camps and among the local Italian population. There was an arrangement for two-hundred illegal recruits to sail for Palestine from southern Italy in June 1946, but the plan aborted when the two boats were sabotaged. Still, in less than six months much was done. Important contacts were opened throughout the new Italian political establishment, including Premier Alcide DeGasperi's daughter. Much of Tavin's clandestine activity was known and tolerated, even when the operations became overt—many Italians, whatever their other motives, had no great love for the British. Tavin, however, discovered several internal problems, because the Irgun had not attempted to monitor diaspora activities until 1946.

Back in June 1939, when Ben-Eliezer arrived in the United States, he assisted in organizing several groups allied to the Irgun: American friends of Jewish Palestine, with Rabbi Louis Newman; the Committee for a Jewish Army, with Pierre von Passen, congressmen, and intellectuals; the Committee to Save the Jewish People of Europe, with Senator Gillette and Ben Hecht; and the Committee for National Liberation, with Peter Bergson and Samuel Merlin. When he returned to Palestine in 1943, these front organizations generated their own momentum, proposed their own programs and policies, and evolved into independent forces usually dominated by a few strong men. Getting all these diverse forces in harness, reducing the inevitable friction, and imposing the high command's vision proved difficult. In particular, the Hebrew Committee wanted to declare a Hebrew exile government and concentrate on illegal immigration—they balked at the high command's orders. They contended that the Irgun was doing Ben-Gurion's shooting for him and kept their extensive funds for their own purposes. In April 1946, Tavin refused to sign an agreement with the committee as long as Bergson insisted on an independent existence and pursued the Jewish-Hebrew distinction. An effort to meld the activities of the Revisionist party, Betar, and the Irgun was reached in an operational agreement in October 1946, but friction continued throughout the diaspora despite the agreement.

In the midst of the wrangling, Samuel Katz arrived from Palestine. Newly appointed to the high command, he was to concentrate on publicity with the diplomatic missions throughout Europe. When he arrived in Paris to meet Tavin, he wore a new pair of shoes to turn over to him and a series of instructions noted in a private code in his address book. In his new shoes Tavin discovered written authorization to begin operations against the British in Italy, a far more congenial prospect than political in fighting with Betar or the Hebrew Committee. In France Ariel, who was fast developing into an unofficial Irgun ambassador, had taken a well-pay-

!

ing position, traveled in the best of circles, and made splended contacts through the aid of Madame Claire Vayada, a former member of the French resistance. He agreed that the Irgun would undertake no operations on French soil, and in return the Interior Ministry produced transit permits for thirty-thousand Jewish refugees, who were to take ships from ports in southern France, ostensibly for South America. Escaped detainees from British camps and prisons received aid and comfort from the French, and there was a promise of much more to come. Unfortunately for Ariel and the Irgun, the rather puritanical French Betar unit had reported Ariel's lifestyle back to the high command. The young French militants could not understand the necessity for Ariel to eat in the best restaurants, live at an excellent address, and travel amid ministers and generals, while the rest of the Irgun made do on modest means. No matter that Ariel spent his own money. Katz brought the word from Palestine that he was to be suspended and replaced by Israel Epstein—it would be a year before his splendid talents as a diplomat were utilized again. In the meantime, he kept his contacts and his good humor.

Back in Rome, away from the politics of Paris, Tavin began to consider the British embassy operation. Early in October direct operational planning began. The basis of Tavin's Irgun strength in Rome was still the detainees, who had filtered down from the various UNRRA displaced-persons' camps. They were Jews from Poland, Yugoslavia, or Czechoslovakia, using various names and tattered identification papers. They were joined by a few agents from Palestine who were constantly on the move, like Israel Epstein, formerly managing editor of *Herut*, then on his way to Paris. Most of the agents were conspiratorial couriers, odd-job men, specialists in this and that. On the evening of Thursday, October 31, two teams set off. One was to paint a large swastika on the British Consulate building, the other to place explosive charges in the British Embassy, timed to detonate when there would be the least chance of casualties. Two valises, each containing a time bomb, were slipped into the entrance of the embassy offices. The bombers withdrew. Within minutes the area was shaken by the explosions. One passer-by was seriously injured and a porter less so. Much of the embassy was a shambles, two floors badly damaged and the formal reception room a wreck. The Italian police rushed to the scene. The chief of the Rome police said the next morning that there was no evidence Italians had been involved. Foreign Minister Pietro Nenni personally visited the embassy. There was no doubt who was responsible after the Irgun sent a communiqué through an American journalist accepting responsibility, and suggesting that the campaign would soon be extended to Britain. An open letter was also sent to Premier DeGasperi. The Italian police began swoops on the known Jewish refugees in Rome, arrested three, detained two others, and announced the name of a wanted man. On November 24, four more Jews were arrested in Genoa. Israel Epstein was picked up. Finally, despite all his efforts to keep out of sight, never meeting a contact for more than a few minutes on erratically chosen street corners, Tavin was arrested in December.[2] Although the pressure in Italy, somewhat *pro forma* to be sure, hindered some Irgun operations, others pushed ahead elsewhere, especially in Eastern Europe, Austria, and Germany.

By far the greatest impact of the Rome embassy bomb was in Britain, where the press immediately seized on the Irgun threat as reality. As soon as he heard the news, Katz took the train for London—he was the first direct Irgun contact with the tiny band of sympathizers. He arrived in the midst of an orgy of journalistic speculation. Riding down Regent Street on a bus, he saw the headline of the day chalked on the blackboard hoarding: IRGUN THREATENS LONDON. It was reliably reported that the Irgun intended to blow up public buildings and assassinate those on the death list: John Shaw, who had recently returned from Palestine, former Colonial Secretary George Hall, now Viscount Hall, and Field Marshal Montgomery, chief of the General Staff. Samuel Merlin of the Hebrew Committee in Paris was quoted as saying that if the Irgun wanted to get into England they could do so without anybody recognizing them. There was immediate speculation on Irgun-LEHI disguises—a typical British Army officer might turn out to be a member of the Stern Gang. It was not all in the newspapers either—security at the ports and airports was stepped up, customs searches became tightened, cabinet ministers were given special guards, troops were on standby orders, Scotland Yard was closed at night, and the press kept up the din. Eventually, Scotland Yard admitted there was no evidence that even one Irgun terrorist was in the country, but a great deal of evidence that the entire episode was the result of press hysteria. Unlike other journalistic seven-day wonders the November press blitz and the official response to the terrorist threat did not simply fade away with the next week's headlines. For the first time the Irgun's presence was felt in Britain. With Zionist assassins supposedly stalking the streets of London, the Palestine problem became far more urgent and visible to the British public, and pressure grew on the government to do something. In a largely unintended deception operation, Tavin's Roman communiqué was spun into an invisible underground in Britain. In time, of course, real assassins with real death lists did stalk London's streets; but in November 1946, there were only the fantasies of the evening press. For the Irgun these fantasies, summoned up at no cost or risk, proved an unexpected gift.

In Palestine the brief pause after the King David operation ended during September. The newspapers gradually filled with reports of attacks on rail lines—three bridges down, an explosion near Bat-Galim, shots into a train outside Jerusalem, a mine on the Ras el-Ain–Kalkilya line. The security forces' casualties mounted—an Arab temporary constable killed, a police superintendent fatally shot, three British soldiers injured removing a mine. The attacks on the railway system grew increasingly audacious. At the Haifa East railway station at midday on Saturday, September 21, the Jewish sabbath, four young men in khaki shorts drove up in a small lorry. They got out and rolled a large oil drum into the central hall of the station. Neatly painted in the three official languages—English, Arabic, and Hebrew—was the word DANGER. It was suggested that the Arab news dealer might like to step outside. He trotted out, followed by the four young men, who hopped in the lorry and drove off. A small crowd of Arabs gathered, shuffling quietly in the noonday sun. Five minutes later there was a heavy crunch, the station bulged out and collapsed in a heap of smoking rubble.

Not all operations were as swift and surgical. A month later, at the end of October, the Irgun command had prepared several widespread incidents—electrically detonated mines on the Haifa-Jaffa road, a buried charge in a parapet of a road culvert, a mine near Kfar Sirkin. Each produced the intended effect, and with it a mounting casualty list. The most serious attack proved the most costly. The Irgun had long been preparing to blow up the Jerusalem railway station. There was considerable evidence that, before he slipped out of the Irgun's hands and was spirited out of the Mandate by the British, Reinhold had passed along the plan. It was decided to go ahead anyway, counting on the fact that the British would assume a cancellation because Reinhold's cover had been blown. They had not, and the attempt to place suitcase bombs in the station collapsed. The British had a carefully placed ambush team on the roof of the station. When the Hok team drove up in a taxi, the British waited until everyone was in the open. A women led the way with two suitcases. A man followed her with another suitcase. Suddenly a suspicious porter tried to stop her. She drew a pistol and fired several shots at him. On the roof the police opened a withering fire down on the Hok team. The woman and a man managed to get back into the taxi. The police still continued to fire into the taxi as the driver took off. The taxi was soon found in the Yemin Moshe quarter by the police. It was riddled, the seats soaked in blood, the floor filled with spent cartridges. A trail of blood led from the taxi to Meir Feinstein, whose arm had been shattered by a burst of police fire. In the Hok team four were wounded and four more captured. The only British loss came when constable Roy Smith was blown up attempting to remove the bombs.

A less costly and far more effective tactic was adopted by the Irgun and employed all over the Mandate—the road mine. Ingeniously detonated by a wire stretched across the road, invisible at night, the mines were deadly to riders in open vehicles, and dangerous in any case. So through the autumn the reports of sabotage, sniping, and arson continued. The British, on November 5, released three members of the Jewish Agency executive, who had been interned for four months and seventeen days; but these and further releases had no effect on the Irgun campaign: three police killed and a British sergeant fatally wounded by a trap bomb in a house in the Bokhara quarter of Jerusalem, more mines, a suitcase bomb with the three-language warning detonated in the Petva Tikva-Ras el-Ain railway station.

As November progressed the tempo of incidents further accelerated, despite the presence of eighty-thousand security forces, including two full-strength divisions. On November 14, the *Palestine Post* reported widespread attacks with electrically detonated mines on the railway system, and serious casualties. On November 17, three British policemen and an RAF sergeant were killed, and four policemen and RAF men wounded, when their 15-cwt. police truck hit a mine outside Tel Aviv at eleven in the evening. The rising casualty rate sparked a violent unofficial British response—troops smashed up several cafés along Tel Aviv's Ha-yarkon street, injuring twenty-nine Jews. The situation was obviously slipping out of control. The chief rabbi appealed for an end to terrorism: "Not by bloodshed will Zion be built, or the nation by murder."[3] The Irgun had long thought otherwise. Increasingly, only the Zionist far left urged a political approach. While condemning terror, the Jewish Agency and the Haganah were willing to resort to violence to impede the exile of immigrants. Violent resistance to the deportation of 3,900 illegals in the *Knesset Israel* on November 26 ended with two Jews dead and forty-five in the hospital. Thirty British soldiers were injured in the process. The Cypriot refugee camps continued to grow. The gunfire and explosions now formed a muted background noise in the Mandate to the increasingly spectacular Irgun operations. The Jewish Agency and Vaad Leumi might announce the "bloodshed must stop," but no one any longer believed it would. As yet no one saw any light at the end of the tunnel. If the British with eighty-thousand troops could could not impose order, who could?

So it continued. LEHI began detonating taxi bombs and truck bombs near British installations. One such charge went off prematurely; already primed, it jogged and exploded, leaving the LEHI taxi a blackened, twisted wreck near the Damascus Gate in Jerusalem. Others took their toll. A two-grenade booby trap was found outside General Barker's residence and dismantled. Barker, in fact, escaped a whole series of LEHI assassination attempts. At one point a placid young lady parked her baby carriage not far from the entrance to his residence for an hour or so each morning. Inside the pram there was no baby, but somehow Barker never passed her. Always he was lucky, changing his schedule, missing an appointment, blocked off by an aide. He was even lucky after returning to England in 1947, for the hunt was not called off even then. Most of the British casualties, however, were not generals or chief secretaries but the anonymous: two RAF other ranks killed by an electrically detonated mine, a British sergeant dead of wounds, a British constable shot and killed.

Then in December the Irgun came up with one more tactic of humiliation. Two Irgun members, Katz and Kimchi, were sentenced to eighteen years in prison for violating the emergency regulation against carrying arms during the Jaffa bank robbery on September 13. To top off the sentence, both were also to receive eighteen strokes of the cat. Begin was outraged. "Was an oppressor now to whip us in our own country? Would the rebels of our generation, ready and willing to sacrifice their lives for the liberation of their people, tolerate this new humiliation?"4 A hurried meeting of the high command agreed almost without debate to issue a warning of a lash for a lash. Since Katz, head of the Irgun's English department, was out of the country, Begin—making use of the English he had picked up listening to the BBC—wrote the manifesto himself. It appeared on the walls of Palestine the next day, first in Hebrew and then in English.

WARNING!

A Hebrew soldier, taken prisoner by the enemy, was sentenced by an illegal British military "court" to the humiliating punishment of flogging.

We warn the occupation Government not to carry out this punishment, which is contrary to the laws of soldiers' honour. If it is put into effect— every officer of the British occupation army in Eretz Israel will be liable to be punished in the same way: *to get 18 whips.*

The wall poster received wide publicity and in one case was marked, "Please don't forget my sergeant major," thoughtfully followed by his name, unit, and regimental number. In this case the British authorities decided to call the Irgun bluff, and on Friday evening, December 27, Benjamin Kimchi received eighteen lashes. Because it was the Jewish sabbath, Begin and the Irgun did not learn of the sentence until twenty-four hours later. Orders immediately went out to issue a second warning, pasted up on Saturday night concluding that "You will not whip Jews in their Homeland. And if British Authorities whip them, British officers will be whipped publicly in return."5 On Sunday morning the legal newspapers reported that Kimchi had been whipped, and the underground poster paper announced the Irgun warning.

That evening Major Brett of the Second Parachute Brigade was standing in the lobby of the Hotel Metropole in Natanya, when five armed men pushed their way through the door. The hotel keeper and the other

guests were held at gun point while the major was hustled into a Dodge sedan. The Hok members followed, and almost immediately the alarm went
up. Hundreds of police and troops descended on the Metropole. Cordons
were ordered established around Natanya, and an intensive search operation was prepared. Almost before this activity had begun, Brett returned.
He had been driven to a quiet road near a cliff and given eighteen strokes.
In Rishon-le-Zion Sergeant Terence Gillam was sitting in a café when
three men armed with revolvers walked in, followed by a man carrying a
Sten. Gillam was taken out, passing two more armed men at the door and
two more outside. Fifty yards away he was given eighteen lashes with a
flexible whip with a weighted tip. In Tel Aviv two sergeants were taken
out of the Armon Hotel and forced into a waiting car by ten members of
Hok. They were driven to the Hadassah gardens near the zoo, and each
was whipped eighteen times with a thin black cable, then released. The
next morning a third warning was up on the walls of the Mandate: "If the
oppressors dare in the future to abuse the bodies and the human and national honour of Jewish youths, we shall no longer reply with the whip.
We shall reply with fire."[6] After attempting to induce Katz to agree he
was too weak to bear eighteen lashes, the British authorities announced
an amnesty for seventeen prisoners, Katz and sixteen Arabs. The maneuver fooled no one, and the world press had a field day with the British humiliation. General Barker later complained that British officers in Palestine had been kidnapped, killed, and even flogged. The whip was never
again used in the Mandate.

The lash-for-a-lash operation did not go without a hitch. One of the
Irgun cars ran into a British roadblock on the Lydda airport road. In the
exchange of fire, one soldier was wounded, one Hok and all four Irgun
men were captured. Three, Yechiel Drezner, arrested and sentenced under the name Dov Rosenbaum, Mordechai Alkochi and Eliezer Kashani,
were sentenced by the three-man military court to be "hanged by the
neck till you are dead." Haim Gorovelsky, under eighteen, was given life.
At the end of December, however, the Irgun did not believe that the only
death sentence to that date—Dov Gruner was still under that sentence—
would actually be carried out. They did not believe the British would kill
men who should be regarded as prisoners of war. There was concern, of
course; but even as a matter of pragmatism the British, after their experience with the IRA, would recognize that the gallows only created martyrs, not order. Therefore the high command concentrated on a new series of operations, planned for early January. On Thursday, January 2, in
Tel Aviv, at seven in the evening, after a diversionary attack on a car park
on Hayarkon Street, there were strikes on the military headquarters in Citrus House, on a police billet in the Importers Building on Haraket, and
on the district police headquarters in Jaffa on the Tel Aviv Road. In Haifa

a British officer was killed by a bomb outside the East Surrey camp near the bay; and at Kiryat Haim five soldiers were bombed and machine gunned from a car which was in turn hit by return fire, blew up, and burned out.

In London, on the evening of January 3, Colonial Secretary Arthur Creech-Jones, Foreign Secretary Bevin, Chief of the General Staff Montgomery, and High Commissioner Cunningham met at the Colonial Office to see if a new British security initiative could be fashioned, and if the London Conference might be revived. When Cunningham returned to Palestine, there was no noticeable easing of the situation. There were the same dismal reports of road mines, shots in the night, sabotage, arson, intimidation, and LEHI lorry bombs detonating beside police stations. There were the same cordon and search operations—248 new détainees since the flogging incident. Cunningham, however, had new plans. On January 15, it was announced that the Third Division would be moved into the Mandate in three stages. Stringent restrictions on the movement of security forces were imposed to lessen their vulnerability. All cinemas were placed out of bounds. British soldiers were instructed to walk in groups of not less than four. Large areas and all cafés were also out of bounds. The army was preparing Operation Polly, the removal of all dependents first to security zones and then from the Mandate. All the security zones were extended—more barbed wire, more barricades, more sandbags, more check points, more guards. On February 2, the evacuation began. In one direction, toward Sarafand camp, went several thousand British women and children. In the other went several thousand Jews, forced to leave their homes in the newly enlarged security zones in Haifa and Jerusalem. Wherever possible, all British personnel were moved inside the security zones, to be isolated and protected. Very few British personnel, civilian or military, could maintain contact with friends among the Yishuv. The British in the name of security had transformed the Mandate into a prison, and locked themselves in as well. At least, Cunningham felt, he was protecting the lives of his men.

In the meantime, on January 26, the second London Conference opened in an atmosphere of muted optimism. It was soon apparent that the Arab representatives had not changed their views from the previous conference. It is difficult to see why Bevin even hoped for new moderation. The muted optimism evaporated. The only slightly cheerful note came out of Palestine, when the Vaad Leumi once again condemned the terrorism:

> Repudiation by the Yishuv and the Zionist movement of murder and the shedding of innocent blood as a means of political resistance.

The Yishuv will defend itself with the necessary force against domination and coercion, intimidation and threats, the extortion of money, and the use of force.[7]

The British had heard all this before and noticed no results. On February 4, the London talks broke down when the Arabs rejected partition. Back to square one. Four days later Bevin announced his own plan. There would be the hundred-thousand immigrants over a two-year period, and a form of Morrison's canton plan. There was no mention of partition or of the Negev. It was a shock to the Jews and unacceptable to the Arabs. The new British diplomatic initiative aborted within days. Bevin said that the choice was now between an imposed solution and recourse to the United Nations. With over a hundred-thousand security troops in the Mandate and more arriving daily, with the country studded by security zones and Tegart fortresses, roadblocks and check points, the British could not even maintain civil order. The odds were against imposing a solution unpalatable to all segments of the Palestinian population.

Palestine had become a grim and expensive albatross at a time when Britain was enduring its darkest days since the war. The country had exhausted its resources and was simply no longer able to maintain its imperial presences. London had already indicated to Washington that British troops would have to be pulled out of Greece, a polite ultimatum that led in March to United States involvement in the defense of Greece and Turkey under the Truman Doctrine. The old British Empire was tottering. India was on the verge of independence and perhaps a civil war. The Egyptians grew increasingly truculent. Everywhere were ominous national stirrings; secret parties plotted in Malaya and Kenya. At home the economy was grinding to a halt as the country slumped deeper into postwar recession. Six years of war and two of peace had brought multiple strains, endless shortages, and spiritual exhaustion. The future seemed only endless, bleak austerity. The winter of 1946–1947 brought the worst storms in years. Wheat imports were down, milk stocks in danger. On February 7, the government announced that coal supplies were critically low and imposed strict rationing of electricity. Factories began to shut down for lack of fuel and power. Unemployment spread. With an agenda full of imminent and crucial decisions, in a cold and exhausted country, the harried cabinet finally gave up on the whole Palestine muddle.

On February 14, the British announced that they had decided to refer the problem of Palestine to the United Nations General Assembly in September. Speaking in the Commons four days later, Bevin explained that the British had been unable to reconcile the Arabs and the Jews—an announcement that lacked all novelty.

There are in Palestine about 1,200,000 Arabs and 600,000 Jews. For the Jews, the essential point of principle is the creation of a sovereign Jewish State. For the Arabs the essential point of principle is to resist to the last the establishment of Jewish sovereignty in any part of Palestine. . . . There is no prospect of resolving this conflict by any settlement negotiated between the parties.[8]

It was also obvious, though unstated, that Britain could no longer impose a decision without alienating the United States and much of world opinion on one hand, or the Arabs on the other. Even more humiliating, Britain had neither the will nor the resources to impose a decision, no matter who might be alienated. Trapped in an impasse only partly of its own making, beset by crises, indignant at the endless criticism, Britain left the baby at the United Nations' door. Or so it seemed.

The Irgun simply did not believe the British intended to get out. Why were they still recruiting for the Palestine police, insisting in a color brochure on the wonders of a lifetime career? Why were the security zones being expanded? Why did military spokesmen insist on the rising strategic value of the Mandate? It seemed more likely that the United Nations would be given the responsibility of negotiating the impossible settlement, while the British would maintain the privileges of occupation, freed of the onus of decision. Colonial Secretary Creech-Jones supplied the hard evidence for this interpretation on February 25, when he told the Commons, "We are not going to the United Nations to surrender the Mandate."[9]

In Palestine things only went from bad to worse. On January 24, General Barker confirmed Dov Gruner's death sentence. He knew the risks he was taking in light of the Irgun's hanging-for-a-hanging threat of the previous year but simultaneously issued stringent restrictions on the movement of British military personnel. Unable to find a vulnerable British officer, on Sunday, January 26, at five in the afternoon, a young woman knocked on the door of Major H. A. I. Collins's flat. Retired and now with various business interests, Collins was expecting no one. His nurse left her tea and opened the door. A young woman, speaking in English, said that she had a message for Collins. The door was suddenly pushed open and three men armed with revolvers grabbed Collins. When he began to struggle, one of the men struck him twice with an axe handle, once in the temple and once on the right arm. Collins was quickly chloroformed, had a sack placed over his head, and was hustled out the door. Eighteen hours later in Tel Aviv Judge Ralph Windham, heir to the Bowyer-Smith barony, was abducted at midday. The Irgun simply walked into the main hall of the court building on Rehov Yehuda Halevi, where Windham was trying a case, and escorted him out of the building. The British immediately declared a curfew for all of Tel Aviv and large parts of Jerusalem and Haifa. Authorities threatened to declare statutory martial law. In London, before the Commons, Creech-Jones repeated the threat. Intensive searches, as usual, produced nothing. Informally, the Jewish Agency learned that Gruner's sentence would not be carried out. After thirty hours, on Tuesday evening, Judge Windham was released. Unlike the five officers who had given their word not to discuss their captivity or identify their captors, the judge had no comment. The next day Collins, whom the Irgun had identified as an intelligence officer, was also released. The British postponed Gruner's execution, they said, because an appeal to the Privy Council was pending. There was no such appeal. Eventually a new attorney, Asher Levitsky, persuaded Gruner that the Irgun wanted him to sign—which was not the case, since irgun policy was to support whatever course the prisoner chose. Levitsky did have the Irgun's permission to get Gruner's signature, which he rescinded once he learned the choice was his alone.

> Of course I want to live. Who does not? . . . The right way, to my mind, is the way of the people in these days; to stand up for what is ours and be ready for battle even if in some instances it leads to the gallows. For the world knows that a land is redeemed by blood.
> I write these lines forty-eight hours before the time fixed by our oppressors to carry out their murder, and at such moments one does not lie. I swear that if I had the choice of starting again I would choose the same road, regardless of the possible consequences to me.[10]

Two appeals were ultimately submitted to the Privy Council, one by his uncle Frank Gruner, an American. When that was rejected, another was submitted by the Tel Aviv municipality. In the meantime Alkochi, Drezner, and Kashani were sentenced to death on February 10, and on February 13, in his last official act before leaving Palestine, General Barker confirmed the sentences. As in Gruner's case, the execution was postponed.

The kidnapping of Windham and Collins, followed by the stay of execution, created consternation—many in Palestine and London were outraged that the authorities had given in to coercion. It was time, some felt, to get terror by the throat. The Jewish Agency was frantic—if the Irgun killed Windham and Collins, the British would inevitably react violently against Zionists. They were most fearful of statutory martial law. The Irgun was not so fearful as curious. It was difficult to see how British security precautions and procedures could be any more stringent. The Irgun decided thus to provoke martial law by launching a series of serious incidents throughout Palestine. Since no one knew whether communication could be maintained, all local commanders were ordered to continue hitting targets of opportunity, without special authorization from the high command. Begin moved temporarily to the house of a Jewish police-

man—a very safe house indeed. On March 1, the Jewish sabbath, the Irgun carried out sixteen major operations. The most impressive was the attack on the British officers club in Goldschmidt House, supposedly totally
secure in the midst of the Jerusalem Bevingrad complex. The Irgun sited a
Bren gun on King George Avenue, opposite the Yeshorun Synagogue, in
an area that jutted close to the northern gate of Security Zone G. Under
the covering machine gun fire a lorry loaded with explosives and Hok men
rammed the barbed-wire barrier. The lorry was driven up outside the club
and the Irgun men rushed the building, tossing satchel bombs in before
them. The explosions brought much of the building down. The club's dining room and reception lounge were a shambles. The bar was wrecked, a
heap of rubble, smashed glass, and broken liquor bottles. In the club
ruins some fifteen people, including three women receptionists, were
trapped and feared dead. The newspapers listed the total casualties on
Sunday morning as twenty killed and thirty wounded, with more to come.

In London the *Sunday Express* ran a banner headline: GOVERN OR
GET OUT. At eight on Sunday morning martial law was proclaimed, with
a full curfew in most Jewish areas. All government services stopped.
There was no postal delivery. Only a few telephones worked. Food was
distributed by the army. There were no trains, buses, or taxis, and only
security motor transport on the roads. Civil courts were suspended and
special military tribunals established. There was no movement in or out of
various closed zones without police authority. Anyone was liable to be
shot for disobeying a soldier, all of whom now had police authority. Two
people were shot and killed almost immediately, but for what infraction
was uncertain, since one was a four-year-old girl. In Tel Aviv the huge
ten-thousand-man cordon and search operation was known as Elephant.
In Jerusalem at dawn, the ten-thousand troops of the First and Ninth Infantry Brigades in Operation Hippo began screening all suspects—every
Jew who could be rounded up and run past a knowledgeable CID eye.
General Gale, commander of Operation Elephant, explained to newspaper correspondents that martial law would continue until the terrorists
had been run to earth. The new military commander, General Sir Gordon
MacMillan, had at last come down hard with the boot.

The boot, Hippo and Elephant, martial law—none had the intended
effect. The Irgun kept up their attacks. On Monday five soldiers and four
civilian employees were wounded in three attacks. The Irgun found no
difficulty in reestablishing communication and control. The cordon and
search operations discovered no one important. On March 5, there were
further attacks in Haifa, Jerusalem, and on the road outside Rehovot. The
Haifa Municipal Assessments Office was destroyed. The following day
the British announced that twenty-five "known terrorists" had been arrested since the declaration of martial law. On March 8, at eight in the

evening, three Hok assault teams attacked targets inside the security zones in Tel Aviv: one centered on Citrus House, the Jaffa police headquarters, and the Sarona co-op building. Brigadier Poole, commanding officer of the Third Infantry Brigade, barely escaped death when his staff car was blown up under him. The next day Irgun and LEHI attacks continued throughout the Mandate—sniping, arson, road mines, hand grenades, and the occasional heavy raid.

The Jewish mayors of Tel Aviv and Petva Tikva, as well as several council chairmen, were called in by the British and warned that terrorism must cease. The next day there was an attack on British Military Camp 87 at Hadera. On March 12, LEHI carried out a pre-dawn assault on the Middle East headquarters of the Royal Army Pay Corps at the Syrian Orphanage—supposedly safe inside a Jerusalem security zone. There were six other incidents in the city the same night. The most damaging was an Irgun assault on the Schneller Building inside the fortified security zone. Led by Yehoshua Goldschmid, the Hok team first broke through the peripheral fortification, cut through the wire, blew up a protective wall, cut through the inside wire, and rushed the building. Once inside, explosives charges were set, while covering units outside kept off British reinforcements. The Irgun withdrew and the charges exploded, gutting the Schneller Building. On March 17, martial law was lifted. Hippo and Elephant were canceled. Seventy-eight terrorists had been arrested: fifteen identified as LEHI, twelve as Irgun, and the rest "connected." The effort to get terror by the throat was a catastrophic failure. Churchill, speaking in the Commons, was not alone in wanting to know how long this squalid warfare with all its bloodshed would go on.

April was the cruelest month. At 2:00 A.M. on March 31, LEHI detonated two huge bombs inside the Haifa refinery. After the flash, a massive sheet of flames shot up several hundred feet. The city was lit blood red by the flames. The fire department was unable to make any progress with the burning oil tanks. Day after day the flames continued, producing greasy black clouds of rolling smoke over the city. Not until April 18, nearly three weeks later, did they begin to die out. By then the squalid war in Palestine had grown more vicious; for the British, after the failure of Hippo, Elephant, and martial law, still wanted to create an impression of control. Haifa lit up, night after night, by an uncontrollable blaze was hardly firm evidence of civic order. On April 2, Britain formally asked United Nations Secretary General Trygve Lie to call a special session of the General Assembly to consider the Palestine problem. Simultaneously, the British representative at Lake Success insisted that London reserved the right to reject any United Nations decision. In order to give weight to British capacity and responsibility in the Mandate, the decision was taken to introduce the gallows into the Palestine equation.

Increasingly, the Irgun had grown concerned about just such a possibility. Well before Dov Gruner's first appeal went to the Privy Council in January, Giddy Paglin had devised a plan to break into the Jerusalem central prison. Essentially, it was a variant of the Ramat Gan raid when Gruner was wounded and captured. This time Paglin wanted to steal a British armored car some distance from Jerusalem, replace the captured British soldiers with other "British soldiers and a prisoner," and drive to the prison at exercise time. On signal, once the car entered the courtyard, the condemned men would rush to the car, where arms would be waiting for them. The difficulty was that the armored car had to be stolen at just the right time and place in order to arrive during the afternoon exercise period before a general alarm went out. This Paglin could not manage. There was a tunnel as well—when two or three Irgun prisoners were gathered together, there was almost always a tunnel. It began in the wall of the lavatory and was pointed beyond the main wall, but going had been slow and the danger of discovery high.

In the meantime Yechiel Drezner, under the name of Dov Rosenbaum, Mordechai Alkochi, and Eliezer Kashani were sentenced to death on February 10 for carrying arms during the December flogging incident. On March 17, Moshe Barazani was sentenced to death for carrying a hand grenade during the assault on the Syrian Orphanage on March 9. On April 3, Meir Feinstein, who had lost an arm during the attack on the Jerusalem railway station, was also sentenced to death—the number of hostages to fate was increasing. Any prospect that Gruner would be summarily executed was ended with the kidnapping of Collins and Windham; but after various delays, on March 26, the appeal failed. Unknown to anyone in Palestine, at almost that same time the British cabinet apparently gave High Commissioner Cunningham permission to carry out the death sentences. Certainly on his return, with the great pall of smoke hanging over the flames of Haifa, it was abundantly clear that *something* had to be done. But on April 8, before any action could be taken, the Tel Aviv municipality's plea for Gruner was dispatched to the Privy Council. On April 14 it was renewed.

By then Yechiel Drezner had managed to smuggle out a report—on tiny slips of paper—from the Jerusalem central prison. The report went to Begin. Even before the three were condemned, clad in the red burlap death suits, they had been brutalized by their captors.

> Before Wilhelma, I decided to stop the car and jump into the orange grove. But the driver lost control of the car and it ran into a barbed-wire barrier set up on the road by the Army. The barrier was dragged along by the car and it was only the second barrier we hit that stopped us. At that moment a Bren gun opened fire on us from behind, and then the car was surrounded by "anemones" with their revolvers aimed at us. We had no choice but to leave the

car with our hands up. Eliezer got a bullet in his back and Mordechai [the driver] in the shoulder. The bullet went right through and came out. As we came out I got a blow in the back and rolled into the ditch. As I lay I heard a revolver shot and I saw a soldier pointing his revolver at Mordechai. He fired, missed Mordechai, and killed his brother Britisher. He at once hit Mordechai over the head with his revolver and threw him onto me in the ditch. We both got to our feet while, with their revolvers trained on us, they kicked us. We heard more shots. I thought they would finish us all off. When they finally took us into an armoured car we found two others. Eliezer was not there. After that we did not see him. The others had also not seen what had happened to him. He had had some difficulty in getting out of the car and they were under the impression that the soldiers had shot him in the car.

Then began the chapter of beatings which ended only the next day at seventeen hours—about twenty hours consecutively.

Amid blows, we were taken into a small armoured car, each of us guarded by a soldier. The guards at once emptied our pockets, ordering us to keep our hands up. They took everything: our watches, about fifty pounds in cash, purses, and notebooks, pens and pencils, even a handkerchief and a comb. When they had done with this, they all began to hit us. They aimed particularly at our faces and stomachs. When we doubled up from blows to the stomach they would hit us in the face to straighten us up again. I remember how my nose ran blood like water from a tap and the soldier called out happily, "I have broken his nose!"

This journey ended in a camp I do not know. They shoved us out and took us to an open field. They stood us in a row, about ten soldiers formed a line in front of us and loaded their rifles. I must mention that we all stood the test, and nobody lowered his head. At that moment an officer came running up and reprimanded the soldiers, who had apparently really meant to finish us off. We were led to a room. They kept us there about half an hour. All the time—from the time we were caught—we had our hands up. After half an hour, when our hands had turned to stone, they put us into a big truck and laid us on the floor. They saw a ring on Mordechai's finger and tried to take it off. When it would not come off they pulled his finger with all their might until they thought it was broken, and then gave up. We came to an anemones' camp and there an officer ordered us to be taken into one of the huts. It was a kitchen which had not been used for some time, about fifteen by forty-five feet. There they undressed us. They took everything off . . . but as we were manacled to each other the clothes remained hanging on our hands. To get them off they pulled with all their strength and injured our hands. What they did not manage to tear off this way they cut off with a razor blade. We were left as naked as on the day we were born.

They began an organized attack for which they had apparently got an officer's permission or orders. They hit each of us in turn and then all together. Four or five soldiers took part in this. When they got tired, they were relieved by others. They hit us with their fists in the head and the feet, and they kicked us in all parts of the body not even omitting the testicles. Among the beaters were two policemen who had apparently been sent to guard us. One of them moved around with a big baton which he brought down on our backs, or legs or stomach. One of these blows broke Eliezer's hand and caused a sprain in Haim Golor's back. One blow I got on my neck almost made me faint. This went on until late at night. An officer came in then and ordered them to stop hitting us, to wash us and give us blankets for sleeping. They poured water over our heads and each of us had to wash the other. The wash did not help much as our wounds were bleeding and we immediately became dirty again. The four of us, wet and naked and shivering with the cold, lay down in one blanket and covered ourselves with two other blankets. (That was all they gave us.) But no sooner had we dozed off than the guard came. We had such visits about every fifteen minutes.

Toward morning they ordered us to get up and "wash" again. The blanket we had lain on was soaked in blood and had changed its colour. After we had washed they gave us clothes so that we should dress. Three of us were not given our shoes. So, covered, in our rags, we were made to run all the way to the "hospital room." On the way every soldier we met hit at us with his fists or his rifle-butt, and our guards did not spare us either. We ran with our hands above our heads. In the dispensary they kept us about three-quarters of an hour with our hands up until the doctor came.

A doctor, a short elderly man, looked at our wounds and asked the soldiers if they wanted to go on "playing" with us. The soldiers replied in the affirmative. "All right then," said the doctor, "I'll bandage their wounds afterwards." (They did not realize that I understood English).

They made us run back the same way to the place we had come from. They again undressed us and took us outside, and there poured slop-water over us. Then soldiers standing around were invited to volunteer to hit us, and there was no lack of volunteers. They then took us inside again and ordered us to wash the floor and scratch our blood off the walls. Only then I saw what that kitchen looked like. There were pieces of dried blood on the walls and we had to scratch them off with our nails. They beat us as we did it. Suddenly the policeman pulled us away and ordered us to kneel and kiss the ground. When we refused we were beaten with a cudgel. But we did not do as he asked. They put another pair of handcuffs on me—apparently they had noticed that I was encouraging my comrades in their rebelliousness. When they handcuffed me I did not want to do anything, and they again hit me. Finally they took off the extra handcuffs.

At about nine o'clock they washed us again . . . and gave each of us a pair of trousers. The same doctor came again and had plasters put on two of us. After that a police officer came, accompanied by the Jewish officer Karlik and several detectives. They hardly questioned us, asked only our names and addresses. All day the police came and went and meantime the soldiers did not stop "playing" with us. Towards evening only Karlik remained in the next-door room and they took us out to get us to sign the chargesheet. While Karlik was sitting in the next room a giant corporal came in and ordered us to do all kinds of humiliating things. When we refused he beat us mercilessly. I told the boys not to keep quiet this time so that our cries should reach Karlik. I had told him clearly that he was the only Jew we had met and that he must do everything to get us out of there, otherwise they would beat us to death. He promised.[11]

Eventually, the four were moved from the paratroopers' camp; but although the identity of the British policeman was discovered, the location of the camp was not. The Irgun could not get to the CID man, for he first traveled only in an armored car, and then after a few weeks was transferred out of Palestine. By then three of the four Irgun men were under sentence of death.

The British have always liked to think of themselves and their army as civilized, restrained, and decent. Their wars are fought within the rules, their conduct is lawful, their standards set standards for others. Strangely enough, their enemies have often thought the same thing. A guerrilla in Ireland, Aden, or Cyprus would usually assume that the British, including the average British soldier, even under provocation in a squalid little war, would play the game, would eschew torture, murder, and wanton reprisal, would neither run amok nor resort to brutality. No one expected the Germans or the Russians to react to provocation with anything but immediate, brutal, compelling force, coupled with institutionalized counter-violence. Thus British cruelty, authorized and tolerated or not, came as a shock to the British themselves. That young soldiers, ignorant of the issues, after a long war, should react with fury to murder from a ditch, random land mines, and all the nasty and unpleasant operations of an underground war could hardly be surprising. That their superiors understood the stress and hence avoided punishment, is again understandable, though less attractive. That the British at home, nurtured on their virtues, were certain that their army reflected in every act British rules of conduct, is not at all surprising. What was special about the British was that ultimately, when the unsavory results of counter-violence surfaced, large segments of the public would refuse to countenance continued rule by terror. Given a choice of governing with violence or getting out, many people wanted the troops out.

In 1921 Ireland had not been worth the price, a price in moral certainty, not British lives. What the paratroopers did could be understood, but not condoned; if discovered, disapproved. During this century almost every rebel against the British Crown has recognized that such recourse to violence is alien to British values, and every incident made public tips the scales to rebel advantage. There is in Britain no possibility of the exquisite logic that would defend torture in Algeria or of the puerile race theories that would permit Germans to murder whole peoples in the name of Aryan purity. The British tried to play the game by the rules; and in Palestine in 1947, this meant they were gradually losing the game. Yet when the rules *were* broken for supposed advantage, those back home in Britain who paid for the game doubted the wisdom of continuing in such an increasingly unsavory enterprise. No wonder that everyone from the high commissioner down to a paratroop corporal grew frustrated and under severe provocation responded, each in his own way, violently. By so doing they only guaranteed further frustration. In the case of the high commissioner, there was a growing inclination to punish the Irgun by recourse to the Crown's justice.

In mid-April Gruner's physician, Dr. Shalit, requested permission to perform a further operation on his jaw to ease his constant pain. The prison authorities evaded the request at first, then on April 13 assured Shalit that he could transfer Gruner to a hospital in a few days. On April 14, Gruner, Drezner, Alkochi, and Kashani were transferred under heavy guard from Jerusalem to the condemned cells in Acre prison. The government information officer announced at a special press conference that there was no special significance to the transfer. The Tel Aviv municipality appeal was still pending. He neglected to mention that the British that morning had secretly enacted a retroactive regulation abolishing the right of appeal from the judgment of a military court. In any case Tuesday was hanging day at Acre—all prisons have their rites and rituals—and the appropriate hour had come and gone by the time the four men arrived. Without much hope in the second appeal, the Irgun suspected that there might not be much time left. Consideration had already been given to the worst possible eventuality—failed appeal, no escape. A Samson strategy was devised for that—to smuggle in a revolver or a grenade to the men, so they could take some of their captors with them. Neither the Irgun high command nor the Jerusalem commander of prisoners hoped it would come to that; for there were still various escape plans. Livni, as Acre Irgun commander, went along with Zettler and Shmulevitz of LEHI in planning a tunnel escape; but since its existence was secret even to the two high commands outside, Livni was certain that Paglin was at work on an escape operation.

Livni, in fact, had not been very enthusiastic about the LEHI tunnel project, preferring to depend on an escape operation mounted from outside. If the tunnel were discovered, they might all be transferred or increased British security precautions might hamper any break. The LEHI people, however, were determined; so Livni went along. He did persuade Zettler and Shmulevitch that, instead of tunneling out of cell 22, which had three windows and was not too secure, they should begin in cell 28 and go straight down, not out—where the tunnel might only lead to the outside yard of the prison. Among the Irgun prisoners was Jerachmiel Romm, a young man who had studied medieval history at the American University in Beirut, whose academic career had been interrupted by the war. He served in the British Army in North Africa and Sicily, deserting with the rank of sergeant major to become the Irgun's Bren gunner and one of the "British soldiers" in Hok. With the help of several volumes from the prison library, Romm had come to the conclusion that the rather scruffy Turkish-built cavalry barracks-turned-prison rested on the crypts of the old crusader fortress of St. Jean d'Acre. A shaft sunk straight down from cell 28 should, according to Romm's calculations, break through the ceiling into a hidden maze of medieval rooms and halls. At worst they might be filled with sand that had sifted in over the centuries, but this would not be a serious problem. Once through and down into the fortress, it would be possible to find a way to the outside walls. If Romm were right, the use of the crypts would eliminate the problems of moving a large number of escapees through the narrow tunnel originally planned by LEHI.

So began the tunnel in cell 28. Simcha Ozer, a professional black-smith, produced a set of digging tools supplemented by cutlery and odds and ends. A trap-opening was cut, not down into the floor, but horizontal-ly into a pillar in the cell. A trap door was made out of stolen cement and slipped into the tunnel mouth. The dirt was scattered in the yard. Pebbles and small stones went first into the kitchen, then out with the garbage. Large stones were boiled in pots over an ancient kerosene stove, bor-rowed each night from the kitchen. When hot they were tossed in cold water, breaking into manageable pieces. The tunnel shaft moved a little further down each night. The digging, at first limited to the thinnest pris-oners, was done by the light of a tureen lamp burning vegetable oil—a di-rect copy of biblical models. At the end of each shift, the base of the tun-nel was soaked in water to soften it up for the next shift, the men, often wearing special clothing, changed in the shaft, the trap door was re-moved, and the "sick" man got up and pulled his bed away. The prison-ers, who had been on guard or whiling away some of the evening hours talking about women to the Arab prisoners and police, moved on to other tasks. By the time Dov Gruner and the rest arrived on April 14, the shaft was two meters down and to the base of the existing basement. Digging, however, was ordered stopped by Livni. Another plan was in the works, and he did not want to risk discovery. Zettler and Shmulevitz agreed.

For the four condemned men there was no immediate danger, at least until the Privy Council rejected the appeal. Gruner's attorney was told he would be allowed to continue visiting his client. Gruner's sister, who had come from the United States and visited him in Jerusalem, was informed that visiting privileges would continue at Acre. And so all was normal there. On Tuesday the four were allowed out for a brief exercise period near the central yard, and Livni, as the prisoners' commander, managed to talk to them briefly as they stood in the sun in their red-burlap suits. Usually, a condemned man spent only eight hours in the two small Acre death cells, but these four were special. While he had the chance, Livni told Gruner that there was an escape plan underway and questioned him closely about the entrances to the death cells—their doors and locks. While prisoners had from time to time made legendary escapes from the prison, none had ever escaped from the death cells. Across the central yard from the LEHI and Irgun cells, entry was through a large iron gate. On the right was a short corridor. At the end of the corridor was a single tiny window through the thick outer wall. Heavily barred, it permitted the condemned man to talk with his last visitor. On the right of the corridor were two smallish cells with heavy-barred grill doors. There was little inside but iron beds attached to the concrete floor. On the left of the corridor was another iron gate, opening into the high-ceilinged gallows room— last visited by an Irgun man when Shlomo Ben-Yosef was hanged.

At four o'clock, Wednesday morning, the little corridor in front of the condemned cells suddenly filled with guards. Gruner was told to stand up, and he refused. He was dragged to his feet. There was no last meal, no final request, no last visitor, no rabbi, no warning. Never before at Acre had more than three men been hanged at once—and now there were to be four. The four men began to sing the "Hatikvah," the mournful anthem of Zionism.

> As long as within the heart
> A Jewish soul yearns,
> And forward, towards the east,
> An eye turns to Zion,
>
> Our hope is not yet lost,
> Our hope of two-thousand years
> To be a free people in our land,
> The land of Zion and Jerusalem.

Across the yard, Chaim Wasserman turned over on his cot. Something had awakened him. He glanced at his watch. It was just after four, yet it sounded as if someone was singing. Then he knew. His cell was at the end of the row, reserved for those who received special treatment, closest to the condemned cells. He heard the "Hatikvah". He began shouting, "Livni, boys! Livni, boys! They are hanging Dov Gruner!"[12] The prisoners—eighty-nine LEHI and Irgun men—stood at the grills in their cells. The yard in front of death row was filled with armed guards. From behind came the "Hatikvah". They joined in, so that the four would not die alone. After a while they stopped and listened. From across the yard the "Hatikvah" was not as loud. A half-hour later only two voices could be heard. Another long, agonizing pause, and faintly a single voice. Then there was silence, the shuffle and click of weapons from the guards, the muted twitter from the Arab cells. Then all eighty-nine men sang once more the "Hatikvah". On Thursday, April 17, the British announced the Gruner, Drezner, Kashani, and Alkochi had been hanged. There would be a curfew until further notice.

The Irgun headquarters in Tel Aviv immediately issued orders to kidnap British soldiers to be hanged in retaliation. In a special broadcast the Irgun underground radio warned the British what the executions would mean.

> We do not want to convey that from now on our struggle will turn into a revenge war. No. We are certain that this is not our fallen heroes' desire. Our war of liberation shall continue in all its fields of activity. We shall strike at the British military bases, at the neuralgic points of British rule.
>
> We will no longer be bound by the normal rules of warfare. In future every combatant unit of Irgun will be accompanied by a war court of the Jewish Underground Movement. Every enemy subject who is taken prisoner will immediately be brought before the court, irrespective of whether he is a member of the Army or Civilian Administration. Both are criminal organizations. He will be tried for entering illegally into Palestine, for illegal possession of arms and their use against civilians, for murder, oppression and exploitation; there will be no appeal against the decision of the people's court. Those condemned will be hanged or shot.[13]

Almost the entire British garrison was confined to barracks or kept within the security zones on alert, to frustrate just such an Irgun tactic. As the days slipped by, with the Irgun patrols fruitlessly wandering the streets in search of a vulnerable soldier, tension and anguish grew in the ranks. What made matters much worse was that Meir Feinstein of the Irgun and Moshe Barazani of LEHI were sitting in Jerusalem central prison under sentence of death. Without British hostages in Irgun hands, the sentence would obviously be carried out on April 21—the new date of the execution announced by the British on April 17. There was no possibility of an instant escape or a break-in operation from the outside.

Feinstein and Barazani realized this, and immediately after the four executions in Acre they smuggled out a request for hand grenades to kill both themselves and their executioners on the way to the gallows. Despite the difficulties, the Irgun managed to smuggle in two grenades, hidden in scooped-out oranges. On Monday, April 21, the night before the execution, Rabbi Goldman spent several hours consoling the two young men.

> The rabbis of old used to say that each man is brought into this world for the purpose of fulfilling some task. Some men fulfill what is given them to do in twenty years, some in seventy, and others never at all. For those who never fulfill it and go on living, life no longer has any purpose. That, too, is a kind of death. But in lives such as yours, my sons, death can get no footing at all, for even your death is turned into life.[14]

Then to their horror, on leaving them, the rabbi announced that he would return at dawn to be with them at the time of execution. Neither Feinstein nor Barazani could persuade the rabbi that they did not need spiritual consolation at dawn. The rabbi assumed they were simply being kind. He insisted. They argued. He insisted again, then left to spend the night in the next cell. The two felt they could not reveal their intentions to the rabbi, thereby compromising him, and they would not risk his life. They would not wait until dawn, but cheat the British—even if they could not get their executioners as well. At 11:40 after the decision had been reached; the two stood side by side in the center of the small cell, their arms around each other. Barazani held the grenade between them and detonated it. The British sentries heard the muffled explosion and rushed to the death cell. The two young men, covered in blood, lay in a heap. Barazani's left arm was torn off and lay in a corner. Both had been killed instantly. Each one-armed body was buried according to the prescription of Jewish law, so that Barazani's arm was placed in a separate coffin. The news only increased the Irgun's determination to find a hostage.

In the meantime the Irgun continued to carry out normal military operations. In the week before Barazani and Feinstein died, there were a series of attacks in Tel Aviv, Haifa, and Natanya. On April 21, military cars were attacked in three places, and two jeeps hit mines near Nebi Samuel. On April 23, Wednesday, the *Palestine Post* reported a major incident on the Cairo-Haifa railway. The train was ambushed from both sides while it passed through orange groves. A land mine was detonated under the first-class coach, derailing the train and making it difficult for the British machine guns to do more than spray blindly into the groves. Total casualties were eight killed and twenty-seven wounded. The next day four soldiers were injured when their 15-cwt. lorry hit a mine on the Wilhelmina-Petvah Tikva road three miles south of Jaffa. While satisfying to headquarters, none of these operations had any direct links to the executions or deaths in Jerusalem central prison. Still no hostages had been taken.

Finally a small group from headquarters, tired of listening to the litany of failure reported back by the Irgun patrols, decided to try themselves. Yaakov Amrami, the high command intelligence officer, and for ten years a member of the Palestine police, and Giddy Paglin, along with Dov Cohen (Shimshon) from the GHQ staff, collected Nauum Slonim, a large, heavily built man, Aaron Mizrachi, Paglin's girlfriend Zippora Pearl, and Amrami's wife Hava. On April 24, divided up in two stolen taxis, they began driving back and forth through the streets of Tel Aviv. They had no more luck than the patrols. Finally they parked on Rehov Hayarkon, and the two girls began making the rounds of the bars. They came back to report that there was a very English gentleman, complete with pipe and accent, drinking in the Park Hotel, urging the girls to sing.

The staff was busy preparing a table for the farewell party by the Palestine Orchestra in honor of Charles Munch. The men agreed they had found their hostage. They rushed into the lobby of the hotel, three with pistols, and Amrami with a mask over his face, carrying a submachine gun. Slonim rushed into the bar, leaped onto the Englishman's table and lifted him up by the collar. The others kept their eye on the staff and checked ID cards. One of the three waiters in the dining room was persuaded not to try and make a telephone call. The wires were cut. The Englishman was hustled out and into the waiting car. Hunched down in the back was the hostage, M.M. Collins, sales manager of the Eralite Manufacturing Company of Surbiton, who had arrived the same day by air from Cairo.

The two cars drove carefully to a nearby orange grove. Collins was pulled out and his blindfold removed. In the dim light he could see a half dozen people. Amrami, the man in front of him, checked his identification. At that moment Shimshon came rushing up from the other car, carrying a rope with a hangman's noose. He insisted on doing away with the formalities and hanging the man at once. Amrami asked Collins who he was and what he was doing in Tel Aviv. Collins said he was a simple businessman who had stopped in Palestine. "Why?" Well, he was Jewish. Amrami was stunned. Collins was not a Jewish name—was there any proof? All Collins could think of was that he had been circumcised. Amrami was not impressed—lots of men were circumcised. At this point Shimshon lost all patience and rushed up again. "Why wait? Let's get this over with!" Suddenly, all at once, Collins realized the meaning of the noose, the drift of the questions, and his own totally unexpected peril. One minute drink and pipe in hand in a warm bar, the next totally alone in the hands of strange men about to be killed for no reason at all. His eyes began to glaze over. The blood drained from his face. Stunned, he could barely answer Amrami's questions. He seemed to know nothing of Judaism. His name had been anglicized. He could think of nothing that might help. He stumbled over his words. Shimshon, standing by with his noose, insisted that Amrami stop and let them get on with the hanging. And this was now Amrami's inclination. Collins had let his time run out. Amrami stepped back, and Shimshon stepped forward.

Collins could no longer talk coherently. Then, at the very lip of death, he began to mutter in Hebrew, "Adon Olam Asher Malakh," the poem learned by very small children to thank God for waking them in the morning. Once he had dragged the faint recollection from the depths of his memory, Collins could not stop. He began in Hebrew the Kaddish, the lament for the dead. There was no longer any doubt. Shimshon dropped the rope. Collins was ushered back into the car, and with Shimshon as his escort, was driven back to the Park Hotel. The whole experience had taken less than an hour. The next morning he left for Syria on his way back to England.

After the latest failure the Irgun gave up efforts to find a hostage, and along with LEHI concentrated again on military operations. Road mines were deposited. Bombs placed. In Sarona a bomb killed four and wounded six in an attack on a police billet on April 25. On April 26, the Haifa CID chief was shot and mortally wounded when a taxi suddenly pulled beside his car near the Applinger Hotel on Carmel Avenue. The same day a police inspector and three constables were killed in Tel Aviv. There seemed no end in sight. Jerusalem was still under curfew. The only prospect of change came elsewhere, when, on April 28, the United Nations General Assembly met in special session at Lake Success, and appointed the Special Committee on Palestine (UNSCOP), entrusted with investigating the Palestinian problem and producing a proposal for the General Assembly to consider. As far as the Irgun and LEHI were concerned, the creation of another commission, committee, or board to investigate and suggest some more was an irrelevant exercise. They believed the British would stay until forced to go. Thus, no matter what the United Nations might do or not do, ultimately any future state depended on their own revolt. Lake Success was very far away from the events in Palestine. The conventional Zionists might be attracted by the possibilities inherent in UNSCOP, might begin at once to crank up their propaganda operations, lobby in the world's capitals, seek a good decision—but not the Irgun and LEHI, although their sympathizers and front groups abroad would follow a similar course. In Palestine there were more important matters. On April 29 in Jerusalem, the British discovered the escape tunnel was only a few meters from the main wall. For the eighty-five Jewish prisoners, a mass break had been a real possibility. What the delighted British did not realize was that elsewhere just such a mass break had entered the final stages.

NOTES

1. *Palestine Post*, 21 August 1946.

2. Israel Epstein was killed apparently in an arranged escape that came unglued. During his Roman adventures once again Tavin had a narrow escape from death when a police officer's revolver misfired at point-blank range.

3. *Palestine Post*, 20 November 1946.

4. Menachem Begin, *The Revolt: Story of the Irgun* (New York: Henry Schuman, 1951), p. 231.

5. Ibid., p. 233.

6.　Ibid., p. 234.

7.　*Palestine Post*, 21 January 1947.

8.　Great Britain, *Parliamentary Debates*, Commons, vol. 433, col. 988.

9.　Ibid., col. 2007.

10.　Begin, pp. 163–164.

11.　Ibid., pp. 269–272.

12.　Jan Gitlin, *Conquest of Acre Prison* (Tel Aviv: Hadar, 1962), p. 98.

13.　Ibid., p. 113.

14.　Geula Cohen, *Woman of Violence* (London: Rupert Hart-Davis, 1966), p. 264.

CHAPTER 4

From the Great Prison Escape
To Lake Success:
May–November 1947

Time has shown a constantly accelerated deterioration of conditions in this country. The sands are running out.
—High Commissioner Sir Alan Cunningham

Those tunneling from cell 28 continued to place their hopes in breaking out of the Acre prison sooner or later, but Livni still expressed little enthusiasm. The chances of getting caught remained high, and the right direction for the tunnel was uncertain. Even if the outer wall could be breached, there would be little opportunity to get many men down the shaft and away. Livni wanted something safer and simpler. In a smuggled letter he suggested to the high command that there was a better chance for a mass escape over the top of the various outbuildings, instead of going under the outer wall. The only comment from the high command was, "not feasible." Work on the tunnel continued. Livni kept turning the matter over in his mind with no result. There were plenty of tales of heroic escapes from Acre (the Arab prisoners could recount dozens), only most were fantasies. The men lacked even elementary information about the fortress. Even with Paglin and the others outside at work on the problem, matters did not look very promising.

One day Livni learned that an Arab prisoner, who supplied the kitchen and cells with kerosene for the stoves, had said he could hear women's voices from the storage room. In a prison holding 613 male prisoners—163 Jews including 58 criminal lunatics, and 450 Arabs including 56 criminal lunatics—guarded by male special police and warders, the Arab's story was most curious. Livni decided at once that what the Arab meant was that he could hear voices, some of which were women's. So the kerosene room must be near an outside street. Livni expressed great interest to the Arab—he was eager to hear the women. A few cigarettes changed hands, and Livni was smuggled to the kerosene room to listen. The other members of the prison command, Zettler and Shmulevitz of LEHI, Dov Efrat, Menachem Shiff, and Arie Malatsky of the Irgun soon were slipped into the kerosene room to listen to the women. There *were* women's voices—the kerosene room was next to a street some place in the old city of Acre. Up near the ceiling was a barred window, but there was no way to climb up and look out. Still it did not really matter. The kerosene room was in the outer wall of the fortress—only a wall separated them from the street. Livni wrote a coded message to Begin. As usual, the tiny figures on toilet paper, folded into a small wad, were picked up by the Irgun's prison postman, an Arab hospital employee who was well paid for his efforts. The wad was delivered to the first station in Haifa; from there Jabotinsky's niece passed it to Begin's safe house. This time Begin's answer was positive: the location and prospects of the kerosene room would be carefully examined.

Examining the room's window from the outside was not all that simple. The old city of Acre was entirely Arab, a warren of tiny, twisting alleys, covered passages, strange levels, and unexpected stairs, the whole maze fitted in, around, above and below centuries of previous building. The original architectural base was the crusader port and fortress built by the Knights of St. John of Malta in the twelfth century, after Baudouin I captured the small port in 1104. Lost to Saladin in 1187, recaptured by Richard Coeur de Lion in 1191, Acre remained a crusader stronghold until internal wrangling opened the way for its recapture by Malik el-Ashraf. For four centuries Acre lay abandoned—the ruins of the sacked city were gradually softened by the drifting sands. In the eighteenth century Emir Daher el-Omar restored the town, and his successor, Ahmed el-Jazzar Pasha, rebuilt the fortifications. Jazzar Pasha, along with Sir Sidney Smith, successfully defended the city against Napoleon, but there was no revival of Acre's fortunes—only another restoration by the Ottoman Turks in 1840. By then very little of the crusader city was easily visible; most had disappeared under the sands, been stolen or altered, or incorporated in subsequent construction by new generations of builders. From the normal, front entrance on the north, the citadel appeared impenetrable—a medieval fortress in perfect condition. The visitor entered a small iron gate in the outside ramparts at the sea entrance, walked up a little road under the walls and crossed a narrow bridge into the fortress. Below the bridge in both directions ran a moat, forty feet deep and fifteen feet broad. From the bottom of the moat to the top of the looming wall, the distance was seventy feet. The wall appeared solid, still studded with Napoleanic cannon balls, with only a few windows fifty feet up. Through a huge iron gate at the end of the bridge lay a short corridor, then another iron gate. Beyond this, a small wall, covered with barbed wire, separated the visitor from the prison yard proper and, here, between the gates, was the visiting room. Obviously, no one was going to break in or out through iron gates, across bridges, and through the sea gate in the outer walls. The north side of the citadel, however, was a secure façade, for on the south and west the old city over the years had crept up the walls. There, according to Livni, was the outside window of the kerosene room.

Set in the midst of a wild hodgepodge of lanes, underground foyers, tiny suqs, and cluttered squares of Acre were several market squares, the most famous of which was the large Khan el-Oumdon, the pillared inn, a two-story gallery built at the end of the eighteenth century by Jazzar Pasha, incorporating all sorts of columns, capitals, and oddments from earlier eras. The chaotic old city had long since crept inside the inner walls of the citadel, which had long been used as a prison by the British. In 1947 the citadel was little more than a Turkish topping over long-forgotten crusader ruins.

The Irgun had first to make order out of the maze of old Acre, then discover a clear route into the kerosene room. They needed to move about in an Arab city at a time of extreme tension. Begin assigned Paglin to study an escape operation. Not long after Livni's letter arrived at headquarters, two Christian Arabs, identically dressed in dark striped suits with round high hats, wandered into the old city of Acre. Paglin was having a first-hand look, and it was a confused one. The warren of the streets was filled with Arabs, some in the elegant suits of the Levantine trader, most in the motley of the Middle East—Western pajamas, old puttees, and jellabas, with women in long black dresses. The noise was deafening. The smells various and not always pleasant. The street teemed with donkeys and splay-backed horses, underfoot were children and curs. Goods tumbled out of the shops to be displayed on the streets: oranges, tinned tuna, radio tubes, melons, sweets, old pipes. Fishing boats were drawn up for repairs in the corners of little squares, surrounded by damp nets and yesterday's fish. Great slabs of purple-dyed lambs hung in the butchers. Flies were everywhere. Wandering in and out of the crowds, the two Christians began to move along the part of the old city that backed up against the citadel. Turning one of the endless corners while trying to stay next to the outer wall, they found they had reached a narrow lane just beneath the wall—there, high up, was the barred window to the kerosene room. And another beside it. Even more astonishing, directly beneath the windows was a strange bridge between the outer wall and an Arab house on the other side of the lane—a perfect platform, permitting access to the windows. Apparently, when some older houses were torn down, a roof was left to form the bridge. In any case, for Paglin's purposes, the windows were ideally located—if there were a way into the lane. After a long delay, while the two bored gentlemen in pinstripe suits yawned and gaped, Paglin decided that a jeep could get down the lane and that he could find some sort of route from the wall gate to the lane. The two then wandered on off toward the new city.

Once out of his fancy dress, Paglin contacted an Irgun man employed in the Ministry of Public Works in Haifa, who managed to get plans of Acre. Unfortunately for Paglin, the plan bore only marginal resemblance to what he remembered from his scouting tour—either the British blueprint was inaccurate, or the neat lines and boxes could not be translated into effective directions. They returned to Acre. This time Paglin posed as a salesman for modern bakery installations (his father's business), and the two wandered about looking for Arab bakeries, until they once more reached the bridge and outside wall. Once more the two began tracking about, putting together a route from the bridge to the outer gate that would take transport. As the route, suitable for a small lorry, began to emerge from the maze, Paglin drew his own plan of old Acre, with each turn and twist well marked and described. There was now a way into the kerosene room. Livni assured Paglin that with a little help from their friends on the outside, the prisoners could make their way to the room. Paglin and Begin agreed. Livni had his escape plan.

Inside the prison, Livni shared his knowledge with as few as possible until the last moment. The only ones told were the Irgun-LEHI prison commanders. The very first bad news was that the total of escapees was absolutely limited by the available hiding places outside: no more than forty-one could be absorbed into the available safe houses of the Irgun and LEHI. The high command decided that thirty Irgun and eleven LEHI people should be chosen. Inside, Zettler felt that the percentages were wrong, and that LEHI should have twelve escapees. Livni would not budge. So Zettler started out unhappy that only eleven LEHI people were to go, and Livni started out unhappy that thirty-one Irgun people had to be left. There was nothing to do but settle down to the inside problems, since Begin absolutely refused to consider more than forty-one. The choice of who would go had to be made by Livni and Zettler. This was relatively easy, since only experienced men were needed outside—trained Hok men, Bren gunners, active service people with British accents or demolition skills. None were told of their selection, to keep down rumor and gossip. A variety of social maneuvers were launched to persuade the elected to begin shaving the glorious beards that had become a prison fashion. Gradually, one by one, the beards began to disappear. Livni did not shave his flowing red one, for as an older man he could not appear to participate in the more youthful fashions. As the beards began to come off in March, Livni even managed to arrange photographs of the escapees, taken with a camera smuggled into prison by the crew of the Irgun refugee ship *Ben Hecht*. These were smuggled out to be used in new identification papers. The prisoners with special treatment—which included civilian clothes—were persuaded to ask for additional clothing, so that the other prisoners would have something decent to wear on the sabbath. The relatives were asked, the new sabbath clothes arrived, and the escapees would be suitably attired when the time came.

The key to the inside escape, however, remained the route to the kerosene room. Normally it was blocked by two iron gates. Livni asked that Paglin smuggle him in enough explosives to blow both gates—the charge would not have to be very large, and smuggling had reached a fine art at Acre. The explosives came mixed in tins of jam labeled Nobel Brothers, Glasgow. When a British officer tasted the wares of the Nobel brothers during inspection of prisoners' presents, he was appalled that anyone, even convicted terrorists, would be interested in using the stuff. As far as eating it went, he was quite right. The detonators came hidden in the false bottom of a seven-gallon oil drum. The whole lot, including homemade grenades and the sabbath clothing, was kept in the tunnel shaft. Livni's remaining and most difficult task was to maintain a semblance of normality, while Paglin completed the more complicated outside operation.

The high command nominated Dov Cohen (Shimshon) as operational commander. His experience in the British army, where he became a staff sergeant and won a Military Medal, coupled wth his British accent, were highly desirable assets. Most important was his singleness of purpose as a commander of the Hok assault squads. In Operation Acre, no matter how many details Livni and Paglin took into account, one man of initiative and confidence would finally have to be in charge. Cohen and Paglin prepared the assault plan. A route was plotted from the Irgun settlement at Shumi at Benyamina in Samaria, about sixty kilometers from Acre. This reduced the chances of running into British blocks or convoys. A thirty-four-man Irgun convoy would consist of two three-quarter-ton lorries and one three-ton lorry, disguised as a British army engineering unit. It would be led by a jeep manned by Cohen, wearing the uniform of a captain in the Royal Engineers, and two British privates. All the drivers and guards would be fitted out in appropriate uniforms, with pips and patches. Another Irgun squad, disguised as Arabs, would move separately to an area overlooking the camp of the Second Battalion of the Sixth Airborne Division outside Acre. As soon as the break began, they would drop in a few diversionary mortar shells—mostly sound and fury, as the Irgun mortars were more noisy than dangerous. Cohen's major problem lay not in getting his men to Acre but in protecting the prisoners' escape route after the break.

He and Paglin prepared a series of holding and covering blocks to isolate the route between the kerosene room and the road to Benyamina. The major danger would come from the British police station north of the citadel toward the new city and perhaps from British security forces moving in from the direction of Haifa. Cohen intended to lay mines on all the access roads, leaving only his escape route clear. The lorries would bring in thirty-four cases of box mines and two cases of kilostone ones. The British would have no difficulty clearing the roads afterward, but the short delay would be all the Irgun needed. The block positions, each manned by three men, had only to keep the roads closed for ten minutes—by then the operation would have succeeded or failed. Cohen and Paglin found one obstacle in getting the small lorries to the side of the citadel through the maze of the old city. Again they visited the area; again they went painstakingly over the route. The drivers and guards were briefed regularly. The second in command, Solomon, dressed as a British corporal, would wind his way in a small lorry past Suq el-Abyad into the narrow lane under the bridge, where his telephone repair crew would raise one ladder and scramble up it. Then a second ladder would reach the outside wall of the kerosene room. This had to be done out of sight of the guards directly above the bridge. Once the wall was blown, Livni's people on the inside could begin operations.

To move thirty-four men and four vehicles into a heavily patrolled British area, blow the side out of a prison in the midst of an Arab city, and anticipate driving out before the British could react was not actually as improbable as it sounded. Inside the citadel were two British officers, two British sergeants, four policemen, and 132 Arab guards—not an overwhelming force. Even if the guards on the roof reacted promptly in the noise and confusion—diversions Livni intended to use to maximum advantage—the intention of the escapees would be unclear. No one would expect a simultaneous breakin and breakout.

Livni decided he could seal off the Jewish cells in the eastern wing from the British quarters and Arab cells in the northern wing with a wall of fire and smoke. For the conflagration Livni prepared a large quantity of olive oil mixed with kerosene. Poured on rags it would create a tall fire, much smoke and confusion. Finally, several homemade grenades were to be tossed at the guards on the roof. When Paglin visited Livni in the room between the gates, bringing along his tin of marmalade, the last details were in place, except that only one of the windows was in the kerosene room. On Paglin's departure, Livni gave him the final piece: "Please go and see my family and tell them I am well. They live in Levaia Okna Street."[1] In Russian *levaia okna* means left window. There was a password, so that the men on the outside could be sure they had reached their own people: "anu" from the outside, "banu" from the inside. All that was needed was the final authorization from Begin and the high command.

With two weeks to go, Livni, whose peculiar requests and strange actions increasingly concerned his innocent colleagues, insisted that during the afternoon some prisoners play noisy games in the yard, while certain others were to sit in their cells reading. The ones in the cells had been chosen to escape, those outside to create a diversion. Still only the Irgun and LEHI commanders knew of the break, along with Michael Ashbel, a demolitions expert who, while in the death cell, had written the popular ballad "On the Barricades." Ashbel was asked to make the charges for the gates between the cells and the kerosene room. Finally, one at a time, the chosen prisoners were brought in and asked if they wanted to remain behind—no one did. Then each was told what was to happen and what his special task would be on the day of the break. As the days slipped by, the other prisoners still did not know there was to be an escape. Not until the very morning of Sunday, May 4, did they learn that they would have to stay, to risk the wrath of the British or attacks by Arab prisoners. It was not an easy task for the commanders, but explaining the priorities helped. Also, the group remaining had a special task. With hard soap in socks, broom handles, and whatever came to hand, they were to bar the way to any pursuit, especially by the Arabs. Although the break was timed for the period immediately after the Arabs were locked in their cells, at 4:15 in the afternoon, there were always a few Arab prisoners wandering in the yard, and the chance of others breaking out in the confusion was excellent. Few Arabs had any love for Jewish terrorists.

The hour was chosen. The Arabs would be locked up; the British blocks would not be up for two hours; the security forces would be at Sunday strength; and inside the prison Livni had access to the exercise yard. (Night, of course, in the old city was hopeless, and the roads would all be blocked.) At 4:00 on escape day, the same group of prisoners began their noisy games in the yard. In the cells the escape groups changed into civilian clothes. The first lorry was to enter the Continental Gate near Kapou Bourj Tower at exactly 4:15. Sitting on the floor of the cells, Livni and the rest could only wait for the detonation. They had been divided into three groups. The first was led by Menachem Malatzky (Arie), twenty-six, who had been commander at Haifa before his arrest, just before the sweep at Bat-Yam. They were to rush down the corridor, with Malatzky and Ashbel in the lead. They would blow the first gate, wait one minute, blow the second gate, wait one minute, then rush on to the kerosene room. This group would have the best chance, since they would be in the small lorry and on the way out before the other two groups reached the kerosene room. The second group of twenty-two included Livni and Zettler. Led by Dov Efrat, armed with clubs and staves, they would hold off any Arab attack and create the wall of fire. Three minutes after Malatzky's group they should be on their way. The last group of eight, under Menachem Shiff, was to toss grenades at the guards on the roof, and hold the end of the corridor until the second lot had gone by. They would be the last out, and would have the most difficult time. Haim Apelbaum, who had been caught after a LEHI raid on the Haifa railway workshops, sentenced to death, and had his sentence commuted, told Menachem Shiff on the morning of the break that he had a premonition things would not go well. Shiff, knowing that Apelbaum's wife was pregnant, reassured him. Livni and Paglin believed that Cohen would pull it off. They waited. Nothing happened. The minutes ticked away. Only Livni knew that if the operation were cancelled it would take place the same time the following day. The rest assumed it was now or never.

Outside, in the old city, Solomon was lathered in sweat and cursing. He had spent much time forcing the lorry through the Arab crowds, jockeying with mules and sweet sellers in the narrow lanes. He finally cleared the Suq el-Abyad and pushed on, up the twisting roads to the rear of the citadel. The lorry stopped. Out jumped a telephone repair crew of the Royal Engineers. Solomon stood back while the first ladder was raised to the bridge. Up scrambled Yehuda Afirion with two heavy boxes of telephone equipment, which on closer examination would have been revealed as two twenty-kilo detonating devices to pierce the three-foot stone wall. Solomon passed him the second ladder, which just reached a ledge beneath the two windows. Festooned with equipment, Afirion started up the ladder. It swayed and there was a sharp crack. A rung had broken. Corporal Solomon hurriedly scrambled up the first ladder to the bridge, rushed underneath Afirion, and provided a new rung with his shoulder. Afirion hurriedly taped his charges not only to the *levaia okna* but, just in case, to the other window as well. With Solomon grunting under him, Afirion inserted the fuse cord and announced he was done. None of the guards on the roof above had noticed anything strange—in any case they could not see directly down to the bridge. Solomon and Afirion moved back down the narrow street to the corner. It had taken Solomon seven minutes to get from the gate to the end of the lane. Inside, the minutes had dragged out like years. Livni had just about decided it was time to change back into prison clothing and wait for the morrow.

At 4:22 a thunderous explosion rocked the narrow lane. Chunks of masonry and rock smashed back and forth in the air and tumbled onto the bridge. Solomon, Afirion, and the rest could see first a billowing cloud of smoke, then a huge hole gaping in the citadel wall. They rushed for the ladder to the bridge. Exactly three minutes from the moment of the blast someone should appear at the hole.

To the prisoners inside, it felt as if the entire citadel had shuddered. Almost at once the Arab prisoners began screaming hysterically. The guards were stunned, unable to decide what had happened. Malatzky and Ashbel rushed from the cells clutching the two detonation charges, followed by their squad. In seconds they reached the first iron gate. The charge was set. Everybody pulled back to the end of the corridor. The charge detonated. The gate was torn loose. They waited, counting out a minute, then rushed down the corridor to the second gate. The second charge was laid. They pulled back down the corridor. The charge detonated. The gate collapsed. This time the minute seemed even longer. Then Malatzky rushed forward into the kerosene room. The outside wall was ripped open. He dashed over and leaned out, nearly butting heads with Solomon who was shouting "anu!" Malatzky replied "banu!"—rather unnecessarily, since Solomon was already dragging him through the hole. Malatzky's men crowded in behind him, filling the kerosene room. They clambered down the two ladders and rushed to the end of the lane and the waiting lorry, free at last.

Dov Efrat's second group split up, one section keeping an eye on the Arab prisoners, the other laying out the materials for the wall of fire. The two explosions that blew the gates simply added to the confusion. There was a huge screen of smoke and fire in the prison yard, which cut off the northern administrative wing and created more chaos among the Arab prisoners. All the Arabs were screaming. Some ran amok directly into the barbed-wire fences. The bewildered Arab policemen assumed a breakout was underway and began firing into the crowd. Some prisoners rushed toward their cells to escape the fire. Others, fearing further explosions, broke out of their cells. The yard was soon filled with a howling mob. By then the excitement had set off those locked in the lunatic cells. Over the din their wild howls created further panic. Meanwhile Efrat's group was groping down the smoke-filled corridor toward the kerosene room. Menachem Shiff's men stepped into the yard and tossed their grenades up at the guards on the roof. These new explosions caused renewed panic among the Arabs, who ran screaming through the smoke and flames, smashing into walls and each other. There was no need to protect Shiff's retreat— the Arabs had still not discovered what was happening and neither had the guards. Shiff's group, too, passed through the corridor and into the kerosene room. Like the others, they piled out through the hole and dropped to the bridge—the wobbly ladder had collapsed into a heap of splinters. The other Jewish prisoners sat out the chaos in their cells. Uncertain as to what was happening below, the British made no effort to enter the yard. The Arabs, dashing madly through the yard and corridors, suddenly discovered the blasted wall. Out of 394 Arab prisoners, 214 made the delightful discovery during the next hour that there was a way out. They jumped to the bridge, then into the lane, and disappeared into the old city.

The last two groups of Irgun-LEHI escapees had a bit more trouble disappearing into the background. While some rushed on toward the Continental Gate, where the three-ton lorry waited, others piled into the smaller lorry waiting at the end of the lane. The driver gunned the engine and the lorry moved off, then sputtered and stopped. The driver tried the ignition, without any effect. He tried again and again. Shiff got everyone out and began to push. Incredibly, with the driver still working at the ignition, the lorry began to move down the narrow streets powered by a motley crowd of civilians, some with long beards, soldiers, and the odd Arab. The Arab crowds took increasing notice of the strange caravan—something was happening at the citadel, and the push-a-lorry crowd did not belong in the old city. Someone leaped up from a café table and tossed a coffee cup. Someone else threw a chair. Livni told Solomon to shoot in the air. The Arabs kept circling them. One, more daring than the rest, boldly reached out and grabbed Livni by the arm. "Enter this shop, where you will find good shelter."[2] Livni pulled his arm away, but the Arab kept insisting. Finally Livni hit him firmly on the jaw, and the Arab staggered back, letting go. Livni ran on after the others. A nasty crowd closed up behind the lorry. Others rushed in front to warn the men clustered near the gate about the strange lorry. On and on the men pushed, as the screaming and shouting crowd edged closer. Suddenly the engine caught. The pushers leaped on board and the driver hit the gas. Odds and ends of makeshift missiles were still bouncing off the cab, but the real danger lay ahead. As the lorry came within sight of the gate, a crowd of Arabs began pushing closed the wooden door. A seething mob separated the lorry from the gate. Shiff ordered a grenade tossed into the crowd—the same noisy but harmless variety used against the guards. The noise was enough. The crowd disappeared into the cafés and down the lanes. The wooden door was pushed open, and the lorry rumbled through to link up with those who had gone before, waiting in the large lorry outside the gate. The two lorries moved off, taking a by-road that would meet the Haifa-Lebanon road at a point free of mines. A single burst of fire hit the second lorry as it moved off—it was the only organized opposition. Inside Haim Apelbaum grunted and leaned forward. He was shot in the stomach, mortally wounded. His premonition had been right. He turned his head and said to Shiff, "Menachem, I told you, remember."[3] Then he died, the only casualty in either lorry. The escape had gone like clockwork.

The diversion party experienced no trouble. They moved into place, waited for the sound of the kerosene-room bomb, dropped in their mortar shells, and withdrew. Unfortunately for them, an Arab on horseback reported his suspicions about the strange "Arabs." The British put up roadblocks to look for what they thought was a green truck. The Arab had said "gris," so when the grey truck filled with Arabs who understood no English passed by the block—"You stupid Arabs, have you seen a green truck?"—it produced only elaborate shrugs and a garble of Arabic. The other diversion parties were successful—five British soldiers were injured by a mine on the Haifa road. In his rush to get everyone away, however, Solomon forgot to call in one of the diversion groups. As the last lorry passed, the men on board called to the commander, Avshalom Haviv, that it was over. Haviv, however, felt he had to wait for a formal order from Solomon to withdraw. He was still waiting when the British arrived. Elsewhere the blocks withdrew in good order. By then disaster had already struck, not to the last lorry, but to the first—the one everyone assumed had driven off free and clear in the first minutes.

Malatzky, Ashbel, Shmulevitz, and the others in the first lorry thought so too. Sitting in the back, they talked and laughed as the lorry twisted through the old city and out the Continental Gate, then along the seashore. There was no reason to suspect the military lorry, with all its lettering neatly painted, driven by a uniformed driver. Someone did. All day Sunday the hot dusty wind, the *kamsin,* had blown into Acre, and seeking to escape the heat, a group of British paratroopers had been on the beach a few hundred yards from the old city. When the charges detonated outside the kerosene room, they ran out of the water, scooped up their arms, and ran across the railway line toward the sea road. They saw the light lorry shoot out of the gate and down to the sea road. One of them opened fire on the lorry, and the others joined in

Inside the lorry Shmulevitz noticed holes appearing in the sides. There were groans from the men. The truck was obviously drawing fire, but from the inside no one could tell what was happening. Dov Cohen in his captain's uniform, along with two others, Nissim Levy and Zallman Lifshitz, was waiting by the jeep at his command block on the Naharia road. He left Levy and Lifshitz at the jeep, and rushed toward the British troops coming up from the beach, shouting, "Stop shooting!" At the same time the driver, trying to dodge the British fire, drove past Cohen and directly into a clump of cactus. The lorry bounced back, teetered, and collapsed on its left side. The men began to stumble out. The British troops thought there was something very strange about an Engineers captain carrying a Bren gun, and then about the crowd of civilians tumbling out of the back of the lorry. They began spraying fire into the rear of the truck. Malatzky was shot in the leg, Baruch Smukler's elbow was shattered. Nearly everyone seemed injured. Gershon Gradovsky, under the name Haim Brener, had been interned in Eritrea, then was brought back and sentenced to ten years. Since 1943 his life had been for the Irgun, and now his death was with it. He was hit through the neck, stumbled a few feet, and collapsed into the roadside ditch. Others were moaning on the ground. No one knew what was happening or where to go. The British continued to spray them with rifle fire. Shmulevitz began running up hill toward the Moslem cemetery. Suddenly a British officer appeared, firing a rifle. Shmulevitz put up his arm to keep the others from running directly into his line of fire. There was a crack, the rifle bullet tore through Shmulevitz's arm, and thudded into the chest of Shimon Amrami. They ran on.

Suddenly the firing slackened off. They realized that the British officer running toward them was Dov Cohen. The British paratroopers were still uncertain about the captain, but held their fire. Cohen yelled in Hebrew for those who could to follow him. Some had been hit in the legs and could not leave the ditch. Itzhak Kuznevsky, also wounded, decided to stay on with them in the ditch. The others rushed after Cohen. They came up to a British patrol lorry with two unarmed troopers aboard. Cohen and most of the men leaped directly onto the lorry, forcing it to move alongside the Irgun jeep. The Irgun arms were hurriedly transferred into it. The driver leaped in, and again the starter ground uselessly. The lorry had been shot up in the burst of fire from the beach, and the petrol tank was pierced.

All was still not lost; for at that moment, from the other direction, came an Arab driving an elderly truck. Cohen fired a single shot in the air, and the truck clattered to a halt. Cohen ordered the Arab out. The Arab was outraged. It was his truck. Meanwhile, Amnon was putting the Irgun arms in the back of the truck, and Shmulevitz arrived with Smukler on one arm and Amrami on the other, both covered with blood. It could be only a matter of seconds before the British troops realized that Cohen was a fake. The driver, Shimshon Vilner, jumped to the cab to pull out the Arab. Cohen then pulled the trigger of the Bren gun, and the Arab driver collapsed onto the road; but the burst of fire also hit Vilner, killing him on the spot. Only two of the others could drive, and both were wounded. Amnon Moshkovitz, dripping with blood, managed to get behind the wheel, start the engine, and roll the lorry across the road, but that was all. The British had opened fire again, and Cohen realized there was no longer any hope. He ran forward with his Bren, to give cover to the men who might try to get across the fields. There was a burst of fire and he collapsed near the Irgun jeep. Lying near him was Zallman Lifshitz, shot down giving covering fire. Nissim Levy, the last of the blocking party at the command post, was shot in the side, through the lungs. He was twisting on the ground in extreme pain, his blood bubbling in his throat.

There were only six left who could move at all. No one was sure what had happened to the others. Nissim Benado was badly hit, but had staggered off some place. Some men were lying in the ditch by the lorry. Nissim Kazas was still beside the Arab lorry. Shmulevitz and Moshe Salomon, who was so far unscathed, followed by Josef Dar, ran into a field of wheat in the faint hope of hiding there. Three others, badly hit, came staggering after them, but were wounded again in heavy fire. The three—

Amrami, Ashbel, and Smukler—collapsed beside the road. The British troops rushed up and found them lying in their own blood. Flushed and excited at having gunned down some terrorists, the British soldiers shot each of them again three times in the stomach. They missed Smukler but guaranteed Amrami and Ashbel a painful death, for their wounds were mortal. The British began spraying the wheat field with fire. The British knew that sooner or later they would get their men. So did Shmulevitz. He stood up and raised his hands.

A British soldier rushed toward him, shouting that the captain was dead and now it was Shmulevitz's turn. The sun glinted on the soldier's red hair and on his rifle. Shmulevitz kept shouting that he was surrendering. The red haired soldier paid no attention—"Shut up, bloody Jew!"—and pulled the trigger. Nothing happened. He pulled it again and again. The magazine was empty. He turned and shouted for another rifle. At that point someone began shouting, "Shmulevitz, don't escape!" The vice-superintendent of the prison, Sedergreen, who had grown fond of Shmulevitz in his role of prisoner's representative, apparently thought he was still attempting to escape and would be shot down. Shmulevitz wanted only to surrender to someone who wouldn't shoot him in the process. Sedergreen stood between Shmulevitz and the British soldiers. Salomon stood up and helped Dar to his feet. They were manhandled to a nearby British lorry, beaten on the way, and tossed in on top of the dead and wounded.

The floor of the lorry was a charnel house, a heap of dead, dying, and wounded. One British soldier still wanted to beat those who were conscious, but an Irish soldier held him off until the lorry got underway. It was obvious that Michael Ashbel was dying, but he kept saying, "It will be all right yet. There is nothing to worry about." The lorry lurched to a stop and Amnon Moshkovitz was thrown into the back. This meant that only Nissim Benado had evaded capture, and he had been badly wounded. All the others in Malatzky's group were dead, dying, or wounded, except Moshe Salomon. The British lorry was still standing in the middle of the road after Moshkovitz had been taken aboard, when an Egged bus filled with passengers stopped alongside. The passengers looked down into the back of the lorry, filled with battered and bleeding men. Ashbel called out, "Jews! See how we are dying for you!" The lorry started up and the Egged bus pulled away with its stunned and horrified passengers. The lorry drew up in front of the Acre police station just north of the citadel. The prisoners were dragged out, staggering and stumbling, those less wounded helping the others. They were shoved into a cell, and collapsed on the concrete floor. They asked for a doctor to tend the wounded and were told to shut up. There would be no doctor. The minutes stretched into hours—it was clear that the wounded would be allowed to die. Shimon Amrami died first. He told Shmulevitz, "Greet all the boys. Tell them to have no mercy, no consideration. Let them carry on.'' His voice ebbed with his strength; then just before the end, "Write to my brother and sisters; try to cheer them up.'' Then very softly, "Mati, avenge, avenge!'' He was dead. Nissim Levy was next, a long and painful death, for the bullet through his lungs created a wound that suffocated him in his own blood. No matter which way he twisted or turned, sat up or lay down, there was no relief. He screamed until the end. Ashbel faded slowly away, his hand growing colder in Shmulevitz's. Cheerful to the last, he murmured, "Don't worry, it will still be good. We'll pay 'em yet.'' Then he too was dead. Six hours after they put them in the cell, the British moved the remaining wounded to the hospital. Of the group that had first come through the hole in the wall the previous afternoon, only Nissim Benado was free, and he died of his wounds on Monday in a hideout in Haifa. Cohen was dead, along with Levy and Lifshitz, five Irgun men from the attack party had been captured, and Apelbaum was killed in the second lorry. It was a bloody day,

For those in the second and third lorry, it had also been a very long day; for their troubles did not end once they crossed the Haifa-Lebanon road, slipping along the back-roads toward the Naharia Road. Almost as soon as the two-lorry convoy turned away from the sea road, an empty British lorry began trailing them. The guard sitting next to the driver leaned out and began firing a revolver into the back of the Irgun vehicle. Livni ordered one of his men holding a Bren to shoot back. The Bren was jammed, the breech filled with sand. It would take a while to unclog, but the trailing lorry had picked up speed, and the soldier was still shooting. Suddenly Efrat leaned forward and tossed one of the homemade noise grenades into the road in front of the British. There was a pause, followed by a loud explosion and a burst of smoke. The trailing lorry braked sharply, and the Irgun convoy pulled away. The two lorries turned off the main road in order to by-pass the Acre-Safad road. They felt lucky at getting no reaction from a British army jeep parked near the crossroads—inside they saw British soldiers and a Bren gun. Actually this was the Irgun jeep, manned only by the dead bodies of Dov Cohen and Zallman Lifshitz. A little later they saw an abandoned lorry skewed across the road, but they had no idea that this was the bloody end of the first group.

About two kilometers further on they caught up with two men in civilian clothes, both known to Livni. He found out what had happened to Cohen and the first group. The convoy continued on the Shfaram-Nazareth road. Livni's big lorry overtook the smaller. Some extra passengers and Apelbaum were transferred to the big one, the canvas sides tied closed, and the convoy drove off. As the road began to climb the hills toward Nazareth, a British convoy—a real one—was sighted moving toward the Irgun lorries. Just as it came opposite, the "British" guard in the small lorry popped his head through the sun window on the roof and snapped off an elegant salute. The salute was elegantly returned, and the two convoys passed. By six that evening, curfew time, they had reached Kibbutz Daliyya, where they were to abandon the lorries and move to Benyamina on foot.

Livni talked to two Haganah men in the kibbutz, insisting they not contact the police until nine. The only trouble was that no one really knew how to get to Benyamina by the back roads. Livni, who had been in the area six years before, set out in the general direction, using a familiar Arab village as a guide. The column moved across the hills, avoiding the road. Although they ran into two Arab workers, no alarm was given—Livni simply asked the way to a nearby Arab village and moved on. Within a half-hour they reached the vineyards of Zichron Yaacov. They moved around them and directly to the Benyamina base, skirting the fence of a brightly lit British army base. Inside Nahalat Jabotinsky they had something to eat, shaved off the remaining beards, and waited for dawn to see if the British would cordon off the area. The LEHI people moved out. At eight the following morning, Paglin arrived with a car and driver; and other cars were available from Nahalat Jabotinsky. The escapees were split up and sent off to safe houses or to places in fighting units for normal military activities. Paglin and Livni drove back to Tel Aviv on Arab secondary roads not patrolled by the British. The great escape was over, and at great cost: five of the attacking party captured and four dead; four killed, seven wounded, and all but one recaptured in the first group; and one killed in the second group.

In part it was the very number of casualties, coupled with the huge number of escapees—251, counting all the Arabs—that produced the world-wide impact. An underground Jewish army had assaulted an apparently impregnable British citadel in the midst of an Arab city. They shot their way in, shot their way out and went to ground. The next morning the security forces were still uncertain what had happened; they assumed that both iron gates had been blown from the outside. The *Palestine Post* reported that 251 had escaped—131 Arabs and 120 Jews, that fifteen were dead—one in a captain's uniform of the Royal Engineers, and that fifteen other terrorists had been captured. British communiqué no. 117 on May 5 stated that 171 Arabs and 21 Jews were still at large. The newspapers afterwards reported daily on the recapture of the Arab prisoners—one eventually made it to Syria. For a week the world's press had another Palestine field day: daring exploit, tragedy on the beach, romantic Acre citadel. The *New York Herald Tribune* reported that the execution of this most dangerous and difficult underground mission was perfect. The attack was spread all over the front of the British newspapers as well. Outrage was expressed in the Commons. Members felt it was impossible for the government to impose order merely by force.

In May 1947, this was the only visible intention of the British government. The General Assembly special session opened on April 28 at Lake Success, twelve days after Gruner and the others were hanged, and six days before the great jail break. While there was no apparent sense of urgency in London or Jerusalem, there was in the United Nations; for here was a great opportunity for international conciliation under the auspices of the new world organization. East-West tension had grown in the past year, but had yet to freeze into the cold war. In March President Truman instituted an aid program to Greece and Turkey to prevent a communist takeover. In June Secretary of State George C. Marshall proposed a massive aid program for Europe—both Eastern and Western Europe; for then the lines were not yet clear. The Berlin blockade, the Czechoslovakia *coup d'état*, and the Korean War were all still in the future. In the spring of 1947, only the pessimists had given up hope for conciliation.

The problem of Palestine, about which few United Nations delegates knew anything but a mix of slogans and biblical references, would make an excellent beginning. Of the great powers only Britain seemed intimately concerned, and the British themselves had called for United Nations intervention. The Zionists were delighted with the new forum, for they had no hopes of British concession or Arab moderation. At Lake Success they pleaded, as a very small remnant of an ancient people, for a homeland in Palestine, mixing moral consideration, interpretations of international law, biblical arguments, and whenever possible, behind-the-scenes politicking. The Arabs, on the other hand, were hampered by their insistence that Palestine was an Anglo-Arab affair, that the United Nations could not decide the destiny of an Arab land, that nothing but an Arab Palestine would do. Although the Zionists were really as rigid as the Arabs, their posture remained flexible, their arguments reasonable, and their admiration for the processes of the United Nations great. Substituting for Ben-Gurion, who did not want to leave the Mandate, Dr. Abba Hillel Silver presented the case for Zionism with eloquence and passion.

> The Jewish people belongs in this society of nations. Surely the Jewish people is no less deserving than other peoples whose national freedom and independence have been established and whose representatives are now seated here. The Jews were your allies in the war, and joined their sacrifices to yours to achieve a common victory. The representatives of the people which gave to mankind spiritual and ethical values, inspiring human personalities and sacred texts which are your treasured possessions, and which is now rebuilding its national life in its ancient homeland, will be welcomed before long by you to this noble fellowship of the United Nations.[4]

An unstated factor reinforcing the Zionist argument was the holocaust: the shadows of Dachau, Treblinka, and Auschwitz lay across the session.

The Arabs seemed truculent and negative. They wanted an independent Arab Palestine—no partition, no cantons, no compromise with justice: the land was theirs. The United Nations had no right to give away what was Arab in history and population. The holocaust, biblical quotations, secret agreements, and specious historical arguments were irrelevant to the basic, obvious fact: Palestine had been Arab for many centuries. Henry Catton of the Arab Higher Committee attempted to explain the Arab arguments and the Zionist position.

> The Zionists claim Palestine on the grounds that at one time, more than two thousand years ago, the Jews had a kingdom in a part of it. Were this argument to be taken as a basis for settling international issues, a dislocation of immeasurable magnitude would take place. It would mean the redrawing of the map of the world. It has been said that you cannot set back the hands of the clock of history by twenty years. What should be said when an effort is made to set the clock of history back by twenty centuries in an attempt to give away a country on the ground of a transitory historical association?[5]

The Arabs wanted all, and justice is indivisible.

In January they turned down the British plan that gave them much and promised them more. What should have been a position of strength—five Arab delegations, sympathizers in Moslem lands, a good case, important friends—began to erode. In a world in which no issue appeared clear cut with justice all on one side, how could the Arabs be so uncompromising?

The delegates, dedicated to compromise, looked to compromise for a solution. Few really knew very much about Palestine, even after the debates and the flood of propaganda, only that it had somehow become their responsibility. The obvious step seemed to be some sort of investigating committee—tactics like that finally led the British to Lake Success and the Mandate to the edge of anarchy. Still, what else could reasonably be done? Although opinion differed on the composition of such a committee, the American preference for a neutral group of small nations gained ground. The British were willing. The Russians seemed less interested in hampering an investigation than in expediting British withdrawal from the Mandate. The result was the establishment of an eleven-nation group, the United Nations Special Committee on Palestine, UNSCOP, composed of delegates from Australia, Canada, Czechoslovakia, Guatemala, India, Iran, the Netherlands, Peru, Sweden, Uruguay, and Yugoslavia. The delegates were a mixed bag: a Moslem Indian without international experience, two embarrassingly pro-Zionist converts from supposedly neutral Latin America, a pro-Arab Persian, and several competent men quite innocent of Middle Eastern matters. Justice Emil Sandström of Sweden was chosen chairman, and Dr. Ralph Bunche, director-general of the Trusteeship Council, was detailed to aid the committee.

There would thus be one more committee, the twenty-second since the establishment of the Mandate. In Palestine few had any faith that such an international expedition would fashion an accommodation of any sort, much less one satisfactory to all. The Zionists, especially the Revisionists, did not believe that the British intended to evacuate the Mandate. They thought UNSCOP a delaying tactic. Actually, High Commissioner Cunningham and the Mandate authorities had no clear idea what London intended, or ever had intended. They had to stumble along day by day, trying to keep the machine running and waiting for a firm directive. On May 29, Bevin insisted at the Labour party conference at Margate that Britain would not give up its Middle East position—whatever that meant. The Arabs had their doubts about the British, knew well enough the intentions of the Jews, and refused to cooperate with UNSCOP. They worried mainly about their own inadequacies and the intentions and capacities of their avowed allies. In Palestine nothing much had changed, except for the worse, as everyone waited without enthusiasm for the expected arrival of UNSCOP in mid-June.

For the Irgun high command the most immediate concern was the capture of the five men in the attacking party during the Acre operation. There was no doubt that they would be charged and convicted of a capital offense under the emergency regulations. Two, Mikhaloff and Zitterbaum, were too young to be hanged, but the three others, Nakar, Weiss, and Haviv, were not. Although Irgun-LEHI operations continued—railway sabotage, mines on the roads, sniping in Haifa and Jerusalem—the Irgun wanted hostages. On Monday, June 9, Police Sergeant E. P. Hackett and Constable P. C. Ward of Ramat Gan station were standing and laughing at the edge of the Galei Gil swimming pool near their beach chairs. They had just had a dip and were toweling off. The pool orchestra swung into a Strauss waltz. At the pool gate a young couple without tickets pushed by the ticket taker. Outraged, he insisted they must have tickets. Suddenly a man appeared with a handkerchief over his face, carrying a white revolver. The ticket taker decided they did not need to buy tickets after all. He and the ticket seller were herded into the office and asked to point out the telephone. They insisted there was none, but one of the men went to the first-aid room, found the phone, and ripped it out. In the meantime two men hurried out to the pool, covered Hackett and Ward with revolvers, and began pushing them toward the entrance. When Ward protested and pulled back, they clubbed him in the head. Dripping blood, he was rushed past the gate. There was a heavy explosion just at the door, and a thick cloud of smoke hung in the air. The two policemen were hoisted into the back of a pickup truck with a canvas hood. On the floor of the truck was a two-door clothes closet, door side up. The two were blindfolded with their own towels and stuffed in the closet. Then an Irgun raiding party of a dozen men clambered in on top of the closet. The pickup truck drove off. Most of the pool customers were very vague about what happened. The band was still playing a Strauss waltz.

Everyone was ordered to dress and leave the pool. When the last man was out of the dressing room, the security forces found out who had been kidnapped. The area commander called in the mayors of Tel Aviv, Ramat Gan, and Petva Tikva, and told them to do something. As always, they insisted that little could be done. Tel Aviv was placed out of bounds; the roadblocks and cages went up. The Haganah called on the Yishuv for help: there could be no profit in one more mad act on the eve of the UNSCOP inquiry. The Haganah alienation from the Irgun and LEHI had grown to the point where some felt that a little Season might be underway. Searches turned up nothing. Then the next day, nineteen hours after they were lifted, the two policemen reappeared. The Third Battalion of Grenadier Guards had thrown a cordon around Herzlia, where Windham had been released the previous January and where the district superintendent of police, J. M. Flanagan, suspected the Irgun had a safe house. Shortly after noon, still in their bathing trunks, Ward and Hackett rushed into the street and up to the troops. They led the Guards back to the first floor of a two-story house, finding odds and ends of armaments but no Irgun members. Ward and Hackett had been tied to beds, blindfolded, in a room with the shutters closed. The guards gave them food the previous evening, and at six that morning tea, biscuits, and cheese. The new set of guards was less interested in talking; and late in the morning, after an excited conversation in Hebrew, they announced they must leave briefly to use the telephone. Ward and Hackett managed to untie the ropes and get away. The nineteen hours thus became an adventure. It was fearfully close to a tragedy, for during a discussion about the five Acre prisoners, they learned what the Irgun had in mind: "Whatever will be done to them, will be done to you."[6]

So the Irgun had to begin again looking for hostages, this time with the security forces alerted and the Haganah apparently close to renewed collaboration. In fact the following week the Haganah thwarted one of Paglin's more ingenious schemes. This time the target was Citrus House in Tel Aviv, headquarters of the British military area, a building surrounded by high fences, concertinas of barbed wire, and interlocking guard posts. In the spring an innocent, balding, middle-aged gentleman called Oppenheim appeared in the district. He spoke only German, was invariably cheerful and talkative, and sought a small storeroom for his wholesale potato business. He discovered just what he wanted in a small cellar opposite Citrus House. Thereafter every day a lorry would arrive; the burlap sacks of potatoes would be unloaded; and the lorry would drive away. Later in the day, when the appropriate orders had accumulated, the lorry would reappear to collect the necessary bags of potatoes. Day by day Paglin's tunnel crept under the street toward Citrus House, while the dirt went out as potatoes. When the tunnel reached Citrus House, a carefully measured explosive charge that would destroy only the building could be laid. The Irgun would then seal off the tunnel and announce on the radio that in forty-eight hours an attack would be made on all Bevingrads in Palestine. The British—after the King David explosion—would have to take the warning seriously, but would not be able to concentrate on any one target. By mid-June the tunnel had reached a point a few yards from the British guard posts. Each night it was sealed, with a small explosives charge left at the farthest point. At this point the Haganah discovered that Oppenheim and his potatoes were not all they seemed. A squad rushed to the cellar to frustrate the Irgun operation. Zeev Werba crawled to the end of the tunnel. The charge went off and Werba was killed instantly. The next day the British newspapers were filled with praise for the heroism of Werba, who had prevented the biggest catastrophe in Palestine history. British representatives appeared at Werba's huge funeral alongside Haganah officers. It was the only good news for the British but most worrisome for the Irgun, who were uneasily toting up the renewed beatings, rumors of informing, and anti-Irgun propaganda, coupled with the release by the British of thirty-two Haganah prisoners sentenced for concealing arms. June's most urgent priority remained the hostage problem.

The trial of the five Irgunists captured at Acre dragged on for two weeks until June 16, the day of the inevitable sentences. With an elegant sense of British timing, it was also the day that UNSCOP arrived in Palestine. The court sat in a large, grim, white building belonging to the Mandate government. On the judges' bench sat Colonel M. E. Fell, president of the court, Major D. Lee Hunter and Captain I. Stewart. The courtroom was filled with the relatives and friends of the five prisoners—Nakar, Weiss, and Haviv, those most threatened, and the two underage prisoners, Mikhaloff and Zitterbaum. They all wore khaki shorts and open-necked shirts. In a pile on the floor beside them were their ankle and wrist irons. To the twenty members of the press, seated at two tables in front of the spectators, none of the five looked like thugs or terrorists—only very young men. After fifteen minutes Fell asked about the two defense lawyers, who were being delayed by a security search. They arrived with Mikhaloff's birth certificate after the court had rendered the verdict. Fell quickly announced that Nakar, Weiss, Mikhaloff, and Zitterbaum had been found guilty on four charges: discharging firearms, being in the uniform of His Majesty's forces, placing mines, and being a member of a group of persons who carried arms and deposited mines. Haviv was found guilty of the first three charges but for some reason not the fourth. The court and the press were herded out onto an open balcony, and the doors to the court were closed. They stood in the boiling sun for three-quarters of an hour. Finally the doors were opened, and Fell reconvened the court. Mikhaloff and Zitterman stood. The other three remained seated.

Almost before the spectators were aware of Fell's intentions, he was reading the first prisoner's penalty. "The court sentences you to suffer death by being hanged." The colonel quickly repeated the same words for the next two. Mikhaloff and Zitterbaum received fifteen years. The five young men began to sing "Hatikvah," and the other Jews in the courtroom, many in tears, joined in. The police again began pushing the singing, weeping spectators, along with the press, out onto the balcony. The courtroom was in chaos; a draft blew Fell's papers to the floor. Without showing any emotion, the three officers hurriedly left the courtroom. A policeman shouted at the crowd, "The first man who tries to cross the line will be shot." Women and other relatives continued to try to see the prisoners. The balcony doors were slammed shut again on the spectators, but they could still hear the five singing as their manacles were fastened again. Ten minutes later the doors were opened. The court was empty; the trial was over.

The trial was an appropriate introduction to Palestine for UNSCOP: jail breaks, armed attacks, military tribunals, and death sentences. Outside the court, the streets were patrolled by soldiers. There were endless roadblocks and barricades, barbed wire everywhere, and even the distant echo of explosions. Several members of UNSCOP were deeply shocked by conditions in Palestine, particularly by British methods of maintaining order. This attitude was especially strong among the members from Latin America, where the difference between a political crime and a civil crime had by necessity long been recognized. In British eyes there was no such distinction. Five terrorists had been found guilty of violating the emergency regulations and properly sentenced. Despite the British contention that the young Irgunists were thugs and murderers, to many observers the young men gave the impression of dedicated patriots and underground soldiers, not criminals. The three death sentences for political crimes did much to turn the Guatemalan representative, Jorge García-Granados into an advocate of Jewish aspirations. "These men are fighting for their ideals as they fought for them in Europe against Hitler. They fight for their people and for their beliefs. In all conscience I cannot pass judgment upon them."[7] Although he tried to remain disinterested García-Granados thus became, as had others before him, emotionally involved in the fate of Palestine. Soon so did most of UNSCOP.

The delegates collectively discussed the British death sentences. After a long and occasionally acrimonious debate, during which García-Granados, the Uruguayan Enrico Fabregat, and the Yugoslav Josha Brilej heatedly pushed the necessity for intervention, UNSCOP decided by the vote of the chairman, Emil Sandström, to take action. UNSCOP cabled Secretary General Trygve Lie, expressing concern at the death sentences on the very day of their arrival. Lie transmitted an appeal to the British government. Unofficially, the British were outraged at UNSCOP's unwarranted interference in the internal judicial affairs of the Mandate. Officially, British Chief Secretary Sir Henry Gurney sent the committee a coldly formal telegram, explaining what should have been obvious: that the case was *sub judice,* and that there was no connection between the sentences and UNSCOP's arrival. The British may have asked the United Nations to consider Palestine, but they had no intention of allowing UNSCOP to interfere in Mandate business. The Irgun then tried a direct approach to UNSCOP, claiming their prisoners had been tortured. Although unhurt when captured, Haviv had spent two weeks in the prison hospital. After recapture, the wounded were given no medical treatment. The Irgun wanted the delegates to call Haviv, Nakar, and Weiss to testify. This UNSCOP declined to do, although the Irgun managed to press their case directly in a secret meeting with Sandström.

Fearful that his colleagues might leak news of any such meeting, Sandström told only Ralph Bunche, and his secretary, Dr. Victor Hoo of China, that he had made contact with the Irgun through Associated Press correspondent Carter Davidson, who had called Samuel Katz. A meeting was set for June 24. Davidson passed on the Irgun's instructions to Sandström at a meeting in the washroom of the British Sporting Club in Jaffa. After a leisurely dinner, Sandström, Hoo, and Bunche strolled out of the Park Hotel in Tel Aviv a little after eight. A car pulled up beside them. The three got into the rear and were quickly driven to the apartment of the poet Yaacov Cahan in Bialik Street, where they met for three hours with Begin, Haim Landau, and Katz. The Irgun found that despite Sandström's previous service as a judge under the British in Egypt, he had an open mind. Hoo asked only one provocative question about a potential population problem in three hundred years—the only hint of a political judgment. Bunche on leaving stopped at the door and said, "I can understand you. I am also a member of a persecuted minority."[8] The Irgun was pleased but cautious—words were only words.

> We are not misled by the cordial atmosphere created in the course of the conversation and we are not blinded by the "impression" our words made. Indeed the atmosphere was truly cordial. . . . Yet there is a great difference between getting a good impression and forming a correct opinion. We know this and we therefore have no illusions about the practical political value of the meeting, just as we have no illusions about the value of the committee's work altogether.[9]

Certainly UNSCOP's work was immediately complicated, if not compromised, when one of the three stopped by the Pilz Café the same night for a drink and let slip what had happened. The news spread, so that the only correspondent who did not file a flash on the UNSCOP-Irgun meeting was Carter Davidson, still in his room writing up his scoop for later publication, as he agreed with Katz.

García-Granados and Fabregat were eager to contact the Irgun too, for both found themselves the leading Zionist advocates on the committee. Katz arranged for them to meet Begin and Meir Cahan (the cheerful Mr. Oppenheim of the Citrus House tunnel) at the apartment of Israel Waks. The meeting was more than simply cordial, for the two had come as friends. When Begin revealed his name García-Granados exclaimed, "So you are the man!" and Fabregat threw his arms around him in a bear hug. Although at the time both García-Granados and Fabregat were more than sympathetic to Irgun aims, they had a problem: "We cannot be more extreme than the Jewish Agency."[10] If they urged a Jewish state for the whole country as a minority report, there might not be a majority for partition. Later García-Granados shifted ground a bit in his memoirs.

> "The views of the Irgun on that [the historical right of the Jews to Palestine] are well known to us," I said. "It is useless to discuss them. We certainly cannot contemplate a solution that does not take into account the Arab rights to self-government and to a free state of their own."[11]

In the summer of 1947, the enthusiasm of García-Granados and Fabregat was a tonic to the Irgun, the more so since the reaction to the UNSCOP meeting produced great indignation at the Jewish Agency and attacks on Irgun personnel during the little Season, a sure sign that the Irgun had scored a political triumph.

For the high command such diplomatic triumphs were transitory. The real problem remained the hostages, and the British were being excruciatingly careful in keeping off the streets, staying in security zones, and moving in groups. To complicate matters for the Irgun, LEHI decided on a series of revenge operations. One of their members had disappeared, a sixteen-year-old boy named Rubowitz. It was feared he was the victim of an anti-Semitic vigilante gang like the British League. The British seemed uninterested in charging Alexander or bringing to trial Captain Roy Farran, who had been positively identified as the officer seen pushing Rubowitz into a car.[12] If LEHI began gun battles in the streets, the difficulties in finding hostages would increase. Already there had been two failures. On June 22, Assistant Superintendent of Police C. J. C. Pound escaped in Jerusalem; and at 1:30 A.M., June 25, Alan Major, an administrative officer, was hit over the head with a hammer while walking down King George Avenue in Jerusalem. He staggered about, but struggled free. LEHI agreed only to hold off for a week. The week passed. At the end of the month in Tel Aviv a LEHI team opened fire on a party of British soldiers near the Allenby Cinema in Tel Aviv, killing one, fatally wounding another, and hitting two more. The same night in Haifa a LEHI car drove up to the Astoria Café in Hadar Hacarmel. Someone leaned out and emptied a Sten gun into the restaurant. Three officers were wounded and the barman, Max Aran, was slashed by flying glass splinters. The British began firing back. The car stalled, and the LEHI people had to escape on foot. The alarm went up all over the Mandate, tighter security precautions were instituted, and the hostage problem became even more difficult. Time was running out. On July 2, the UNSCOP plea was rejected. On July 8, the British confirmed the death sentences. The Irgun again threatened to meet hanging with hanging. Finally on July 12, the Irgun found the means to carry out the threat.

That Saturday evening two Palestine policemen in the intelligence branch left the Café Gan Vered in Rehov Samuel, in the seaside resort of Natanya, with Abraham Weinberg, a War Department clerk in Leave Camp 79. The two sergeants in mufti had decided to walk Weinberg home before returning to their post. To the innocent eye the three seemed quite ordinary, but there were less innocent eyes in Natanya. A black sedan pulled up alongside the three men just as they passed the town hall. A number of young men tumbled out and covered them with submachine guns. They were ordered in English to put up their hands. Unarmed and unprepared, there was little else Sergeants Cliff Martin and Mervyn Paice could do. When the Irgun men attempted to search them, stepping into the covering line, both attempted to break free. They were clubbed over the head, shoved into the car, and quickly chloroformed. Weinberg pleaded that he was a civilian, had asthma; he knew nothing. He was simply gagged—the Irgun did not need a clerk. The car drove for about fifteen minutes, finally stopping in an orange grove. All three had their hands and feet tied. The last Weinberg saw of Martin and Paice, they were lying on the ground unconscious. He was pushed into the car for another fifteen minute drive to another grove outside Natanya. At 5:30 the following morning, July 12, the grove watchman found Weinberg. By then the security authorities already knew they had a kidnapping on their hands.

Sergeants Martin and Paice were tumbled into the back seat of an Irgun car, then driven to a carefully prepared hideout under a Natanya diamond factory. It was an underground bunker, a three-meter cube. The roof was covered by three feet of sand that baffled down any noise. At one corner was an aluminum-rimmed escape hatch on two tiles. There were sandbags beneath the lid to prevent any hollow sound if it were tapped. The bunker was totally sealed, without air or light; so Paglin had prepared two bottles of oxygen. The two men were told how to use the bottled oxygen and how long it would last. There was food for a week and a canvas bucket for a toilet. Once sealed, the bunker was secure for twenty-four hours. At first the sergeants complained of the lack of air; and twice Paglin, who agreed that the bunker smelled dreadful, took them out while it aerated. Later the two appeared dazed, complained less, and seemed to accept their fate. They had been told what it might be if the three Irgun men were hanged.

Meanwhile, beyond the bunker, the response to the kidnapping and the possible fate of the two sergeants was immediate and intense. Martial law was imposed on Natanya and twenty outlying settlements, an area of fifteen thousand people. Operation Tiger, involving five-thousand troops, was laid on, and simultaneously the British authorities demanded that Natanya must produce the two sergeants unharmed by seven that evening. The town officials protested that they were not to blame, that they did not support the Irgun. The British, suspecting there would be little help from the population, intensified the searches. Natanya was a ghost city; its streets deserted except for patrolling armor and squads of heavily armed soldiers. All the inhabitants were under house arrest. The city remained paralyzed while the searches continued. One after another, the troops brought in groups of thirty and forty Jews to be questioned. The number interrogated finally climbed to 1,427. No one knew anything. The hostages could not be found. The Irgun radio had already announced that the two sergeants would not be released until the sentences of the Irgun men were commuted. In this one case, at least, the British cordon and search operation did have the full cooperation of the recognized Jewish authorities.

The mayor of Natanya, Oved Ben-Ami, insisted from the first that all hope of a reprieve for the three would be lost. The Jewish Agency deplored the dissidents' provocative act. The Haganah, still involved in the little Season, unofficially joined the search—their people knew every house, grove, and potential hideout within a ten-mile radius. Yet neither they, the CID, nor the Jewish settlement police found a trace of the two sergeants. Only once was there a hint of a break. Just as a British army patrol pushed open the door of the diamond factory, there was a scuffle and a thud from inside. Apparently someone had gone through a back window, but there was no sign of anyone outside. The British had in fact caught an Irgun guard inside, but a painstaking search failed to reveal the shaft hatch. The diamond factory was actually searched twice without results. Finally, on July 16, the British declared a three-hour break in the curfew, then forty-five hours old. The full-scale searches were called off. Nineteen suspects out of the 1,427 questioned were kept for further investigation. The next day in London Richard Crossman and Maurice Edelmann, members of Parliament, appealed for the release of the sergeants, as did a variety of public and private figures, all to no effect. Then on the evening of July 17 came news that completely overshadowed the drama of the sergeants.

Once again the street newspapers were pasted up in all the Jewish quarters of the Mandate; handbills were passed out by Haganah boys racing about in the darkness to avoid the police.

> The refugee ship called *Exodus 1947* is headed for the shores of Palestine, after having succeeded in breaking through the blockade upon emigration from ports of exit.
> The Haganah ship *Exodus 1947* has 4,554 refugees:
>> 1,600 men
>> 1,282 women
>> 1,017 young people
>> 655 children
>
> The ship has been spotted by the British navy. A naval force, five destroyers and a cruiser, are now closing in on her from all sides, and leading her on her way.
> At 2200 hours tonight, and tomorrow morning at 0730, the refugees will broadcast a message to the Jews of Palestine from the deck of the ship on 35 meters wavelength. The broadcast may be picked up on the Haganah secret radio, Kol Israel, 45 meters wavelength.[13]

The refugee ship *Exodus 1947,* formerly the American excursion steamer *President Garfield,* was the last in a long line of Aliyah Bet's blockade runners. In 1946, well past its prime, it was sold for scrap. A keen-eyed Haganah arms agent appeared in Baltimore and offered $40,000, a tidy profit for the scrap dealer, who prudently had no quibbles or questions. Bernardo Marks, a merchant seaman from Cincinnati, recruited a crew of sixty nine, and the *President Garfield* was ready to sail for Europe. Most Haganah ships were smaller, and few managed to unload their passengers. There were already over ten thousand Jewish refugees interned in camps on Cyprus. The *Exodus,* however, was special; for the Haganah expected that this time the British would make an example of the latest attempt to break the law. Headed by six members of the Haganah, the crew had already been forced to return the ship to America for refitting after a mid-Atlantic hurricane. By the time the ship reached the Azores on her second attempted voyage to Italy, British intelligence had moved in, and tried to prevent the purchase of supplies. Then, when the ship arrived in Italian waters, they found their way out of La Spezia blocked by a gunboat. With no shore leave the crew sat for seven weeks during April and May. The ship was at last released, and sailed to the French port of Sète. There they loaded 4,500 refugees from the displaced-persons' camps—all carefully supplied with visas to Columbia, a ploy that made their presence in France legal but hardly convinced the British. This time the British had no intention of standing idly by while the Haganah slipped out of Sète.

On June 12–13 in Paris, Bevin and French Foreign Minister Georges Bidault opened a conference of European nations to discuss the application of the Marshall Plan. On June 13, Bevin received word from British

intelligence that the ship had arrived at Sète. He insisted that Bidault prevent it from sailing. Bidault diplomatically replied that the passengers had
valid Latin American entry. Bevin was outraged. He knew as well as Bidault that the destination of the ship was not Latin America. In Paris British Ambassador Duff-Cooper immediately pressured Premier Ramadier
to prevent the departure. Rumor reached the Haganah in Sète of the maneuvers in Paris, and they immediately sailed away before any police
could arrive. Flying the silk flag of Zion, presented to the crew by the Haganah on February 25, the *Exodus* immediately became the object of an
intensive British naval search organized by Bevin when he returned to
London on July 14. There was never much hope that the *Exodus* could
evade the British. Soon a small flotilla, the cruiser *Ajax* and five destroyers, trailed the ship just over the horizon. Bevin felt the time had arrived
to come down hard on the Haganah. Support for Zionism seemed to be
ebbing. The Italians were concerned about Irgun activities. The Yugo-
slavs had agreed, after negotiating a favorable trade treaty with Britain, to
deny port facilities for Jewish immigration. Even President Truman was
persuaded by the pragmatists to issue an appeal to Americans not to aid
illegal Zionist activities. Bevin had increasingly become obsessed with the
continued Zionist provocations in Palestine.

At 2:00 A.M. on Friday, July 18, before the first light, the *Exodus* was
running east toward Gaza about twenty miles offshore, well in international waters. A British destroyer came alongside and trained a search-
light on the ship. "You are in territorial waters. Stop your ship. We are
going to board you."[14] Another destroyer came along the other side.
More blue-white lights focused on the cluttered deck of the *Exodus*. The
two destroyers moved closer. The bow of one tore into the flimsy bul-
wards with a shattering crash. Wood splinters flew everywhere. The *Exodus* began to lose way. Over the side came long strings of firecrackers
that sounded like machine guns. Tear gas grenades followed. Next came a
group of sailors with hard leather shields on their left arms, carrying clubs
in their right. The Jews fought back with a hail of potatoes and tinned
food. The sailers clubbed their way to the wheelhouse, shot off the lock,
and rushed in swinging. An American volunteer, Bill Bernstein, was
smashed on the left temple and collapsed on the deck, mortally wounded.
Outside, the boarding party shot and killed a sixteen-year-old orphan,
Hirsch Yakubovich, who had been watching the action from behind a big
life raft. A sailor, claiming he saw a hatchet, fired his pistol into Yakubovich's face from a range of six inches. The fight continued all along the
boat deck and the hurricane deck, as the Jews refused to give ground,
kept up the potato barrage, and fought back with clubs chopped from ban-
isters.

The British destroyers continued to ram the *Exodus,* smashing again and again into the heavy fender of the American ship, which became her salvation, for her sides already resembled crushed matchboxes. Things did not go at all well for the British. Many of the sailors were captured and locked in cabins. Those in the wheelhouse who tried to set a course for Haifa found that the Haganah had uncoupled the steering cables. In the radio room an American student preacher, John Stanley Grauel, was broadcasting the news to Palestine.

> This is the refugee ship *Exodus 1947.* Before dawn today we were attacked by five British destroyers and one cruiser at a distance of 17 miles from the shores of Palestine, in international waters. The assailants immediately opened fire, threw gas bombs, and rammed our ship from three directions. On our deck there are one dead, five dying, and 120 wounded. The resistance continued for more than three hours. Owing to the severe losses and the condition of the ship, which is in danger of sinking, we were compelled to sail in the direction of Haifa, in order to save the 4,500 refugees on board from drowning.[15]

In Tel Aviv a general strike began spontaneously. Nothing moved except crowds of Jews on the streets. Buses were stopped in the middle of road; cars pulled to the sides. No shops or factories opened. There was no swimming on the beach. The hotels closed; the verandas and restaurants emptied. Everything was shuttered. At sea, listing slightly, the ruined *Exodus,* led by the *Ajax* and followed by the five destroyers, made slowly for Haifa. Just past four in the afternoon the crowds, waiting beyond the great coils of wire and the checkpoints manned by the Sixth Airborne, CID, military police, and the constabulary, sighted the *Exodus.* The blue and white flag of Zion still flew from the mast. On the side was painted "Haganah Ship Exodus 1947." The rest was mostly rubble—a huge hole in one side, a muddle of broken pipes leaking water and steam, scattered possessions, splintered wood, dangling railings. The rafts and lifeboats hung at strange angles; the decks were canted and covered with rubble. On the decks were also thousands of people, clad in bits and pieces of clothing—shorts, dresses, ragged trousers—all singing "Hatikvah"— home at last, but hardly free. On the other side of the pier were moored three zoo-cage prison ships: *Ocean Vigour, Runnymede Park,* and *Empire Rival.* If the past were any indication, the refugees would wake up next week in a Cypriot detention camp, the biggest single load scooped by the British security forces during the entire illegal-entry campaign.

Soon the refugees began to move down the tilting gangway, the wounded first, then women with children, then the others. They were people of all sorts and conditions: Hungarians with gypsy eyes, dark North Africans, thin men in shorts nursing bruises, giggling Polish girls. Few had possessions, some carried shoddy satchels; there was the odd straw baby carriage, the green water bottles carried by each refugee, a blanket here, a few books there. They were searched—they could have no film, cameras, razors, knives or scissors, and no fountain pens. Then the British herded them across the pier and up the gangplanks of the prison ships. At 9:00 P.M. the *Ocean Vigour* sailed, then the *Runnymede Park,* and finally, at 5:40 the following morning, the *Empire Rival.* All that was left was the crushed hulk of the old excursion ship and a few bored British guards. The saga of the *Exodus* appeared over. It was not a particularly attractive British exercise, since it seemed unlikely to teach the Jews a lesson. Watching from outside the rolls of rusting wire was Justice Sandström, chairman of UNSCOP. No one knew what lesson he had learned.

If the adventures of the *Exodus* passengers had ended in the detention camps of Cyprus, British credibility would probably not have been too seriously damaged. The old ship was not the first seized nor were the refugees the first sent off to exile. Admittedly the Yishuv seemed especially outraged at this deportation, so much so that the Haganah, for the first time since the united resistance, undertook offensive operations. They twice attacked radar stations near Haifa, and sabotaged and sank the transshipment vessel *Empire Lifeguard* on Haifa harbor.The British simply listed them along with the weekly schedule of fifty-one terrorist attacks. The general strike was over. The press had other matters to report. Unfortunately for the British officials seeking an easier life, Bevin had decided the saga would not end in Cyprus. The three cage ships simply disappeared into the Mediterranean. Observers on Cyprus awaited the convoy's arrival as the days slipped past. While the ships sailed aimlessly through the Mediterranean, Bevin sought to implement the new illegal refugee policy: illegal immigrants would be returned to the countries from which they had come. French public opinion violently opposed any forceful repatriation; and the French goverment, while willing to give asylum to the Jews, would not force them to land in France against their will. The British decided to bring the three cage ships back to Sète and see if most of the Jews would land voluntarily—after nine days of sailing about the Mediterranean in midsummer, continued confinement would be most unattractive. Early on the morning of July 29, the *Ocean Vigour, Runnymede Park,* and *Empire Rival* dropped anchor in Sète. The international press arrived in droves to report the miserable conditions on the cage ships—cramped and confining wire cages, hardly room to stand, not enough water, inadequate sanitary facilities, no place to wash, no privacy, no exercise. Aryeh Felblum, London correspondent of *Haaretz,* like the other reporters hired a launch and got a first-hand look.

On approaching the *Ocean Vigour* I witnessed the most terrible spectacle I have ever seen in my life. It was a spectacle I shall never forget. On the deck, in narrow, very high cases, worse than those in a zoo, surrounded by barbed wire, were crowded together my brothers and sisters of all ages. There the sun had beaten down on their heads for eighteen days at sea. They had not even been able to lie down at night. Between the cages stood red-bereted guards isolating each cage. I called in Yiddish, "Will you leave the boat?" They answered in unanimous chorus, "No!" Then I called to them in Hebrew, "Shalom!" Again they answered in chorus, "Shalom!"

The Britons on the deck turned their arms on me and I had to retreat. As I drew away I heard calls from the boat: "Lehitraot!" Then they sang "Hatikvah," while I, choking with tears, blew them kisses.[16]

Not all the correspondents were so involved; but it was a French abbé, responsible for arranging medical aid and food supplies, who dubbed the ships a floating Auschwitz.

The entire operation seemed increasingly mean spirited and unsavory. The three cage ships remained anchored during a searing heat wave. Despite British efforts few Jews would leave. The sick remained. Five children were born; each qualified for British citizenship. Then came four days of teeming rain, lashing across the open cages, dribbling down into the sodden and suffocating holds, covering the decks with slime. The British authorities on the three ships made no secret that the purpose of maintaining the increasingly dangerous conditions on board was to force an evacuation. And yet, sodden and miserable, jammed in their cages, the Jews would not leave. A hunger strike was declared. The stories began to sift out to the press. Almost day by day the saga of the *Exodus* was becoming a new Zionist epic: a run-of-the-mill blockade breaker had given birth, with a British midwife, to a new legend. The French government opened a series of initiatives, hoping that the British would remove the vessels and end "l'affaire *Exodus*." The British stalled. They finally announced to the refugees: "Those of you who do not begin to disembark at Sète before 18 o'clock tomorrow, August 22, will be taken by sea to Hamburg."[17] The Haganah sent a boat with a loudspeaker to urge the refugees not to leave. They did not, and the three ships sailed for Hamburg on August 22.

The world's press was once again waiting at the dock in Hamburg on September 9, along with a thousand British troops, fully armed, backed by fifteen-hundred German police with another fifteen hundred in reserve. They carried high-pressure hoses, steel-tipped truncheons, and riot shields. Loudspeakers blared jazz, not unlike the music used to herd other Jews to death camps. The refugees from the *Empire Rival* offered no resistance. In fact they quickly evacuated the ship, mainly because they had left a large time bomb ticking in the hold. There was violent resistance from the other two cage ships. Screaming defiance, men, women, and children tossed bottles and cans, battered the British with clubs

wrapped in barbed wire. On the *Runnymede Park* fifteen-hundred Jews re-
pulsed the four-hundred-man boarding party. The British water hoses
then opened up, forcing everyone up against the wall where they were
truncheoned. Drenched and battered, they were dragged off, some unconscious, some still struggling. Beyond the docks-five hundred German police, led by a British colonel, broke up a protest demonstration of 1,300
displaced persons. Finally it was over. The three cage ships were empty,
filthy and foul, their decks covered with debris.

The refugees were safely settled in two camps at Poppendorg and
Amstau—the all-too-familiar watchtowers, with German police reinforcing British guards, the long barbed-wire fences, the searchlights, the dismal and shoddy barracks, the miserable routing imposed from above.
Concentration camps in Ethiopia, Cyprus, or Palestine were unpleasant
enough. In a world still horrified by the holocaust, concentration camps in
Germany filled with Jews snatched back from the Promised Land were
shocking. These Jews had already been punished in the purgatory of the
cage ships before being beaten into submission on the Hamburg docks.
What enemy of Britain could have conceived so desperate and futile a
policy as that chosen by Bevin? Long before the gates closed in the wire
fences of Poppendorg and Amstau, Bevin's Palestine policy—part pique,
part pragmatic prejudice, part muddle— had brought Britain nothing but
humiliation and anguish.

The departure of the three cage ships from Haifa was a signal for escalated violence. The Haganah undertook their three operations, and both
LEHI and the Irgun increased the pace of incidents. On Friday, July 18,
with the *Exodus* moving toward Haifa, attacks in Jerusalem had wounded
four British soldiers near Kfar Bilu, while one British soldier was killed
and three were wounded. On the following day six attacks took place in
Jerusalem, and in Hehalutz Street in Hadar Hacarmel a three-man attack
team shot and killed one British constable and wounded another. The
next day, July 20, a curfew was placed on Hadar Hacarmel. There were
seven Irgun attacks on the railway lines, and the headquarters of the First
Infantry Division at Tel Litwinsky came under mortar fire. There was a
report of a British soldier killed and a British constable and three soldiers
wounded in the Haifa district. A mine killed one soldier and wounded
three near Raanana. A British staff car moving along the road north of
Natanya was sprayed with automatic fire. In Jerusalem a police armored
car detonated a mine near the Syrian Orphanage. All through the night of
July 20, the day UNSCOP left Palestine for Beirut, there were shots,
mine explosions, and the grumble of British armor through the deserted
streets. In Natanya Operation Tiger, still in full swing, had produced
nothing. In Haifa there was a total curfew and continual sniping. The
month of July finished with ambushes, mine explosions, night raids, and a

long butcher's bill for the security forces: two British soldiers killed and eight injured by a mine explosion on the Jaffa road, nineteen British soldiers injured when the Haganah sank the *Empire Lifeguard* in Haifa harbor.

The British had no intention of reversing course. True, in the last two weeks of July, the total losses were thirteen members of the security forces killed and seventy-seven wounded, two civilians killed and fifteen injured—and only one terrorist killed in over a hundred incidents. Two more Haganah ships were intercepted, but this time the refugees were sent to Cyprus after a struggle along the gangways and pier. Operation Tiger finally had to be called off and the curfew on Natanya lifted. The two sergeants and the three condemned Irgun men in Acre began again to attract the attention of the Mandate. After the debacle of the *Exodus* and past concessions whenever the Irgun held hostages, the Irgun high command did not think the British would go ahead with the executions. Nearly everyone in the Mandate, except the most self-righteous members of the British establishment, believed that so far all the executions had been exercises in pressure politics, not acts of justice or even acts of vengeance. The jails and camps were filled with men equally guilty of capital offenses or found guilty and sentenced to death only to be reprieved. The Gruner case ended at the gallows not because of a crime but because of the British need to project a certain image. Even after their experience in Ireland, the British refused to accept that the Crown's justice was a farce in rebel eyes, and that the gallows bred martyrs. At his trial Avshalom Haviv drew just this parallel.

> When the sons of Ireland rose up against you, when the Irish underground started their fight against you, you tried to drown the rising in rivers of blood. You set up gallows, you murdered in the streets, you exiled, you ran amok and stupidly believed that by dint of persecution you would break the spirit of resistance of free Irishmen, the spirit of resistance which is God's gift to every man worthy of the name. You erred. Irish resistance grew in intensity. The blood of the fighters and the tortured rallied the people to the banner of revolt, until you were forced to withdraw, leaving behind you ineradicable bloodstains and unforgettable memories. Free Ireland rose in spite of you. . . .[18]

At least the British authorities recognized their dilemma—give in to blackmail or risk the sergeants' lives. The chance for a swift reprieve had slipped away. Operation Tiger had aborted. The Jewish Agency and Haganah had come up with nothing. The plea for restraint by Vaad Leumi brought no response. The plea by the chief rabbi brought no response. There was nothing to do but carry out the sentences on hanging day, July 29, as scheduled. To do less would be a public concession of British impotence, which was long recognized by all but Bevin and the optimists.

It was a foolish display of inflexibility. The officer responsible for the execution of Dov Gruner and the others, Major Charleston, superintendent at Acre, had already refused to hang the men because no British lives were lost in the escape operation. He was dismissed and sent back to England. Major Clow was ordered from Nablus to Acre with orders to hang the three as scheduled on Tuesday morning. Early Monday evening the three were told the sentences would be carried out the following morning between four and five. They immediately broke into the "Hatikvah," followed by Michael Ashbel's "On the Barricades." They shouted the news to the other prisoners, adding, "Avenge us!" Then they continued the strange songfest, three young men standing in the mean whitewashed walls of the condemned cells, singing to a listening prison of Jews and Arabs, plus the British army and police units who had come in with the hangman.

At two in the morning, a Sephardic rabbi, Nissim Ohana, visited with them for a few minutes. He carried out a message to their family and friends: "Do not grieve too much, what we have done we did out of conviction."[19] At the trial Haviv had told the court that it could never understand the spirit of free men going to death.

> And this too you will probably not understand: I, a young Jew, facing the sentence of death, lift up my heart to God, and give praise and thanks for the privilege of suffering for my people and my country, and say with all my heart: "Blessed art thou, O Lord, King of the Universe, who has kept us alive and maintained us and enabled us to reach this season."[20]

At 4:00 in the morning, Haviv's season came to a close. The Jewish prisoners, jammed against the bars, heard him begin the "Hatikvah." His voice was strong and clear, fading slightly as he moved into the gallows room. The Jewish prisoners joined in. Haviv's voice stopped at 4:03. His body was left dangling at the end of the rope for twenty minutes. At 4:25 Nakar began the "Hatikvah;" the others joined in, and three minutes later he was gone. Twenty minutes later his body was cut down. At 5:00 Weiss began to sing and was joined by the chorus. In two minutes he too was dead.

news seeped out of Acre prison, Paglin was at a movie. He was called out and told that the British were going to hang the boys, then put a curfew on the country at eleven that evening. Paglin hurried to Begin's safe house. There was no doubt in Paglin's mind that the Irgun threat had to be carried out as a matter of policy, not vengeance. Samuel Katz had just written as much in the underground *Irgunpress.*

> We recognize no one-sided laws of war. If the British are determined that their way out of the country should be lined by an avenue of gallows and of weeping fathers, mothers, wives, and sweethearts, we shall see to it that in

this there is no racial discrimination. The gallows will not be all of one colour . . . Their price will be paid in full.[21]

When Paglin reached Begin he was meeting with a few members of the high command. The only doubts were technical. Paglin moved into the kitchen with Begin to urge instant action. Begin wanted to know if it would be possible to hang the sergeants—the roadblocks would be up, the Haganah alert. Paglin said it could be done if he could take personal charge—for six months the high command had not allowed him to go into British-controlled areas. There was some danger in failing with the attempt, but Paglin insisted the risk be taken. To hesitate would seriously damage Irgun prestige, and a revolutionary organization breathes prestige. Paglin felt it could be done in the diamond factory and the bodies moved to an orange grove; moving the two would be taking too great a risk. Begin agreed. Paglin slipped out of the house on his way to Natanya.

Paglin drove his Morris 8 up to Natanya and collected the others. The roads were filled with British security traffic. Standing by the hatch in the diamond factory floor, they could hear the British vehicles patrolling all around them. There was a desperate rush to get the hatch open. Paglin was afraid of being caught in the act before anything could be done. Once the hatch was clear the first sergeant was rushed out. After hours and hours in the dugout on limited oxygen, he could hardly make sense out of what was happening. He stood swaying, his face blank and covered with stubble, gasping the fresh air. Paglin pulled a homemade hood over his head. He was hustled into the next room and lifted onto a small chair. A rope with a looped noose dangled from a hook in a rafter. As his wrists and ankles were bound, he spoke for the first time. "Are you going to hang me?" No one answered. "Can I leave a message?"[22] Paglin told him there was no time. The noose was around his neck. Paglin gestured, and one of the men kicked the chair away. The body swayed back and forth, the hook creaking in the rafter. The rumble of British traffic searching along outside was the only sound. The sergeant's fingers grew limp, his trousers became stained by his voided bladder. Paglin made another signal. The second sergeant was brought out, hooded, bound, and placed on the chair with the second noose about his neck. Another signal, and he too swung at the end of the short rope, the hook creaking. After twenty minutes the two bodies were taken down, placed in the rear of a jeep, and driven to an eucalyptus grove at Umm Uleiga. The ropes were tossed over a tree limb. The bodies were quickly jerked off the ground and left hanging there. Paglin and the rest moved off, leaving a mine on the small access road—two hanged men was one fewer than three. The Irgun secret radio broadcast the news that the sentences had been carried out. Many refused to believe it.

Irgun notices of the executions appeared on the walls of the Mandate. British searches, however, missed the bodies; so the Irgun, fearful that the Jewish settlement police aiding the search would set off the mine, called police headquarters and gave the location of the orange grove. When the British arrived, they suspected the bodies were mined and kept their distance. With a knife on a pole, the two ropes were cut. Hooks were fastened from a distance into the sergeants' clothing and roped to the rear of a Land Rover. As they were being dragged away from the site of the execution, one of the bodies hit the mine, which exploded—the British were correct in taking precautions. The Irgun had answered the gallows with a gallows and hanged two innocent young men. In British eyes the sergeants were only doing their duty. Everyone was horrified. The Jewish Agency condemned the act, calling it a vile murder by a set of criminals. In London Creech-Jones spoke for most Britons.

> In the long history of violence in Palestine there has scarcely been a more dastardly act than the cold-blooded and calculated murder of these innocent young men after holding them hostage for more than a fortnight.
>   I can only express the deep feeling of horror and revulsion shared by all of us here at this barbarous crime.[23]

The London press was uniform in condemning the hangings. *The Daily Telegraph* wanted the security forces to "take the gloves off." The *Times* felt that the Jews' cause had been harmed. The *Daily Express* insisted that "not in the black annals of Nazi wickedness is there a tale of outrage more vile." There were anti-Semitic demonstrations in London, Manchester, and Glasgow. Jewish shop windows were broken. In Liverpool Jewish stores were looted by mobs. Slogans were smeared on synagogues and Jewish cemeteries desecrated. The Jewish Agency had feared as much. In Geneva Shertok announced, "It is mortifying to think that some Jews should have become so depraved by the horrible iniquities in Europe as to be capable of such vileness."[24] In Palestine the security forces were not interested in such fine distinctions—their friends had been murdered in cold blood. In Tel Aviv British soldiers, some in uniform, ran amok along Ben-Yehuda and Allenby streets. Armored cars began shooting into civilian buses and private cars. The troops attacked cafés, smashed shop windows, and beat passers-by. Five Jews were killed and fifteen seriously injured, and scores of others bloody and bruised. At the funeral of three of the five killed, an RAF armored car fired into the funeral procession. On August 5, thirty-five prominent Jews, mostly Revisionist politicians, but including the mayors of Natanya, Tel Aviv, and Ramat Gan, were arrested. It might have appeared that the death of the two sergeants vitalized British resistance to the Irgun rebellion, smeared all Jews with the terrorist label, and set back the dream of a state. This was not so; in fact, it was rather the reverse: the two sergeants were the straw that broke the Mandate's back.

In Britain there were full-page pictures of the two sergeants; their bodies hanging like strange fruit in an orchard. The papers, with heavy black headlines and outraged editorials, reported the anguished speeches in Parliament, the mobs daubing swastikas on synagogues, and the looting attacks on Jewish shops. Few in Britain took time to notice the reaction of the *Manchester Guardian*—"Time to Go." The Guardian's writers felt the only hope was the United Nations, which might find a way to release Britain from responsibility, giving Jews and Arabs an opportunity to start afresh. The *Guardian* was perceptive; for the wave of revulsion in Britain was directed as much against British presence and tactics as against Jewish terror: the exhausted *Exodus* refugees dragged screaming back from the Promised Land, the death of two young men trapped in a humiliating and pointless struggle against a persecuted people, the weekly lists of dead and maimed that brought no thanks from either Jew or Arab. So, instead of adamant demands for vengeance and reprisals, as some expected, the consensus gradually formed, as the *Guardian* predicted, that the time for evacuation had arrived. The news out of the Mandate was always bad. On August 5, three British constables tried to drag a bomb out of the Jerusalem Labor Department. There was a huge roar and all three were dead. One of them, blown over a ten-foot wall topped with wire, lay smashed on the ground, the other two were somewhere under the ruins, their bodies in shreds. It went on and on. Bevin and the others might still hope for British advantage, but increasingly the only reasonable hope seemed the United Nations.

After visits to Beirut and Amman, UNSCOP arrived in Geneva on July 27. By a vote of six to four, they decided to send a subcommittee to visit the Jewish displaced-persons' camps in Germany and Austria. Some members claimed that the displaced Jews did not really want to go to Palestine, but at the camps the subcommittee found that most of the survivors of the holocaust were unalterably determined to emigrate there. Should they be asked to return and rebuild an anti-Semitic Poland, whose communist government did not want them? Should they be sent back to a divided and sullen Germany, whose former leaders had tried to destroy them right under the eyes of the people? Should they return to their ghettos of rubble, and become again an unwanted minority in the ruins of Vilna or Lvov?

When the subcommittee returned from Germany and Austria, the eleven delegates had privately reached a consensus on at least some vital points. They had to produce a solution of some sort despite the fact, as the British high commissioner told them, that a peaceful solution seemed unlikely.

> No solution can be found which gives absolute justice to everyone. It is clear, too, that no solution can be found which will be wholly agreed to by everyone. Therefore, it seems that to a greater or lesser degree whatever solution you find must be imposed.

There must be a solution, however. Time has shown a constantly accelerated deterioration of conditions in this country. The sands are running
out. The only answer is an early political solution.[25]

Since their departure on July 20, conditions in the Mandate had further
deteriorated. It was bankrupt, and the British would have to withdraw.
The idea of a withdrawal appeared to gain impetus, when, in August,
Prime Minister Attlee had announced a new Battle of Britain, this time to
conquer the worsening economic situation. One of the savings announced
was the return of 200,000 of the 450,000 soldiers stationed abroad—and
95,000 were in Palestine. The delegates continued meeting with representatives of the Foreign Office, but there appeared to be a curious ambiva-
lence, and no firm future British policy took shape. UNSCOP decided
that the Mandate must end, while maintaining the economic unity of
Palestine.

The delegates basically agreed to partition the Mandate into two
states with an economic union. There were differences among them on
the size of the new states and the conditions for their establishment. The
majority proposed a Jewish territory to include eastern Galilee, the central coastal plain, and the Negev Desert. The Arabs would have western
Galilee, central Palestine, and the coastal plain in the far north and far
south. The Jerusalem-Bethlehem area would be an international zone.
There would be a two-year probationary period, and Jewish immigration
would continue at a monthly rate of 6,250 in the first two years and 5,000
after that. The minority report, sympathetic to Arab aspirations, suggested a three-year United Nations administration, with both Jewish and Arab
regimes, and a single capital at Jerusalem. Jewish immigration could continue but no quotas were set. The two reports were submitted to the General Assembly at 11:55 P.M. on August 31, the deadline for UNSCOP.

Arab and Zionist diplomats closely monitored the Geneva deliberations during August. The Zionists had two first-rate foreign policy advis-
ers on hand in David Horowitz and Abba Eban. Samuel Katz arrived to
represent the Irgun. The Arabs, still uneasy about UNSCOP, were represented only by an agent of the Arab Higher Committee. Various experts
and spokesmen appeared from time to time, including the British, who remained excruciatingly vague. In Palestine Ben-Gurion was growing increasingly more militant. On August 8, he felt the time had come to demand the liquidation of the British regime in Palestine without any delay.
On August 17, he accused Britain of conducting a war on the Jews. On
August 26, he insisted that Bevin wanted to remain in Palestine at all
costs. All this sounded like last-minute militancy to his Irgun listeners,
and only words at that. When the cage ships left Sète the Jewish Agency
declared a day of fasting, and when it arrived at Hamburg a single day of
mourning. The Irgun assumed that Ben-Gurion was speaking for the his-

tory books, so as to claim that he, not the Irgun, had forced the British withdrawal. In Geneva the Jewish Agency was working so hard for partition that those on UNSCOP sympathetic to the Irgun's maximum demands felt they could not be more Zionist than the Jewish Agency, and so they joined the majority of seven advocating partition. If the Irgun got only a piece of the loaf they felt was theirs in the UNSCOP report, the Arabs were even more disappointed. The Arab League information office in New York warned the United Nations that acceptance of either proposal would mean violence in the Middle East.

Indeed, almost for the first time since the beginning of the Irgun revolt, there was violence traced to Arabs. On August 11, an Arab gang had shot up the Café Hawaii on Yarkon Street, killing four Jews, mortally wounding one, and injuring twelve more. On August 14, between Tel Aviv and Jaffa, Jewish and Arab crowds attacked each other with knives and stones, and shooting and arson began. Three Jews and one Arab were killed, nine Jews and seven Arabs injured. Two days later a Haganah group attacked the camp of the Arabs who had shot into the Café Hawaii. Four Arabs were shot dead and a family of seven killed when their house was dynamited. These were ominous signs that the Arabs had lost patience: they had watched the long struggle between the Irgun and the British from the sidelines, but now that distant forces were about to decide the fate of Palestine, something had to be done.

In June 1946, the Arab League had met at Bludan in Syria and resolved to uphold a series of secret agreements: the denial of economic concessions to the United States and Great Britain, the withdrawal of the Arabs from any international organization, and the need to make war in Palestine if the Zionists remained. It was significant that a British observer was present—Brigadier Iltyd N. Clayton, a prominent Arabist; for the Arabs in 1946, like the Zionists, assumed that the future disposition of Palestine rested with the British. By the summer of 1947, however, this was no longer the case. UNSCOP seemed to take its assignment seriously. No one could tell what Britain intended. The Arabs might have to depend upon their own resources, not an especially attractive prospect. Although all the Arab leaders, in power and out, agreed that the Zionists should not have Palestine, beyond this they had little in common but mutual rancour, suspicion, and mistrust. Within Palestine, the Mufti had ruthlessly removed most opposition to his followers, who remained organized in traditional ways for traditional purposes—brigandage, riot, and revenge. Even in the cities there were still only weak political structures, and most of the middle class feared and abhorred politics. The Mufti wanted an Arab Palestine, *his* Palestine, with no Jews. Hardly anyone else wanted the mufti to have anything. His major rival and long-time foe, Emir Abdullah of Transjordan, wanted as much of Palestine as he could get and most particularly Jerusalem. He was willing to make a deal with the Jews. The Egyptians, when the feeble government and venal king could spare the time to consider it, wanted more. The Iraqis wanted the Egyptians, the Syrians, and Abdullah to have less. The Lebanese wanted the easy life; and the Saudis worried about the holy places, mistrusted the Palestinians, and abhorred Abdullah. No one wanted to make serious sacrifices or contribute to any common cause. On September 16, the Arab League again met at Sofar, Lebanon. The secretary general had not called the meeting, Iraq had. Neither Egypt nor Saudi Arabia favored another session, and everyone knew that Baghdad simply wanted to distract attention from the Anglo-Iraqi treaty negotiations that had caused serious popular discontent. No one wanted to worry about Palestine. A *pro forma* note was sent off to Washington and London, warning that the creation of a Jewish state would inevitably bring violence with it. Everyone went home to tend to more vital matters.

The Palestine problem simply could not be evaded so easily. The Arab people—the poor in the suqs, the intellectuals sipping endless black coffee in the cafés opposite the universities, the nomads in the hills and deserts—expected *something* to be done to prevent the shame of a Jewish state in the Holy Land. So did the Arabs in Palestine; but they recognized that, whatever the martial virtues of the Mufti's people, mobs alone could not defeat the Jews. All the Arabs knew that the Haganah was a vast, heavily armed underground army, fifty- to-seventy-thousand strong, just waiting to rise if the British left. There were also the Irgun and Stern, and offshore refugee ships crammed with volunteers and arms. Thus, if UNSCOP·and the General Assembly voted, despite Arab warnings, in favor of a Zionist state, and if Britain tolerated such an action, an Arab Palestine was doomed unless the Arab states intervened. Those states continued squabbling and circling for national advantage.

For the Jews in Palestine, the intentions of the Arab League, the Mufti, or the Arabs next door remained of secondary importance. Where the key factor for them had always been in Britain, now the focus had shifted to the United Nations. The Jewish Agency in particular, after publication of the UNSCOP proposals, geared up for a diplomatic propaganda campaign in favor of partition. From August 31 until the opening of the General Assembly on September 16, the agency marshaled its worldwide forces to back partition as the best possible solution. This was anathema to the Irgun, LEHI, and the Revisionists, who still wanted at the very least the entire Mandate. They still refused to believe that Britain would leave.

Certainly British statements were less than candid. At Lake Success Creech-Jones and British Ambassador Sir Alexander Cadogan remained vague. They noted only that London would not support any solution not acceptable to both parties involved. As no such solution would ever exist, Britain's attitude remained an enigma. On September 23, Creech-Jones informed the General Assembly that Britain would not implement partition. What did this mean? According to Begin and the Irgun, since there was no possibility of any international armed force implementing partition, "The British Government's plot is clear for all to see." The British would continue to seal off the Mandate, permitting their Arab allies to invade Palestine, while they would retain key strategic positions.[26] The Irgun thus opposed partition. First, Eretz Israel had to be restored intact to the people of Israel; second, partition was simply a British plot to continue, by alliance with the Arabs, as the occupying power. Thus the Jewish Agency's lobbying for partition was one more example of arrogant innocents deceived by the British, selling out the Promised Land for promises.

As always, the Jewish Agency felt reassured by the Irgun's criticism: partition must indeed be the appropriate course if Begin opposed it. More Jewish money and talent was funneled into New York. Lobbying in delegates' lounges, securing favorable editorials from major newspapers, and buying glowing endorsements from the mighty were the ways to produce a Jewish state. The special session ground on through the same old arguments, meeting as an ad hoc committee fourteen times in twenty-four days. There were old arguments but a few novel developments. The United States support of partition on October 11 came as no surprise, but it was still a disappointment to the Arabs. The announcement on October 13 by the Russian delegate, Semyon K. Tsarapkin, endorsing partition put Moscow and Washington on the same side, something the Arabist establishment in London had believed impossible. When the General Assembly as ad hoc committee voted favorably on the majority report, twenty-five to thirteen, with seventeen abstentions, there was not yet a two-thirds majority. The Arabs had a chance, but matters had grown serious for all. In Palestine Ben-Gurion ordered the Haganah to produce a general mobilization plan and sent a secret arms-buying mission abroad to prepare for a real war. The Arabs met again in Aley, Lebanon, set up a military committee, called for the procurement of ten-thousand rifles for the Palestinian Arabs, and made efforts to acquire fighter planes. In Lake Success three new subcommittees were set up—more to delay a decision than to devise a more satisfactory majority proposal.

The United Nations delegates had to make a decision on Palestine in the world's most Zionist city. With only the odd exception, New York's huge Jewish population was deeply committed to Zionism. The combination of the holocaust and a decade of careful Zionist organization had created a massive, articulate, wealthy, and influential pressure bloc. Politicians of all varieties, party-givers, unions, and church groups were coöpted for the cause. Sure evidence of the effectiveness of this effort was the endorsement of a Jewish state by both the Democratic and Republican national conventions in 1948: in an election year the Jewish vote, which all politicians assumed existed, might be crucial. While there were those, especially in non-elective office or within the foreign policy and defense establishment, who saw pragmatic virtues in the Arab cause, most politicians favored the Zionists. The non-Jewish public, pockets of anti-Semitism aside, had been swayed by the death camps, by a biblical romanticism, and by the effective lobbying of Zionist advocates.

The orthodox Zionist organizations left little to chance. Cut off from intimate contact with the Mandate for much of the war, the American leaders had created a vast, overlapping complex of influence and enthusiasm, which they used to collect and dispatch funds and to maintain Jewish morale. Irish efforts in the 1920's seemed primitive and ineffectual in comparison with the Zionist program in the years before 1948. Exploiting the Zionist presence in the entertainment industry, the press, and the academic establishment, making use of all the reservoirs of sympathy, the dedicated shaped a massive and effective propaganda effort. The Revisionists' work, occasionally impressive, in reality stood on the shoulders of a giant. The Zionist impact in public and private during 1947 and 1948 grew after decades of careful sowing by the orthodox groups, and flowered in an immense spate of publicity, marshaled votes and influence, newspaper editorials, petitions and mass meetings, and cunningly structured dinner parties. As the great Zionist machine ground toward the General Assembly vote, even those knowledgeable about Palestinian events paid little attention to the positions and political postures of the Irgun—they were wild men on the fringe of real events.

The Irgun's press and radio, "The Voice of Fighting Zion," continued to warn against partition and the British plot, but for the high command Lake Success was very far off. Although Ely Tavin, Samuel Katz, and Eitan Livni had created an Irgun presence in Western Europe, in America the advocates of the Irgun were not only distant but also out of touch. There were, however, some outside the orthodox organizations who pushed the Irgun's case. Ben Hecht's American League for a Free Palestine had a spectacular career. Hecht wrote and Billy Rose produced "We Will Never Die," an extravaganza that once played to forty thousand people and included chorus girls, dancers, celebrity appearances, and at one improbable point fifty rabbis praying in unison. Hecht's impact was such that Zionist rivals founded Americans for the Haganah in response. Hecht and his organization, however, had little influence at Lake Success, underwrote only limited emigration, collected few arms, and had no leverage in Palestine. Begin and the Irgun pursued their own course, anticipating only reinforcements and armaments at some later date. In the meantime the major responsibility of the Irgun was to maintain the pressure, devise and carry out spectacular armed operations, and warn against the facile optimism of the Jewish Agency.

During the negotiations at Lake Success, the Irgun produced one operation that attracted considerable notice, not (for a change) because it was bloody or ruthless but rather because it was technically fascinating. During the summer one of the innumerable Irgun spotters, always on the lookout for chinks in the British armor, noticed that the Northern police headquarters on Kingsway in Haifa was protected by a high wire fence and sand-filled barrels, but that it might be possible to devise something to go over the fence and roll to the entrance of the building. Paglin did not see why not and set to work on a complicated barrel bomb. First the exact height of the fence was checked by watching cars and trucks moving in and out of the yard. Then on top of a heavy lorry Irgun engineers constructed a launch ramp so that the barrel bomb would roll off at a forty-five degree angle at just over the height of the perimeter fence. On two tires from a three-ton lorry, the bomb would then roll straight towards the building, stop, turn at a ninety-degree angle, and continue on to the target, where a lock would hold the barrel against the wall. In the final model it was possible to cut out the ninety-degree turn.

On Monday, September 29, pedestrians in Kingsway noticed a large grey lorry, loaded with a huge piece of tarpaulin-covered machinery, moving slowly down the street from the direction of the German colony. The lorry stopped by the eight-story building at the corner of Khayat Street. Inside, the Irgun operator pulled the cord release. The barrel bomb began rolling out from under the canvas, and by the time it hit the ground the lorry, armor plated on the windows and engine, had moved off down the street. The ponderous bomb, trailing a wisp of smoke, rolled up to the wall and stopped. It rocked back slightly and the lock held. There was a pause, then a huge explosion. Much of the building came crashing down in a heap of masonry and plaster dust. A shower of glass splinters tore out through the street. An Arab coffee vendor, who had watched the huge barrel appear out of nowhere and rumble up to the wall on rubber tires, still had his mouth open when flying glass cut him in two. A car was lifted off the street and smashed into a passer-by. The final casualty toll was ten killed and fifty-four wounded, thirteen seriously. On October 1, the British authorities and the newspapers received the photographs and diagrams that Paglin had made of the device and mailed to them.

As Jews and Arabs followed events at Lake Success, the underground in Palestine pursued their own violent course, often without the spectacular results of the barrel bomb explosion, but with sufficient impact to heighten the chaos in the Mandate. At 12:10 P.M., October 13, a mills bomb was tossed over the seven-foot wall of the American Consulate on Mamillah Road, Jerusalem. Two employees were injured. At the end of the month came renewed Haganah-Irgun clashes. The Haganah shot two Irgun men at Rishon-le-Zion, but, despite scathing Irgun wall-poster attacks on Ben-Gurion and the Jewish Agency, the Season sputtered out and the Irgun and LEHI returned to the campaign. Two British police were shot and wounded on Allenby Street near Barclay's Bank. In Jerusalem LEHI broke into a flat and cut down a Jewish CID man, Corporal Shalom Gurewitz: he was hit with eighteen bullets from a Thompson. The security forces got revenge when they encircled a LEHI safe house in Raanana on Wednesday, November 5. Twenty soldiers poured in a withering fire, killing five teen-agers, including three girls. Two girls and a young man were killed outright, one girl and a boy fatally wounded when they tried to flee, leaving the remaining boy and girl, shocked and unbelieving, to surrender. The same night an automobile drove slowly down Kingsway in Haifa. A metal snout poked out a back window as it came up to an outdoor café, and a single burst of fire into the tables killed a British sergeant and three policemen. The car accelerated down Kingsway. On November 13, at nine in the evening, two British policemen were walking slowly down a Jerusalem street toward a small cluster of Jews. As they drew even the Jews drew revolvers and fired, killing one and wounding the other. Almost at the same time at the Ritz Café on King George Avenue a large crowd of British soldiers were trying to forget their troubles with beer and talk. The flurry of shots that took out the two policemen did not alarm the crowd—gunfire was almost a normal Jerusalem night noise. Suddenly six grenades tumbled in from the darkness beyond the café's lights. The soldiers leaped up, breaking tables and glasses. There was a brief sound of breaking glass and British cursing; then came a long heavy burst of automatic fire and the chain of grenade explosions, each sending shrapnel into the cornered men. One was mortally wounded and twenty-seven were injured. In Haifa at almost exactly the same time, four British civilians were standing at the corner of Hechalutz and Shmaryahu Levin streets. The usual nondescript sedan pulled up to the curb. There was a long burst of automatic fire. All four lay sprawled in the gutter. Two were killed instantly, one died in a taxi on the way to the hospital, and the last two hours later in the hospital. The next day two more British policemen and two soldiers were shot down in the streets. So it went: a plainclothes detective killed on Jaffa Road, wild shooting most nights, more curfews and searches, a LEHI killing of four people suspected of divulging a safe house. There were always incidents, the echo of gunfire and mines detonating, trials and long sentences, sabotage, increasing evidence of Arab snipers. There seemed no end to the agony; and the debates of the United Nations were a far, faint hope.

The United Nations was still the only hope left, no matter what the British intended. No one at Lake Success could fathom British policy. Although Bevin, his Arabist adviser Sir Harold Beeley, Creech-Jones, and Ambassador Cadogan seemed to oppose partition, they offered no alternative, and would implement nothing unacceptable to both Arabs and Jews; in effect they would implement nothing. Those who suspected that Britain had shifted all but openly to the Arab side had ample evidence—Brigadier Clayton was present once again at the Arab League meeting at Aley in October. Those who suspected that Britain intended to stay no matter what happened at Lake Success had ample evidence too—recruiting in Britain was continuing for the Palestine police, with placards, posters, and ads in the London and provincial papers.

The United Nations debate struggled on. The three subcommittees, one on partition, one sympathetic to the Arabs, one for conciliation, continued to meet between October 21 and November 10. There was little hope for the conciliation subcommittee, and a general acceptance that the Arab sympathizers would construct a minority report. The key was the subcommittee on partition, where the delegates sought to make partition palatable to a two-thirds majority of the General Assembly. The size of the Jewish state was reduced from six thousand to fifty-five hundred square miles by the removal of part of the Negev and the city of Jaffa. The Mandate would end May 1, and the transfer of power to the Jews and Arabs would take place July 1. On November 13, Cadogan announced that British troops would not leave until August 1, and until then no agency of the United Nations could exercise power in the Mandate. The subcommittee adjusted its timetable and agreed that the Mandate was to end not later than August 1, but that a United Nations commission would administer the Mandate during transition. The following day Cadogan repeated that Britain would be the sole judge on timing the end of the Mandate. García-Granados was not alone in assuming that this British truculence was solely the result of resentment and hurt pride.

> In a word, from the moment the United Kingdom brought this problem to the United Nations, its statements have been vague and its policies tantalizing.
>
> We can only conclude that, although the United Kingdom had said that it will not oppose the partition plan, it is, in fact, opposing it. The British say they will respect the report and hand over authority to the commission, but, in fact, they refuse to hand over anything, they will not agree to give the Commission an area in which to start work.[27]

Britain was not motivated solely by resentment and hurt pride but by the attraction of a pro-Arab posture long urged by the Arabist establishment. What Bevin hoped would happen was not too far different from what Begin suspected him of plotting: the collapse of order in Palestine, with or without partition; either no Zionist state or a small remnant of one, and always the possibility that Britain would have to intervene openly. Some in Washington and New York continued to see the advantages of an Arab alignment and the dangers of advocating partition. In the State Department Loy Henderson, chief of the Near and Middle East division, feared that Arab resentment might open up the area to the Soviet Union. He had an ally in Navy Secretary James V. Forrestal, as well as in a group of pragmatists who feared Russian intentions and were unmoved by Zionist rhetoric. Their problem was simply that President Truman, who had met with Chaim Weizmann in November, favored partition. So did a substantial portion of the American political establishment, in some cases with a fervor equal to any Zionists'. The most Henderson managed was to persuade the American delegation under Herschel Johnson not to lobby in favor of partition. But Johnson had pro-Zionists in his delegation, none more so than Eleanor Roosevelt, and a president who thought otherwise. The Zionists in New York continued to employ every gambit learned in a generation of pressure politics, persuasion, and conversion. They capitalized on everything from Hitler's crimes to biblical quotations. They used the support of American friends, from Robert Taft to Robert Wagner. Truman ordered Johnson to lobby for partition—it might well be necessary despite everything the Zionists had done.

On November 24, the three subcommittees' reports were presented to the General Assembly. The conciliation subcommittee reported no progress. The vote on the Arab resolution came first and as expected was defeated twenty-five to twelve, the rest abstaining. On the partition report the Arabs collected one previous abstainer, and the vote was twenty-five to thirteen, sufficient as a majority vote to carry partition to the formal General Assembly, but one vote short of the needed two-thirds. The Arabs actually had a razor-thin edge. A period of intense lobbying began, this time with the Americans leading the way, along with the committed delegations from Guatemala, Uruguay, and Czechoslovakia. On Wednesday, November 26, the General Assembly met to vote. The Zionists were not sure of their two-thirds, a difficult majority to fashion and hold. Haiti had spoken against partition in debate. Paraguay had sent no instructions to their delegation. Liberia was unsure. Greece had decided to vote no, as would the Philippines. Some delegations in favor were contemplating abstention. No one could be sure what the French intended. Hour by hour, the speakers strode to the rostrum to put their views on the record, while in the lobbies the conferences and caucuses went on nonstop. At five in the afternoon, with speeches still to come, the General Assembly decided to recess until Friday, because Thursday was Thanksgiving. For forty-eight hours, with the help of the Americans and their other friends, the Zionists shored up their position. Antonio Vieuz of Haiti, who had spoken eloquently against partition, received instructions to vote for it. Pressure was turned on Liberia and Greece. General Carlos Romulo of the Philippines suddenly departed on an Atlantic voyage, and his replacement agreed to abide by the wishes of Ambassador Elizalde in Washington and vote yes. Belgium, the Netherlands, and New Zealand, instead of abstaining, reluctantly agreed to vote yes. Paraguay finally received instructions to vote yes. The new revolutionary regime in Thailand removed its old Ambassador. Thailand would not vote. France remained uncertain. Ambassador Alexandre Parodi on Friday requested a further delay of twenty-four hours. Apparently Paris wanted to show her Islamic colonies that every avenue was being explored, but this gave no clue as to the ultimate intentions of France. Washington had indicated further aid might depend on their vote. Finally the delays and postponements ended. On Saturday afternoon, November 29, at Flushing Meadows in the huge grey building that once contained a skating rink and now housed the General Assembly of the United Nations, fifty-six of the fifty-seven delegations met to decide the future of Palestine.

By five in the afternoon, the three hundred seats reserved for the delegates were filled: Saudi Arabia's Emir Faisal ibn Abd al-Aziz, austere and brooding in his black and gold abayah, a figure from another world; Sir Alexander Cadogan, cool, indifferent; France's Alexandre Parodi, his vote still in doubt. In the jammed spectators' gallery sat Moshe Sharett, counting his votes over and over. Some of his colleagues were crammed into the press section; but Weizmann had remained in his hotel, exhausted, too overwhelmed to appear at the vote. Further along in the spectators' gallery sat Jamal Husseini, representative of the Palestinian Arabs, who, like his colleagues, sat impassively. In the delegates' lounge he had just warned once more that partition would mean war. The Arabs could do no less if justice were denied them.

Just after five, Assembly President Oswaldo Aranha of Brazil announced the vote on the partition subcommittee resolution. Afghanistan voted no, as expected. Argentina abstained. Chile switched to abstention. A majority was assured, but two-thirds uncertain. France voted yes, and a small wave of applause swept through the spectators' gallery. Finally it was over: thirty-three yes, thirteen no, and ten abstentions. Thailand was absent. The United Nations had authorized a Jewish state. The British delegation had abstained. Now they were stern faced; Sir Harold Beeley, next to Cadogan, was grim. The Arabs showed no emotion. Six-thousand miles away, at two in the morning, crowds abandoned their radios and swept into the streets of Jerusalem, Tel Aviv, and Ramat Gan, shouting and dancing. Their Arab neighbors turned off their radios and went to bed. Such injustice at the hands of strangers would not go unpunished.

At Lake Success, in the old ice rink, the Arabs made it clear to the excited and flustered delegates that the vote was a beginning not an end.

The government of Saudi Arabia registers, on this historic occasion, the fact that it does not consider itself bound by the resolution adopted today by the

General Assembly. Furthermore, it reserves to itself the full right to act freely in whatever way it deems fit, in accordance with the principles of right and justice.[28]

Iraq does not recognize the validity of this decision, will reserve freedom of action toward its implementation and hold those who were influential in passing it against the free conscience of mankind responsible for the consequences.[29]

Nations are not created by majority vote. In the delirium of their triumph, the Jews of New York, Tel Aviv, and Ramat Gan seemed to think so. They had a state. The hora went round and round, and the songs went on. "A Jewish state! Long may it live!" Standing on the rooftop in downtown Tel Aviv, Geula Cohen, the LEHI radio announcer who had escaped from prison with the help of the Arabs of Abu Gosh, looked down in despair at the celebration. "A Jewish state without Jerusalem, without Hebron and Bethlehem, without the Gilead or the Bashan or the lands beyond the Jordan."[30] Samuel Katz, back in the Mandate, was no less depressed. When his neighbors pounded on his windows urging him to come out, he felt no jubilation. "There was nothing to sing about. I knew we had a new war on our hands."[31]

The next day, less than twenty-four hours after the partition vote at Lake Success, a group of Arab irregulars opened fire on a bus on a road outside Jerusalem, killing seven Jews. At the United Nations Amir Arslan of Syria warned, "Let the consequences be on the heads of others, not on ours."[32] Seven Jews lay bloody on the floor of a riddled bus. Spontaneously and violently, the Arabs of Palestine acted. The Mandate collapsed into anarchy. Palestine once again became a battleground.

NOTES

1.   Jan Gitlin, *The Conquest of Acre Fortress* (Tel Aviv: Hadar, 1962), p. 74.

2.   Ibid., p. 153.

3.   Ibid., p. 150.

4.   *Official Records, First Special Session of the General Assembly,* vol. 3 (Lake Success, N.Y. 1947), p. 116.

5.   Ibid., p. 197.

6.   *Palestine Post,* 11 June 1947.

7.   Jorge García-Granados, *The Birth of Israel* (New York: Knopf, 1949), p. 59.

8.   Samuel Katz, *Days of Fire* (London: W. H. Allen, 1968), p. 160.

9.   Ibid., p. 161.

10.   Ibid., p. 162.

11.   García-Granados, p. 157.

12.   Farran was court-martialed on October 1 and found not guilty on the following day. Convinced of his guilt and that the verdict had been a cover-up, LEHI decided to take matters into their own hands.

13.   Ruth Gruber, *Destination Palestine: The Story of the Haganah Ship Exodus 1947* (New York: Current Books, 1948), pp. 17–18.

14.   Ibid., p. 47.

15.   Ibid., p. 18.

16.   Katz, *Days of Fire*, p. 168.

17.   Gruber, *Destination Palestine*, p. 109.

18.   Menachem Begin, *The Revolt* (Los Angeles: Nash, 1972), p. 284.

19.   *Palestine Post*, 30 July 1947.

20.   Begin, p. 285.

21.   Katz, p. 169.

22.   Dan Kurzman, *Genesis 1948: The First Arab-Israeli War* (New York: World, 1970), p. 173.

23.   Great Britain, *Parliamentary Debates*, Commons, vol. 441, col. 636.

24.   *Palestine Post*, 4 August 1947.

25.   García-Granados, p. 157.

26.   Begin, *Revolt*, p. 333.

27.   García-Granados, p. 257.

28.   *Official Record of the Second Session of the General Assembly*, vol. 2 (Lake Success, N.Y., 1948), p. 1425.

29.   Ibid., p. 1427.

30.   Geula Cohen, *Woman of Violence* (London: Rupert Hart-Davis, 1966), p. 271.

31.   Katz, *Days of Fire*, p. 184.

32.   *Second Session General Assembly*, p. 1427.

רק כך

NOTICE	הודעה

1. On the Day of Atonement, multitudes will assemble on the Mount of the Temple, before the Wailing Wall, and evoke the memory of millions of our fallen brethren, victims of German cruelty and British treachery.

2. The principles of civilized humanity demand that the sacred prayer should not be hindered and the sacred place should not be profaned.

3. The Government, which rules, against the will of the Hebrew Nation, **temporarily** in our homeland is asked not to violate these principles.

4. Every British policeman, who will dare to intrude into the yard of the Wailing Wall on the Atonement Day and hinder the traditional prayer, **will be recorded as a criminal and punished accordingly.**

Hairgun Hatzevai Haleumi
B'ERETZ-ISRAEL

א. ביום הכפורים על הר-הבית, ליד הכתל המערבי, יתייחדו המוני העם עם נשמות קדושי ישראל, שנפלו קרבן לאכזריות הגרמנית ולבגידה הבריטית.

ב. עקרונות האנושות התרבותית מחייבים, כי לא תופרע התפלה הקדושה ולא יחולל המקום הקדוש.

ג. הממשלה, **השולטת זמנית** – למורת רוחו של העם העברי – בארץ מולדתנו, נדרשת לא להפר עקרונות אלה.

ד. כל שוטר בריטי, שיעיז להתפרץ, במשך יום הכפורים, לרחבת הכתל המערבי ולהפריע את התפלה המסורתית – **יירשם כפושע פלילי ויבוא על ענשו.**

הארגון הצבאי הלאומי
בארץ-ישראל

(above) The Yom Kippur wall poster, September 27, 1945. *(right)* CID Building in Jerusalem after the December 27, 1945 raid.

(left) Menachem Begin. (below) Menachem Begin with wife and son Benjamin in 1945.

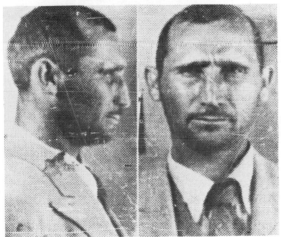

(above) Police mug shot of Yeshua Zettler. (right) Amihai Paglin.

(above left) Guela Cohen. *(above right)* Eliahu Lankin. *(right top)* Captain K. H. Spence, G. C. Warburton, A. E. Taylor just before being kidnapped. This photo was taken without foreknowledge by a press photographer. *(right bottom)* The same three kidnapped officers after they were released in July. *(facing page, top)* The ruins of the King David Hotel, Jerusalem, 1947 *(facing page, bottom)* "Bevingrad," the barbed wire zone in Jerusalem during Jewish-Arab conflict, 1947-1949.

רק כך

אזהרה!

חייל עברי, שנפל בשבי האויב, "נידון" ע"י "בית-דין" של צבא הכבוש הבריטי למלקות.

אנו מזהירים את ממשלת הדכוי מפני הוצאה לפועל של עונש משפיל זה.

אם הוא יוצא אל הפועל, יוטל אותו עונש על קציני הצבא הבריטי. כל אחד מהם יהיה עלול ללקות 18 מלקות.

הארגון הצבאי הלאומי
בארץ-ישראל

כסלו תש"ז

WARNING!

A Hebrew soldier, taken prisoner by the enemy, was sentenced by an illegal British Military "Court" to the humiliating punishment of flogging.

We warn the occupation Government not to carry out this punishment, which is contrary to the laws of soldiers honour. If it is put into effect — every officer of the British occupation army in Eretz-Israel will be liable to be punished in the same way: to get 18 whips.

HAIRGUN HAZVAI HALEUMI (N. M. O.)
b'Eretz-Israel

Warning by the Irgun, written by the beginning of December, 1946.

TO MEN BETWEEN 18 AND 28
(INCLUDING THOSE ABOUT TO BE CALLED UP)

How to Get Into a Crack Force
–Earn £20 a month & All Found

A Vital Job — a MAN'S Job —
Ask yourself, "Would I Suit?"

If your health and intelligence are good, if you're single and want a *man's* job — one of the most vital jobs in the British Empire — if you like the glamour of serving in a crack force in a country of sand dunes and orange groves, historic towns and modern settlements — if you prefer this type of life on good pay *that you can save* . . . here's how you can get into the Palestine Police Force.

A typical job of work in Jerusalem — a smart, well-trained constable controls traffic of all kinds in the sunny streets of the capital.

THE FACTS
(Parents also please read)

The Palestine picture is not as some often imagine —one of constant turbulence, but young men of integrity and intelligence are needed to police it —fairly and firmly. Men of the right character (toughness alone is not called for) are hand picked and carefully looked after. If you think you're the right type of young man for the Palestine Police send off this coupon now.

CONDITIONS: You must be physically fit, be 5 ft. 6 ins. or over in height and have normal-eyesight.

PAY: £20 a month *to start with.* Extra pay for specialists (you are given training first!) Pensions for long service.

ALL FOUND: Smart uniform. Good rations, excellent accommodation, skilled medical treatment. (Your pay is your own!)

LEAVE: 2 months at home after 2 years. 3 months after 3 years. 2 weeks per year local leave (visits to Egypt, Syria, Cyprus, etc.) Camels, horses, cars, motor-cycles, speed boats, radio, sport, etc.

The Desert Patrol on the watch for hashish smugglers. On this job camels are more suited than are modern trucks.

JOIN THE

COUPON

To Dept. W/I Crown Agents for Colonies, 4, Millbank, London, S.W.1.
Please send me illustrated prospectus and application form.

NAME...
ADDRESS...
.... *AGE*...............

PALESTINE
POLICE FORCE
AND HAVE A **MAN'S** JOB!

(Remember this when registering for National Service)

British Palestinian Police recruiting poster.

AP

(above) British troops overlooking the Old City of Jerusalem, 1948. (below left) The hanging room, Acre Fortress. (below right) Moshe Barazani of LEHI, and Meir Feinstein escorted in chains by British security forces.

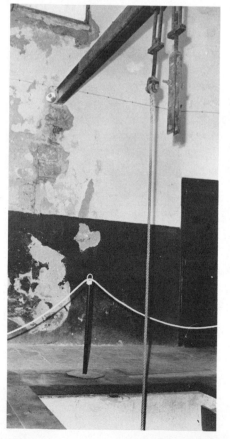

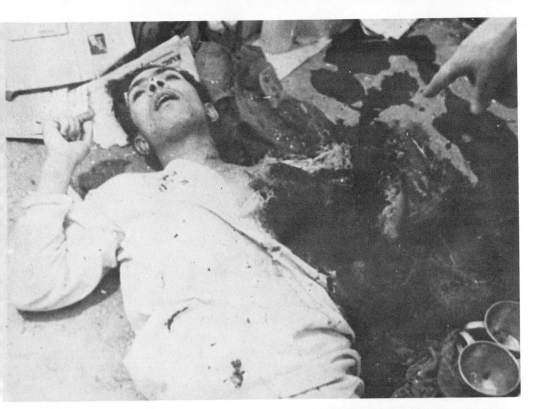

(top) The death cell of Barazani and Feinstein after the grenade detonation. *(above)* Crew captured from the "Ben Hecht" and held in Acre Prison through March and April of 1947. From left top: M. Shmulevitz, K. Amrani, J. Romm, Yosef Morach, Yohav Levi. Bottom: Menachem Schiff, Palech Tamir, Gershon Gradovsky. *(right)* The tunnel mouth in the cellars of Acre.

(top) Exodus, 1947, in Haifa Harbor. *(right)* Irgun railway operation at Benyamina, June 1947. *(below)* Hangings in Palestine: The bodies of British sergeants Clifford Martin (left) and Mervyn Paice as they hung from Eucalyptus trees, July 30, 1947, near Natanya, Palestine.

To the People of England !

TO THE PEOPLE WHOSE GOVERNMENT PROCLAIMED "PEACE IN OUR TIME"

This is a Warning !

YOUR GOVERNMENT HAS DIPPED his Majesty's Crown in Jewish blood and polished it with Arab oil — "Out damned spot — out I say…"

YOUR GOVERNMENT HAS VIOLATED every article of the Eretz-Israel Mandate, flouted international law and invaded our country.

Oswiecim, Dachau and Treblinka made way for the "Exodus"

To the Hitler–Bevin Alliance — To the murder of the

survivors whom Hitler's wrath could not reach

We are resolute
that it shall not come to pass again !

We will carry the war
to the very heart of the Empire !

We will strike
with all the bitterness and fury of our servitude and bondage.

We are prepared to fight
a war of liberation now to avoid a war of enslavement tomorrow.

PEOPLE OF ENGLAND !

Press your Government to quit Eretz-Israel NOW !
Demand that your sons and daughters return home
or you may not see them again.

FIGHTERS FOR FREEDOM OF ISRAEL

A pamphlet the LEHI planned to be dropped in London, August 9, 1947.

(above) Paglin's truck bomb, September 29, 1947. *(below left)* Truck bomb results, Haifa, September 29, 1947 *(below right)* Salen Harb brandishing a revolver and a Koran at the Congress of Arab People in Cairo, October 12, 1947.

PART 4

THE UNDECLARED WAR

The Arab world is not in the mood to compromise. We shall fight. You will gain nothing by peaceful means and compromises. . . . It is too late to speak of peaceful solutions.
—Abdul Rahman Azzam Pasha
Secretary General of the Arab League

CHAPTER 1

The Arabs Attack,
December 1947 — March 1948

Drive the Jews into the sea.

—*Haj Amin al-Husseini*

At first light on December 1, dim figures began slipping through the alleys and side streets of Jaffa. They moved into the Manshiya quarter past the Hassan Bek Mosque and up to the edge of Tel Aviv, in some places within a few blocks of Allenby Street. There was a shot, the first in tens of thousands that would be fired out of the Manshiya into Tel Aviv. The single figures turned into groups; and the mob swept against the first Jewish shops, burning and looting. Not wholly unprepared, the Haganah and Irgun arrived on the scene. There were sharp, vicious fire fights all day. The security forces kept a discreet distance, losing only a single British constable. By the end of the day, the first reports were five Jews and three Arabs killed. The next day, with the Arabs still on a general strike, fighting continued all along the edge of Manshiya; six Arabs were killed and twenty-three wounded, fourteen Jews killed and twenty-one wounded. The attempt by the Arab mobs to push through toward Allenby Street collapsed as the Haganah and Irgun came out into the open. By then the fighting had spread throughout the Mandate.

In the countryside Arabs left their villages, crept toward their local kibbutzim, and fired into them. In the towns the Arab suqs were crowded with men looking for new cartridges. In Haifa sniping led to open battle at the edge of the Jewish city. Everywhere part-time snipers crouched in the hills and potted away at the Egged buses, at Jewish cars and transport, at any promising target. The best target range was the Tel Aviv-Jerusalem road, beyond Latrun, that snaked through the mountains to the New City's western approaches. There was sniping throughout Jerusalem, and from the first week in December the position of the 1,700 Jews isolated inside the Old City was perilous. Despite the seeming chaos and violence before November 30, the Arab reaction to partition was nothing less than a small scale, irregular war. The British simply stood by and observed, having no intention of risking further lives to monitor Arabs or defend Jews.

During the first two weeks after the partition vote, ninety-three Arabs, eight-four Jews, and seven members of the security force died. The Arab/Jewish edges of the divided cities—Jerusalem, Haifa, Tel Aviv-Jaffa—were battlegrounds. The roads were unsafe, especially for Jewish traffic. The isolated kibbutzim had come under siege, as had separate Jewish quarters in the Old City, Safed, and elsewhere. Attracted by the action and the prospect of loot, self-appointed guerrillas from Lebanon, Syria, and Transjordan began to drift across the borders, coalescing into bands and then melting away. Jewish road traffic could move only in armed convoys. On December 10, ten Jews were killed and four wounded when their convoy was ambushed between kilos fourteen and fifteen on the Jerusalem-Hebron road, during an attempt to get through to the Etzion bloc of kibbutzim. In Haifa six Arabs were killed and thirty-two wounded by Haganah fire. In the Old City three Arabs were killed during a clumsy attempt to break into the Jewish quarter. Over the next two days thirty-six more Arabs and eleven Jews were killed, along with two British soldiers.

Although Creech-Jones insisted that British acceptance of the United Nations partition resolution "was not a grudging acceptance. . . . We wish our authority transferred to our successor in an orderly manner,"[1] this was not exactly the case. High Commissioner Cunningham had at last received a firm policy directive from London. He was to keep the situation as calm as possible with minimal British invovement. He was "to have nothing to do with Partition in any way, shape, or form."[2] Cunningham had grown increasingly gloomy about the prospects for Palestine. He had been sent off without any clear directive—Attlee simply suggested he "just go out and govern the country"[3] and went on to more serious social matters while Bevin and his Arabist advisors constructed what policy there was. The present policy, according to Cunningham's undersecretary Sir Harold Beeley, was to align Britain's interest in the area with those of the Arabs. Implementing partition, accepted, as Beeley noted, "with an absolute minimum of enthusiasm,"[4] was out. On December 6, a three-page secret British Army order arrived, setting out the principles that would govern withdrawal—there was no mention of any continuing army responsibility for maintaining order. So each night just before dinner, his one private time, Cunningham sat slumped in an armchair before the fire in his sitting room, listening to Bach and Vivaldi, trying to forget the casualty lists, the swift decay of thirty years of British effort, and the grim prospect of worse to come. He could do no more than he was ordered to do, watch and wait until the time came to leave. And what would be left?

In London Bevin, the Arabists, Montgomery, the military strategists, and the smart money in general foresaw a variety of promising options. Although evacuation had been announced for May 15, the local Arabs might create sufficient chaos so that Britain would stay. Until early December London continued the construction of new British bases in southern Palestine. Britain might leave by one port and be asked back by another. The Arab Legion, under Sir John Glubb Pasha, directed by British officers, might pull back over the Jordan one day and come back the next. Even if the local Arabs muffed their chance, the Jews would stand little hope against regular Arab armies. Illegal immigrants were still being shifted to Cyprus, where all potential volunteers were kept behind wires. The naval blockade would continue to prevent modern arms from reaching the Haganah. All that had to be done in the Mandate was to maintain an even-handed, neutral posture. This would favor the Arabs, who were receiving arms and volunteers over the open borders, who were ambushing convoys and settlements that were prohibited by law from possessing arms. Even when attacks on Jewish convoys became routine, London would not budge "since the carrying of firearms by vehicle drivers does not constitute effective protection against small-arms fire from ambush."[5] So Britain at last had a Palestine policy that apparently offered a variety of promising options by condoning an irregular war in Palestine. It was not one of the empire's finer moments.

The events in Palestine, after the partition resolution brought the naive singing into the streets, confirmed the Irgun's analysis. There was no need to dismantle the anti-British campaign. There was the added dimension of Arab irregulars recreating the tactics and techniques of the 1936 revolt, but this time directed solely at the Yishuv. As the prospect for partition grew during the autumn of 1947, the Irgun high command increasingly focused on the problem of Arab resistance. The Arabs had been practically ignored during the revolt, but the incidents of August attracted Irgun attention. These, coupled with the repeated threats by spokesmen of the Arab League and the various Arab regimes, meant that the Irgun would have to adjust first to an irregular war, and then to a conventional one. The first prospect was daunting and the second dreadful. Recruitment had climbed to two thousand members, but only seven hundred could be armed at one time, none had been formally trained, and there was almost no heavy equipment. As an underground organization fighting the British, this had not been crucial, but to participate in the defense of the Yishuv and to contemplate effective offensive operations required much more.

The news from the diaspora was not unpromising. Tavin, Livni, and Katz were in Europe setting up supply nets, recruiting volunteers, preparing for the moment when reinforcements could be sent. In the meantime the Irgun would have to make do with the arms on hand, with those that could be produced in the underground factories, and with those that could be stolen, looted, or bought in the growing chaos of the Mandate. Taking advantage of that chaos and the growing British caution, Bezalel Amizur of the high command began to set up regular, open-tented camps for the new volunteers, out in the orange groves. The number of volunteers increased almost weekly, as did the budget, which rose from £3,000 to £10,000 a week, money that, excepting some South African contributions, had to be found in Palestine. A few donations dribbled in from Latin America and $10,000 came for the United States in 1948, but much of the overseas money had to be funneled into arms procurement in Europe. The high command hoped that European arms, and especially European volunteers, would permit an offensive that would sweep forward to the Jordan, even if the regular Arab armies did invade. The high command remained optimistic about the Irgun's capability against the Arabs; and, with the Irgun out in front, the cautious Haganah would have to follow. Before the arrival of the diaspora forces, however, the Irgun intended to concentrate on two fronts: Jaffa, a snipers' nest that could cut off both the Negev and Tel Aviv from the Jerusalem corridor, and the Ramele-Lydda Arab sector that dominated the Jerusalem road from the north. With only seven hundred armed actives, even operations on these two fronts could be little more than counter-raids. The prime necessity was to enlarge, train, and equip a more orthodox army as fast as possible.

In Jerusalem Yehuda Lapidot was ordered into teaching. He had been director of the foreign-press section of propaganda, languishing there while recovering from a wound at Bat-Yam that prevented him from using a gun. The high command decided that a course should be set up to train local commanders from around the country and promising recruits, particularly with rifles and Brens. Jerusalem was hardly the ideal place for the course—mostly the Irgun used Stens and revolvers in city fighting rather than the more visible rifles and heavy Brens—with the British jammed into the city, training camps were impossible. The Irgun had been using schools and synagogues during slack hours, often without the permission or knowledge of the regular occupants. Lapidot, however, was game, and he began to look for a flat to hold his first class of fifteen. He eventually made contact with a rich young man who, to spite his disapproving father living in the same building, turned over his elegant flat near the edge of Katamon to Lapidot. All the expensive furniture was moved out so that the fifteen candidates could move in. With his mind on military matters, Lapidot arranged for sandwiches instead of proper meals—after five weeks of sandwiches three times a day, cooped up in the unfurnished apartment, his first class looked forward eagerly to the pleasures of a real war.

Lapidot's most serious problem was not avoiding the British, despite two nearby posts, but getting along with the Haganah. The sudden appearance of a relatively large Irgun unit in a mixed area under Haganah control caused difficulties. They were told not very diplomatically that the Irgun was running a training center, nothing more. The area was filled with snipers, and the British had placed two cannons on a roof, warning the Haganah they would open up. The cannons proved too much for Lapidot, and he asked Jerusalem Irgun headquarters for permission to nip over and steal them after his class was completed. His poking about alerted the local Haganah commander, who warned him off the cannons. The warning would have had little effect, except that Irgun headquarters had already turned him down. Lapidot's apparent acquiescence greatly eased the tension caused by an incident that Lapidot thought inane, but the Haganah had taken very seriously.

While his pupils were sitting on the floor, methodically taking apart and reassembling the Brens, one of the recruits waiting his turn was peering out below the shades. Suddenly he noticed, directly across the street, someone else peeking out from under the shades of a second-floor flat. After the two had peeked back and forth for a while, Lapidot agreed that the young man could slip out and investigate. He returned to announce that the chap seemed most uneasy, and, besides, he didn't look Jewish. Several of the recruits went across the way to the second floor, where they found a man "visiting" a woman, as one disapproving young volunteer put it. He did not speak Hebrew; and a search of the apartment produced a revolver, but nothing really seemed amiss. The couple were obviously not snipers, and both seemed quite embarrassed that their visiting hours had been interrupted. Lapidot simply warned the man off, sent the recruits back to the flat with the revolver and went about his business. When he returned to the training flat, he found a violent argument taking place between a crowd of Haganah men and his recruits. The Haganah commander said that the peeping man was an Armenian—of course he did not look Jewish. He was bringing information to the Haganah, not "visiting" the woman; and of course he was nervous with the bloody Irgun peeking at him from under a shade. The affair trailed off in mutters, and the Haganah departed with the revolver. Soon the Haganah commander reappeared and formally announced to Lapidot that the affair was not over. The woman had been insulted by the Irgun assumption about "visiting" with an Armenian and demanded an apology. Lapidot agreed to go back with the Haganah officer. They found the woman red and weeping. The Haganah officer immediately apologized for both organizations; and Lapidot, who could hardly muffle his laughter, dutifully nodded his head. His duty done, the Haganah officer stalked down the stairs, but he suspected he had been made to look an ass in front of the separatists. The result was weeks of suspicion and tension, while the Irgun recruits learned their trade and ate their sandwiches.

As a reward and final examination Lapidot decided to take the fifteen men out to the countryside to some waste ground to the west of Katamon. There, beyond the interest of the Arabs or British, the recruits could fire their rifles and Brens for the first time. They were delighted at the chance. They arrived at the impromptu firing range. Lapidot had scavenged five cartridges for each—seventy-five rounds was an impressive hoard. They rattled off their practice rounds with considerable enthusiasm. Lapidot then lined them up in more or less regulation order with sloped arms, and they marched back toward Katamon for new orders. Nearly there, Lapidot's little formation almost met disaster head on. The column turned a corner with great precision to face a British patrol car, containing four men armed with submachine guns. With dismay Lapidot realized his Brens and rifles had no ammunition—all the rounds had been used up in practice. It was clearly no use to run; the British would simply open fire. So he ordered the column to continue in step, arms sloped. On they marched, every eye on the British soldiers. The patrol car moved smoothly alongside. The British watched the sixteen heavily-armed Irgun men, who in turn watched back. The British patrol, outnumbered, outgunned, and unchallenged, rumbled on down the street. The Irgun column returned to the flat, graduates into a new irregular war.

This was the kind of war that was developing for the Irgun: desperate efforts to catch up in training, appalling shortages, and a new uneasy relation with the British. They were adjusting. The question was, would the adjustment be swift enough and effective enough if the Arab attacks escalated? The reaction to the new situation was quite different for LEHI; for that organizaton had not attempted to adjust to the new reality and had nearly collapsed. The Irgun had immediately refused to accept partitioned Palestine.

> A tiny little state, . . . a mutilated Eretz Yisrael without Jerusalem and without Haifa, without land and without water, without freedom and without a future.[6]

Begin and the rest insisted the eventual Zionist state would be limited only by the capacity of Zionist rifles. States were made with arms, not votes—against the British, against the Arabs, against anyone standing in the way of the future. Matters were not so clear within LEHI.

A deep unease began to spread within LEHI as the Yishuv sat rapt before the radios, listening to the news from Lake Success, hearing the words "evacuate" and "withdrawal." Like the Irgun, LEHI suspected a trick, a plot, and could not envision a real end of the Mandate. Yet now the possibility existed. After the partition vote there was the prospect of a Jewish state, one that would have to be made real by force of arms; but it was real nevertheless. Yet much of LEHI's struggle had been otherworldly. There were the endless ideological debates, the carefully honed positions and postures; but the cement that held the organization together was a shared dream, a will to sacrifice, a dedication to a vision too luminous to detail. They sang, "Only death can free us from the ranks."

> In our ecstatic vision of Redemption it had always seemed to us that victory in war would coincide with the fulfillment of the dream of ages. Somewhere beyond the realms of cold reason, we had believed that, when the last British soldier left the country, messianic times would arrive.[7]

There would be no messianic times, no ideal state, no more blood spent on dreams. The end of the long night, lived with fierce intensity, was about to end inevitably. There would be only a narrow state, with the prose of bureaucrats, careers incrementally advanced, wages and regular hours. There would no longer be the shared exhilaration of danger, the narcotic of the underground, no longer any hope of making history. Almost from the first Begin had paved the way for the Irgun to move out of the shadows. The Irgun would disappear with the proclamation of the state. Betar had already been dissolved the previous August. Those who wanted to go into politics could do so. Those who did not could move on, their sacrifices made. Not so in LEHI. Now the British were to go, and suddenly it appeared that the Arabs were the enemy. Eldad had not wanted to see an Arab enemy; Yellin-Mor continued to believe a Jewish-Arab clash could be avoided. Shamir was interned in Africa. Zettler was not interested in ideological discussions. For two months LEHI evaded accepting the new reality of an Arab war, then defined as a facet of a general British plot.

> The events in Palestine since the United Nations decision prove that British imperialism has decided, after its military and political defeat, to move its Arab allies into action with direct and open British support. Aided by terrorist measures, the Arab Higher Committee has succeeded in making itself supreme over the Arab masses. Were the Arab people acting of their own free will, and not in accordance with their own interests, they would not have supported the rioters. Indication of weakness on the part of the Hebrew people will only weaken the determination of the Arab masses to resist the dictates of their leaders . . .
>
> The FFI have decided to open an offensive against the rioters and their accessories.[8]

By the time the LEHI high command had decided on a correct position during the irregular war, the wrangling over the future had grown very bitter.

The first split came over the future structure and role of the organization. Yellin-Mor believed that the time for politics had arrived. LEHI should move above ground, become a radical political party, not stolidly old-line "socialist" like the Zionist left, but dynamic, seeking to exploit the changing world scene, the rise of anti-imperialism, and the interest of Soviet Russia. Zettler thought Yellin-Mor a fool and wanted to get on with the struggle, to maintain LEHI as a military underground to counterbalance the pacifists of the Jewish Agency and the Haganah. Eldad, still wrapped in the glowing biblical dreams of a Third Temple and the redemption of the Hebrew nation through blood sacrifice, could not imagine any end to the struggle either, any degrading withdrawal into politics. Throughout the membership division appeared. Families wanted the volunteers home now that the revolt was as good as over. Soon there would have to be a real army to repulse the armies of the Arab states; soon the British would be gone; soon things would change. All at once they realized that they had survived. They had a future with special limits and opportunities, not a revolutionary destiny. In December Zettler went to Jerusalem to direct operations—there at least there would be no politics, no dithering over revolutionary destinies.

The Jewish Agency's tendency to continue Zionist politics as usual—after all, such a strategy had just won the promise of a state—began to erode during December. Some had not lost hope that the British would protect the Yishuv and maintain order. Some remained confident that the United Nations would protect the emerging Jewish state. Some hoped the Palestinian Arabs, would, as they had done before, return to their villages and suqs after the brief ecstasy of violence. Some hoped that the Arab states' threats were no more than bombast. Not all were so optimistic. Ben-Gurion, the executive of the Jewish Agency, and Israel Galili and his Haganah had concluded by December that a massive effort was necessary to prepare the Haganah for any eventuality, including a war with five Arab states. Ben-Gurion had people working on acquiring arms and equipment in the United States. His special agent, Ehud Avriel, arrived in Paris in December with full authority and considerable funds. In the meantime the military situation seemed to decay daily.

The Haganah was not really a waiting army but a lightly armed militia, tied to settlement and quarter defense. There were only 400 full-time Haganah members. The mobil Palmach force under Yigal Allon had a strength of 3,100, but could not be fully mobilized at any one time. There were not enough arms for the other 32,000 Haganah people, and almost no heavy arms—700 light machine guns, 200 medium machine guns, 600 two-inch and 100 three-inch mortars. There was no armor, no air force, no artillery, and only ammunition for a three-day conventional war. By the end of the month, the first illicit shipment from the Haganah base at Magenta outside Milan came into the Mandate, mostly Brens, rifles, and .303 and 9-mm. ammunition.

The crucial defense decision had to be made with only these limited resources in hand. And Ben-Gurion would make it, for he increasingly came to dominate all the institutions and agencies of the inchoate state. There could be no struggle to independence without him, and his decisions were not always based on sound military principles or even, his critics contended, objective reality. His first principle was that there must be no retreat, no matter how isolated the kibbutz, how vulnerable the quarter, how defenseless the settlement. There would be no concentration of resources, no temporary evacuation of endangered women and children, no cutting of inevitable losses. Next, if possible, the Haganah would hold onto the mixed districts, especially in western Jerusalem, and keep the Arabs off balance by the odd grenade and shots at night. Convoys with armored buses and trucks were to be organized to preserve the isolated settlements. Mostly the immediate policy was to hold on.

Such a seeming return to havlaga at such a moment of crisis was no more than the Irgun had expected—Ben Gurion still seemed the same old cautious politician, now dependent on United Nations good will. The Irgun wanted action. On December 11, it mounted a series of offensive operations throughout the Mandate. At ten on Thursday morning, an attack squad moved into the village of Tireh, near Haifa, warned the women and children to get out, and blew up the main house—thirteen Arabs were killed and six wounded. Similar attacks took place at Yazur near Tel Aviv, Shaafat near Jerusalem, and Yehudiyeh on the Tel Aviv-Lydda road, all centers of irregular activity. The same afternoon a bomb was detonated in the Haifa suq, killing six Arabs and wounding forty. In Jerusalem another bomb detonated in the crowd in front of the Damascus Gate, "traditional gathering place of the Arab terrorists."

It was like the glory, gory days of the Arab revolt, terror begetting terror; but the Irgun felt it was time to act. Even Ben-Gurion praised the operation at Tireh before he learned that the Irgun was involved. The next day the orthodox line appeared in *Davar:* such acts were "senseless provocation." Yet the era of havlaga had at last passed, if not for *Davar* then for the Haganah, whose patrols were soon blowing up houses to encourage Arab evacuation, attacking Arab villages, and ambushing Arab patrols.

Within the Jewish Agency, under the shadow of the Arab threat, there were those who felt the old divisions between Haganah and Irgun too great a luxury. The Irgun had already called for a provisional government and the union of all fighters. This was sufficient for some in the Agency to make a direct approach to Begin. On December 15, Begin, Landau, and Katz went to the Tel Aviv home of the Mizrachi leader, David Zvi Pinkas, to meet a delegation from the Jewish Agency, Mapai, and Mizrachi. Nothing very concrete came from the discussions. The Irgun could not convince them that the British would not open up a port on February 1, as the United Nations had requested, or that a real war was in the offing. They agreed on some technical matters concerning defensive positions in Tel Aviv, but that was it. Neither Ben-Gurion nor many of influential Haganah commanders wanted any such initiative. They did not trust Begin and the dissidents, nor did they seek an alliance that would recognize the separatists. In fact Haganah-Irgun relations again became tense with the renewal of the Season of beatings, spying, and even kidnappings. At last the Haganah agreed to end the kidnappings. Then, two weeks later at the beginning of January, Yedidiah Segal, an Irgun officer in Haifa, was kidnapped by a Haganah unit. In retaliation the Irgun lifted one of the Haganah intelligence officers in Haifa. On January 12, the Irgun Haifa commander Ammon received a letter from the Haganah commander suggesting a prisoner exchange. The Haganah man was released. According to the Haganah the Irgun man was released. But Yedidiah Segal did not return. Three days later his body was found in the Arab village of Tireh. On January 16, the Haganah announced that Segal had escaped before he could be released. Many within the Irgun wanted reprisals; Segal's mother came to plead for moderation: "I do not want the shedding of my son's blood to cause a civil war."[10] Instead the Irgun high command requested that the Jewish Agency appoint a public inquiry committee. This was done, but early in February another serious incident postponed serious discussions. Increasingly, as British security forces moderated their activities and withdrew from the Jewish sectors, the Irgun had come out into the open. In order to push their drive for arms, the high command decided on an above-ground campaign for funds. At a rally around an Irgun sound truck in Mograbi Square in Tel Aviv, Haganah men threw hand grenades into the crowd. No one was killed, but there were some serious injuries. On this particular night Begin, for the first time since the opening of the revolt, came above ground and walked openly down Allenby Street. Since early 1947 he and his family had been living in a house in the center of Tel Aviv near the Hasimah theater. No one recognized him but a few very startled Irgun people. He had come out to listen to the general criticism of the Haganah action. Despite the death of Segal, the Mograbi incident, and a long series of minor provocations, Begin felt that negotiations with the Jewish Agency should continue; but progress remained halting.

Though no political settlement was reached, if the state was proclaimed there would be no need of one, since Begin had promised to dissolve the Irgun. An operational agreement was eventually reached on March 8: in static defense, the Irgun would be under Haganah orders through Irgun officers. The Haganah would approve Irgun offensive operations against the Arabs or reprisals against the British. The Irgun would carry out operations assigned by the Haganah but would continue to resist efforts at disarming by the British. Arms raids would be joint, carried out by mutual agreement. The Irgun would not be hampered in raising funds, except there would be no confiscation, and the Jewish Agency would announce that the Irgun was not getting funds from Agency sources—a very sore point with Irgun fund raisers in the diaspora. The agreement was to come into effect when ratified by the Zionist General Council. Weeks passed. Ben-Gurion and his friends wanted no agree ment, and ratification was postponed again and again.

If a united front eluded the Jews, the Arabs had even more difficulties in fashioning a single policy in response to the partition resolution. Without any apparent sense of urgency, the prime ministers of the Arab League states met in Cairo between December 12 and 17. Iraq, still plagued by domestic difficulties, had become even more militant. Baghdad wanted immediate intervention by volunteers. Arab armies should move to the Mandate borders at once. Iraqi General Sir Ismail Safwat Pasha, chairman of the league military commiteee, estimated the Zionists had fifty-thousand troops with armor, artillery and a secret air force. Something must be done to save Arab Palestine. The most militant supporter of intervention, Riad Solh of Lebanon, came from a country without military resources balanced on the cusp of schism. The most Islamic state of all, Saudi Arabia, wanted no volunteers and no regular army to intervene. Old King ibn-Saud had told his son Feisal that he would lead his army personally to Palestine, but the "army" was a motley collection of tribesmen on camels. Transjordan wanted no volunteers, especially under the control of the Mufti. The Mufti wanted no regular armies intervening, especially the Arab Legion of Transjordan. Egypt supported the Mufti, thereby helping to thwart Abdullah of Transjordan and avoiding committing the woefully unprepared Egyptian army. Syria wanted volunteers but no Mufti. Eventually an unsatisfactory compromise was reached. The Arab states would supply ten-thousand rifles and arrange for the training and equipping of three-thousand volunteers in Syria. There would be a war chest of a million pounds. The fifty-two-year-old Safwat Pasha would be supreme military commander. The volunteers would be led by an anti-Mufti appointee. No one was very pleased, least of all the Mufti, who had already sent his own candidate into Palestine to lead the struggle.

In December the Palestine grapevine came alive with the news that "Abu Moussa" had returned after nine years of exile. Without orders, without order, the militants began drifting out of the Arab villages and down to Jerusalem to greet Abdul Kader Husseini, the Mufti's man in Palestine. Just over forty, a stocky solid man, he had long since become a legend. During the Arab revolt he had been wounded leading his fedayeen. He had been captured by the British but escaped to fight again. Wounded once more, he was smuggled out of the Mandate, bleeding and unconscious, slung over the back of a camel. From Syria he had gone to fight the British once again in Iraq. Captured again, he spent nearly four years in prison. With a degree from the University of Cairo and a brief career as a nationalistic journalist, he was not the typically ill-educated, limited follower of his cousin the Mufti; but he was just as rabid. Most important, in a land without structure, he could command the loyalty of the Palestinian Arabs, and build an army around him. He told the eager volunteers what they wanted to hear, what they knew to be true: "We shall keep our honor and our country with our swords."[11] The day of swords had gone, and no modern army could be created overnight from hordes of illiterate, ill-disciplined, emotional tribesmen, from bits and pieces of equipment, vast enthusiasm, a love of display, and the prejudices of the last century. Abdul Kader did not plan such a modern army. He was sufficiently sophisticated to know his materials, and he did not need a Prussian army. In Palestine the practices of the past, the congenial old ways, could prove as effective as panzers. All Abdul Kader needed to do was urge the Arabs to ambush, to loot trapped convoys, to snipe from safety, to attack at the edges, to burn, to lie in the hills and fire on the roads, to murder from a ditch. No target was more tempting than Jerusalem, with its hundred-thousand Jewish hostages clumped at the end of a narrow ribbon of road running from the hills of Latrun, past Bab el-Wad and Kastel, under the hateful eyes of the Arab villagers. "We will strangle Jerusalem."[12]

The Mufti could be well content that Abdul Kader was in Jerusalem. His ally, Kamal Irekat, who had first promised to throw the Jews into the sea, had organized the villagers along the Jerusalem-Hebron road to block access to the Etzion block. In the Jaffa area another old friend, Sheik Hassan Salame, could squeeze Tel Aviv from the south and from Lydda-Ramele to the north. The one serious rub was that the Arab summit had insisted on appointing as commander of the volunteers his old rival, Fawzi el-Kaukji, whose long career in intrigue and war was quite different from that of Abdul Kader. Born in northern Lebanon, Kaukji had served in the Ottoman army in another Palestine campaign, alongside General Otto von Kreiss's German Army. There he had won the Iron Cross second class and developed a lifelong admiration for all things German. After the war he had spied on the Turks for the British, on the French for the British, on the British for the French, and on the French and British for the Germans. He, not the Mufti, had led the village fedayeen during the Arab revolt against the British, and now he had returned to lead them again in a third Palestine campaign. A heavy, erect man with a thick neck and bristly short-cut red hair, clad in shiny black jackboots and an elegant suede jacket with a sheepskin coat thrown over his shoulders, he appeared more Prussian than Arab, the very man to weave an army out of whole cloth. After his arrival in Syria volunteers of all sorts and conditions began to stream into Damascus: Albanian and Yugoslavian Moslems who had supported Nazi Germany, tribesmen from Syria and Lebanon, reluctantly retired brigands, the odd Druze, Bedouins from the edge of the desert, suq Arabs with smuggled rifles. Amid the motley of clothes and customs, the variants of small arms, Kaukji's Arab Liberation Army began to take shape. Some volunteers could not be bothered with the delay and drifted across the unguarded borders into the Mandate. They were afraid the war would be over before they had their shot.

Within the Mandate, during December, there seemed to be war enough for all. Official communiqués could only take note of the more serious incidents. There was constant sniping in the mixed cities. Medical convoys to the Hadassah hospital, on the slopes of Mount Scopus inside an Arab area, were fired on repeatedly: one nurse was killed and other personnel were wounded. A Jewish doctor was shot down visiting an Arab patient. Trusted employees slipped back to murder their employers. Funerals drew sniper fire. The light-blue Egged buses had to have protection—British or armor plate—or they ended riddled in roadside ditches. The silver buses of the Arab National Company became moving targets whenever they passed near Jewish quarters. On December 15, the Arabs blew up the water pipes into Jerusalem. A National Company bus was shot up the same day outside Petah Tikva. The next day two Negev kibbutzim came under Arab attack. In Jerusalem six people were hit and killed by snipers. In Tel Aviv there was constant firing from the Hassan Bek Mosque and from nests along the edge of Manshiya. On December 21, the toll was eleven dead—sniping in Jaffa; a bus ambush; firing in Haifa; a gunfight on King George Avenue in Jerusalem between a British officer and an Irgun man. Fifty Jews a week were being killed in what was still largely a random campaign of violence. Irgun attempts at retaliation were brutal, ruthless, and ineffectual. On December 29, a bomb at the Damascus Gate in Jerusalem detonated in the midst of a crowd. Fifteen Arabs were killed and over fifty wounded—the square was turned into a slaughterhouse, the pavement slippery with blood. Two British policemen, rushing to the scene, were shot and killed. The next day a car slowed down as it came alongside a large crowd of Arabs in front of the Haifa oil refinery. A bomb was tossed into the crowd. The two-thousand Arab employees ran amok in the refinery, killing any Jews they could find. Forty-one Jewish workers were slashed or clubbed to death and seven were mangled but lived. The same day the Hadassah hospital bus was shot up again, all fourteen passengers and the driver wounded.

The Irgun struck back again. At four in the afternoon of January 7, a police van, stolen from a Ford garage, drew up in front of a high school in the Rehavia quarter of Jerusalem. On the van floor were two bombs constructed by the Jerusalem engineering section, each a fifty-gallon oil drum filled with scrap metal around a TNT core. Poking out of the top was a simple cotton fuse girded with wooden kitchen matches. To activate the bomb all that was needed was to draw the striking section of a matchbox across the top and get out of the way. The young man assigned to light the fuse in his first operation, was Uri Cohen, a young biology student. He crouched over the drum, protected on each side by a Hok member armed with a submachine gun. The unit commander sat in front next to the driver. The van moved off, passed through the Arab Legion check point without question, then another Arab check point, ignoring a request to stop, and on along the walls of the Armenian quarter. As the square in front of the Jaffa Gate came into sight, the commander ordered Cohen to light the fuse. There was a frantic scramble, then an embarrassed pause. Cohen had no matchbox. The commander slipped back into the rear of the van, leaned over next to the drums, and handed Cohen his own. Cohen quickly scratched it across the match heads. There was a flare and the fuse began to burn. He swung open the rear doors and grabbed the drum. Just then he looked into the faces of the startled Arab crowd standing at the No. 3 bus stop. They did not move or speak; they just watched. Cohen slowly shifted the bomb down onto the pavement. The crowd stood stunned, staring first at the twinkling fuse, then at Cohen. He closed the door. The van accelerated. The crowd stood motionless. The van passed beyond the square. Then the bomb detonated, and the pavement became a bloody shambles. A shop owner smashed into his shutter, crucified on the twisted metal. Those at the bus stop were shredded, bits and pieces of them scattered in bloody smears across the square. There was a tinkle of falling glass, a few groans, and then the long screams of pain and horror. A few hundred yards away, the Irgun van swerved and ran into a traffic island before Cohen could light the second bomb. The driver could not get the van off. A crowd began to gather, and the police moved in to see what had happened. All five decided to run. They threw open the doors and headed for the Mamillah cemetery, toward the safety of the New City. A glance showed the British security forces why the men had deserted the van—the drum bomb sat near the door, the white fuse surrounded with unlit matches. They turned and opened fire on the fleeing men. Zigzagging in the open, the Irgun men made excellent targets. One after another they staggered and fell as the British rounds hit home. In the cemetery Uri Cohen collapsed, his leg smashed. He was scooped up and taken to the hospital, where the Irgun later rescued him. Only one man got away clear from the Jaffa Gate operation. He died in an Irgun action a few months later. Seventeen Arabs were killed in the explosion and over fifty wounded.

Inside the Old City, in a bomb factory not far from the Church of the Holy Sepulcher, the Arabs' explosives expert was preparing an answer.

Fawzi el-Kutub was a most unlikey Arab: tall, blond, with green eyes, he had been in a Jewish concentration camp outside Breslau, and arrived in Palestine on a refugee ship with fifteen-hundred Jewish companions. The remainder of his credentials were more conventional: he had taken an active part in the Arab revolt, specializing in tossing grenades into Jewish quarters (fifty-six times according to his own count), had seen exile in Syria, the usual spell with the Mufti in Iraq, and an SS commando course in Holland. For his first major operation Kutub had chosen the building of the *Palestine Post.* There would be no tiny fifty-gallon drums here, but a serious device. Kutub acquired a British police pickup and packed it with half a ton of TNT. Abdul Kader sent him two British deserters, Eddie Brown, a police captain who claimed the Irgun had killed his brother, and Peter Madison, an army corporal. The two men would drive the truck to a point directly in front of the *Post,* park it, then get out and wander off. It worked like a charm. On the evening of February 1, the *Post* building went up in a sheet of flame. The street was covered with masonry, broken glass, and burning bits and pieces. On Feburary 22, Kutub used Brown and Madison again to detonate another car bomb in Ben-Yehuda Street in the midst of a shopping crowd; fifty-two people were killed and more than a hundred injured. On March 11, he constructed his masterpiece, a grey-green Ford with a quarter-ton of TNT and an elaborate detonator—a mixture of mercury, nitric acid, and alcohol. The car moved off, flying an American flag on the front fender. Along with his driver Daoud, Kutub drove triumphantly into the courtyard of the Jewish Agency, and parked directly in front of Haganah headquarters. The two walked off, leaving the clockwork detonator ticking away. A suspicious Haganah guard came alongside the Ford, peered in, and decided that, American flag or no, something was odd. He took off the handbrake and pushed the car across the courtyard, away from the Haganah door to another location until he could check matters out. He never had the chance. As he reached inside to put the hand brake on again, the clockwork ticked out, the detonator went off, and the Ford disintegrated. Thirteen people in the civilian wing of the Agency were killed almost instantly. Kutub and the Irgun were not alone in concentrating on the bombing campaign—the Irgun had bombed the Hotel Semiramis in Katamon, supposed headquarters of the Arab irregulars, killing twenty-six people—and no Arab irregulars. But bombs, however dreadful and spectacular, were not the key to the irregular war.

Kader had found the key in the simple sniper. As the weeks passed, his irregulars were slowly strangling Jerusalem. Outside the Jewish New City, the four kibbutzim of the Etzion bloc to the south, Nebi Yaakov to the north, the Mount Scopus complex, and the Jewish quarter of the Old City were each in turn cut off by the snipers. With the water pipes cut and the food vendors transmuted into fedayeen, everything had to come over the Tel Aviv road or out of existing stocks. Early in February Ben-Gurion appointed a new Haganah commander, David Shaltiel. Shaltiel had once been a sergeant in the French Foreign Legion, and had spent time in Dachau before arriving in Palestine to join the Haganah. Ben-Gurion chose Shaltiel to defend Jerusalem because he was an advocate of orthodox military procedures, not of the equalitarian Palmach tactics of spontaneity. Ben-Gurion foresaw a real war, not a campaign of commando raids. Unfortunately, Shaltiel, as head of Haganah intelligence, had played a major role in the Season, so the prospect of intimate Irgun-LEHI cooperation in Jerusalem was poor. They did not trust Shaltiel, whom they saw as a Ben-Gurion pawn, not a military commander. Shaltiel, in turn, apparently still loathed the dissidents. To complicate his problems, he had no old Zionist ties, no leverage with the Jewish Agency in the city and no real military assets.

Shaltiel had trouble not only with the separatists and the Jewish Agency bureaucrats, but also with the British. Many felt the new British neutrality was sufficiently partisan, but there was also increasing evidence of British complicity in the Arab irregular war. No effort was being made to stop the drift of irregulars across the border; in fact, a private arrangement with the British army permitted Kaukji on March 6 to move his first battalion from Syria into the Mandate in return for his quiescence. There were repeated reports that British faces had been seen in Arab mobs, that British soldiers or police had been involved in the *Palestine Post* bomb, that British security forces were abandoning Jewish convoys. And it was undeniable that the British would allow no one aboard the No. 2 bus, the last link into the Jewish quarter of the Old City, except civilians without arms. Almost as soon as he arrived, Shaltiel discovered just how deep was the hatred of sections of the British Army for the Jews. On February 12, the Highland Light Infantry arrested four Haganah men, and turned them over to an Arab mob near St. Stephen's Gate in the Old City. One was shot down instantly. The mob tore the clothes from the other three and held them on the ground while volunteers castrated them, then hacked them to death. It was not the first such incident, but it ended the last trace of Haganah havlaga. Henceforth the Haganah would resist being disarmed.

The British felt ill used at the rising criticism of their procedures. They had fought a long and difficult guerrilla campaign with what their leaders felt was remarkable moderation. There had been no official reprisals, no authorized resort to torture. The army, with orders to avoid trouble, was only trying to run out the clock, not abet the Arab attacks. There were admittedly a few rotten apples in the British barrel, and some wild men who had deserted, but most men were doing their grim and unpleasant duty. They were at least trying to protect the Jews, if not fight their war for them. Without this protection there would be no No. 2 bus into the Old City, no convoys out to Etzion and Nebi Yaakov. Glubb Pasha and General MacMillan had even intervened personally to salvage a trapped convoy. The Arabs had closed in on a convoy to Nebi Yaakov, riddled and burned the two trucks and poured fire into the one homemade armored car, when Glubb and MacMillan arrived.

> When we rounded the bend in the road, we saw a large Jewish armoured car halted in the middle of the village street. The street was wide, and the houses on each side had small gardens in front of them. The houses and gardens were full of Arabs firing their rifles at the armoured car. Every now and then, the muzzle of an automatic was thrust through a loophole in the side of the armoured car and fired a few bursts at the Arabs, and was then withdrawn. There were obviously living Jews inside the armoured car, but we could not tell how many. The noise of the firing was deafening.[13]

MacMillan called up a nearby unit of the Household Cavalry. He and Glubb persuaded the Arabs to stop firing. The British would take away the Jews, and they could have the armored car. The Arabs grudgingly agreed, and the British troops formed a cordon around the car. Glubb shouted for the Jews to open up, they were safe.

> At last the Jews ventured to open a crack of the door. One by one we got them out, passing them between us into the British vehicle. Two could hop. Several were dead. It was difficult to see whether some were dead or alive. Their clothes were torn, they were little more than a heap of lacerated meat. It was like a butcher's shop—so much torn flesh and pools of blood. Dragging, carrying, pushing, and covering them with our bodies, we thrust them into the British vehicles, which drove off. I called our soldiers over to one side. I waved to the villagers—"It's all yours," I shouted.[14]

Similar convoys to Etzion in the south had run similar obstacle courses. In December, outside Bethlehem, ten Jews were killed and all the vehicles lost in an early convoy. In January a unit of Palmach and Haganah men, mostly Hebrew University students, were sent to reinforce the bloc, after a heavy attack by Abdul Kader's irregulars had been driven back. The local Arabs discovered the Haganah column and closed off any retreat. There was a brief advance down the mountain road before this too was closed off. The grapevine reported the Jews trapped, and villagers began to rush to the scene. Soon the hills were covered with riflemen rushing to a certain victory, the shrill undulating of triumph could be heard above the thunderous rattling of their rifles. All the thirty-five Jews were killed. On January 24, the British intervened in a Haganah attempt to clear the slopes above the Tel Aviv-Jerusalem road after forty Arabs and ten Jews had been killed. They ended the attempt by opening fire on the Haganah. The Arabs kept the heights. During February only two full convoys of gray buses and khaki trucks came in from Tel Aviv. Every armored lorry drew fire. The run under the heights of the Bab el-Wad and Kastel produced the echoing rattle of the Arab rifles, the clank and twang of ricochets off the armor plate. Inside the heavy lorries grinding through the pass there were occasional thuds and groans, as slugs found their way through the gun slits. There was always the thump of bursting tires and the grim prospect that a lorry would fall by the wayside, a tomb for the Jews, a trophy for the Arabs. Even when the convoys slipped into Jerusalem, there was never enough to go around: a hundred-thousand Jews had to eat, drink, and occasionally fire back at the Arabs.

So there was less of everything. Water from the cisterns was doled out from tank trucks. Communal kitchens and bakeries produced what little they could. There was only sporadic electricity and telephone service. Cinemas closed, restaurants and cafés served ersatz sweets and artificial coffee. There was little cooking fuel and gasoline, and dwindling ammunition. Everywhere the Haganah was weak. The same was true for the Irgun and LEHI. And the weakest chink of all was the Old Cty. For over a century the Jewish population within the walls had been dwindling, as new immigrants built houses in the airy garden city to the west. Even the most orthodox rarely chose to live in the cramped, twisting alleys of the Jewish quarter. In 1895 there were twenty-eight thousand Jews in the Old City, in 1939 five thousand. As Abdul Kader began to strangle Jerusalem, there were only seventeen hundred left, crowded into the old houses, the synagogues, and yeshivas. There was Eliyahu Naavi, where Elijah had appeared to complete a minyan, the Stambuli Synagogue for Turkish Jews, where Christ appeared before Herod and where the Teutonic Knights began. There too, in 1267, Moshe Ben-Nakhman built a synagogue with marble pillars and a school, and gradually the Jews settled around it. They crowded in between the Armenian quarter and the Arab houses to the east that cut them off from the Wailing Wall, from the old wall to the south, and the Arab quarter to the north. There was no gate for the Jewish quarter. The Dung Gate led only to the Wailing Wall and a nearby entrance to the Dome of the Rock. The Zion Gate served the Armenian quarter. This meant that once the Arabs began attacking the Jews in the Old City, the only link was the No. 2 bus line, that covered the half-mile to the Jaffa Gate in five minutes.

In December the total armament of the quarter consisted of sixteen rifles, two of which did not work, twenty-five pistols, and three Suomi submachine guns, relics of Tehomi's Finnish purchase for Haganah-bet. There were eighteen Haganah men and a handful of Irgun-LEHI. In two weeks the Haganah had managed to smuggle one-hundred-twenty people into the quarter. A few more Irgun-LEHI men slipped in. British guards were bribed. Devout rabbis, doctors on emergency calls, women with heavy builds and powdered beards, overage yeshiva students, all made a one-way journey to the Jewish quarter on bus No. 2. Along with them came hand grenades in purses, rifles under the floor of the bus, ammunition in pockets, and explosives in market baskets. Inside the quarter an arms industry produced bombs in cigarette tins and grenades out of cans. Children bought bullets from the British. A maze of tunnels was created, linking all parts of the quarter. Since the two telephones were tapped by the British, messages were smuggled out in the ear of a dog who had a friend in the New City. It was all very makeshift, but there was no other way. Few thought a real defense of the quarter was possible. Anyway it might make no real difference. March came, bitterly cold and bleak, and the convoys staggering through the gauntlet could not keep up with the needs of all the Jews.

By March there was no meat, eggs, milk or vegetables. Rations were minimal. Everyone was cold and hungry, and many were frightened. Elsewhere the story was not much better. The Jews in Safed, like those in the Old City, were cut off and nearly defenseless. Many kibbutzim, like the Etzion bloc, depended on erratic convoys and their own resources to fight off Arab irregular attacks. The sniping continued in all the mixed cities. Kaukji decided to go into action, and attacked the religious settlement of Tirat Zvei. A mass of some five-hundred Arabs simply ran pell-mell toward the kibbutz perimeter wire. As Kaukji watched from a hill his army came apart; the Jews methodically fired into the undisciplined crowd. By the time the British arrived, Kaukji had lost a dozen killed and thirty-six wounded. The Arabs hailed this as a victory to equal those of his rival Abdul Kader. Kaukji's attacks in March against Magdiel and Kfar Saba went no better. His men rushed at the perimeter, howling and firing in the air. Cut down, they withdrew as swiftly. Kaukji felt certain that the sorely pressed Jews, with little ammunition, cut off and uncertain, would collapse. Settlements defended by farmers and their wives could not fight for long. Yet they did, and again Kaukji had to pull back before his army disintegrated into independent bands of brigands. His difficulties were about the only good news for the Jews during March.

The worst news of all came from New York. At the State Department, Loy Henderson and his pragmatic supporters had never given up hope that American policy could be shifted from Truman's blatant pro-Zionist posture. His ally was still Secretary of Defense Forrestal, who feared that the growing Arab animosity would cut off the United States from Middle East oil and even open the area to Soviet penetration. Washington had become increasingly concerned about Soviet intentions, and the coup in Prague in February intensified the fear that Moscow had aggressive aspirations everywhere. Thus Palestinian partition had a cold-war role, and State, Defense, the new Central Intelligence Agency and the National Security Council wanted the United States to propose a shift to trusteeship or an approach to the International Court of Justice. Partition could not be imposed by United Nations resolution, but only by force. If the force were international, the Soviet Union would be involved, and if not, since Britain had opted out, only the United States had the troops. Such an intervention was unthinkable. In a complex series of bureaucratic maneuvers, after Truman had glanced over a draft speech to be given at the United Nations that passingly mentioned a trusteeship, the opponents of partition froze the draft into a final version. Secretary of State George Marshall, assuming Truman's authorization, informed Ambassador Warren Austin to go ahead and deliver the speech, advocating a trusteeship in Palestine.

The drift toward American disengagement had been noticed by the Zionists as early as January, but their efforts to reach Harry Truman, their best and most powerful friend, had aborted. The president was tired of Palestine, the incessant lobbying, the repeated arguments. As a last ploy, his old haberdashery partner, Eddie Jacobson, was brought in from Kansas City to see if he could get an appointment with the president for Chaim Weizmann. Jacobson managed it, but only at the last minute. The president had first turned him down. "I don't want to discuss Palestine or the Jews or the Arabs or the British. I've discussed it enough. I'm just going to let the matter run its course in the United Nations."[15] On Thursday, March 18, Weizmann finally saw the president, who said, "You can be sure that I will work for the establishment and recognition of a Jewish state that will include the Negev."[16] It was not absolute support for the partition resolution as written, but it was good enough to allay Weizmann's and his colleagues' fears that partition would be sold out. The next day, March 19, Warren Austin asked the Security Council to suspend partition and call a special session of the General Assembly to consider trusteeship. In Palestine the news was greeted with volleys of Arab bullets, fired off to celebrate this new victory. In New York the Zionists were shattered. Weizmann had been sold out in less than twenty-four hours. Truman was furious. He could not instantly disown Austin, but there would be no trusteeship. As soon as Truman discovered what had happened, he appointed Loy Henderson Ambassador to Nepal, the slopes of the Himalayas being about as far from the center of the stage as it was possible to arrange on such short notice.

Austin's speech intensified Jewish anguish in Palestine. Even the most optimistic had lost faith in resolutions and votes, in the authority of the United Nations, in the decency of the British. Some British troops actually began leaving Palestine. On March 5, eighteen hundred left Haifa, and two days later two thousand more shipped out, but doubts about a real evacuation persisted. The Arab Legion was still inside the Mandate, assisting in security duties. Although the Legion was supposed to be withdrawn along with the British, the Jews expected that even if it were, Glubb's troops would soon be back. Strained to the limit by the irregular attacks, no one looked forward to an assault by the Legion, which was a real army, unlike Kaukji's massed brigands or Kader's tribesmen. In fact Abdullah had already decided to act alone and planned to move the Legion back across the Jordon on May 15 to occupy the assigned Arab areas, thus thwarting his rival the Mufti, the vile Farouk in Cairo, the Syrians, and the rest. Late in February, Glubb and Transjordanian Prime Minister Tewfic Abdul Huda met with Bevin in London. Tewfic revealed Abdullah's intentions, stressing that the only alternative was the anti-British mufti. After a pause, Bevin replied, "It seems the obvious thing to do, but don't go and invade the areas allotted to the Jews."[17] It was all the authority Abdullah wanted for his invasion, assuming that the Jews held out long enough to prevent an irregular triumph.

By mid-March there was little doubt that the irregulars had bright prospects. The situation in Jerusalem was grim. The roads were very bad and getting worse. The isolated settlements could not hold out forever. With the British still in position, patrolling, arresting, trying to maintain order, it was difficult for the underground to train the new volunteers, and despite the illicit factories, impossible to arm the men. It would be two months before the British evacuated and the ports opened up, and two months seemed forever. Some arms were trickling in from various sources, but the most productive source proved to be the British Army. Many disgruntled soldiers were willing to turn a blind eye to theft. A few helped out because they backed the Jews, disliked the Arabs, or abhorred their sergeants major. In the chaos of closing down a vast military presence thirty-years old, a great deal slipped through chinks, and not just bits and pieces. The Haganah managed to steal an armored car in Jerusalem and two tanks in Haifa. There were repeated raids on British camps by the Irgun. After an earlier failure at Haifa on March 19, a Saturday with no troops about, the Irgun raided a NAAFI warehouse. Arriving in Haifa at seven in the morning in several trucks, the Hok unit found no one present but a sleepy watchman brewing his morning tea. He was bundled to one side and kept under a gun, taking all incoming calls with an innocent tone, while his guards listened on the extension. The few callers suspected nothing. The trucks were loaded up with stores. It took about forty minutes for each one. Each driver then drove to the Irgun base at Shuni near Benyamina. There the truck was unloaded and sped back to the NAAFI warehouse. Finally a call came through at noon from the British. An officer announced that he knew someone was holding a pistol on the watchman, and consequently the police were on the way. Taking him at his word, the remaining Irgun men piled into the trucks and hurriedly drove off, passing the British block just before it closed. They sat on Mount Carmel for a couple of hours until the British gave up looking for them, then drove back to the base at Petah Tikva, a good and rather typical Irgun day.

Equally typical of underground activity in Palestine were the never-ending plans for prison escapes: the tunnels dug and sealed, dug and discovered, dug and used; the secret communications nets based on bribery and cunning; the hidden workshops; and most of all the prison plots, as the British adjusted their defenses to each new technique. The previous November a major tunnel out of the Latrun detention camp had been discovered only at the last minute, when cracks in the hut floor revealed a hundred-meter affair complete with escape chamber. At the same time in Acre, another attempt was thwarted quite unwittingly by the prison authorities. After the great escape in April, the remaining Jewish prisoners were shifted to new cells, a minor matter except that the sealed tunnel shaft was off limits. The prisoners had to begin a series of violent quarrels, which so upset routine that the superintendent agreed to separate one lot by opening up another cell.

Once the tunnel was unsealed the old routine began again, as the shaft daily deepened past floors and recent foundations, toward what the prisoners hoped would be the sand-filled crusader cellars. One day a digger saw a piece of stone just at his feet disappear without a sound. He reached down and poked at the floor of the shaft. More masonry and dirt disappeared, and a hole opened. There was no indication of how large the cellar would be, or how deep the sand. When the hole was enlarged the diggers could peer down into the darkness. Pebbles dropped through the hole made no sound. Eventually a light was lowered. Suddenly, as the dim light moved away and the twisting shadows took form, they realized the shaft had pierced the roof of a huge, empty crusader vault, perhaps seventy feet high. The vault had been sealed eight-hundred years before, after the fall of the fortress. There was no sand. The diggers clambered down a makeshift ladder and looked around. It was soon apparent that they had entered not a single room, but the major floor of the old castle. The Turkish and British construction had gone up not on ruined cellars, but on top of the crusader fortress. They had broken through to all the lower floors, empty and forgotten for centuries. In one room Shmulevitz came upon several huge cedar logs. He touched one and the entire log crumbled to dust.

The escape plot grew apace. All but one prisoner would be able to get out through an exit in a nearby stable, which was reached by a side tunnel through the vault walls. The escapees could be met at the stable and whisked away in cars before the British knew they were missing. Left behind would be a double amputee, who could not really make the tunnel-vault trek. He would seal the tunnel entrance in the cell wall. The Jewish prisoners would vanish into thin air. The shaft seal was so elegant that it seemed unlikely anyone would find it without instructions. The break was planned for December 5. Then came the partition vote, and the Arab prisoners rioted. Outnumbered ten to one by the Arabs, the Jews' position was sufficiently precarious for the prison authorities to move them all to the Jerusalem central prison, a compassionate gesture completely lost on the prisoners, who were only a few days from the greatest prison break of all.

In Jerusalem Shmulevitz found himself in cell 23, where it appeared he would stay for some time. The cell looked out across a prison yard, several hundred meters to the nearest wall. Even if a tunnel could be constructed, which, given the dirt disposal problem, was unlikely, on the other side of the wall was the Arab Legion broadcasting station, an area filled with security forces at all hours. Consequently Shmulevitz gave up on tunnels for the time being and concentrated on his guards. He worked on one sympathetic Jewish warder, urging a simple plan. Shmulevitz would shave his flowing black beard and take the place of a short-term prisoner due to be released. The warder could innocently escort Shmulevitz out, thereby covering his own tracks. The other prisoner, when the error was discovered, would be released anyway. Reluctantly the warder agreed. At the last minute he backed out, pleading the risks to his wife and children. Shmulevitz was suitably annoyed and promised that he would escape, would do it when the warder was on duty, and in such a way that the clues pointed to him. In the meantime he and the others sought another way out.

Word on the communications net, from a LEHI man in the Public Works Department, revealed that a plan of the central prison sewer system indicated that if a short six-meter shaft were opened at a certain angle it would pierce a pipe wide enough for the men to move through, exiting in the security yard. Once there several prisoners could mingle with the workers leaving the compound. So once more work began on a tunnel head. The site was partially under an iron double bunk bed, firmly cemented into the concrete floor. It was swiftly uncemented and the tunnel begun. Some of the dirt could be scattered about the yard, but not much; some could go down drains, but not enough. After a time work was impossible because the bags of dirt waiting in the tunnel for disposal took up too much room. The prisoners then announced to the warders that those in cell 23 were having difficulty keeping things clean. Theirs was the only cell in the row two inches lower than the corridor. When they tried to wash it out, they could not simply sweep the water down the drain like the others. They suggested a sump hole under the watertap to collect the water. Having little else to do, they would be quite willing to do the digging.

The prison superintendent agreed. It would keep the chaps busy, and improve the efficiency of the clean-up routine. One morning an Arab prisoner appeared with a wheelbarrow filled with tools and cement, followed by an Arab police escort. Since only one or two could work at once, the others moved over into the far corner and began a shim-shon game in the corner. The click and rattle of the thrown pieces gradually had the desired effect on the remaining bored policemen, who like most Arabs, were addicted to the game. Slowly they drifted over to kibitz. In the far corner, under the bunk bed, the top of the tunnel slid back. A pair of hand appeared and pushed out a bag of dirt. One of the workers lifted it up and dribbled the dirt into the pile from the sump shaft. Another bag appeared and the contents were poured into the sump shaft. Soon the tunnel top slid softly shut, and the workers poured the cement into the sump shaft. The shim-shon game came to an end. The Arab policemen watched dully as the Arab prisoner reappared with his barrow and trundled away a rather heavy load. They did not have far to go to reach the sewer, and they could dispose of the remaining dirt.

Then, quite unexpectedly, two British officers appeared one day with an Arab police escort. One was a specialist on escapes. He had learned his trade in a German stalag during the war. He began to poke holes in the plaster walls and take up the stones from the floor. The prisoners slipped out into the corridor under the eyes of the police to wait for what would be the inevitable discovery—the man was clearly a professional. Refusing to give up hope, Shmulevitz stayed in the cell. The officer climbed on top of the double bunk to pry at a stone on the wall. The bunk wobbled and Shmulevitz, ever helpful, gave him a hand. The officer thanked him. Shmulevitz said it was nothing, that after he had finished investigating cell 23 he would inform him how foolish he was. Stone by stone, the officer moved along, arriving one stone from the tunnel shaft. Still intrigued, he stood up and noted he was through—one could not look at every stone. Shmulevitz asked, "Did you ever build a tunnel?"

"Yes."

"Then we are colleagues. How long was yours?"

"Two hundred yards."

"Ah, then you are the specialist. Ours at Latrun was only seventy-five meters. But look out the window. How far would a tunnel have to be for an escape?"

"Well, three or four hundred yards."

"How many cubic feet of dirt would such a tunnel need?"

"Eighty to a hundred."

"Where would we put it? The cell is impossible. The exercise yard is too small and has a concrete floor anyway."

"But I heard someone scratching under the walls last night."

"Well, then, why didn't you come and investigate?"

"It was too late and I didn't have my own key. But I did go to the medical room and get a stethoscope. And I *did* hear tunneling."

All this was very bad news for Shmulevitz. It was going to be difficult to cope with a tunnel expert using a stethoscope. Putting on his grim, white-faced look, and with a bit of a tremble, Shmulevitz said that if they were not tunneling, it must be the Arabs. And if the Arabs were digging, it was only to get into the Jewish prisoners' section and leave a bomb under the cells. Quite logical, but not quite convincing to the British escape specialist, who left musing on Arab tunnels and piles of dirt. The prisoners anticipated that he would return. Very late that night, as soon as he crept into the far end of the long corridor, word was flashed to cell 23. Slowly, cautiously, in gumshoes and dark clothes, he slipped past the "sleeping" prisoners. When he peeped around the door into cell 23, he found two frightened prisoners taking the watch. Huddled in blankets, they were listening at the wall for the sound of Arabs digging. The specialist crept back, convinced that the chaps in cell 23 had nothing to do with the scratchings his stethoscope had picked up.

Escape day was February 20, and although there were twelve people involved (eight LEHI and four Irgun, the reverse of the ratio at Acre, since this was a LEHI operation) the assumption was that only three would get away. There would be just three real LEHI workers with proper papers in the yard for the three prisoners to replace. Since the odd opportunity might turn up, they decided to make twelve sets of identity papers anyway, to hold out hope for all twelve. The wall of the sewer was breached. Shmulevitz crawled down it, followed by the other eleven. He popped out unnoticed from the drain exit, only six meters from the window of cell 23. He scampered out and strolled over to the guard at the compound gate. The guard wanted to know if he had finished work, since it was only nine in the morning. Shmulevitz assured him the job was done and that the rest of the workers, who had entered by the other gate, would be along soon. Then he walked out. One after another, the others moved toward the gate, straggling through in ones and twos. Then, just as the very last one reached the gate, for no good reason an Arab constable began to ask questions. One of the workers, already away free and clear, returned and stopped a passing British officer to complain about this rank discrimination. His fellow worker was being held up just becuse he was a Jew. Always for fair play, the British officer called off the Arab constable and waved the last worker out of the yard. Four hours later the BBC's newscast announced the escape. A warder had found cell 23 bare, the bed pulled back, the tunnel entrance open. Bound and gagged in the tunnel was the Jewish officer who had backed out of Shmulevitz's exchange-prisoners ploy. Suspecting something odd in cell 23, he had showed up after the last man had disappeared into the sewer. The other prisoners had grabbed him before he could spoil the plot, tied him up, and stashed him in the tunnel.

Shmulevitz made his way to a meeting point on Ben-Yehuda Street, and from there was directed to a safe house in the home of a LEHI friend, Rabbi Gorontzik. The Palestine he found was vastly different from the one he had left when arrested. The Jerusalem commander, Zettler, filled him in on recent events. The old underground struggle had been transformed into almost open warfare with the Arabs, and the Arabs were winning. The run through the mountains below Bab el-Wad and Kastel had become a dreadful valley of fire. Eventually the thin line back to Hulda and Tel Aviv would be cut, a truck would stall, or the Arabs would push through a full-scale attack. The convoys would end and the city would strangle.

On March 24, the Arabs learned from a secret transmitter that a major convoy was on the way. They built a blockade of logs and stones across a narrow section of the gorge; and three-hundred riflmen crouched on the slopes to wait for the long, vulnerable snake of slow-moving armored vehicles to creep into range. The lead armored car came under sniper fire when it was just beyond the pumping station at the entrance to the gorge. The convoy crept on under increasing fire. Two Vickers machine guns, one on each slope, began to rake the first vehicles. Arabs leaped up from the roadside ditch and tossed grenades onto the armored car, forcing the gun slits closed. The car came to the roadblock and pulled to one side. A huge bulldozer, a blockbuster, lumbered slowly past to scoop away the Arab barricade. There was a huge explosion as a mine detonated under it. The blast threw the blockbuster off the road into the gulley, a smoking ruin. A truck moving up behind the leading armored car hit a second mine and was thrown across the road. The way to Jerusalem was cut, but the convoy kept on moving. The level of Arab fire rose. All up and down the convoy was heard the thump of exploding tires, the hiss of steam from pierced radiators, the clatter of rounds off the armor, and the faint rattle of defensive Sten fire out of the tiny gun slits. The convoy commander, moving up and down in his Hillman, tried to maintain an effective defense. The five men from the blockbuster managed to get into the leading armored car despite the rain of bullets. The smashed truck, leaking blood through its back door, disappeared in a ball of flame when the gas tank went off. The Arabs cheered.

As the minutes passed, more and more villagers rushed to the slopes. The firing was unremitting and deafening, yet the shrill Arab battle cries still floated down from the heights of the gorge in broken Hebrew: "Yitzhak, Yitzhak, today death will find you!"[18] Death found many Jews that day. After a dreadful six hours the survivors of the forty-strong convoy reached Hulda. They left behind sixteen trucks, two armored cars, and the little Hillman. The Arabs rushed howling down the slopes and set upon the wrecked trucks. Sacks of flour, cans of meat, tins of sardines, butter, oil, beans, all were grabbed and borne up the slopes to the villages. At one point along the road, a sea of oranges poured out of the shattered side of a supply truck, rolling into eager Arab hands. All night they would cook, eat, and gloat. For the first time a convoy had failed to reach Jerusalem. Now it was a real siege.

Jewish reaction was swift. All night the Haganah worked to put together another convoy. Just before dawn on March 25, an eighty-vehicle snake, stretching for two miles along the road, moved off from Hulda toward the gorge. This convoy got through at the cost of five Jews killed and nine wounded. The Jerusalem Haganah now faced a serious problem. The situation at the Etzion bloc had become untenable. Without immediate reinforcements they would be lost. If the armored vehicles that had arrived from Tel Aviv could be used to push through aid, the situation would be greatly improved—it was never going to be very good. Yet this meant risking all the armored vehicles. Shaltiel felt it was too great a risk. His commander in Tel Aviv, Yigal Yadin, did not—Kfar Etzion was the southern bastion of Jerusalem's defense. The convoy would go. Shaltiel, however, insisted to the convoy commander, Mishael Shacham, the man who directed the Hotel Semiramis operation, that the turn-around time in the bloc could be only fifteen minutes. Some supplies would even be tossed out before the trucks stopped moving. This way, while the Arabs would discover the convoy, they would not be able to concentrate in time to block the escape route. Shacham reluctantly agreed. He would command the convoy from the air in a tiny Auster, so he could keep an eye on the Arabs. On March 28, Easter Sunday, at six in the morning, the convoy moved out: a barricade blockbuster, a crane, four armored buses, nineteen armored cars, and forty trucks, plus the best arms in the Jerusalem command, including eighteen machine guns and two mortars. The convoy passed down the roads to the south, past the obvious curves and gulleys, past the sharp angle at Nebi Daniel, all empty of Arabs, and on into Etzion, right on schedule. Shacham glided his Auster into the Etzion strip. The alarm was up all along both sides of the road, and the Arabs were rushing for their rifles. The grapevine was pulling them in toward the road for miles around. The district commander, Irekat, would have liked to concentrate his army in a single blocking point; but he had no army, only a growing mob. In Hebron and Bethlehem honking trucks and shouting runners spread the news as hundreds rushed home to snatch up a rifle and a handful of cartridges. Without orders the locals began tossing stones on the road of Nebi Daniel.

Inside Etzion the minutes ticked away as Shacham tried to load two precious but disparate bits of return cargo—a damaged Haganah plane that had crashed on landing several days before, and Zimri, the kibbutz' pride seed bull, whose pastures had come under sniper fire. The loading proved difficult. Zimri would not cooperate. The minutes slipped by, an hour, another hour. The Haganah headquarters in Jerusalem became frantic. The British had discovered the existence of the unauthorized convoy and wanted the Jewish Agency to order it to remain at the settlement. Shaltiel could not agree. Every vehicle he had was isolated in Kfar Etzion. Above the bloc Daniel Beckstein came flitting over in a Haganah spotter plane. Shacham's Auster was still on the strip. When Beckstein looked down he could see the Arabs moving toward the escape road, hundreds and hundreds of crawling black dots, an ant army creeping towards the road, clumping into groups as it came nearer. Finally the convoy moved out and met an ambush at Nebi Daniel, the ideal spot at a sharp bend of the road, where the local Arabs had automatically collected in the greatest number. The blockbuster managed to cut through six barricades, one after the other, as the level of fire increased. The hundreds of Arabs increased to a thousand, then another thousand. The seventh blockade held. Five armored cars and five trucks managed to break free and get back to Kfar Etzion. The remaining movable vehicles were positioned to make three sides of a square, using a ruined Arab house for the fourth. Hedgehogged in an all around, the Jews turned back repeated Arab forays. There was little Shaltiel could do to help. Uzi Narciss and Amos Chorev flew over in a Tigermoth and an Auster, dropping a few pipe bombs. The Arabs hardly bothered to look up. Pleas for the British to intervene before the Arabs massacred the 180 men and women trapped at Nebi Daniel ran into difficulties. MacMillan and his deputy, Colonel George W. Harper, were both in Athens; and the acting commander proceeded cautiously. He pushed a heavy patrol up the road until it ran into Arab mines. Just after midnight the Arabs, under Sheik Hamoud of Hebron, tried to rush the ruined house, but were driven off. In the hours before dawn there was a pause. Lying inside the hedgehog, the Jews heard all around them the murmur of the Arabs, waiting for dawn, the final charge, the blood and booty. Dawn came and the Arabs charged. They were driven back. They charged again and were driven back. The hills all around the tiny house were full of Arab irregulars. Inside the hedgehog the ground was covered with the dead and dying. Without water or food, exhausted, with dwindling ammunition, the Jews kept firing, waiting for the last great attack. A second British column had been stopped; but Colonel Harper had nearly reached an agreement with Irekat, who called Cairo for the Mufti's authorization. The British could take the Jews out, but everything else would be turned over to the Arabs. The Mufti agreed. Harper's column pushed on through the madly excited crowds of Arabs, made the sharp turn past the blackened and burned vehicles. Along the roadside were the burned and castrated bodies of dead Jews, their faces mutilated according to the Arab wont. Ahead was the house, "small and alone in the middle of hell."[19] When Harper arrived, the Arabs were already moving toward the promised loot. Thirteen dead and forty wounded Jews were carried out of the house and placed in the British trucks. The survivors tossed their arms away and climbed up. The Arabs had lost 135 killed but won a victory. Harper moved out and the Arabs moved in. For the Jews it was the worst day so far. Shaltiel had lost his best arms, all his vehicles, some of his best people, and the confidence of many of the Jews he was defending. Etzion was cut off. There could not be another convoy. Jerusalem was cut off until new vehicles could be found. Matters could not go on as they had much longer.

Everywhere the Jews had been successful in defense, as the Arab volunteers' crude attacks broke apart before disciplined dug-in fire. Yet everywhere the Arabs had appeared to attack again. No kibbutz had fallen; but the successes of defense had all been in vain, because the roads had been closed. Unless the links among the Jewish communities could be reëstablished, hopes for a Jewish state would die long before the formal end of the Mandate on May 15. The time had come for the Jews to go on the offensive, to clear out the Arabs' secure areas, to destroy the roadblocks. And none too soon, for there would be no reinforcements from the diaspora, none of the arms the dozens of agents had been purchasing and stockpiling, and not even the arms and vehicles that had gone out to Kfar Etzion on Easter Sunday. Like the Haganah, the Irgun also was concerned about the progress of the agents in the diaspora. On the day the convoy left Jerusalem for Kfar Etzion, Samuel Katz flew to Paris to check the progress made in Europe and then on to America to attempt to sort out the conflicting programs of the pro-Irgun groups. In Paris Katz learned from Shmuel Ariel and Lankin that there was a good possibility of official French help in establishing a base for training. Arms and supplies necessary for two infantry brigades would be provided. On the day Katz arrived Ariel's request was formally acknowledged by Jacques Boissier, chargé de mission in the office of the foreign minister. It was good news to send back to Palestine and to take across the Atlantic. If Katz had stayed longer, he would have had even more reason for celebration. A week later on April 4, Lankin was called to a meeting at a Paris hotel—oddly enough the same hotel where Herzl wrote *The Jewish State*. When he opened the door of the hotel room, he found himself staring at Yaacov Meridor, Shlomo Ben-Shlomo, and Reuben Franco, all supposedly prisoners in the Gilgil camp in Kenya. All Lankin could say was, "My God! It can't be. It's impossible."[20] Their escape was the culmination of an African epic, an Irgun campaign thousands of miles distant from the King David and the death cells at Acre; but a campaign still very much a part of the revolt. In that African campaign no man's adventures were more remarkable than Meridor's, who had, according to the British count, already escaped seven times previously.

Meridor had been arrested at 3:00 A.M. on February 13, 1945, in the midst of the Season. There was a rap on the door, and a detail of the British police strike force, accompanied by a Haganah informer, took him away to Jerusalem for questioning. He was the biggest catch of the Season, Begin's second in command and the former commander of the Irgun. He was flown off to Cairo in a special plane on February 22. There, British intelligence again tried to pry something useful out of him. From the first moment, Meridor intended to escape. In Cairo he carefully stole British Army stationery while writing a statement—it might come in handy. He suborned a British soldier to send a coded letter to Begin in Palestine. Begin misread the code but answered, so communication was established, money could be sent to Cairo, and the small Irgun net could be activated. Proper contact was soon set up, but before any firm plans could develop the contact sergeant was caught and confessed. Meridor hurriedly set to work on his window bars, certain he could drop out and simply walk away into the dusk. Moved out of his old cell, he had one last go at the window bars in his new cell, realizing that there were only a few hours left. There would have been no hope at all if he had not discovered that the Greek ELAS prisoners kept in the cell previously had almost gotten one of the bars out. All his frantic last-minute work with a razor blade was in vain. His escort arrived, and he was driven off to the Almaza airfield.

By dawn he was in Khartoum on his way to the Cartago camp in the Sudanese highlands inland from Port Sudan, a very long way from Palestine. Here the remainder of the original 251 deportees had been sent from their first confinement outside Asmara in Eritrea, and were joined from time to time by others. Although most prisoners were Irgun or LEHI, a few were not, detained on suspicion, or in error, or for some political sin other than open revolt. Meridor arrive late in May, eager to get escape plans under way. Eventually, on September 29, Meridor and two others were driven out of the gates, crammed into the tank of a water truck. They took a train, reached Port Sudan, and managed briefly on their forged identity papers. They could find no way out of Port Sudan by boat, so took the train back west. At Adbara their luck ran out, and the British detained the three strange travelers. Their story collapsed; and after ten days of freedom, they were returned to the camp. Two days after their arrival, the British shipped everyone south to Sambal camp, a mile and a half from Asmara.

Immediately on arrival the three escapees were separated from the other prisoners and, as punishment, placed in Baldizer fortress overlooking Asmara. Instead of being returned to the Sambal camp on November 11, as promised, the three were kept an extra day at Baldizer. During their exercise period they learned why. Four men, led by Eliahu Lankin, had escaped: Rahamin Mizrachi, Benjamin Zeroni, and Yaacov Gurvitz. The last two, disguised as Moslem women, tried to make their way to Ethiopia, but apparently their disguise was unconvincing to real Moslem women, and they were re-arrested. Lankin and Mizrachi stayed in hiding in Asmara, and would be a valuable asset if there were to be a big escape. As soon as Meridor returned to Sambal, work began on the tunnel. All the traditional obstacles were solved: the disposal of the dirt, ventilation, a lighting system, a warning system, how to bleed off electrical power, acquire cement, seal the tunnel shaft, distract British interest, fashion tools from bedsteads, steal wood, make hand drills. Simultaneous preparations were undertaken so that the escapees could disappear once they popped out of the tunnel. In British occupied Eritrea, which consisted of a few heavily patrolled towns, nearby Asmara, and endless miles of unknown wilds, this was more daunting than pushing a tunnel under the wire.

Shimon Shiba made a solitary nighttime break, contacted Lankin at camp, and returned before dawn; but the British discovered his bed empty. The search found him still in camp, however. Uncertain, they herded the prisoners into the football field, and locked up Meridor separately. Hours of searching revealed nothing. Meridor was still in solitary confinement when he learned that the Sudanese guards had fired into the compound of the fifty-five new prisoners who had arrived in December. Two were killed and twelve wounded. It was the Irgun's worst day in Africa. The prisoners, after a variety of protests and confrontations, decided that the best response could be made with the tunnel. By February there were two tunnels, giving back-up protection. Work was intensified, for the tunnels had to be completed before the heavy rains came to Eritrea: June 15 was judged to be the deadline. After that, both tunnels would probably collapse. In the meantime, the post-escape preparations began. One group of escapees would go directly into Asmara, where Lankin and Mizrachi were preparing a hiding place with an underground shelter. Later they could try to rech the port of Massawa, and from there make their way north up the Red Sea. The other group required more elaborate preparations; for they would go out as fully uniformed British soldiers, hijack the local bus, and drive south to Ethiopia. The prisoners' factories produced everything—compasses, uniforms, berets, belts, regimental emblems, rank badges, kit bags, even revolvers in regulation green soldier holsters. Finally the entire lot was ready. The main tunnel was beyond the wire and ready to open. The uniforms and documents were finished. The fifty-four-man escape team was chosen and divided into two lots. For a week there was light rain, and then on June 29, the very last day thought possible for the escape, heavy rain fell.

The escape committee decided that the tunnel could be used. Soon after the evening roll call, the men began moving out through the tunnel, a long muddy snake, head to toe. They all got out. The Asmara group set off in the direction of town, and the "British" unit drove off in the bus toward the Ethiopian border. The bus group had bad luck almost from the first. In driving over a landslide, the bottom of the oil pan was pierced, and they had to abandon the vehicle and march overland. When the alarm was sent out, it was a simply a matter of time before they were scooped up by the British—"My God! Royal Artillery badges! Our full army uniforms! Where did they get them?"[21] On their return Meridor discovered that seven men had been recaptured just outside camp, but there were still twenty-three free in Asmara.

The thirty-one escapees were transferred to Baldizer fortress for safekeeping—no escape from there. Not only was there elaborate physical security—concrete, thick bars, thickets of wire—and a guard equal to that of the entire Sambal camp, but the British also had a sergeant and corporal live in the same building with the prisoners. Within twenty-four hours the escape committee decided the tunnel would begin in the kitchen, out of sight of the soldiers. The dirt would be hidden in the fortress ceiling. Everything worked smoothly; the dirt went upstairs; the tunnel crept along, and it was assumed that a few more weeks would see them through. Then they were ordered back to Sambal. There they found more bad news. Five of the Asmara men had been arrested trying to get to Massawa. Lankin had been arrested in Ethiopia, and would certainly be turned over to the British. Soon three other men were captured in a house on the outskirts of Asmara. The great escape was gradually coming to a sorry end.

The prospects of escape were dim from the special quarters prepared for Meridor and the eight others recently recaptured. In each of the two cells, two soldiers with machine guns were stationed in relays, day and night At night the room was lit. Trips out of the cells were made with a guard of two armed soldiers. Meridor had already devised an escape route—up through the ceiling, under the roof to a big hall, poke a hole, jump down, walk through the door to the courtyard of the camp and on into town. The only hitch continued to be the two guards in the cell. The key break came when the British soldiers, for unknown reasons, were replaced by Sudanese. The prisoners, after the January massacre, insisted they could not have Sudanese guards in their cells, and the authorities agreed to move them into the corridor. The escape plan went ahead. On September 3, Shimon Shiba and Meridor made their hole, scrambled under the roof over the heads of the guards, dropped into the hall unnoticed, sauntered out the door, across the courtyard, and away. Once out of sight, they discarded their military clothing and walked into Asmara as civilians. They stayed out only until September 24, when the British picked them up, along with the last of those still free from the great escape. There was some good news. Lankin had wangled his way out of Addis Ababa to French Somaliland. After considerable bureaucratic discussion and British entreaties, the French decided that Lankin's papers were valid; and he sailed from Djibouti for France. The goal beyond the next tunnel mouth thus became Djibouti.

The new tunnel was started, but with excavation only on Sunday. Then the prisoners could work rapidly and almost undisturbed. On the evening of January 14, 1947, Meridor, Arieh Ben-Eliezer, Reuben Franco, Rahamim Mizrachi, and LEHI's Shamir crawled out of the tunnel. They walked off at 8:20, discarded their filthy tunnel clothes, and in twenty minutes reached Asmara. Ben-Eliezer was smuggled into Addis Ababa in a secret compartment under a lorry. Then the other four rode out of Asmara in a small room built into an oil tanker. It was a long purgatory of thirst and heat, as the driver dawdled down to Addis Ababa, a week behind schedule. A new purgatory began—failed plots, legal maneuvers, delays, missing documents, confused communication. Ultimately Ben-Eliezer and Shamir managed to get to Djibouti, but the British were adamant about their return. Their only option was imprisonment for illegal entry. The Djibouti exit appeared sealed. The weeks stretched into months. There was supposed to be a plane, but it never came; documents did not appear; and the three left in Addis Ababa could not devise a way out on their own. Mizrachi at last prepared to try for Djibouti, but the other two had to wait for the long-delayed plane. All three were arrested by the Ethiopian authorities in the middle of July, were tried for illegal entry, but the case was postponed, and they were turned over to the British. They were taken to the Asmara central prison and from there to the empty Sambal camp. The other prisoners had been moved to Kenya. They found that serious preparations had been made for their arrival.

> On entering a small room inside one of the large empty barracks, we were struck by its resemblance to a cage. The ceiling had been covered with a closely meshed barbed wire. The windows, too, in addition to the bars, were screened with the same familiar material. The door had been removed and the doorway was also filled with barbed wire, covering the entire opening except for a space approximately 20 inches from the floor, where a movable carrier had been attached. We had to enter on hands and knees. The barrier was closed behind us and the cage sealed. In the corridor a British soldier stood guard, his Sten directed towards us: and at the two windows two other soldiers manned Sten guns which had been mounted in the window, pointing at us. One of the first things we noticed as we looked around were the electri-

cians setting up searchlights outside in such a manner that the light flooded the room through the window. A detachment of soldiers with full kit had been accommodated in the large hall next to our room. They formed the guard shifts and were held in reserve for any emergency. Between the fences of the camp, motorized patrols of another unit had been stationed, and the guard towers near our barracks had been manned by soldiers armed with Sten guns. Final conclusion: Exemplary security measures.[22]

The three thought it a splendid compliment, better than a commendation.

A few days later they were taken out and flown to Nairobi. From there they were moved to Gilgil camp. On August 19, 1947, as Meridor entered the camp, before he could move more than a pace, someone whispered in his ear while pounding him on the back, "We are digging. We have gone 12 yards and already passed the fence."[23] And so it began again. Meridor was quickly taken off to see what had been accomplished.

Down inside the tunnel, I found the most extraordinary room I have ever seen in all my experience digging. In the earthen walls, cupboards had been built for tools, first aid equipment, electric installations, etc., and there was even a handmade, manually operated fan . . . to supply with air the men who were working 16 to 17 yards inside the tunnel.[24]

The problem was that the proposed exit had suddenly become the site of two tents full of native soldiers. It was decided to seal the tunnel and hold it in reserve.

A second shaft was promptly opened. Meridor and the others became increasingly impatient; for the news out of Palestine indicated that the revolt was coming to a climax, and a real war was in the offing. There was much to be done in the diaspora, and many who could do it were behind barbed wire in Kenya. As the digging continued, the escape committee devised a method to use the tunnel more than once. Previous escapes had been concealed only long enough for the men to get well away. This time the escapees' places would be taken by cunningly constructed dummies. Nearly as complex was the long process of forging the appropriate documents with all the proper stamps and seals. They would go out on Honduras passports, carefully created by the camp's skilled forgery team. In South Africa, the Irgun representative, Raphael Kotlowitz, had made preparations to fly a plane to one of the small airports near the camp. The pilot would arrange to meet the first six escapees, drive them to two taxis specially hired to take a party of Latin American tourists to Uganda. From Kampala they would cross into the Belgian Congo, acquire the appropriate new visas, and fly on to Brussels. A week later a second group of six "Salvadorians" would follow the same route. A pilot, Bernard Wolff, was found, and contact was made with various Revisionist groups in helpful places.

The break was set for Saturday night, March 27. The dummies were slipped into place, and the escape team—Meridor, Reuben Franco, Yaa-kov Hillel, Shlomo Ben-Shlomo, Nathan Germant, and David Yanal—crept to the tunnel, crawled to the end and waited for the signal to go. It never came. There were native soldiers above the exit. The next night the dummies were again in place. The six again crawled to the tunnel end, and this time the light blinked. They found their way to the meeting place, and there was the car driven by Bernard Wolff. He was vastly excited. The prisoners had a thousand questions. In the babble and confusion, Wolff drove straight through a stop railway crossing; and with a scraming roar the locomotive tore by, a yard behind the car. It was Meridor's closest es-cape in Africa. They were driven to the taxis and motored into Kampala. After registering at the hotel, they cleaned up and had breakfast. Then they started off again. They reached the Congo border at midnight, seven-hundred miles from Gilgil. Their papers were checked and the barrier was lifted. The Irgun agents were waiting for them, and matters went quite smoothly. The visas were granted with interest and enthusiasm. "This is the first time in my life that I have seen a Honduran passport, and I have been in the business for years."[25] On Sunday, April 4, their Constellation landed at Brussels airport. Meridor, Shlomo, and Franco flew on to Paris the same day.

A variety of snags kept the six Salvadorians out of the tunnel. In Palestine, delighted with the news out of Paris, Begin permitted the Irgun propaganda machine to announce that Meridor and his five comrades, now escaped from Africa, participated in an attack on the British army camp at Pardess Hannah. In London, on April 8, the *Daily Mail* duly re-ported the news. Somehow the news did not reach Kenya, where the dummies still filled in for the absent six. Eventually, letters revealing the escape reached the camp. The Irgun quickly canceled the second escape and destroyed the dummies. The British began a prison count. The first counts, on April 13, revealed six prisoners missing. The officer in charge, Captain Clark, fearful that he would be blamed, discovered detainees only too eager to give evidence that the six had been in the camp during the five o'clock roll call. After that, it was not Clark's responsibility. The evening roll calls still came up six short. On April 15, the *East African Standard* broke the story of the escape in Kenya. The British, on Clark's roll-call evidence, assumed that the break had been made on April 13, but gradually new evidence turned up. Clark's story began to sound most pe-culiar to suspicious British security people. The escape investigation was kept open for the time being.

When Meridor and the others arrived in Paris, they found, as they ex-pected, that there was much work to be done in the diaspora. They also discovered that matters were not going too well in Palestine. The news of the Nebi Daniel disaster had arrived. It was not the last bad news out of

Palestine, but it was the last dramatic success of the Arab irregular war. Ready or not, the Jews had to move. They could no longer remain on the defensive and lose the battle of the roads.

NOTES

1. Great Britain, *Parliamentary Debates, Commons,* vol. 445, col. 1212.

2. Larry Collins and Dominique Lapierre, *O Jerusalem!* (New York: Simon and Schuster, 1972), p. 84.

3. Ibid.

4. Ibid.

5. *Palestine Post,* 21 December 1947.

6. Irgun Zvai Leumi, *This is the Way,* n.p., n.d., p. 10.

7. Geula Cohen, *Woman of Violence* (London: Rupert Hart-Davis, 1966), p. 269.

8. *Jerusalem Calling,* 1, no. 1, February 1948.

9. Samuel Katz, *Days of Fire* (London: W. H. Allen, 1968), p. 189.

10. Menachem Begin, *The Revolt* (Los Angeles: Nash, 1972), p. 343.

11. Collins and Lapierre, p. 88.

12. Ibid.

13. Sir John Bagot Glubb, *A Soldier with the Arabs* (New York: Harper & Row, 1957), p. 75.

14. Ibid., p. 77.

15. Dan Kurzman, *Genesis 1948* (New York: World, 1970), p. 95.

16. Ibid., p. 97

17. Glubb, pp. 63, 66.

18. Collins and Lapierre, p. 220.

19. Ibid., p. 238.

20. Yaacov Meridor, *Long is the Road to Freedom* (Johannesburg: NEWZO Press, 1955), p. 353.

21. Ibid. p. 181.

22. Ibid. pp. 306–307.

23. Ibid., p. 313.

24. Ibid., p. 315.

25. Ibid., p. 351.

CHAPTER 2

The Jews Attack,
March 1948–May 1948

You are being attacked by superior forces . . . The west exit of Deir Yassin leading to Ein Karim is open for you! Run immediately!
—LEHI loud-speaker, 4:35 A.M.,
April 9, 1948

Sitting on Ben-Gurion's desk was the Haganah's overall offensive plan, Dalet, which would begin when there was no more danger of British intervention. In March Ben-Gurion accepted that Jerusalem could not be relieved unless they activated the relevant operation from Dalet—called Nahshon, after Nahshon Ben-Aminadav, the first Jew who walked into the Red Sea when Moses ordered the waters parted. He first insisted that one plane load of the new arms must be secretly flown from the base near Prague into the Mandate. And on the night of April 1, a Dakota DC-3, jammed with rifles and German machine guns, glided into the Beit Darass airfield, which had recently been evacuated by the British. The arms were hastily unloaded, and the DC-3 was fueled and waved off before dawn. The British arrived early the morning of April 2 to find nothing on the abandoned airfield. Ben-Gurion had the arms for Nahshon, but not the men. On March 21, Shaltiel had reported from Jerusalem to the Haganah high command that he could not undertake offensive action. "Our forces are hardly sufficient for defensive warfare."[1] That was even before the Nebi Daniel disaster.

When the Haganah high command met on April 1, they reluctantly consented to Ben-Gurion's demand for an immediate attack to open the road but could promise only four-hundred men. Ben-Gurion insisted on fifteen hundred, and the next day, with the arms in Palestine, the Haganah commanders tried harder. They managed to piece together a force of fifteen-hundred men, more or less organized on formal army lines. On April 6, this force would strike east from Hulda and clear the Bab el-Wad gorge. Shaltiel, ready or not, would simultaneously move west against Kastel. A huge convoy would be in place at Hulda, ready to move. It was rather a complex operation to undertake in less than a week, but Ben-Gurion felt a deep sense of urgency. Jerusalem seemed to be slipping away.

While preparations for Nahshon continued, news from the front was most encouraging. On April 4, a Haganah sortie patrol crept up the twenty-five-hundred-foot heights and surprised the Arabs at Kastel. Stunned at the Haganah attack, they fled down the hill, called for aid, and prepared a counterattack. For the moment, however, the Haganah controlled one of the two key heights, even before Nahshon. Then a Haganah bomb demolished the headquarters of Hassan Salame's Druze volunteers, killing most of the staff but missing Salame. In Jerusalem Shaltiel found himself scraping the bottom of the barrel for troops. In absolute desperation he contacted the Irgun commander, Mordechai Raanan. He had already quarreled with the LEHI commander, Yehoshua Zettler, and in no time he was shouting at Raanan, who had made it no secret that he loathed Shaltiel—a prissy, authoritarian hypocrite sent in by Ben-Gurion, probably to make a deal with Abdullah. At twenty five, as an Irgunist maximalist, Raanan had no intention of accepting Haganah orders, especially coming from Shaltiel, an architect of the Season. So Shaltiel ended up in a fury, shouting at Raanan, "I'm here to protect the life of the Jews in Jerusalem, not to initiate any attacks! If you're not going to cooperate, I'll deal with the LEHI and you'll be cut off from supplies."[2] Raanan went directly to see Zettler, whose story was much the same. The two agreed to launch a joint operation of their own, but in tandem with Nahshon. They also had limited resources and no formal military experience. They decided the best bet would be Deir Yassin, a small Arab village to the west of Jerusalem, near the kibbutz Givat Shaul. There had been rumors of Arab snipers using the village, and the four clans living there had been involved in the 1929 disturbances. The likely result was that a swift descent, a loud warning, and a rattle of machine gun fire would probably spark an Arab flight.

When Shaltiel heard that the Irgun and LEHI intended to attack Dier Yassin, he felt that for the moment he would have to swallow his loathing for the thugs and criminal dissidents. On April 6, Nahshon began with attacks at both ends of the corridor, and the fighting around Kastel was heavy. The Arabs drove out the Palmach unit. Abdul Kader was on his way back from Damascus to lead the struggle. The villagers were again rushing to the front from Bet Safaf, Malkeih, Ein Karim, and Deir Yassin. The Haganah retook Kastel, but the Arabs counterattacked again and again. On April 7, Shaltiel dispatched identical letters to Raanan and Zettler.

I learn that you plan an attack on Deir Yassin. I wish to point out that the capture of Deir Yassin and its holding are one stage in our general plan. I have no objection to your carrying out the operation provided you are able to hold the village. If you are unable to do so I warn you against blowing up the village, which would lead to the flight of the inhabitants and the occupation of the destroyed and empty houses by foreign forces. This situation would increase our difficulties in the general struggle and a second conquest of the place would require heavy sacrifices.

Furthermore, if foreign forces took over, this would upset our general plan for establishing an airfield.[3]

Neither bothered to answer; they were too busy preparing for the attack to worry about Shaltiel.

On the morning of April 7, an event of crucial importance for Nahshon and for Jewish Jerusalem occurred on the main street of Kastel. Abdul Kader had returned to Jerusalem the previous day. He ordered his commanders to collect all the arms and men possible, then went to the headquarters of Ibrahim Abu Daya, who had led earlier ambushes. Kader wanted an immediate night attack on Kastel, and so, without further preparations, 150 men and several supply donkeys set out for the slopes of Kastel under the command of Abu Daya. Kader, who was too valuable to lose, would wait at the jump-off point with his civilian aide, Abdullah Omari, whose main duty was to see that Kader stayed put and did not rush to the battle. The column moved off and the little group around Kader sat and waited. The firing spread and grew louder. Suddenly a messenger appeared. "Ibrahim sent me. He says he is in trouble and needs more help!"[4] Omari insisted that Kader stay put. Kader reluctantly agreed not to go too close but would just find out what was happening. He stepped outside with Omari and two others almost into the path of a mortar shell, which burst to one side, showering the four with shrapnel and wounding everyone but Omari. Kader was unfazed, though, and with Omari's brother Moussa, he limped on toward Kastel. Just below the village, at four in the morning, they heard the Arab fire sputter and begin to die. One or two more shots were heard, then nothing. Kader sent Moussa on ahead to find out what had happened. An hour later a second messenger arrived at Kader's headquarters and reported that Abu Daya had been wounded and ammunition was short. He had not seen Kader.

Kader had by then reached the first houses of Kastel. Apparently the firing had died out because the last assault had swept the Jews off the heights. Accompanied by two irregulars, he walked on down the short main street to find Abu Daya. Someone ahead called out in Arabic, *"Ta-'al ya gama'a!"* Kader answered in English, "Hello, boys."[5] He had found his men. He stepped forward. Suddenly, ten yards ahead, just outside one of the solid stone houses, a man stepped out of the darkness.

Sergeant Meyer Kamiol tracked the three for a moment with his Sten and then fired a long burst. Kader disappeared down the slope and into the darkness. The unit commander, Mordechai Gazit, went through the dead man's papers but on discovering his Egyptian driving license in the name of Abdul el-Kader Salim—not Husseini—assumed that while his Sergeant Karmiol had hit a fat fish, it was not *the* fat fish. He reported the killing by radio to Haganah headquarters. A little later Uzi Narkis arrived at Kastel with three armored trucks loaded with sixty-thousand rounds of ammunition and took away the papers of the dead Arab, leaving the body in the street.

From the moment Omari heard that Kader had disappeared, word spread through the villages and to the Old City—Abdul Kader needs help. By mid-morning Gazit at Kastel could see them coming, thousands of irregulars, creeping up the slopes like a great swarm of locusts that grew by the minute. The firing grew louder. None of the Jews could move in streets swept by fire. Narkis's ammunition was passed from house to house in bags. The thousands of Arabs crept closer, pouring in the rounds they had rushed to buy in the Jerusalem market on their way to help Abdul Kader. Reinforcements did not arrive in time for Gazit, and when they did, they could not get through the hail of fire. The Arabs reached the mukhtar's house. A coherent defense was no longer possible, and Gazit and the survivors pulled out, tumbling down the slopes. From above, a cheer of triumph went up as the Arab irregulars rushed through the streets, shouting and waving their rifles. An Arab banner was run up on the mukhtar's house, and more and more men crowded the streets, laughing and firing rifles in the air. Others from outlying villages and Jerusalem began to arrive—Kastel was Arab again. A coffee boy from the Old City, Nadi Daies, who was following the crowd, stumbled over a body lying sprawled on a flight of stairs in front of a small stone house: an Arab martyr, his pockets turned inside out by Jewish looters. Then Nadi Daies looked down into the face of Abdul el-Kader Husseini and howled. The hysteria of victory, in a moment, became the hysteria of grief—first the stunned silence of horror, then the narrow streets of Kastel filled with men screaming, "Allah akhbar! Allah akhbar!" Some fell on the body to kiss the dead face, others tore at themselves, beating their heads and groaning. Down from Kastel the dreadful word spread; and down, passed hand to hand over the heads of the moaning crowd, came the body of Abdul Kader. He was followed by the great sobbing swarm that his magic had conjured up from the suqs and villages. Only a small band of fifty men under Bahjat Gharbieh remained in Kastel. The death of a hero had priority over tomorrow's battle. Those men in the empty village and the Mufti's men in Damascus all knew that only Abdul Kader could evoke the spirit they needed to win that battle.

The battle that came that day, April 9, would in time become more fa-mous than Kastel or Bab el-Wad. Abdul Kader's name and fame would, like his army, fade and be forgotten, but not Deir Yassin. For millions upon millions of Arabs that tiny village, a clutch of attractive flat-topped stone houses atop a slight ridge, would become a symbol of Zionist perfidy and cruelty. But 2:00 A.M. that day when Raanan and Zettler sepa-rately began to brief their men, Deir Yassin was still little more than a name and an objective—and for the Irgun and LEHI an easy operation.

Just before 4:30 the Irgun moved out of the Jewish suburb of Bet Hakerem to swoop on Deir Yassin from the east and south. The LEHI group, following their armored car with a mounted loud-speaker, started out from kibbutz Givat Shaul. As soon as the LEHI car reached the edge of the village, a warning would be broadcast that an attack was under way, and the way to Ein Karim, five miles to the south, was still open. Followed by a heavy volley of shots from three sides, there should be lit-tle left to do but rush into the deserted village. Operation Achdut (unity) would commit 132 men, with LEHI supplying the explosives, the Irgun Stens, and the Haganah some rifles. Problems began almost at once. The Irgun people under Ben-Zion Cohen arrived at the edge of the village at exactly 4:30. They had no contact with the LEHI people under David Gottleib and had to assume that everyone was on schedule. Some of the Irgun people began firing into the village. The three-man village guard in-side a concrete pillbox immediately returned the fire. The Irgun concen-trated on the unexpected defensive work, pouring in a hail of fire. The cry went up in the village, "Yehud alain!"—the Jews are coming. The Arab return fire continued and began to spread, and the heavy crump and flash of the old Mausers and Ottoman rifles indicated that no one was fleeing to Ein Karim. On the other side of the village, Gottleib's people were late. By the time the armored car came creeping up the trail, the fire fight was well under way and all the Arab guards alert. Instead of being able to smash right into the center of the village to make the loud speaker an-nouncement, the armored car plunged into a homemade tank trap, direct-ly in front of the first row of houses. As the LEHI people struggled to move the car, the Arabs opened up on them. The loud speaker suddenly activated:

> You are being attacked by superior forces . . . The west exit of Deir Yassin leading to Ein Karim is open to you! Run immediately! Don't hesitate! Our forces are advancing! Run toward Ein Karim![6]

In the rising din, no one heard the warning but the LEHI men, who were trapped in the car by the waves of Arab fire zapping in around them. They struggled to get the car out; the time for a warning had obviously passed.

The LEHI people ran toward the first row of houses, firing as they went. Shots seemed to be returned from every window in every house. Above the roar of the old rifles and the stutter of Stens came the howls of the Arabs, determined to defend the village to the last. Each house had to be taken; and each was filled not only with Arab defenders, but also with women and children. They was nothing to be done but toss in grenades and then spray the small rooms with automatic fire, but both the LEHI and Irgun men found it difficult to get close enough to the houses to be effective. The attackers were repeatedly hit. The operational commander, Ben-Zion Cohen, went down, and his place was taken by Yehuda Lapidot. Arab fire seemed endless. It took two hours to reach the center of the village. The atmosphere was hectic. When the men finally reached an Arab house, they became increasingly ruthless in spraying the inside with Sten fire. Lapidot decided that such house-to-house fighting was costly and ineffectual. He sent word to Raanan, who was anxiously watching the lack of progress from Givat Shaul, to send up explosives. Raanan and his aides soon appeared with knapsacks filled with TNT. The new orders. were to dynamite each house, one by one. Following close behind the dynamiters, the Irgun and LEHI people fired on anyone who moved, anyone in the sniper houses, anyone who might be a threat, and increasingly anyone at all. The fighting and firing went on and on. By early afternoon fifteen houses were dynamited to rubble. The sniping ended. After a fierce and tenacious battle, the mukhtar's house fell, and the last Arabs were shot. The survivors were rounded up and loaded onto trucks. Dazed and shaken, they were driven slowly through the streets of the New City, then released near Mandelbaum's house. They disappeared into the Old City.

By then the nature of the Irgun-LEHI victory had become clearer. At 5:30 Shaltiel appeared at the edge of Deir Yassin, a smoking ruin filled with the corpses of men, women, and children. Raanan announced that the village was under his control, and he wanted Shaltiel to send in a Haganah unit to take over. Shaltiel replied, "We're not going to take responsibility for your murders!"[7] and he withdrew his men from the edge of the village. He left Raanan with the bodies piled in a quarry. A few were charred after an attempt was made to burn them. The next morning Dr. Jacques de Reynier, the Red Cross representative, arrived and amid the ruins found three people still alive, a ten-year-old girl and two women. There was ample evidence of the ferocity of the attack. The British authorities in Jerusalem were already taking down atrocity stories from those who had survived—murder, rape, loot, mutilation. The Irgun and LEHI denied the charges, denied that the last men captured in the village had been shot, insisted that the operation was a straightforward attack that had run into heavy resistance—40 percent casualties—and been salvaged only by dynamiting the sniper houses. Some privately admitted that men, women, and children had been shot on sight, but denied the more macabre survivors' tales of raping and mutilation.

A Haganah unit under Yeshurin Schiff moved in to replace Raanan. With a group of schoolboys, they dug a mass grave and buried about 250 corpses. Schiff noted, "It was a lovely spring day. The almond trees were in bloom; the flowers were out, and everywhere there was the stench of the dead, the thick smell of blood, and the terrible odor of the corpses burning in the quarry."8 The Arab propagandists snatched up the massacre of Deir Yassin and with elaborate and gruesome detail sent off the news. Now the timorous Arab regimes would have to act. The British briefly considered an air strike on the village, but dropped the idea once the Haganah moved in. On April 10, Shaltiel issued a statement, putting as much distance as possible between him and the attackers.

> The splinter groups did not launch a military operation . . . they chose one of the quiet villages in the area that had not been connected with any of the gang attacks since the start of the present campaign; one of the few villages that has not let foreign gangs in.
> For a full day, Etzel and LEHI soldiers stood and slaughtered men, women, and children, not in the course of the operation, but in a premediated act which had as its intention slaughter and murder only. They also took spoils, and when they finished their work, they fled.9

Raanan and Zettler immediately released Shaltiel's letter to them, a revelation that greatly disturbed Ben-Gurion, who had seized the opportunity to dispatch a cable to Abdullah expressing horror and regret. He feared that Deir Yassin might end any chance of an understanding with Abdullah.

The Arab's attention was not on the fate of Deir Yassin, but on the funeral of Abdul Kader. Thousands of tribesmen who had fought the battle of the roads came into the Old City, still dazed with grief, to pay their last respects. As Abdul Kader's coffin came into sight at the door to his brother's house and was passed hand over hand through the Damascus Gate, a single shot rang out, followed by the heaviest concentration of gunfire ever heard in Jerusalem. As the coffin bobbed down Solomon Street and up the Via Dolorosa to the great open quadrangle around the Dome of the Rock, the firing went on and on—enough ammunition to conquer half of Palestine. As the firing died out and the mourners began to drift home, they passed Gharbieh, who had stayed at Kastel with his fifty men. The Haganah opened up both ends of the corridor and jammed through a huge convoy. Three more followed on April 12, 17, and 20, although the Arabs regrouped around Latrun and shot at the last convoy of three hundred trucks. The siege of Jerusalem had been lifted, if only temporarily. Jewish morale was restored, and the Haganah were battle tested.

Elsewhere, the news for the Arabs was equally bleak. During the first week in April, Kaukji failed to take the strategic settlement of Mishmar Haemek, the gateway to the costal plain but as usual claimed a victory. When the fighting began along the Jerusalem corridor, he felt he had to compete and so launched a second attack on April 14. With a thousand men and six French 75 mm. artillery pieces, he planned to sneak up the heights and sweep down on the surprised Jews. Instead, the Palmach, aware of his intentions and intimate with the terrain—it was an old Haganah training ground—laid an ambush. The Arabs, concentrating on Mishmar Haemek, crept past the Palmach and, at a range of three-hundred yards, came under withering and unexpected fire. The attack collapsed. The Arab Liberation Army retreated all the way back to the main camp near Tubas. The village irregulars were shocked at the collapse of the regular army and imediately disbanded.

Kaukji reported to Safwat Pasha that the Jews had 120 tanks, the lightest six tons, plus twelve batteries of 75s, six bomber and fighter squadrons, and a complete infantry division, one regiment composed solely of non-Jewish Russian Communists. Despite all this he had won through at Mishmar Haemek. After the battle a Beirut paper reported that the Jews had surrendered in the presence of the British commander. When foreign correspondents asked Kaukji how long it would take the Arab Liberation Army to sweep the Jews into the sea, he replied, "I took Mishmar in ninety minutes, so all you have to do is to find out how many other Jewish settlements there are and multiply them by ninety."[10] It takes more to make an Arab into a Prussian than an Iron Cross second class, and much more to transform Arab volunteers into disciplined soldiers than wishful thinking. The "victory" at Mishmar Haemek marked the beginning of the end for the Palestine irregulars and for an Arab Palestine.

Despite Kaukji's facile optimism, most Palestinian Arabs recognized disaster looming. The Arab Liberation Army was shattered, Abdul Kader lost, the battle of the roads lost. Without help from the Arab regimes, the future was bleak. Already the British, set to evacuate on May 15, were pulling back from exposed positions. Where once the Arabs had waited eagerly for the opportunity to pounce on the defenseless Jews, now they waited in increasing agony for the reverse, their minds turned to the blackened ruins on the hill west of Jerusalem. At Tiberias the Arabs were most uneasy. The British were leaving there on April 18. The more numerous Jews lived in the new city on the hill overlooking the Arab old city on the shore of Lake Tiberias. The tiny Jewish quarter in the old city had been isolated for months, but the local irregulars had not pushed through their attacks. Once the British evacuated, the Haganah opened their attack from both directions. Abdullah had arranged for thirty trucks to evacuate the women and children. The men would stay and fight. On the afternoon of April 19, the trucks arrived. Soon every woman and child had climbed aboard. There was a pause. No one wanted another Deir Yassin. One after another, the men began clamboring up. Excess baggage had to be dropped over the side as every man came aboard. The convoy moved out, leaving Tiberias to the Jews.

As early as December 1947, a gradual exodus of individual Arabs from the Mandate had begun. The first refugees were the prudent with funds, who intended to wait out any trouble in Beirut or Cairo. Politics in Palestine had for years meant the mufti, and the mufti meant shooting. They had no interest in politics. Many of the monied Arabs were local notables, the potential leaders of the community, who thus removed what guidance might have been available for the people. The Palestinian Arabs, without real direction from above or institutions of their own, were left at the mercy of rumor, anxiety, and fear. When the fighting spread, the Arab families in mixed districts began to move out—there was no Ben-Gurion to impose a no-retreat policy. All believed evacuation would be only temporary. Every Arab believed that if the Jews were not actually swept into the sea, at least they would be badly handled, first by the irregulars and then by the regular armies of the Arab regimes. Then, too, it was unwise to be in areas under Jewish control. Besides, there were rumors that the Arab League or the Mufti approved of evacuation. So the cautious moved to safer quarters. When the Haganah offensive began early in April, coupled with the news from Deir Yassin, the Arabs, regardless of their leaders' intentions or the issues of the moment, began to flee because they were afraid of the Jews. They left homes and businesses to save their lives, first in a trickle under direct threat, but increasingly on the basis of rumor. As Begin noted, some good came out of Deir Yassin for the Jews. In any case, even when the British tried to help the local Arab commanders, by tipping them off in advance about evacuation plans or even allowing them to move in beforehand, that advantage was jeopardized by public panic and the Haganah's quick action.

Two days later, April 21, Haifa's turn came, when Major General H. C. Stockwell, the British commander, ordered the Sixth Airborne out of the city. He assumed that the Haganah would be able to take over within a week. The Haganah unit, under Moshe Carmel and Mordechai Makleff, had prepared Operation Misparayim (scissors), a two-pronged attack from the heights of Hadar Hacarmel and the old commercial center. The Haganah assumed that the Arabs had made similar preparations and would have superior forces. Instead, there was only a scratch force of some five-hundred irregulars under the command of Captain Amin Izzedin, a Lebanese Druze, who had brought in forty volunteers to bolster the defense. Stockwell spoke with Izzedin at British headquarters on Stella Maris Road at 11:30 A.M. but either Izzedin misunderstood the timing of withdrawal or felt he could be of more use elsewhere, for he immediately left for Damascus.

When the Haganah attacked, the Arabs resisted stubbornly, despite the lack of leadership and the growing civilian panic. Haganah sound trucks blared warnings. Hearing them, the civilians began to move down toward the port in search of safety. The trickle became a flood, and all during the night the crowds grew on the dockside. By morning Arab resistance was flickering out, and the population was hysterical. Ultimately an emergency Arab committee refused to agree to Carmel's truce terms: surrender of all weapons, immediate curfew, and Haganah control of the entire city. Instead all the Arabs would be evacuated: better a dignified refusal to accept injustice than an accommodation with the Haganah. Efforts to prevent evacuation by Jewish spokesmen failed. By the end of April, sixty-thousand Arabs had left the city.

For some while, as the direction of events became clear the number of trained volunteers increased, and the Irgun high command had considered operational possibilities. There was talk of a move north to clear the Tel Aviv-Haifa road, but during an informal conversation with Israel Galili stress was placed on the Tel Aviv-Jerusalem connection. Rather than Galili's somewhat indirect nibbling operation, the Irgun decided, without informing him, that a far more tempting target was Arab Jaffa, a fervidly nationalist Arab city outside the United Nations partition boundaries, which remained a potential threat to the Jerusalem connection. In fact, the Irgun suspected that the Arabs, with British complicity, wanted to drive a column from Jaffa to Jerusalem, cutting off the Negev, splitting the Jewish territory and heralding the end of any Jewish state. Moreover, in the months since the partition vote, Arab snipers in Manshiya had inflicted approximately a thousand casualties on Jewish Tel Aviv. The minaret of the Hassan Bek Mosque became an especially obnoxious symbol of the irregular war. On April 21, the Irgun high command agreed on the Jaffa operation. Begin appointed Paglin as commander. It would be the largest Irgun operation to date.

Paglin planned to deploy some six-hundred men in two groups. One would be mobile, loaded on nearly a hundred trucks and two Bren gun carriers, which would be stolen from the British. He would also reap the benefit of the raid on the British Army Camp no. 80 at Pardess Hanna, and material confiscated from the British train raid the week before. There the Irgun had made off with twelve tons of two-inch mortar shells. Paglin would thus have artillery support of a sort. He concentrated his men at the Irgun's Camp Dov—named after Dov Gruner—in Ramat, and prepared a two-pronged attack, including a drive straight through the neck of the Manshiya to the sea, cutting off the entire area around Hassan Bek Mosque. In the ensuing Arab panic the mobile force would drive on through into the center of Jaffa. At two in the morning of April 25 Begin arrived at Camp Dov for his first public appearance. There was no introduction, but the Irgun people recognized that the pale, bearded man who spoke to them must be the commander.

> Men of the Irgun! We are going out to conquer Jaffa. We are going into one of the decisive battles for independence of Israel. Know who is before you, and remember whom you are leaving behind you. Before you is a cruel enemy who has risen to destroy us. Behind you are parents, brothers, children. Smite the enemy hard. Aim true. Save your ammunition. In battle, show no mercy to the enemy that shows no mercy to our people. But spare women and children. Whoever raises his hands in surrender has saved his life. You will not harm him. You will be led in the attack by Lieutenant Gideon. You have only one direction—forward.[11]

A little after 3:00 A.M. they moved out toward operational headquarters at the Alliance School—a little behind schedule, for Paglin had hoped for a night attack, and with dawn at 4:30 there would not be time. There was not much point in waiting twenty-four hours, since the Arabs who watched from Manshiya knew an attack was coming.

At 8:00 the Irgun's two two-inch mortars opened up a heavy barrage, dropping in all over the city, and particularly in the center south of Manshiya. The three Irgun gunners, hour after hour, dropped the shells down the tubes and listened to their high whine as they were launched. Inside Jaffa the endless whine and crunch of the incoming rounds had a devastating effect on civilian and irregular morale but little effect on the direction of the battle at Manshiya. There the Irgun found that the Arabs were amply prepared. Cement pillboxes had been constructed at strategic street corners and on the roofs of many buildings. The Arab Spandaus could match the Irgun Brens, and the Arabs were firing from cover. Arab fire almost at once began to take a toll of the attackers with no visible returns. The first day's losses for the Irgun were four killed and six seriously wounded. On the second day the Irgun pushed on, breaking into some of the first rank of houses and driving out or killing the Arabs in room-to-room fighting. But that was all, as the mortaring went on. Arab civilians were reported boarding boats in Jaffa harbor, but along the edge of Manshiya there was no hint of weakness.

The gloomy reports from Jaffa had not disquieted the Jewish Agency. Many felt that this ill-advised spectacular—a typical Irgun exercise—would destroy the dissidents' prestige. The Haganah, however, were more concerned with military than political factors, and felt that if the Irgun broke off the attack, their own preparations to seal off Jaffa by loop-ing, flanking attacks would be that much more costly. Better that the Ir-gun hammer away and tie down resistance. Galili and Yigal Yadin met with Begin and approved of the continuation of the attack under the terms of the long-delayed March 8 Irgun-Haganah agreement. It had been ac-cepted two weeks previously by the Zionist General Council but ignored by Ben-Gurion, who did not want any accommodation with the Irgun. Be-gin, however, had grave doubts about further frontal fighting. When he returned to the Alliance School, he felt that with no hope of progress op-erations should be suspended. "We shall defend the line we have taken with a strong holding unit. The rest of our troops we shall withdraw."[12] Some of the Irgun commanders agreed. Some did not, especially Paglin, who slipped out and began sending in officers to lobby for another try. He had been searching for a way through the Arab defense, and on his return insisted to Begin that there was still a possibility. Begin reluctantly gave him twenty-four hours.

What Paglin decided to do was drive a corridor through to the sea by blowing a passage through the houses, building sandbag walls across the streets, and using heavy covering fire and explosives to protect his men. The distance to be covered was about three-hundred meters, and twenty-four hours was hardly time to construct an artificial above-ground tunnel under heavy fire. At 4:00 P.M. on the third day, April 28, the Irgun began digging and bombing their way forward, yard by yard. At some points buildings were mined so as to collapse on Arab pillboxes, at others the sandbag walls had to be constructed by men lying on their backs under withering fire, lifting one bag forward at a time. Just at dawn the man at the head of the tunnel looked up and saw the sea just ahead. After twenty-four hours of unremitting work under brutal crossfire, they had made it al-most to the shore. Without waiting, the men rushed shooting and shouting at the final Arab position. The Arabs were at last aware of what had hap-pened, and turned and ran. The Manshiya quarter was cut off and the Ir-gun began clearing out the remaining pockets of resistance. The militants in the Hassan Bek Mosque held out to the last, but by mid-morning the Zionist flag flew from the minaret. Soon the Irgun men gave up looking for Arab snipers and began collecting souvenirs and valuables, rampaging through the deserted quarter hauling off loot, large and small. Meanwhile the Irgun command had switched its two mortars to give aid to a bogged-down Haganah attack.

By April 30, the Irgun rounded out their hold on Manshiya, took the Jaffa railway station, and strengthened their blocks on the Jerusalem road. The way into the center of Jaffa lay open. The Irgun success caught the British by surprise. General MacMillan was concerned with his eva-cuation route from the Sarafand camp. In London Bevin was again outraged. The British had already been accused of selling out the Arabs in Haifa; and now the Jews were about to take an entirely Arab city outside the partition boundaries—and not just any Jews, but the Irgun. MacMillan was ordered to retake Jaffa and hand it back to the Arabs. The second section of the order was really difficult, for the quarreling and splintered Arab volunteers had given up the fight. Their leaders charged each other with treason, and evacuated the city. Increasing numbers of civilians followed them. Retaking the city would present problems as well.

On the morning of April 30, British tanks moved out from the Jaffa city center on the three main roads toward Manshiya. Paglin immediately sent out a bazooka team to block the main road. When the first British tank rumbled into sight, they made a direct hit with the first round, disabling the vehicle and blocking the road. A demolition team on the second road cropped the facade of a building on top of another lead tank. Things went better for the third armor proxy. The first British tank hit the Irgun's Bren carrier, killing the four-man crew; but with the other two streets blocked, the column leader pulled his tanks back into central Jaffa. The next morning a British air strike hit the Bat-Yam quarter, and MacMillan's twenty-five pounders began a desultory shelling of Tel Aviv. Spitfires began strafing runs on the Irgun positions in Manshiya. A British destroyer appeared offshore. Tanks, supported by infantry, began moving out again from central Jaffa. Artillery fire, mortars, and machine guns raked the Irgun positions. With no antitank guns, Paglin directed sapper teams to create blocks in front and behind the first five British tanks. Uzi Levy exploded a house into Hassan Bek Street, sealing one of the two parallel exits out of Manshiya, then rushed up Hacarmel Street to place the second charge. Meanwhile, the Irgun men were creeping up and tossing lit dynamite sticks onto the tanks. The British tanks found the going very slow, the streets clogged with smashed masonry, and the Irgun fire heavy. Realizing after nearly two hours that the Irgun was still resisting and the way out was in danger, the tanks pulled up and began to retreat, spraying the side streets with machine gun fire. As they pulled past the partial block on Hacarmel Street, Uzi Levy was hit and killed. His brother, a member of the high command, was still in Gilgil when the news reached him.

MacMillan was now in a hopeless position. The news of the British setback completed the panic generated by the Irgun's mortars. The Arab civilians began fleeing to the waterfront. Order collapsed. Old scores were settled in shootouts. Looting began and fires spread. Soon MacMillan had no Arabs to return the city to—even if he had wanted to risk more head-on assaults against the Irgun. He flew to the Suez Canal Zone and explained his dilemma to the British Middle East commander, General Sir John Crocker. Crocker agreed in turn to explain the situation to London. MacMillan returned to negotiate with the Jews on means to stabilize the situation. The British wanted the Manshiya police station and the right to send armored patrols through the Manshiya quarter. Begin did not want to accept, but agreed that the Haganah could replace his men. If the Haganah wanted to let in patrols, that was their business. As for the police station, the Irgun called a press conference to discuss the terms of the British proposal. At exactly 10:00 A.M., after the foreign correspondents arrived, the first question was whether the Irgun would accept British terms. Paglin looked at his watch and waited. There was a huge explosion just at the moment he began to talk. There was no longer a Manshiya police station. The Haganah moved in to take over the Irgun sandbagged positions along Azen Street. The Irgun commander, Shraga Elis, insisted only on a receipt. Written on a page torn from the Haganah commander's notebook, it was the epilogue for the battle of Jaffa:

Received from Irgun Zvai Leumi: One Jaffa

Only five thousand of the original hundred-thousand Arabs remained in the city. The Irgun had lost forty-two killed and four-hundred wounded— one-third of the nearly fifteen hundred involved.

Elsewhere the news was mixed. Despite a seemingly hopeless situation, reinforcements had arrived and Safed was held. The Palmach cleared out further areas in Galilee. Operations in the Negev strengthened the position of the isolated kibbutzim, and on the coast north of Haifa a scratch Haganah force captured Acre. The situation around Jerusalem, however, had again deteriorated. On April 13, a convoy of professors, doctors, and hospital personnel was ambushed and, when the British would not intervene, was finished off by the Arab irregulars after a seven-hour battle. Mount Scopus was cut off, and on April 18 the Arabs seized August Victoria hospital. No convoys at all had reached the Etzion block. Kibbutz Nebi Yaakov could be reached only at night by small patrols, and the situation in the Old City as always was poor. Operation Jebusi by the Haganah at the end of April did not open the corridor, but captured Katamon and the Greek quarter of western Jerusalem. On May 4, the Arab Legion, escorted by British tanks and followed by a swarm of irregulars, attacked the Russian monastery in the Etzion block. They were driven back, but the Jews lost twelve dead, twenty-eight wounded, and expended much irreplaceable ammunition. It seemed likely that Glubb wanted to clear out the Etzion block so that his "British" army could withdraw into Transjordan one day before evacuation, then return as an Arab army the next. The Jews were hardly any better prepared for a real war at the beginning of May than they had been a month before. They still had only tiny single-engine planes, stolen Bren carriers and armored cars, a few more mortars and machine guns, but not enough of anything. Aid from the diaspora would be crucial.

When Tavin was dispatched to Italy by the high command in January

1946, he was forced to create an organization from scratch. In a year he fashioned an underground from displaced persons, volunteers, and a few aides sent from Palestine. It was sufficiently effective to bomb the British Embassy on October 31. That operation, however, loosened the ties Tavin had with the Italian government and led to arrests. To counteract this, in January 1947 pamphlet bombs were detonated simultaneously in eight Italian cities, explaining the aims of the Irgun to the Italian people and calling on them to join the struggle. By then the Irgun underground had set up branches in Germany and Austria, run a commanders' battle school at Tricasa and Ladispoli in Italy, and soon moved the diaspora headquarters to 18, Avenue de Messine in Paris. The most fruitful recruiting ground discovered was the remnants of Betar; for despite the holocaust many had survived. One Irgun unit of five in Poland had remained intact throughout the war, and sailed for Palestine as a group as soon as the opportunity arose. Eventually there were Irgun units in twenty-three countries, including a North African group to defend the local Jews, and even a Chinese unit in Shanghai, commanded by two men trained in Europe and sent back to China. The Prague office grew until it became a subheadquarters for all Eastern Europe. These European operations were tied together by Tavin, endlessly crossing the continent, always without a proper passport, relying on Red Cross papers, a ready tongue, and a growing net of smugglers willing to aid the Irgun.

With the Irgun growing in the diaspora almost beyond the capacity of the Paris headquarters to cope with it, Tavin had the help of Samuel Katz, a roving ambassador in Paris until his dismissal, and of Ariel, the Irgun ambassador to the French government. Also, after the Acre break, Lankin supervised recruiting and training the volunteers. Repeated efforts to give organizational coherence to the entire diaspora movement collapsed under the weight of competing groups, personality clashes, and the strains of differing perspectives and priorities. The Irgun in the diaspora remained an integral part of the Palestine organization. Despite the increasing number of high command people stationed abroad, Palestine decided all policy matters. In March 1947, another effort was made when an Irgun legation in the diaspora was set up in Paris with representatives of the Betar executive, the world executive of the Revisionist party, and the Irgun under Hillel Kook, who used the name Peter Bergson. The Irgun high command soon became disenchanted, as the component parts of the movement continued their independent ways—funds were not channeled to the Palestinian struggle, and there was still pressure for some sort of Hebrew government in exile. The attempt to coöpt the other organizations having failed, the legation was closed down in October. Betar, the Revisionist party, and the Hebrew Committee for National Liberation went their own ways.

If relations within the movement were difficult, those with the orthodox Zionist agencies were dreadful. There was constant friction: the Jewish Agency pretended that funds collected by them were also distributed to the Irgun; there was suspicion that the Czechs' decision to sell the Irgun arms only if the Jewish Agency agreed had not originated in Prague; the Revisionists and Betar wanted more visas for the legal immigration, and the incidents of the various Seasons poisoned most attempts to cooperate in the diaspora. The worst single incident ended with a bloody clash and several arrests in Innsbruck in September 1947. Thus Irgun activities in the diaspora were almost always isolated from those of the other Zionist organizations.

Beyond the world of Zionism, the Irgun headquarters made an impressive and ultimately profitable number of diplomatic contacts. In fact one of the major purposes of the diaspora headquarters was to build up such contacts, to win friends and influence regimes, to play the part of a quasi-state, knitting together covert pacts, arms agreements, military aid deals, and acquiring the freedom to act openly. Thus, although the early contacts in Italy had been severed after the British Embassy operation, renewed attempts were made to get in touch with old Italian friends and, through the apostolic nuncio in Paris and the assistant secretary of state in the Vatican, to maintain contact with the Roman Church. The result was a remarkable toleration of Irgun activities, training centers, movements, and personnel—those arrested in the autumn of 1946 were soon released. In Czechoslovakia the government was even more forthcoming. Irgun training camps were set up with Czech officers acting as instructors. Despite currency problems, the Irgun fund drives of Keren Habarzel took place openly, as did the distribution of propaganda. Representatives of the Defense and Interior ministries met regularly with Irgun agents. But there was no open arms sale. Despite the negotiations between J. Klarman of Budapest and War Minister Budneraz, the Rumanians too were reluctant to become openly involved. In Paris Irgun discussion with members of the Polish security authorities also failed to produce arms. Contact was even made with the Kurds. All the constant diplomatic activity, however, eased the illicit purchase and covert shipment of arms, and did produce two intelligence coups, when highly placed officials in Paris and London independently contacted Irgun headquarters, supplying detailed information until late in 1948.

During much of 1947, the arms problem was only one of many. Headquarters was monitoring the Geneva meetings of UNSCOP, where contact was maintained with Ralph Bunche. The propaganda mills had to be fed: the weeklies *Zion in Kampf*, *Zum Sieg*, and *La Scala*, the steady stream of bulletins, manifestos, announcements, and pamphlets. Aid was given to sympathizers' publications, *The Jewish Struggle* and *The Legion-*

naire in London, *Answer* in New York, and *La Riposte* in Paris. The branches had to be supplied with instructors, propaganda, fund raisers, and in some cases money. The volunteers had to be processed and trained with the available arms. Intelligence information from a variety of sources had to be gathered and sent on to Palestine. And there was never enough time, money, or talent. Despite all this, arms were gradually accumulated in dumps in Austria, Italy, and France. In France former members of the resistance proved most helpful, donating arms and ammunition. In Canada agents purchased two Lodestar planes for $19,000 each, one Hudson plane for $7,000, fifteen parachutes, additional equipment, and spare parts. A Piper Cub was bought in Paris, and in South Africa two Oxfords were acquired for £ 2,000. When five Bren gun carriers owned by a French agricultural cooperative came on the market, they were picked up for 350,000 francs. Explosives left by the Germans in Nancy were removed and brought to southern France. Powder was removed from war-surplus shells. All over Europe the bits and pieces piled up: new Brownings, TNT, used M-1s, grenades, old German and Italian rifles, new bazookas and Piats, military tents, gelignite, uniforms of varying makes and models, medicine, mills bombs, tools—eventually there was even a blood bank in Paris. Very little of this could be forwarded to Palestine. Between February and March 1948, Tavin managed to arrange forty-three tiny shipments from New York to Tel Aviv. Most packages contained two revolvers and two hundred rounds of ammunition, though three contained a dismantled broadcasting station. All forty-three were smuggled out of the Tel Aviv customs warehouse. Not all went so well in New York. On April 27, 1948, two men were arrested—one was the son of Louis Untermeyer—in a fur loft on West 28th Street with 144 machine guns, 203 rifles, and 268 pistols, along with other arms and ammunition. Their attorney, Paul O'Dwyer, managed to get them acquitted a month later. The only other matériel to reach Palestine came when Yoel Amrami arranged to stuff the luggage of new immigrants. The rest stayed in dumps, often in the open, and always at risk. Twice the French confiscated arms under the impression that the Irgun was a communist front, but both times the matériel was returned.

Not all the arms were stockpiled, for the Irgun intended wherever possible to strike at the British in the diaspora. Fearful that the British might revoke the declaration of evacuation and prolong the naval blockade, the Irgun prepared a series of operations against British merchant shipping, the most advanced one being in Shanghai. The warning of Irgun intentions was passed on to the British by Ben Hecht through the American consul general in Munich, Sam Woods, at the Hotel Crillon in Paris. Woods sent it on to the State Department, and from there the warning went to the Foreign Office. Three days later Woods reported to Hecht that

London had informed Washington Britain had no intention of prolonging the blockade. Usually the Irgun did not limit military operations to warnings. In March 1947 an active service unit attacked a British officers club at the Sacher Hotel in Vienna. In May explosives were confiscated from the Austrian quarry at Saalfelden and in August from Salzburg. A mining attempt was made on a British military train near Hanover in June, and two months later another British military train was mined and derailed near Melnitz. In March 1948, there was another attack on an officers club in the Park Hotel in Vienna, and on a sergeants club in Germany in April 1948. In London, in August 1948, Monty Harris attempted to sabotage British military lorries due to be shipped to Iraq. In Italy preparations were made for attacks on a British army headquarters, near Mestro, grounded military aircraft at Fiumezzino, and the admiralty building at Naples, but these operations were canceled. In Brussels an attempt to kidnap the informer, H. Reinhold, in order to carry out the death sentences passed in Palestine ended in the arrest of the Irgun people involved. The British once more spirited Reinhold out of the country. Of all these military operations, perhaps the most daring was the attempt in England on the life of General Barker.

For the Irgun Barker was a peculiarly odious opponent. His secret reports while commanding British forces in Palestine revealed his basic anti-Semitism, as did the regular reports of his outbursts against Jews. As his parting gesture, in February 1947, he had signed the death warrants of Alkochi, Kashani, and Drezner. The major difficulty was that the Irgun did not really exist in Britain, and after February 1947 Barker was there. The Irgun man in London, Yocl Bela, was engaged in the cosmetics business and had no training for such an operation. On his arrival in Paris, Lankin decided that someone must be smuggled into Britain, and that the man for the job was Yoel Eilberg. He had been in the British Army—the Guards no less—had a Welsh accent, and had participated in the Rome embassy operation. At a time when the newspapers regularly reported that every British port and terminal was constantly and carefully watched for suspected terorists, Lankin intended to fly his man into England.

After the war a young South African pilot in London, Boris Senior, had purchased for £1,000 a small three-seater with an eye to its possible political use. He made one or two flights to Le Bourget north of Paris and to Barcelona. In contact with Lankin in Paris, he began to scout about. In northern France, near Tous-le-Nöel, he discovered a rarely used glider field surrounded by trees. Naturally there were no customs, as there were in England. There was, however, a way around English customs, and the operation was scheduled down to the minute for April 20, 1947. As Senior brought his little plane into the French field, he saw parked to one side a Citroën, innocently loaned by a friendly communist. Inside were Lankin and Eilberg, along with two young ladies, Zipora Levy and Lee Stern, to give a picnic-like atmosphere of innocence. While Senior swung the plane about, Eilberg ran over and climbed in. Senior revved the engine and took off, just over the trees, with no one the wiser. Back in England a British car was parked in a lane by a stone wall running alongside a farmer's field in Kent. Seated inside this car were a young couple, Ezer Weizmann and Deborah Landman, apparently deeply interested in each other, actually listening for the putter of Senior's engine. Right on schedule, he swooped over the field. The girl waved her scarf. His plane slipped in over the trees and coasted to a stop. Eilberg leaped out and clambered over the stone wall. By the time Eilberg was in the car, Senior had the plane in the air and was on the way to Lympe, where he cleared customs ten minutes later and flew on to Croydon. He taxied in, left his plane in the hanger, and made his way back to his flat in Bayswater. When he arrived Eilberg was already there. The flight turned out to be the easy part.

Eilberg found no real organization, no explosives, and limited intelligence. The CID was suspicious of Yoel Bela, and followed him everywhere. A few days after his arrival Eilberg returned to Senior's flat to find a police inspector asking questions. Irgun literature was scattered about the flat. Eilberg was promptly and formally introduced to Inspector Dyer of the Palestine desk at Scotland Yard. Senior said that Eilberg was his friend Gibson from Jersey, which would cover lapses in the Welsh accent, and the girl with him was Hazel, a friend. The combination of Hazel and the accent must have done the trick; for Dyer was much more interested in Senior, who he suspected was flying for more than pleasure. The inspector made a passing reference to Senior's friends in Paris, and soon thereafter Senior had his license revoked. He waited two or three weeks and then went back to South Africa to look for airplanes for the Haganah or the Irgun. Eilberg on his own decided explosives were out and gradually pieced together a mode of operation. Barker and his family lived in an area of Northampton close to the Houndslow camp, and Eilberg planned to shoot him on the road as he drove to the office. Anxious to speed up matters, he risked contacting Yoel Bela. The police immediately picked him up. His Welsh-Jersey cover collapsed, so he admitted to being a German refugee illegally in England. He spent a few months in jail for illegal entry—how he had got in did not seem to bother the British—and then was deported to Germany. Bela was arrested and the Irgun was closed down in England, despite continued journalistic reports of terrorists stalking the street.

Actually there were others on the streets. LEHI had a British branch as well, just as small as the Irgun's. In 1946 Yaacov Heruti was called away from his explosives factory and sent to London. His target was Bevin, although Major Roy Farran and General Barker were on his backup list. He arrived on his own passport as a student to find that LEHI consisted of one girl in London, Betty Knut. He had a list of potential friends, members of Betar, those personally recommended or some Palestinians who might sympathize with LEHI. Ultimately he built up a unit of twenty-four people in London. He had a free hand in administration, operations, the size of his unit, the hideouts, money, equipment, and timing, which meant in effect that he was pretty much on his own, although he could communicate with Palestine in code letters, cables, and sometimes by courier. Mostly he concentrated on compiling a detailed account of Bevin's public movements. Bevin had an office in Admiralty House, opposite 10 Downing Street, and a home in Regents Park. Heruti felt that the easiest plan was to wait for Bevin to drive up to his office, preferably during a foreign ministers' conference, when there would be a small crowd and an exact time of arrival. One had only to lean forward and shoot him as he got out of his car, then turn and walk away toward Piccadilly. The risk appeared very low. At the last minute, to Heruti's disappointment, Yellin-Mor cabled to cancel the operation. Not too many other LEHI British operations went much better. A series of letter bombs caused minor injuries to those on an enemies list; and a book bomb exploded and killed Farran's brother, who misread the address. Two plans for sabotage operations remained on the drawing boards. At least Scotland Yard never picked up anyone; but in May 1948, Heruti left Britain, took a ship from France to Israel; and LEHI too was closed down.

By early 1948 the Irgun had accumulated substantial resources in the diaspora. A special arms procurement department was set up, and funds from Keren Habarzel were channeled into purchases. With the Arab irregular attacks increasingly threatening the Yishuv, the Paris office realized that a very substantial effort was needed. In March the decision was made to form an International Division, equip it, and ship it to Palestine to arrive as the state was proclaimed. Without it the state might not last much beyond the first days, but with it all of Palestine might be won.

The high command in Palestine also asked the diaspora headquarters to formulate ideas on the future of the Irgun and proposals for operations before and after the establishment of the Jewish state on May 15. The Paris headquarters proposed the establishment of a quasi-interim government, the Comité du Salut Public, and the rejection of the partition scene. This was mainly the program of the Hebrew Committee of National Liberation. There were also proposals for sabotage operations against the British and Arabs outside Palestine, and for bacteriological warfare against the Arabs. The high command rejected all of the proposals and insisted that the primary mission in the diaspora was to raise the forces necessary for the International Division's invasion of Palestine.

Training camps, geared to produce regular rather than underground soldiers, were set up in Austria, Italy, Germany, and later Czechoslovakia. Efforts for a major arms breakthrough were stepped up but with disappointing results. The contacts in Rumania, Hungary, and Czechoslovakia did not produce the desired results. In Paris Shmuel Ariel remained optimistic that the French government would in time prove forthcoming, but weeks were slipping away. The one certain asset was a four-thousand-ton LST, bought in America in November 1947 by the Hebrew Committee for National Liberation. The vessel was in excellent operational shape, could make fourteen knots and load five-thousand men without luggage. In February Abraham Stavsky of the Arlosoroff affair, who had been with the ship in America, was put in charge of Operation Palest. The LST, renamed *Altalena*, Jabotinsky's pen-name in Italy, would be under the command of Monroe Fein, an American from Chicago. The *Altalena* arrived in the Mediterranean in February 1948, but there was as yet no International Division and no arms. So, ever ready to turn the odd penny, the Irgun began using the *Altalena* to make commercial runs between Italy, North Africa, and France until the end of April. Some of the volunteers trained at Genoa came aboard to learn seamanship and influence the volunteers from the United States. Early in May the *Altalena* was moved to an anchorage off the French coast to wait for the arms.

Still the arms did not come. Lankin, Tavin, and Katz were joined first by Meridor and the Gilgil escapees and then by Ben-Eliezer. He and Shamir had been dispatched by the French from Djibouti on a destroyer, after the British had stopped a French ship off the Suez Canal to search for Palestinian terrorists. The French had not taken kindly to the exercise, and Ariel felt his request to the French government now had an excellent chance. On May 7, the permanent chief of the Foreign Office, Jean Chauvet, informed Ariel that the Irgun request would be formally discussed by the cabinet. Ariel had meetings with Chauvet, Pierre Boursicot, director general of the Sûréte Nationale, Marc Pages, head of the aliens department of the Interior Ministry and his assistant, François Rousseau. Ariel was convinced that agreement was only a matter of time. A superb and subtle diplomat, Ariel knew the long-standing French imperial grievances against the British—Syria and Lebanon snatched away, the snubs of the war years, the sinking of the French fleet—all these had been stored away. The French cabinet was all but ready to play the Irgun card in the Middle East—a few arms smuggled out would win a friend and put Paris one up on London.

The arms that did exist were moved south to dumps near Marseilles. Elsewhere the search went on. The Irgun had expanded sufficiently even to contemplate an air force to go with the purchased planes. Pilots and mechanics were brought into France, mostly from the United States and Canada, and attached to the special Irgun air force branch under Chomski. All were paid $60 a week after an initial $2,000 bonus, except for three professionals at $700 a month and one at $1,000. The Irgun knew that Haganah agents were scouring Europe and America for arms as well, but they had amassed no great quantity and had the same shipping difficulties facing the *Altalena*. The British naval blockade would not end until May 15. They did get one ship past the blockade but did not want to risk more. There were many in the Irgun who doubted it would end then. There was more talk in New York and Washington about an alternative to the partition resolution. The high command did not trust Ben-Gurion and the others not to give in to pressure. The British response to the Jaffa operation appeared ominous. Thus, however comforting the news that the Irgun had twenty-two pilots in the pipeline, or a four-ton Dodge truck in storage in southern France, or a huge assorted collection of arms, this was not enough. The French had to come through or the state would be in danger; and with only a few days to go before May 15 any decision would come too late for the *Altalena* to arrive off the coast the moment the blockade ended. The diaspora high command decided to charter a Dakota DC-3 and fly into Palestine the moment the British had evacuated, in order to report directly to Begin.

In Palestine Begin's problems and worries were little different from those of his commanders in Paris. For weeks he fretted and fumed, wrote scathing editorials in *Herut* and juggled his options because he was not convinced that Ben-Gurion would not scuttle the plans at the last moment and postpone the declaration of the state.

> If next Sabbath the message goes out: "The Hebrew State is hereby established," the whole people, the youth will rally and fight shoulder to shoulder for our country and people.
>
> If on that day a declaration of shameful surrender is published, if the leadership succumbs to the tactics of the enemy and Hebrew independence is destroyed before it comes to life—we shall rebel. There will be no surrender except by the "Vichy" leaders. The Hebrew Government will certainly be established.[13]

Just in case, the high command undertook preparations to declare the Hebrew state unilaterally in Jerusalem at the Edison cinema, at Chancellor and David Yellin streets. On May 12, the Jewish National Executive voted six to four to proclaim the Jewish state, despite American pressure to postpone the decision. Ben-Gurion had voted with the six, and the week before had even sent Eliezer Liebenstein to Begin to express his appreciation of the Irgun pressure for a state. After May 12, there were intensive preparations by all factions of the Jewish underground to rush into the vacuum left by the British.

At precisely eight o'clock on a cool, clear Friday morning, High

Commissioner Cunningham stepped out of Government House in Jerusalem to review an honor guard of the Highland Light Infantry. He said a few words, then stepped into his black bulletproof Daimler to the sounds of the Highlander bagpipes playing a Scottish dirge. He was driven to the airport and flew on to Haifa. There at the dock, the Irish Guards played "God Save the King." Back in Jerusalem the last Union Jack came down at one in the afternoon, but hardly anyone watched. There were more important matters than the rituals of evacuation. "They shuffle out in darkness and chaos, almost unnoticed." Three hours later, and, to avoid the sabbath, eight hours before the formal end of the Mandate, David Ben-Gurion read the Declaration of Independence to a packed audience in the Tel Aviv Museum.

> With trust in Almighty God, we set our hand to this declaration at this session of the Provisional State Council on the soil of the homeland, in the city of Tel Aviv, on this sabbath eve, the fifth of Vyar, 5708, the fourteenth day of May, 1948.[14]

The Etzioni Brigade was already involved in Operation Pitchfork to seize the evacuated zones in and around Jerusalem. The Arabs had only rudimentary plans, since they intended to wait for the invasion of the regular armies that would sweep the Jews into the sea and with them the Zionist state of Israel.

The Arab armies that appeared so formidable to both the Haganah and the Palestinian Arabs would not have borne close examination. First there was no united command left, not even on paper. Abdullah, who had spurned a deal with the Jewish Agency, decided to go it alone, to send in the Arab Legion and annex the Arab partitioned areas and whatever else he could manage. The Lebanese would send down some troops but not very many or very far. The Syrians and Iraqis would attack with only three-thousand men each. Egypt would have the largest expeditionary force, nearly ten-thousand men; but Farouk only decided on invasion at the last minute, thus committing an unready army. The Arab total, including irregulars and volunteers, came to about twenty-five thousand men. Except for the Arab Legion of Abdullah, these were armies more in uniform than in practice. The soldiers were uneducated, often untrained, and viewed with contempt by their officers, who themselves were often corrupt, lazy, and without combat experience. The armies, however, looked like regular armies. They had planes and a few ships, artillery, tanks, though all was poorly maintained. They could acquire more arms through conventional channels. The more astute Arab officers and statesmen were aware of the appalling military deficiencies and of the dim prospect for success, especially since they assumed that the Haganah had sixty- to eighty-thousand well-trained troops. They knew that their long-heralded invasion was hardly going to be a massive holy war waged by forty million Arabs. The Jews did not know this; for they knew their own paucity of arms. The Haganah was everywhere weak and still had no planes, artillery, or armor. In the last days of the Mandate, the Arab Legion had wiped out the Etzion bloc, indicating what might be in store for the new state of Israel.

At 5:00 A.M. on Saturday, May 15, just at first light, three Egyptian Spitfires swept in from the Mediterranean and made a single bombing run over the Tel Aviv airport at about a thousand feet. They swooped around in a tight turn and flew back out to sea and over the horizon. There had been no resistance, no antiaircraft guns. It was a gloomy beginning to the real war.

NOTES

1.   Jon Kimche and David Kimche, *Both Sides of the Hill: Britain and the Palestine War* (London: Secker & Warburg, 1960), p. 133.

2.   Dan Kurzman, *Genesis 1948* (New York: World, 1970), p. 140.

3.   Ibid., p. 141.

4.   Ibid., p. 132.

5.   Ibid., p. 133.

6.   Ibid., p. 142.

7.   Ibid., p. 147.

8.   Larry Collins and Dominique Lapierre, *O Jerusalem!* (New York: Simon and Schuster, 1972), p. 280.

9.   Kurzman, p. 148.

10.   Alec Kirkbride, *A Crackle of Thorns* (London, John Murray, 1956), p. 157.

11.   Menachem Begin, *The Revolt* (Los Angeles: Nash, 1972), p. 354.

12.   Kurzman, p. 177.

13.   Samuel Katz, *Days of Fire* (London: W. H. Allen, 1968), p. 225.

14.   *Official Gazette* (Israel), no. 1, 14 May 1948.

(above) Arabs looting Jewish business district in Jerusalem, December 2, 1947. (right) Displaced Jews, December 15, 1947. (facing page, top) Arabs overturning a Jewish taxi near Damascus Gate, Jerusalem, January 3, 1948. (facing page, bottom) British Soldiers searching Jews, December 20, 1947.

(facing page, top) Abdul el-Khader Husseini inspecting Arab irregulars of Nablus, January 3, 1948. *(facing page, bottom)* The debris of the Atlantic Hotel explosion in the Jewish business district that killed 35 people, February 22, 1948. *(above)* Jewish volunteers on the front lines. *(right)* Emir Abdullah and Sir John Pasha Glub.

AP

(right) Death for sale at local shoe store in Jerusalem's Arab section, February 23, 1948. (below) Arab volunteers in Syria, March 3, 1948. (facing page, top) Arab volunteers in southern Syria on their way into Palestine, March 11, 1948. (facing page, bottom) Arab volunteers on the road to Damascus, 1948.

(above) Bodies in road after the attack on Jewish convoy, April 1, 1948. *(below)* Irgun-Haganah line between Jaffa and Tel Aviv. *(facing page)* Mosque of Hassan Beis at Jaffa from which the Arabs fired on Tel Aviv. Hebrew sign was put on after the Haganah took possession.

(top) Tunnel
entrance used in Meridor's
Kenya escape.
(middle and bottom)
Yaacov Meridor entering
the tunnel.

PART 5

The War for Israel

The Jews must become a nation once more, a people with its own land.
—Leon Pinsker

In a sense the declaration of the state should have ended the underground role of the Irgun, for Begin had repeatedly insisted that the group would be dissolved. Such a dissolution would have been almost unique in revolutionary circles. Such organizations are often more difficult to dismantle than construct. More often than not the usual course has been a bitter civil war or the transformation of the covert movement into a conventional army or party. Begin had always looked beyond the state to a new and legitimate role for the underground as the core of a new party, perhaps an opposition party, but a loyal one. The agreement with the Haganah signed in the midst of the battle for Jaffa was thus a step in the anticipated direction. After May 15, the Irgun high command, now fully above ground, increasingly concentrated on the absorption of their cadres into a united military force.

The same was the case for LEHI. Soon after the proclamation of the state the LEHI council, usually eight or ten people, met around one table. For the first time in two years Shamir was present. It was agreed that LEHI would disperse, and the members individually join the new army, the Zahal. This decision angered the section of the membership that wanted to go on as a unit. As with the Irgun, Jerusalem was excluded. Somewhat later a majority decided on the formation of a political party, Miflegeth Halakanin (Fighter's Party), a decision that led to a deep schism, since many believed with Eldad that LEHI was a revolutionary arm not a political party or an underground army. Others felt with Zettler that the future direction of LEHI was less important than getting on with the war. So LEHI remained intact in Jerusalem but dissolved elsewhere without formalities.

The Haganah-Irgun worked out the details, and a formal agreement was signed on June 1. While many individuals went directly into joint units, many Irgun people joined as a group, retaining their arms, officers, and often their independence of spirit. In the chaos of the early invasion days, this was the general pattern everywhere except Jerusalem, for this was the first two snags that held up the disappearance of the Irgun.

Jerusalem was not included in the partitioned Jewish state and lay in a legal limbo. Everyone now recognized that the ultimate boundaries of Israel would be drawn not by resolutions but by force of arms. The United Nations had decreed a completely international city. Ben-Gurion and the Jewish Agency were determined to keep Jerusalem without alienating international opinion. Thus the new provisional government took no overt posture, did not annex the city, and made no statement. Begin and the high command suspected that, while Ben-Gurion might want the New City, he would not make the supreme effort to seize it all. Consequently, both Irgun and LEHI maintained their men in the city, cooperating with each other and, whenever possible, with Shaltiel and the Haganah. Jerusalem gave the Irgun a welcome opportunity to postpone the inevitable self-liquidation, which in revolutionary politics is a painful process. The second snag was that 25 percent of the Irgun strength was in the diaspora, where recruiting was continuing. With or without French arms, the *Altalena* would sail and the International Division would arrive. Given the past record of new provisional governments, no one in the Irgun high command wanted to cancel any future options or for that matter even to let the Jewish Agency and the Haganah commanders know about the *Altalena* operation until it happened.

The *Altalena* and Jerusalem aside, the old days of the revolt had passed completely. Diaspora headquarters might still be concerned with operations against the British, but the Irgun in Palestine had been preparing for a real war for months. Paglin had discovered, as did Raanan and Zettler, that street fighting and urban warfare pose different challenges. In the battle of Jaffa, ingenuity, old techniques, and bravery had won the day, but this could not become habit. This was why the high command had insisted that the diaspora camps train real soldiers in conventional ways. In this, at least, the Irgun and Ben-Gurion agreed. The new premier felt the era of the Palmach had passed: dash, equalitarian spirit, and bravery had a place in the real army he was planning, but the era of elite units was gone. In this Ben-Gurion was quite perceptive, for some of those dashing Palmach people had opened secret discussions with LEHI in Jerusalem about possible cooperation. What Ben-Gurion would have preferred, as far as the Irgun-LEHI was concerned, was instant and total dissolution and enlistment in the Zahal, formally established on May 28. Begin and the others accepted the need for amalgamation, but felt that the long struggle underground should give the Irgun people the privilege of fighting the war with their own. In the agreement on June 1, the Agency and Zahal command consented to this. By then the real war was well under way.

The war was fought by two very small armies of nearly equal size, each with counterbalancing strategic and tactical assets. The Arabs were far better equipped, could move through friendly areas and strike at will. The Israelis had all the tangible and intangible assets of the defense and, most especially, a zeal and determination not matched by the Arabs in most encounters. The Arabs might want to win, but the Israelis could not afford to lose. In retrospect it is clear that the Arabs simply did not have sufficient men to attack the defended Israeli strong points effectively. A single defense position like the Etzion bloc was vulnerable to Arab attack, but only at very considerable cost and at the risk of draining off all the reserves. The war was not a struggle between David and Goliath, but a series of disorganized clashes between small units, rarely of even regimental size. There were no conventional front lines, but key areas dominated by police stations, hills, or a village. Neither side could long maintain an offensive, so most engagements could not last for more than a few days without bleeding away the attacker's strength. The result was dozens of independent battles without much pattern or plan.

An important factor during the real war was the international climate; for seldom was a military campaign so hedged about by resolutions and intervention from afar. Commanders had to fight with one eye on deliberations at the United Nations or on government statements in Washington, London, or Moscow. As the war continued, it became clear that the United Nations was going to insist on a cease-fire; and that both Arabs and Israelis sooner or later would accept such a truce. After nearly four weeks of fighting, a pattern developed. There were three Arab thrusts, uncoordinated and without central control. In each case there was first an Arab advance through Arab areas, then their offensive momentum was blunted after some local success, and finally came the unsuccessful Israeli counterattack, eroding Arab strength but not capturing much ground. The Egyptians reached the bridge beyond Ashdod, after securing much of southern Palestine, but stopped there when they came under attack by two Israeli Messerschmitt-109 fighters, one flown by Ezer Weizmann. The Syrian and Iraqi drives in the north failed to secure major objectives, although the Israelis were hard put to hold firm. In the center Abdullah, at least, had a victory in the capture of the Old City and the defeat of the two Israeli attacks at Latrun which had attempted to open the way to Jerusalem. Although the two battles of Latrun were costly and bloody failures, a new alternate route—the Burma Road, by-passing the Latrun bloc—was created so that the New City could be supplied. On June 11, both sides were strained and exhausted and accepted the United Nations truce with relief.

By then the epic of the *Altalena* was well under way. On May 15, the Irgun DC-3 from Paris—the first commercial flight into Israel—landed at the Tel Aviv airport, bringing Begin the news of continued French delay. The Irgun high command felt that there must be some way to load the *Altalena* swiftly—even a thousand rifles or so would make a great difference. They decided to go to the Haganah. The Irgun attack on Ramele, under the operational agreement with the Haganah, was already in difficulties because of a shortage of ammunition: at least the *Altalena* could bring in something. At midnight at the Irgun headquarters in the Freud Hospital, Begin, Landau, Meridor, and Katz met with Israel Galili, Levi Shkolnik, and David Cohen. The Irgun wanted $250,000 to equip the men waiting in France, who would go directly into the Zahal when they arrived. The Haganah could put one thousand armed men on board, and take over the *Altalena* when the LST arrived in Israeli waters. There seemed no reason why the Haganah should not agree. That evening Begin spoke over the radio, taking the first step to dismantle the underground.

> The Irgun Zvai Leumi is leaving the underground within the boundaries of the Hebrew independent state. We went down into the underground, we arose in the underground under the rule of oppression. Now . . . we have Hebrew rule in part of our Homeland. In this part there is no need for a Hebrew underground. In the state of Israel, we shall be soldiers and builders. We shall respect its Government, for it is our Government.[1]

On May 17, two days later, Galili told Landau that Ben-Gurion had turned down the Irgun offer. A generation's suspicion and enmity could not be lifted so easily. Ben-Gurion did not trust Begin or the Irgun. He noted the quibbles in Begin's speech and saw no reason for accommodation or conciliation. In Paris negotiations by G. Rothschild and Arthur Koestler to bring about Haganah-Irgun cooperation and Haganah men on the *Altalena* also failed. The new Zahal could be armed, would be armed, without any such arrangement.

On May 16, in Paris, Ariel met with Jean Morin, director of the foreign minister's cabinet. France had decided to give arms to the Irgun. On May 19, the decision was confirmed in writing, when Ariel met Bidault at the Foreign Ministry. Katz arrived on the same day from Israel to find the diaspora headquarters on the Avenue de Messine seething with activity. Agents were dispatched to transport the volunteers to the south of France. All the purchased and donated arms were concentrated near Sète. The French felt less urgency. It took ten days before Ariel could see General Revers, chief of staff of the French Army, about the arms transfer. No final date had been set. General Coudraux was placed in charge of the transfer, but the French Army only received final instructions for the June 5 transfer on May 31. By then Ben-Eliezer and Nathan Germant, one of the Gilgil escapees, had flown to Israel to make final arrangements about the landing site and recognition signals. This time the Irgun high command did not bother to inform the Haganah of the French government's decision. When Begin signed the formal merger agreement on June 1, he again neglected to mention the *Altalena*. There were enough complications already. The Israeli government had accepted United Nations cease-fire proposals on May 23 and May 29, and it was only a matter of time before the Arabs did as well. The terms of the truce would un-

doubtedly hamper an overt arrival of the *Altalena,* but the diaspora headquarters decided to go ahead in any case. Then the French government
postponed delivery for three days. Next the French police, ignorant of
the Irgun's authorization, discovered a load of arms that had somehow
ended up in the baggage room of the Marseilles railway station. The Irgun
claimants were arrested, and a complex diplomatic effort had to be
mounted to get agents and arms released. Finally, Coudraux fixed Tuesday, June 8, as delivery day.

    Katz and Ariel arrived at Sète that day. Nothing happened. The
hours passed and June 8 ended. Katz, exhausted, was asleep in the car.
Monroe Fein and Ariel were still on the *Altalena.* Finally, along with
Stavsky, they came ashore and stood on the dock, waiting. At last they
saw a long string of lights winding toward them. The French had arrived.
The convoy drew to a halt. Major Sasso, divisional commissioner for the
Surveillance de la Territoire of the Sûreté, dismounted and put himself at
Ariel's disposal. In two hours the French soldiers unloaded the arms. Ariel gave Sasso a receipt for 5,000 rifles, 300 Bren guns, 150 Spandaus, 5
caterpillar-track armored cars, 4 million rounds of ammunition, several
thousand bombs, and a variety of other equipment. At two on Wednesday
morning, the stevedores began loading the ship, but nothing was easy. A
case broke open. The arms were discovered, and the stevedores went on
strike. Many were Algerian, and had no intention of helping Israel. Ariel
managed to get the assistance of French soldiers and rounded up some Irgun volunteers. By noon on Friday, June 11, the loading was complete.
The Irgun recruits arrived by truck from Marseilles and hurried aboard.
The French port authorities gave the *Altalena* a cursory glance and
cleared it for sailing. Fein, recognizing that time was running out—a
newspaper article appeared on June 10 about an Israeli ship loading arms
in a French port—stalled until the last of the recruits arrived. At eight-
thirty the *Altalena* sailed from Sète. Its destination was the beach at the
end of Frishman Street in Tel Aviv, according to instructions that Germant had brought on Wednesday. BBC news later the same evening reported the departure of the *Altalena* and the details of the final truce
agreement, which contained a pledge by both Israel and the Arab states
not to introduce additional arms into the area. The troubles of the *Altalena* had just begun.

    In Israel Begin heard the BBC broadcast. He was stunned, having ex-
pected to be told of the sailing ahead of time. Suspecting British provocation to halt a real sailing, he cabled Katz not to send the boat and to await
instructions. Two days later he learned that the *Altalena* had really sailed
and that Katz could not make radio contact. Begin then radioed directly
to the *Altalena:* ''Keep away. Await instructions.'' He was fearful that
Ben-Gurion might prevent the ship from landing, as a breach of the truce.

On board the *Altalena* there was no contact with Israel or France, but on the third day the faint and garbled message came through. Lankin recognized the voice of the secretary of the Tel Aviv office just before the transmission faded out. Fein tried to acknowledge the message and ask for a re-transmission of the order to keep away—all he got was static.

Begin met with Israel Galili, Levi Shkolnik, David Cohen, and Pinhas Vaze, a security official, and revealed the existence of the *Altalena*—somehow the Israeli authorities had missed the BBC broadcast. Begin noted that the ship was carrying enough men and arms to win the war and would arrive in five days. Galili and the rest were shocked. Nine-hundred trained men and arms for ten battalions might not win the war but still would make a major difference. So far very little had come into Palestine from the diaspora, despite the triumph of Haganah agents abroad. Yet there were two great risks. A breach of the United Nations truce might endanger the state but so might a heavily reinforced Irgun. Galili stalled. He asked Begin to get in touch with the ship and tell the captain to slow down. Immediately after the meeting he telephoned Ben-Gurion who, not unexpectedly, was outraged at Begin's deception. Still, the arms existed, and only five days away. Ben-Gurion opted for the arms, telling Galili and his staff to work out the details.

The next morning Galili met with Begin to prepare for the landing of the *Altalena*. Begin wanted to know about the arms that would go directly to Jerusalem. Galili agreed that they could work this out, but said he thought 20 percent would be about right. What he did not say, and what Begin did not ask, was to whom the 20 percent would go. Begin assumed they would go to the independent Irgun units, but Galili and Ben-Gurion had already decided on the Zahal. Then Pinhas Vaze met with Begin and his people to decide on a landing site. Instead of Tel Aviv, Vaze insisted on Kfar Vitkin further north, a Mapai settlement loyal to Ben-Gurion. Vaze wanted the arms stored in government warehouses. The Irgun agreed on Kfar Vitkin but not the government warehouses. Begin was adamant. Vaze telephoned Galili and arranged another meeting at army headquarters in Ramat Gan. This time the distance between the positions became clear—there was no agreement. Galili passed along Ben-Gurion's warning.

> You will have to accept our demands or you will bear full responsibility for the consequences, and the responsibility will be very heavy indeed. Unless you change your mind, we wash our hands of unloading of the arms.[2]

Begin was relieved. He did not mind accepting the responsibility of unloading the arms. He did not grasp that neither Galili nor Ben-Gurion proposed to tolerate such an Irgun action. On June 18, Ben-Gurion had not quite made up his mind exactly what to do about the *Altalena*, but his suspicions of Begin and the Irgun, already intense, had been strengthened. He had no intention of standing idly by while the Irgun became a military threat to the new state. Begin would have to recognize legitimate authority or pay the consequences. It might be preferable to make him publicly pay the consequences for his willful challenge to proper authority.

The next morning, June 19, when the *Altalena* was 220 miles from Tel Aviv, Fein received his landing instructions: Kfar Vitkin. Lankin was delighted—a Mapai settlement meant Haganah cooperation. At nine that evening the *Altalena* hove to about forty yards off the two red lights at the end of the Kfar Vitkin pier. The LST could get no closer because of shallow water. The sea was too rough to land the recruits. There was no Irgun welcoming party on the pier. Lankin decided to pull back out to sea, beyond sight of the United Nations observers and wait until the next evening. At 5:00 A.M. on June 20, the *Altalena* began moving to a spot fifty miles off the coast. In the meantime, at Irgun headquarters at the Freud hospital, the Zahal liaison officer, David Cohen, met with Bezalel Amizur of the high command and learned that the *Altalena* had arrived, and would return the next evening. Cohen repeated his promise to help unload the ship and indicated he would mobilize trucks himself. He spoke only for himself. Once the *Altalena* arrived, Galili wanted swift action against what he chose to see as an Irgun threat. During the afternoon the cabinet met on the *Altalena* question. Moshe Sharett, like Galili, conveniently forgot the danger of a cease-fire violation if the arms went to the Zahal. He deplored the situation, but noted that the government would not be responsible. The question was not really the cease-fire violation but whether to resort to force to prevent the arms from landing or to seize them. Sharett suggested sending five-hundred men to Kfar Vitkin to scatter the Irgun people drifting in to watch the unloading, and to arrest anyone disembarking. Yigal Yadin reported that he already had six-hundred men in the area but did not know whether the army would carry out a threat to use force. Ben-Gurion supported Yadin. The cabinet unanimously agreed to give the Zahal high command the authority to use whatever means necessary. Since everyone present knew that the Irgun would unload the arms—or at least would begin to do so—the cabinet decision meant a vote for civil war.

At the time the cabinet was meeting in Tel Aviv, Fein had brought the *Altalena* into the same mooring position he had used the previous night. All but about fifty of the recruits disembarked and moved off to Irgun camps. The remaining men began unloading the arms. As Irgun people continued to make their way to the beach, they saw Zahal troops barricading the road. No one paid much attention. At first light Begin decided that Paglin should continue the unloading during the day. Very soon, however, reports reached Paglin that the Zahal had the beach surrounded and were moving closer. It was only a matter of time before they swooped down and collected the arms. Paglin radioed to Begin on the ship, urging that everyone and all the arms on the beach be ordered back to the *Altalena*. Begin was dismayed. He had no longer any worries about the Zahal, only about the United Nations reaction. He came to the beach and when Paglin could not be swayed replaced him with Meridor. Paglin walked up the beach to a friend's house in Natanya. The unloading continued. The Zahal unit was formally under the orders of Moshe Dayan who had left the area to escort the body of the American commander of the Jerusalem front, Micky Marcus, back to the United States. In any case the commanders were authorized to take whatever measures were necessary. A Zahal officer appeared on the beach and delivered an ultimatum to Begin signed by Dan Even, commander of the Alexandroni Brigade. Even wanted the arms turned over to the Zahal; if Begin refused, force would be used. Begin had ten minutes to reply. Begin insisted that such matters could not be decided in ten minutes. The envoy departed, and there the matter rested. Meridor and the others felt that the only option was to take the *Altalena* to Tel Aviv as originally planned. There would be more Irgun people to help unload, and the government could hardly begin a civil war in the midst of Tel Aviv. Begin disagreed; such a withdrawal might be construed as dishonorable. At about five in the afternoon, Begin ordered a break. Everyone was exhausted.

In a short-sleeved shirt and dirty khaki trousers, Begin met with Stavsky and Fein, who had rowed from the ship. They too wanted to move to Tel Aviv. Fein went back to the ship. As he climbed aboard and looked back, he heard the rattle of machine gun fire. People on the beach began diving for cover. Lying in the sand with Zahal fire cutting up the beach, Begin still refused to leave. Stavsky and several crewmen grabbed him and dragged him to the motor launch. He fought and cursed in Yiddish, pleading to stay. Stavsky paid no attention. He had other problems. Two Israeli corvettes appeared and opened fire on the launch. Fein maneuvered the *Altalena* between the motor launch and the two corvettes. Begin, still complaining bitterly, was hauled aboard. Fein moved off for Tel Aviv, weaving and turning the *Altalena* to avoid the corvettes' fire.

On shore the Irgun people remained pinned down on the beach. Eventually seeing no point in the struggle, Meridor arranged a cease-fire. The Zahal people collected the arms on the beach—a fifth of the total— and took the Irgun people into custody. The Irgun had lost six killed and eighteen wounded, Zahal two and six. In Natanya, when the news of the firing on the beach reached Paglin, he decided to go immediately to Tel Aviv—there were enough Irgun troops in the city to seize the government. Two could play Ben-Gurion's game. Paglin could not reach Tel Aviv in time; for over the next crucial hours he was in the hands of the

Zahal, engaged in one escape attempt after another. Finally he pried open the lock of an underground bunker in a kibbutz near Tulkarm and raced to freedom past the stunned guards, over a barbed-wire fence and across a mine field. Meanwhile, with the *Altalena* twisting south in a cat-and-mouse game with the corvettes, word of the fighting at Kfar Vitkin spread through the grapevine. Irgun soldiers began to leave their units and move toward Tel Aviv. In Tel Aviv the commander of Israel's tiny air force prepared his pilots to bomb the LST. One, Boris Senior, who had served under Lankin in the diaspora during the attempt on Barker, had no intention of carrying out any such order. He did fly over the *Altalena* soon after she was beached on top of an old illegal immigrant boat less than a hundred yards from shore. Senior sought to signal encouragement to those below, but, exhausted by the events of the day, no one looked up into the night sky. The crew and remaining volunteers with the *Altalena* stayed put, waiting for dawn to see what the government would do.

At an early morning cabinet meeting, Ben-Gurion received a vote of seven to two authorizing all measures necessary to assure that the ship was turned over to the government. Ben-Gurion, in his capacity as defense minister, telephoned Yigal Allon at Palmach headquarters in the Ritz Hotel in sight of the *Altalena*.

> Yigal, we are being faced with open revolt. Not only is Tel Aviv in danger of falling to the rebel forces, but the very future of the state is at stake. You are to take command of the Tel Aviv area. Your new assignment may be the toughest one you've had so far. But I'm depending on you to do what is necessary for the sake of Israel.[3]

Although Ben-Gurion ordered Allon not to start firing unless fired on first, or unless the Irgun began to unload the arms, despite "our warnings," this was window-dressing. As always Ben-Gurion wanted no accommodation with the dissidents, only a showdown—even one carrying substantial risks; for he knew the Irgun was stronger than the Zahal in Tel Aviv. Out on the *Altalena* Begin broadcast over a loudspeaker to the people of Tel Aviv, asking for help to unload the arms. Watching all this from the veranda of the Kaete Dan Hotel, directly opposite the ship, were the United Nations observers. The adventures of the *Altalena* were rapidly becoming a spectator sport, as foreign correspondents followed the curious crowds down to the seashore. Some reporters combined an open-air breakfast on a hotel terrace with news coverage. A little to the north of the Kaete Dan, at the Ritz Hotel, Yitzhak Rabin, deputy commander of the Palmach, began to distribute hand grenades to his staff. The first motor launch was lowered from the *Altalena* and plowed through the shallows to shore. The Irgun men jumped out and unloaded several wooden crates of arms. Watching twenty yards away were a group of Zahal men.

A few Irgun men stayed on the beach, as the boat returned to the *Altalena*, the test run a success. Fein ordered it loaded again. The worst was over, except that through his binoculars Fein saw Zahal troops flooding the beach front.

At one in the afternoon the second test run began. The motor launch moved away from the *Altalena*. Begin, Fein, Stavsky, and Lankin stood on the bridge and waited. Yigal Allon stood atop the Ritz Hotel and watched the launch move toward the beach. When it was twenty yards out, Zahal machine gun fire swept the beach and the launch without warning. Fein, over the ship's radio, heard the pilot cry, "I'm hit in the chest!" Somehow the launch reached shore. Begin radioed Landau at Irgun headquarters to try and get a cease-fire, then rushed to the loud-speaker, shouting for the troops to stop shooting. The *Altalena* immediately came under heavy fire. The loudspeaker was blown off its mounting. Men began dropping on the deck. Stavsky fell, mortally wounded. The heavy barrage continued to sweep across the deck of the ship, intensified every time Begin appeared on the bridge. On the beach the Irgun men held on, gradually joined by colleagues from Tel Aviv. All morning the Irgun people in Zahal had continued to leave their posts and move toward Tel Aviv. One Irgun battalion withdrew from positions near the Lydda airport, another fought its way through from Ramele when the Zahal put up a block at Beit Dejen, and still another was isolated and kept in place near Sarafand camp. Enough reached Tel Aviv to transform the situation. Allon and Rabin were isolated in the Ritz. Their machine guns could continue to rake the *Altalena*, but they could not control the ground. No one knew it, least of all the Irgun; but Tel Aviv had been lost to the Zahal. Paglin's idea of rushing Ramat Gan and seizing the government had become a reality. Ben-Gurion had his open revolt, and the dissidents were in danger of taking Tel Aviv.

Yet it did not seem this way on the *Altalena*, where the deck was a shambles. The discarded gear of the nine-hundred passengers was bad enough, but the heavy machine gun fire had created chaos. It was difficult to treat the wounded, and no one was sure how many were dead. After forty-five minutes Allon agreed to an Irgun request for a cease-fire, so the wounded could be removed. The cease-fire would go into effect at four. Then Allon noticed some Irgun people setting up a fifty-caliber machine gun on the deck aimed at the Ritz. He telephoned Ben-Gurion for permission to use cannon and mortar fire—first as a warning, then to sink the ship. Ben-Gurion agreed. At approximately the same time a delegation led by Tel Aviv Mayor Israel Rokakh arrived at Ben-Gurion's office to urge a cease-fire. Ben-Gurion insisted he had no authority to interrupt military operations without a cabinet decision—a unique disclaimer on his part. Fein, still on board the *Altalena* was waiting for the Zahal boats to evacuate the wounded. At four, instead of the truce coming into effect, the first shell from Allon's artillery produced a waterspout off the *Altalena*. Two more shells landed near the ship before Fein received assurances the firing would stop. It did for a moment. Then the *Altalena* was bracketed. A shell tore through the soft deck and exploded in the hold. The ammunition cases began detonating one after another. A huge cloud of smoke drifted up over the *Altalena*. Allon telephoned Ben-Gurion, who turned to the mayor's delegation to announce the climax of the crisis. With the *Altalena* on fire, the corner was turned. Zahal reinforcements were moving into Tel Aviv. Although Begin insisted on no surrender, Fein was more practical. He ran up a white flag. Begin continued to demand that it be taken down, but Fein paid no attention. The wounded were bleeding to death. It was only a matter of time before the *Altalena* blew up. The shelling continued. Another hit would be fatal.

Fein managed to get through to Zahal headquarters at the Ritz. He wanted to know why the artillery was still shelling the ship after the white flag had gone up. The answer was ingenious: "There is a general ceasefire, but the order has not reached all units of the army."[4] The main deck was a seething ball of flame, and ammunition in the hold continued to explode. Fein and the rest began to abandon ship. The wounded went in rafts; others jumped in and swam. Some were picked up by Irgun boys paddling out from shore on surfboards and rafts. Finally only seven were left on the deck. Fein and Lankin insisted that Begin jump, but he refused—he would be the last off. Fein ordered two seamen to toss Begin over the side. He could be heard cursing until he hit the water. The last two off were Lankin and Fein. The flaming *Altalena* remained under the pall of smoke, ammunition and bombs detonating all during the evening. On shore the firing dwindled away. The Irgun people were interested only in helping the survivors. The total losses at the end of the day were fourteen Irgun killed and sixty-nine wounded. Zahal lost two killed and six wounded.

Ben-Gurion euphorically announced before the National Council, "Blessed be the gun which set the ship on fire—that gun will have its place in Israel's war museum."[5] Zahal continued to hunt down any visible Irgun people in Tel Aviv. Begin broadcast that evening from the Irgun underground transmitter.

> Irgun soldiers will not be a party to fratricidal warfare, but neither will they accept the discipline of Ben-Gurion's army any longer. Within the state area we shall continue our political activities. Our fighting strength we shall conserve for the enemy outside.[6]

At the thought of the men already killed and wounded in the fratricidal warfare along the beach front, his voice broke and tears came. The prag-

matic felt Begin had been broken; Ben-Gurion's orders had paid a handsome dividend.

Two days later, at a press conference, Galili produced what was to be
the orthodox version of the *Altalena* incident.

> The crisis broke out because of the grave fact of a boat's arriving on the
> shores of the country during the truce without our prior knowledge, without
> our being asked, without our agreeing. About a month ago the Commander
> of the IZL signed a document in which it was stated that the members of the
> IZL would enlist in the army and take an oath of loyalty to the Government.
> The IZL members enlisting would in the transition period constitute separate
> regiments to be incorporated in various brigades on various fronts. The doc-
> ument also laid down that the IZL would cease separate operations for the
> acquisition of arms and their contacts in this field would be transferred to the
> army. The IZL and its Command were to cease operating and existing in the
> State of Israel. . . .
>
> Two or three days before the boat arrived we were surprised in the dead of
> night by news that the boat was approaching our shores. Our demand that the
> boat be handed over unconditionally to the government and army was reject-
> ed. They demanded that the arms be taken to the stores of the IZL and used
> primarily to arm the IZL regiments.[7]

This did not satisfy everyone. Galili himself had given a different briefing
to Even. There was the matter of who fired first. And if, at Kfar Vitkin,
the Irgun intended to force the issue, why had all the recruits moved away
from the beach to inland camps? Why had Palmach units of Zahal opened
fire at Tel Aviv, and why had the cannons broken the cease-fire? Two cabinet ministers resigned. Awkward questions were asked. Ben-Gurion put
the matter behind him and went on to dismantle the Palmach within Zahal: first the rightist dissidents destroyed, then the leftist. There would be
no private armies in Israel. But if in the process Begin had been discredit-
ed or killed, the future would have been easier for the new government.

Yet there was every evidence that Begin was finished. After his
broadcast he waited in a hideout in Jaffa, as the Zahal searched for him.
Eldad of LEHI found his way to him and insisted that the time for action
had come. All the Irgun and LEHI people, strangers in their own land,
should combine and break through to Jerusalem. With their united forces
they could establish Free Judaea, an independent city-state like Danzig or
Trieste. Eldad was convinced that the operation was possible. Zettler had
long insisted on something of the sort. There could be a Third Temple and
a new beginning. Begin would not listen, would not leave his men even to
avoid arrest. To Eldad Begin was a romantic, putting honor over practicality, an idealist as much as a revolutionary: he had none of the pragmatism of Lenin. Without the Irgun LEHI could not act alone. There could
be no Free Judaea born in Jerusalem, no Third Temple, no Israel stretch-

ing from the Euphrates to the Nile, Eldad's luminous dreams flickered and faded. Still, even with the Irgun and LEHI broken and scattered, all was not lost: the units cut off in Jerusalem remained intact. At least there something could be done.

To the dismay of both Irgun and LEHI, very little had been done during the four-week war in Jerusalem. The Etzion bloc had been lost even before the formal invasion by the Arab Legion. The settlements to the north, Nebi Yaakov and Atarot, had been evacuated. There seemed to be no offensive spirit. Once the evacuated British zones had been seized in Operation Pitchfork, Shaltiel seemed content to hold on in the New City, and hope for the best in the Old City. Shaltiel, on the other hand, found working with the independent armies in Jerusalem, including the Palmach as well as the Irgun and LEHI, frustrating beyond belief. He could not find out their roster strength. He could never be sure they would cooperate in a joint action. Neither Zettler nor Raanan could conceal his distaste for him. There was Deir Yassin. Then Shaltiel would not occupy the Armenians' buildings near Zion Gate for "religious reasons"—that did not bother the Arabs. Irgun telephone lines were tapped.

When Shaltiel finally decided to respond to the hysterical pleas from the Old City, where in the first twenty-four hours of the real war the Arab irregulars had taken 25 percent of the quarter, no one trusted him. The Irgun and LEHI, assigned to a diversionary assault on the New Gate, did not believe his assault on the Jaffa Gate was serious. The Palmach under Rabin was assigned to attack on Mount Zion, but did not believe the attempt should be made at all. The overall commander of the operation withdrew, saying it would not work properly. The Palmach diversionary attack at the Zion Gate was carried through, and opened a way into the Jewish quarter. Reinforcements and fresh troops under Mordechai Gazit discovered that the operational commander, Uri Narciss, felt he had to withdraw the exhausted Palmach men from the breach. By dawn the Old City was again isolated. Gazit brought in eighty-six men, new weapons, ammunition, and supplies. It was not enough. The Arab Legion had crossed the Jordan. Shaltiel felt he would be fortunate to hold the New City, much less relieve the siege of the old. The Irgun was again outraged. If they had been asked, reinforcements could have been rushed to the Zion Gate from nearby units. Irgun-LEHI relations with Shaltiel continued to deteriorate.

Inside the Old City, along with Gazit's new men and the Hagana unit under Moshe Russnak, was an Irgun group of forty under Isser Nathanson holding the northeastern boundary. Nathanson and the others recognized that unless Shaltiel mounted another serious offensive, defeat was only a matter of time. When a second assault on the Zion Gate failed the next night, the situation within the Jewish quarter grew desperate and the anguish of the Irgun and LEHI in the New City intense. Without Shaltiel's cooperation there was no way to break through to Nathanson. With the armor of the Arab Legion probing Jewish Jerusalem, Shaltiel had other priorities. The result was that the Jewish quarter had to be left to its own limited and irreplaceable resources. The Arab Legion poured in a seemingly ceaseless stream of artillery and mortar fire. All along the perimeter the Arabs pushed forward against scattered and isolated posts, nibbling away, absorbing one house at a time. Slowly the district was reduced to smoldering rubble. By day a pall of swirling smoke hung over the Old City. At night the fires beneath turned it into a glowing, dark red cloud, roiling and twisting, slashed by the quick bright flashes of the gun muzzles. Day after day, the Legion and the Arab irregulars kept up the deafening machine gun and small-arms fire. There were hardly any defenders left. The civilians were crowded into a few synagogues, often only a few feet from the advancing Arabs. If the last coherent resistance collapsed, there was bound to be a massacre. On the morning of May 28, two elderly rabbis crept out of the ruins to negotiate details of the surrender with officers of the Arab Legion. At 3:25 that afternoon, it was over. The Jewish quarter was a blackened ruin: charred buildings, hot bricks, broken temples, spent cartridges, glowing embers, and the unburied dead. Strategically the loss was hardly important, but the end of a Jewish presence within the walls was an emotional defeat of untold proportions, a lament for a generation.

It was the greatest Israeli loss of the first round, the four-week war. The major powers, acting through the United Nations, finally managed to impose a truce on the two exhausted opponents. The Arabs had few victories, and those were concessions more than triumphs. The Egyptians had moved up from the south in two prongs. One halted north of Gaza and the other advanced to the southern reaches of Jewish Jerusalem. Most kibbutzim had been by-passed, and the future of the south and the Negev remained in doubt. The Arab Legion had moved around Jerusalem, but not into the New City. Mostly Arab areas had been occupied and defended successfully, especially at the bloody battles of Latrun. The contributions of the other Arab armies were even less impressive. Essentially the Israelis held almost all their own and occupied some adjacent mixed areas. Both sides felt that their resources had been strained to the limit in confronting a superior enemy, and both grasped the truce as a recess. This was particularly true of the Irgun, for the dream of Jerusalem remained unrealized. The impact of the *Altalena* disaster, the dissolution of most of the military units, the realization that a state extended even to the Jordan might prove impossible, simply heightened their determination to seize the Old City, only a few hundred yards away behind the medieval walls—Jerusalem the Golden.

Thus, when the United Nations truce came on June 11, many were determined that the Old City should be reclaimed. Jerusalem, the real city of their dreams, not the neat garden suburb to the west, must be redeemed. There would be time, for not even the most optimistic assumed that the cease-fire meant the war was over. The Arab regimes remained unrepentant: they were no better organized, united, or effective, but no less adamant that injustice would not go unopposed. Despite the truce, every report indicated that new recruits and arms were reaching the Arab commanders. In Cairo the king and his regime felt much had been won in southern Palestine, and the gains needed to be consolidated. Abdullah was heartened by the results of the battles of Latrun, and could foresee the Arab Legion rounding out his new territories across the Jordan. Both Syria and Iraq believed they had come close to victory, but as yet nothing tangible had been won. None recognized that the tide had turned. Ben-Gurion was at last the beneficiary of the flood of arms from abroad, the Zahal was mobilized, experienced, and rested. The threat of the private armies had been removed. There would be another round.

At Lake Success the appointment of Swedish Count Folke Bernadotte as the General Assembly's mediator, along with the creation of a truce commission, gave hope to the optimists. Rushing against time, Bernadotte prepared his own solution to replace the terms of the partition resolution. He rested his plan on what he saw as the realities: the existence of Israel, the power of the Arab Legion, and the interests of Great Britain. On June 27, his plan was made public and managed to antagonize everyone. Gains would be lost, aspirations denied. The Arab League rejected it, and the Israeli government followed suit on July 6. For a great many Israelis and all of Irgun-LEHI, the Bernadotte Plan was especially abhorrent—the Negev and western Galilee would be lost, but so would Jerusalem. Many saw Bernadotte as a pawn of Britain, acting in Abdullah's favor for London's benefit. Too much of Jerusalem had been lost already. In the second round, with their independence in the city still intact, the Irgun and LEHI wanted the Old City and an end to Shaltiel's delays.

After the repeated explanations of Israeli weakness in Jerusalem, Raanan seized the opportunity of the truce to seek real help from Irgun headquarters in Tel Aviv. He had only 150 men, and not enough arms to go around. LEHI had even less. If Jerusalem were to be redeemed, there would have to be reinforcements from somewhere. He hitched a ride on a convoy truck and ended up driving the strange five-ton vehicle all the way to Tel Aviv, stripping its gears along the way. He rushed to Begin and asked for everything he could get. With the arrival of the *Altalena* imminent, Begin for once had something to offer. He emptied the Jaffa arsenal and gave Raanan the units that had not yet been incorporated into the Zahal. Three days later Raanan had his arms convoy—four trucks loaded with one hundred men, ten Brens, the two three-inch mortars from the Jaffa attack, three-hundred shells, two-hundred Stens from the underground factory, a Piat, over one-hundred rifles, and ten-thousand rounds of ammunition. Actually his greatest problem was getting his convoy through the Burma Road, for Ben-Gurion vetoed Galili's permission to use the by-pass at the last minute. Begin rushed from Tel Aviv to confer with Raanan and the Palmach commander at the steep escarpment where tractors were needed to pull up the trucks. Between Begin's sweet reasonableness and the gradual realization that Raanan commanded a great many more men than he did, the Palmach commander reconsidered. The convoy was permitted through. Shortly after dawn, with the convoy safe in Jerusalem, Raanan appeared at Shaltiel's office.

> I've come from Tel Aviv with a convoy of arms and men. As soon as the truce ends, we're going to attack the Old City. I suggest we carry out the operation together. If you don't agree, we'll do it now even against your opposition.[8]

Shaltiel, who in four weeks of the real war had grudgingly learned to live with the dissidents, agreed that everyone—Irgun, Haganah, Palmach, and LEHI—would attack the Old City in a joint operation. Actually, no matter what Raanan, Zettler and the others thought, he had been deeply committed to the attack on the Jaffa Gate, even acquiring a baby lamb to sacrifice at the base of David's Tower. This time, with Raanan's arms and men, a united effort, and good luck, he might push on as far as the site of the fallen Temple. Others had even more grandiose plans. Some of the LEHI people, dissident to the end, intended to blow up the Mosque of Omar, on the Dome of the Rock, so that a new Third Temple could arise.

To make reality out of the disparate dreams, the three commanders met and, to their amazement, agreed. There were too few men to cut off the Old City from the countryside by means of a flanking attack. Surprise would be lost and the Arab Legion, hampered in city fighting, would be deadly beyond the walls. Thus the option was again a frontal assault at one of the gates. Shaltiel offered the intriguing news that Professor Aaron Kachalsky of the Weizmann Institute had nearly perfected a huge, V-shaped, hollow-charged bomb called Conus, that could easily blast through the Old City wall. LEHI turned over some six tons of explosives from their stores—Heruti, their expert, had returned from London to Jerusalem as commander of the technical department. Kachalsky got to work on the final version of Conus. Shaltiel, however, had other objectives—the Sheik Jarrach quarters and the Tel Aviv-Jerusalem railway. On July 9, the Oded Brigade began to move on the Arab villages of Malha and Ein Karim, the first step in linking up with the Harel Brigade to the west for the joint capture of the railway. Reluctantly LEHI and the Irgun agreed to help. The fighting was limited, but the Egyptians did carry out the first air raid in history on Jerusalem. Over the next two days, the Jerusalem front was relatively quiet, but Israeli successes around Ramele and Lydda, the decay of the Arab Legion position, and the prospect of massive Arab losses escalated pressures for a new cease-fire. Shaltiel assumed that when the fighting began again he would have time to shift his limited resources between the three major objectives.

By July 14, a truce was not only imminent, it might first be enforced in Jerusalem. Before Shaltiel could move, the Arab Legion attacked near the Mandelbaum house and seized some houses south of the Damascus Gate. Shaltiel ordered a counterattack, made some local gains, and once more postponed the offensive against the Old City. On July 16, Ben-Gurion informed Shaltiel that a truce would be imposed in Jerusalem just before six the next morning. Time had about run out, and none of the three objectives had been taken. Yadin ordered Shaltiel to try and take both Sheik Jarrach and the Old City, but if there was not enough time to concentrate on Sheik Jarrach. Shaltiel decided instead to concentrate on Operation Kedem, the assault on the New Gate, and Zion Gate, making use of the Conus device. By this time Raanan and Zettler were infuriated by the endless delays and evasions. Things had not gone well. LEHI, in cooperation with Shaltiel, won a victory at Ein Karim, but after occupying Malha the Irgun troops were badly mauled in an Arab counterattack. The Irgun blamed Shaltiel for withdrawing artillery support too soon. Paglin and Katz came into Jerusalem, learned of the problems with Shaltiel, and devised an Irgun attack through the New Gate, an attack that would require the occupation of the church of Notre Dame de France, then occupied by the Haganah. When Shaltiel learned of this venture, he managed to persuade Raanan to wait until Friday night for the joint Operation Kedem. The only change was that the Irgun, under Yehuda Lapidot, would assault the New Gate from Notre Dame instead of the Zion Gate from Mount Zion. At the last minute Lapidot and Paglin decided to use conventional satchel explosives instead of the ponderous Conus device. Haganah at the Zion Gate decided to depend on the Conus.

At the Jaffa Gate a special unit of LEHI from the orthodox Mea Shearim quarter, their skullcaps and long curls incongruous beside the helmets and Stens, were stationed in an abandoned house near Barclay's Bank. While they waited, since it was the sabbath, services were held. There was plenty of time. At the New Gate, Lapidot began to fret. Nothing was happening. Then a stray Arab shell hit the Conus truck. The secret weapon detonated with an immense roar, and all the New City trembled. The second Conus was ordered up to Mount Zion. Nothing else happened. Raanan at Shaltiel's headquarters was furious: no artillery, no excuses, more delays and evasions. No one could make contact with the artillery, and no messengers were sent. Raanan chain smoked, stalked back and forth and shouted. Finally at midnight the artillery bombardment began. An hour passed, then another. Still the artillery pounded the Old City. As long as the Israeli fire continued to drop behind the wall, there would be no attack. Raanan was frantic. He threatened that if the bombardment did not end, the Irgun would go in anyway. At three in the morning, the bombardment ended. Five-hundred shells had been dropped into the Old City. Raanan ordered Lapidot to send in the three Irgun battalions. There were fewer than three hours left until cease-fire time. Around the edge of the wall at Mount Zion, the other Conus had arrived. The LEHI people moved out toward Jaffa Gate.

On the wall the Arabs knew that the end of the Israeli bombardment meant an inevitable Israeli assault. Those opposite Mount Zion suddenly saw a strange apparition lit by the flicker of tracers and the light of the moon. Conus was coming. A truck had brought the device up to within two-hundred yards of the wall, but it would have to be carried the rest of the way. No one had given the problem of moving the device any thought, and the defensive trench leading almost to the wall was exactly one foot too narrow. The Haganah men slipped two iron bars under the V-shaped Conus and lifted it. Conus, like some great prehistoric insect, began to creep up toward the Zion Gate. Eight men staggered with it for a few yards, while another eight gave covering fire. Then they changed places. There was mounting Arab fire, with tracer light sweeping back and forth across the device. Grenades set fire to thistles, and soon the front was brightly lit. Slowly, slowly, Conus crept closer. At last the men moved it under a bulge in the wall, where it was at last protected from the enfilade, but still harassed by splinters from the grenades dropped by the Arabs directly above them. The base of the Conus was too short. It had to be raised on stones. Finally it was in place. The three fuses were connected. The men dashed away across the slope, seeking cover.

There was a long pause. It seemed as if everyone was waiting, even the doomed Arabs on the wall above. Then Conus exploded with an incredible roar, a massive flash that lit up the sky over the entire city. Then came the faint shouts of the Haganah men in the sudden silence as they rushed the Zion Gate. David Shaltiel at the base of Mount Zion was awed by the tremendous flash. With his radio man panting behind him, he began to run up the slope toward the Old City and his long-denied victory. LEHI's attack had run into heavy resistance at the Jaffa Gate, so the huge explosion was welcome—the Haganah was in for sure. At the New Gate, Lapidot in Notre Dame had watched his men blow in the gate, then the next small wall, and push on into the city. Now there would be at least two prongs inside the Old City. Lapidot radioed headquarters to see how LEHI and the Haganah were doing. The first word was that they were both inside the city. Then there seemed to be some doubt. No, LEHI was not in. Then came the word from Zion. The first attackers, pushing through the Armenian cemetery, expected to rush straight through the smoke still billowing around the explosion site, on through the breach, and mop up any demoralized Arab resistance. The first men had almost reached the wall when the smoke drifted away. The wall was marred only by a large black smudge. There was no breach. The Arabs above began to fire again. A messenger rushed to Shaltiel, who still believed the wall had been broken. When he learned that Conus had failed, he was shattered. There was now no hope for the Zion Gate attack. It was almost five in the morning. Shaltiel had no alternative attack plan, no hope for improvisation. LEHI had failed. He hardly gave a thought to the Irgun. It was all too late. "We have no choice. Now we must follow the cease-fire."[9]

At five o'clock, Shaltiel's chief of operations at headquarters ordered a general retreat. Standing near him, Raanan heard the order and nearly had a seizure. LEHI may have failed, and Haganah may have failed; but Lapidot had reported the Irgun inside the Old City. His men were not going to surrender. He was told that if the Irgun disobeyed orders all supplies would be cut off, no wounded evacuated, and the men inside cut off from Notre Dame. In the meantime, Lapidot felt that the attack had bogged down. It was not a matter of surrendering, but without reinforcements those inside the New Gate would soon be eliminated. Neither Paglin nor Raanan received the news gladly. Lapidot insisted that there was no hope, but that everyone would stay if ordered. Since they would be killed, there could be no possible recriminations against the Irgun command. This gave the others pause. Lapidot was told to make up his own mind. He withdrew his men. Jerusalem would not be redeemed. The bitter Irgun men huddled in Notre Dame were the last remnant. The orthodox LEHI men began making their way back to the Mea Shearim quarter on foot—it was still the sabbath. It seemed to Raanan, Zettler, Lapidot, to all those in LEHI and the Irgun, that Jerusalem had not been worth the risk for Shaltiel. Even the military governor, Dov Joseph, a sound Jewish Agency man, felt that Shaltiel could have stretched matters, since the Arabs had not formally agreed to the cease-fire. Shaltiel insisted, like any regular army man, that he had followed instructions. "My instructions were not to fire if the Arabs stopped firing, and they stopped firing."[10]

Elsewhere, the ten days of war did not end on such a bitter note. Israeli troops took over a large slice of central Galilee, enlarged the Jerusalem salient, and held on elsewhere. The map was not greatly changed, however. The Egyptians were still in the Negev. The Syrians had their captured settlement of Mishmar Hayarden. The Lebanese were in central Galilee. The Iraqis still occupied the Arab heartland in the center. What had changed was Abdullah's ambition. The Legion was no match for the

Zahal—one more encounter and the main prop to his throne might disintegrate. Abdullah was finished fighting. The others ignored the evidence that the Zahal was daily growing larger, more effective, more experienced, and could now overwhelm the various Arab forces, even the Egyptians. The second truce brought not peace, but armed provocation and covert campaigns—a limited war, monitored by international opinion and the United Nations; for Bernadotte still had faith in a negotiated settlement. Ben-Gurion felt that the situation and the boundaries were inherently unstable. He wanted the Zahal unleashed. In August his party and cabinet opposed his plan to attack in the Jerusalem area and the Hebron hills. A military victory might lead to a diplomatic defeat. Ben-Gurion bided his time. During September tension increased all along the Arab Legion front, especially in Jerusalem. The Israelis released a report to foreign correspondents that an Arab offensive was planned for September 15. On September 15, the correspondents were informed the offensive had been postponed until September 21. On September 16, mindful of the rising tension, Bernadotte landed at Beirut airport on his way to Damascus and Jerusalem.

LEHI thought Bernadotte's mission a travesty, his proposals only implementation of British policy, and even his selection as mediator an outrage. They were convinced that Bernadotte had cooperated with the Nazis during the Second World War, sheltered Walter Scholenberg, and had undoubtedly been a German employee. Furthermore, since his appointment he had acted in British interests, devising a plan little different from one Bevin might have proposed—no Negev, the return of 300,000 Arab refugees, Arab rule in Jerusalem disguised as internationalization, and the absorption of the Jewish state into some sort of hybrid federation. LEHI had not yet given up the dream of a Jewish state on both banks of the Jordan. The high command—Eldad, Shamir, and Yellin-Mor—had come to three general conclusions after watching Bernadotte in action. First, the LEHI unit in Jerusalem would remain independent until the city was incorporated into the state, and if the United Nations did not work to Israeli advantage Bernadotte might have to be eliminated. Second, there was no place for any United Nations force in Israel, and it should be expelled, even at the risk of war. Third, LEHI insisted on the territorial integrity of the Jewish state—that is, both banks of the Jordan—and would continue to fight for the independence of the entire area.

Increasing evidence accumulated that Bernadotte was a malignant influence. If the world at large thought Ben-Gurion and his colleagues aggressive expansionists, LEHI did not. A secret Irgun report claimed that Shertock had assured Bernadotte that the Israeli government would not object to having Palestine form a federal Jewish-Arab state, but that prudence would be necessary, because the Irgun and LEHI could cause serious trouble. Rumor reached Israel that Bernadotte had been critical of Ben-Gurion's government at Arab League headquarters in Cairo, that he had made scathing comments about how Dayan *"s'est conduit comme un gangster."*[11] Bernadotte had nearly become enemy number one to certain of the LEHI commanders. Eldad had already made up his mind that the mediator would have to go.

By early September the intrinsic divisions within LEHI were pronounced. Yellin-Mor clearly was going to make the transformation into politics easily and smoothly, taking as many members with him into a position well to the left of the spectrum. Eldad, with his vision of a Third Temple and a greater Israel, could not so readily perceive such a conventional role or any end of the long struggle short of the ideal. Shamir and Zettler, less concerned with ideological or political niceties, felt that pragmatically Bernadotte was a danger. None saw clearly that their revolt against the foreign oppressor, initiated by Avraham Stern, was now over: the foreign oppressor was gone, and a new and no less dangerous world had evolved. The Arab enemy could not readily replace the British, nor could service in a conventional army recompense the sacrifice of the underground. Assassinating Bernadotte could provide again the old cement—he was a surrogate foreign oppressor. Thus eroded down to the faithful few in Jerusalem, LEHI could organize a deed that would change history. They would again find a purpose and shape the future. They would act, not disband. Without Bernadotte there would be no Bernadotte Plan, no prospect of the Israeli government yielding to international pressure, and no possibility of a federation-type settlement imposed by distant powers.

On Friday, September 10, Zettler drove Eldad from Jerusalem to Yellin-Mor's apartment on Ben-Yehuda Street in Tel Aviv. There the triumvirate met to resolve the Bernadotte problem. The mediator had already finished his revised plan and sent it on to the United Nations General Assembly. Nibbling on fruit and sipping wine, they went over once again the ethics of personal terror, the potential benefits of the deed; then they developed the details of the operation. The only innovation was the decision to use a cover name, Hazi ha-Moledeth (Fatherland Front), an obscure Bulgarian organization, instead of accepting responsibility as they did in the case of Lord Moyne. This was so the LEHI people outside Jerusalem would be protected.[12] Word was immediately sent to Zettler, back in Jerusalem by then, of the decision. Zettler was to plan the operation with the aid of Joshua Cohen, the man in the orange groves in 1942, and Stanley Goldfoot, an immigrant from South Africa and a devout advocate of apartheid. Things had come full circle for Cohen as well, for he had trained the two Eliahus in 1944 for the Moyne assassination. The three would have to hurry: although they had solid intelligence and even an inside man, Bernadotte was expected in Jerusalem the following Friday.

On Thursday, September 16, Bernadotte's white United Nations Dakota taxied to a stop at Beirut airport. He picked up his Swedish chief of staff, General Aage Lundstrom, held brief talks with Arab leaders, lunched at the St. George Hotel, then at 2:00 P.M. flew on to Damascus for further talks. There he was presented with a magnificent piece of brocade, and replied that he looked forward to presenting it to his wife on her birthday. At five he called on President Koualty, then saw Prime Minister Mardam Bey and Foreign Minister Barazi. He held a press conference, but would not comment on his plan. He sandwiched in a trip to the Archaeological Museum and Omayyade Mosque before his dinner with Mardam Bey at the Club de Damas. He spent the night at the Oriental Palace Hotel. His Dakota took off for Kadandia airport in Jerusalem at 9:30 Friday morning. On board as usual were his personal staff, his adjutant Red Cross Major Jan de Geer, his secretary Miss Wessel, Dr. Ullmark, and his valet Kull. Forty-five minutes later the Dakota touched down at Kadandia. Colonel Abdullah el-Tell of the Arab Legion and several observers were there to meet him.

There was some concern about his plan to visit Ramele, sixteen kilometers to the north; for there had been snipings along the roads out of the city, and recently United Nations personnel had come under fire near the Mandelbaum Gate. Bernadotte insisted; they went out to Ramele and back with an armored-car escort and then on to the United Nations headquarters at the YMCA, opposite the King David Hotel. A shot had actually hit one armored car, but other than that the day was uneventful. The party had lunch at the YMCA; and before his 4:30 meeting with Dov Joseph, Bernadotte decided to visit Government House, a potential headquarters for the United Nations mission that Lundstrom felt was unsuitable and dangerous. While Bernadotte was in the tower of Government House looking out over Jerusalem word came in by radio that Dov Joseph requested a postponement of their meeting until 6:30. Bernadotte agreed and in the meantime decided to visit the Jewish Agriculture School nearby, which the Israelis refused to evacuate in violation of the truce agreement. After discovering the Israelis in place, Bernadotte decided to return to the YMCA and pick up a copy of the truce regulations so that a formal complaint could be made to Dov Joseph.

The little convoy moved off slowly. In the first car was Belgian Major Massart, who was driving, Miss Wessel, Swiss Lieutenant Colonel Flach, Major de Geer, and the Jewish liaison officer Captain Hillman, who was to shepherd them through Israeli lines. Next came the white Red Cross car of Dr. Facel, the Swiss director of a clinic at Government House. Finally came the mediator's sedan driven by Colonel Begley, United Nations security chief. There was a large United Nations flag to the left of the radiator and a white flag on a long staff to the right. In front with Begley was the American Commander Cox, chief observer on the Jewish side. In the rear Bernadotte was sitting on the right-hand side, French Colonel André Pierre Sérot, chief observer in Jerusalem, in the center, and Lundström was on the left. The convoy quickly picked up speed to hamper any snipers. At the barrier of the Greek quarter the Israeli guard let down the pole halfway, then raised it again, and finally let it down all the way. Captain Hillman leaned out the window of the first car and shouted in Hebrew to let them through. Up went the barrier and the convoy went through. They passed several lorries filled with Jewish soldiers, then Dov Joseph's armored car going in the other direction. They drove through the Katamon quarter, passed another Zahal roadblock, overtook a brokendown lorry also filled with Jewish soldiers, and began to climb a steep incline through a shanty town by open fields. It was just before 5:00. Over the top of the rise, Major Massart lifted his foot from the accelerator. An Israeli military jeep was stopped, partially blocking the road. Apparently the driver, who certainly appeared nervous, had tried to turn and stalled in the middle of the road.

Zettler had barely managed to get the jeep in place. The ambush had been set for Bernadotte's scheduled meeting with Dov Joseph. The delay until 6:30, coupled with the unexpected return to the YMCA, upset his operational plan. The route problem was not difficult. Anticipating last-minute change, Zettler had made plans for roadblocks at all likely routes into the New City. Whether Bernadotte would come at all was the problem. Goldfoot, who had been nervously quarreling with Zettler as the minutes crept by with no convoy in sight, drove off to the government press office to see what news he could pick up. In the pressroom he managed to overhear that Bernadotte would arrive at the perimeter of the New City at 5:00 and pass over a route near a LEHI camp. Just after 4:00 the jeep, with four men aboard, pulled out of the LEHI camp, drove five-hundred yards along the road, and stopped. The four got out and built a makeshift roadblock that permitted one-lane traffic. Then they got back in the jeep and waited. About a hundred yards away Zettler and Goldfoot stood beside the road; they did not want to miss the deed. As the United Nations convoy began to move up the slope, an hour later, the jeep pulled across the road and stalled.

The United Nations party saw four men in khaki uniforms, shorts, and peaked caps sitting in the jeep watching them. Three climbed down and began walking toward the convoy, two on the right and one on the left. The driver stayed in the jeep. Hillman called out in Hebrew to let the cars through, that everything was all right. The man on the left moved swiftly past the first two cars and came up alongside Bernadotte's sedan.

Everyone suddenly noticed that all three had Schmeisser automatic pistols, and they were paying no attention to Hillman. The single man peered in the window. He was clean shaven, dark, thin, about thirty, and seemed quite fit. He was standing directly by Lundström. Everyone began to take out their passes; for they had obviously run into one more check point. The thin man thrust his Schmeisser in the window. It was just 5:03. He squeezed off a long burst, moving in an arc from Bernadotte's chest to Sérot, holding it on target at a distance of less than three meters. He stepped back and finished the magazine, firing into the radiator. Colonel Begley, who had leaped out as the thin man began firing, tried to grapple with him, but was badly burned in the face by the last gun flashes. The two other men standing at the head of the convoy began firing at the same time, riddling the wheels of the first car. The two then turned and ran back to the stalled jeep. The driver, suddenly far less incompetent, accelerated and the jeep disappeared at top speed down a side road. The thin man ran off across the roadside field discarding the magazine and detachable barrel. In seconds he had disappeared. Behind the convoy the breakdown lorry stopped thirty yards behind Bernadotte's riddled sedan. It was 5:04.

The long burst of fire was devastating. As soon as the muzzle was jerked from the window, Bernadotte bent straight forward. Lundstöm, still dazed, asked, "Are you wounded, Folke?" Bernadotte may have nodded, but the thin man's second burst into the radiator made it difficult to hear. Immediately Bernadotte raised himself to a sitting position, then sank back unconscious. He sprawled in the corner, his head back, his uniform soaked in blood. Colonel Sérot lay twisted and torn in the other corner. He had been hit in the head and chest seventeen times and was obviously dead. Hillman rushed back and Lundström asked him for directions to the nearest hospital. Colonel Begley drove at full speed to the annex of the Hadassah hospital on Mount Scopus. Water was pouring from the radiator. Major Massart followed, his tires coming apart in shreds. At the hospital Bernadotte was rushed to the casualty room. Lundström tore away his shirt. He had obviously been hit in the heart and was still bleeding profusely from a wound in the abdomen. A doctor rushed in, took one look, and stopped. "Can't you do anything?" pleaded Lundström. The doctor stepped forward and listened briefly for a heartbeat. "It's too late." Bernadotte had been hit six times, and the wound in the heart had caused almost instantaneous death. His body was moved back to the YMCA, where his room soon filled up with flowers. On Saturday, September 18, his body was moved to Haifa and then back to Sweden. He was buried on his wife's birthday.[13]

The world reaction to the assassination of Bernadotte was immediate and universal horror and disgust. The deed seemed so pointless: the victim was a man of peace. In Israel the reaction was considerably more muted. The year had been filled with blood and trauma. One more death could be easily absorbed, especially since Bernadotte was less than friendly to Israeli aspirations. The only serious concern was that an adverse international response would be provoked by the assassination. Thus the Israeli reaction was correct and prompt. No one believed that the Hazi ha-Moledeth really existed; so Israeli security people began rounding up LEHI members, a congenial occupation for many of them. LEHI was outlawed. The LEHI-Irgun units in Jerusalem were dissolved. Zettler, Cohen and Goldfoot went into hiding. Eldad and Shamir were in two safe houses in Tel Aviv. Yellin-Mor, who had heard a radio news bulletin of the assassination while sitting with his wife and Samuel Merlin in a café in Haifa, went into hiding but was soon arrested along with Shmulevitz.

Most of the LEHI people in the Zahal were shocked by the assassination. They did not understand the purpose of killing Bernadotte or any reason for the continued existence of LEHI. It was this lack of relevance that destroyed LEHI, not the arrests, which many accepted as pro forma, a sop to world opinion. They were detained in Jaffa, where the guards maintained lax discipline—at one point the LEHI prisoners took over the old Turkish fortress, held a press conference, and served beer from a keg. Ben-Gurion was furious, and those who had not already escaped were moved to Acre. The arrests seemed to serve little purpose during the tense no-war-no-peace situation. Eventually only Yellin-Mor, Shmulevitz, and a few others were left to be tried under the Emergency Regulations. The LEHI leaders were still sought by the police, but not very vigorously. It did not really matter, for LEHI was finished. Many of the escapees even went into the Zahal under assumed names. A few were still detained in Acre. Yellin-Mor and Shmulevitz came to trial in January 1949. Few were very interested as Yellin-Mor summed up for the defense with an amalgam of political theories, biblical references, and personal reminiscence. On February 10, Yellin-Mor received eight years and Shmulevitz five, with special treatment as political prisoners for both. No one expected them to serve their sentences, especially Yellin-Mor, who had just been elected to the Knesset.

Long before the LEHI trial, Israeli politics, priorities, and boundaries had shifted. The underground had become a historic artifact, a subject for scholarly dispute and political adjustment to contemporary purpose. By then Bernadotte's assassination was only a distant, minor incident. More important were the results of a renewed war, fought as the international community sought to reimpose a cease-fire that depended on the returns from the battlefield. No one had really believed the second truce would last. There were too many loose ends. The Arab leaders had not revealed their inadequacies to their people, who still anticipated some sort of victory. Ben-Gurion, recognizing the shift in the military balance, wanted to round out the boundaries of the new state, particularly in the center along the Jerusalem corridor, and in the northern Negev. He was persuaded by Yigal Yadin to forgo an attack on the center and permit an operation in the south against the Egyptians, whom many, including Yadin, considered the main enemy. The continued probing attacks by the Egyptians would supply an excuse to break the truce, and then the front commander, Yigal Allon, could activate Operation Ten Plagues. On October 15, the Israelis struck. The fighting lasted until October 22, when a new truce was imposed, although the Israelis kept occupying vacuum areas for some while longer. The week of heavy fighting in the south was an unmitigated disaster for the Arabs. Although the Israeli gains had not come easy, and the Egyptians put up a fierce defense, the end result was the collapse of the Egyptian hold on the south. Their units, as at Iraq-Suldan and Faluja, were either surrounded, or forced to withdraw, and the Israelis occupied a large slab of territory almost up to Bethlehem, including Beersheba. The loss was a traumatic shock to the Arab states and produced another summit conference, this time in Amman. As usual there were recriminations rather than reform. In the midst of this agonizing reappraisal, Kaukji, still seeking the elusive victory, attacked Manara, a small, isolated kibbutz almost on the Lebanese border and seven miles from the nearest Israeli settlement. In a hastily organized attack the Israelis responded to provocation—actually they seized a golden opportunity—and crashed into Arab Galilee in Operation Hiram. In sixty hours the Israelis destroyed the Arab Liberation Army, occupied all of Galilee, and seized a strip of Lebanon.

The diplomats took over again, seeking a permanent cease-fire, but without notable success. The Israelis again attacked the surrounded Egyptian garrison at Iraq-Suldan in the northern Negev and captured the Monster on the Hill. Under the Sudanese commander, Taha the Black Tiger, the Egyptian garrison in the other pocket at Faluja refused to surrender. Allon sent in a delegation led by Yeruham Cohen to seek the pocket's surrender. Cohen met one of Taha's staff officers, Gamal Abdel Nasser, who arranged a Taha-Allon meeting the next day. Taha, though his situation was hopeless, refused to surrender, insisting that he would save the honor of the Egyptian Army. Faluja never surrendered, and Taha indeed salvaged the only honor for Egypt during the war for Palestine. Yet, even then, the war was not over. The Arab leaders still could not admit defeat, although their refusal to treat with the enemy almost guaranteed further defeats. The Israelis also had problems; for although they now had the power to inflict defeat on the Arabs, they were afraid of international repercussions.

In December the Israelis decided to risk one more operation in the south, not only to secure control of the Negev and defeat the Egyptian Army, but also to force a truce on Cairo. Farouk would be given the choice of an end to the war or an end to his army. An added benefit of the offensive would be the occupation of all the Negev and the near certainty that the other Arab states would follow the Egyptian lead in seeking a truce. Operation Ayin began on December 22. In a series of complex and elegant attacks the Israelis cut through the Egyptians into Sinai. By December 29, Allon's troops were three miles south of El-Arish. Within hours the town would fall, the collapsing Egyptian Army would be destroyed, and the war over. Then Britain threatened to intervene, and Ben-Gurion insisted that Allon hold off and attack Rafa instead, which was on the international boundary instead of inside Sinai. By then news of the disaster had reached Cairo and the mobs were out. Allon was driving his wedge toward the coast. The Egyptian Army barely held on. On January 6, 1949, the Egyptian government announced it was willing to open armistice discussions at the United Nations mediator's headquarters on Rhodes. Ralph Bunche, Bernadotte's successor, at last had an opportunity to negotiate something more than a fragile cease-fire. As one Arab state after another reluctantly agreed to a cease-fire, the Palestine War came to an uneasy end. Iraq, with no common boundary, did not bother to appear at Rhodes. The others would go no further than a cease-fire. The boundaries of Israel became not those of the United Nations partition resolution, but those secured by the Zahal—they rounded out the last corner in March, when an Israeli column moved south through the Negev to the tip of the Gulf of Aqaba. Of the original Mandate the Egyptians occupied a truncated Gaza strip, crammed with refugees without hope of productive lives. Abdullah's Arab Legion held the central bulge, the Arab portions of the West bank, and the Old City of Jerusalem. When annexed these would form the richest portion of the new Hashemite Kingdom of Jordan. The Israelis had the rest: far less than the Revisionist dream of a state on both sides of the Jordan, far less than the Irgun had hoped when the *Altalena* sailed, but far more than some had feared before the proclamation of the state, when five Arab armies were moving toward a defending force untrained in real war and without real arms.

By then Begin and most of the others had made their peace with reality, lowered their sights, and turned their attention elsewhere. Long before Israeli armored columns swept into Sinai, Begin had been busy dismantling the Irgun. Although there were detentions after the *Altalena*—Meridor, Lankin, Hillel Kook, Amizur, and others—and some talk of retaliatory kidnapping in the diaspora, Begin was determined—except as regards Jerusalem—to turn to politics. Not everyone within the Irgun was so inclined. The Irgun commanders in the diaspora felt that Begin and some members of the high command might let slip the opportunities still available to create Zionist facts. True, the French government no longer had any interest in the Irgun after the *Altalena* debacle, "How could you have been so foolish?" but there were other options. Paglin was sent to Europe to consider possibilities. Begin, however, would have none of this. Paglin was ordered back. The Irgun account in a Swiss bank was closed out, and the money returned to Israel. After Bernadotte's assassination and the end of independent Irgun operations in Jerusalem, Begin began pressing the diaspora headquarters to give up all operational plans, to turn over arms and aircraft to the Israeli government, to close down as an underground, and become a formal branch of the new political party, Herut.

The response from the diaspora to the requests from Israel was less than enthusiastic. The various local commanders and the people at the Paris headquarters refused to accept the instructions of an emissary from Israel. The aims of the Irgun had not been achieved. There was still much to do in the diaspora. A group of commanders went to Israel to examine operational possibilities, then returned to Europe for consultations in Paris, Rome and Munich. Begin would not be swayed—the days of the underground had ended. He arrived in Paris and, in a series of meetings on December 22–24, listened politely to his diaspora commanders. He was as always politic, gentle, thoughtful, but firm. He would oppose any effort to continue the Irgun as an expatriate organization. He flew on to New York. When he returned to Paris, the Irgun of the diaspora accepted the inevitable. On January 12, 1949, they formally disbanded. The Irgun's Paris headquarters became the official European bureau of the Herut movement. The war was over.

As with every war, there were tag ends still about. Many in the diaspora Irgun withdrew into silence and exile, stunned at the betrayal of their dreams. Some still refuse to live in Israel. Once a few reunited to make use of the old smuggler's net in a flawed assassination attempt against Konrad Adenauer during the negotiations between the German Federal Republic and Israel—in their eyes a reconciliation that came much too soon after the holocaust. The others avoided politics and their old friends of the underground. Some, of course, did come to Israel. Those arrested in Austria were eventually set free, smuggled out to Italy, and then on to Israel. In 1950 the Israeli Foreign Ministry intervened and three Irgun prisoners, serving twenty-year terms in Germany for mining a military train near Hanover, were deported to Israel. The three men involved in the attempt against Reinhold were released at the same time. Monty Harris, however, when released after his sentencing for the operation against the military lorries for Iraq, moved to Dublin and opened a shop. In Israel the loose ends were tied up. On July 13, 1948, the British cage ship *Ocean Vigour* brought the African detainees home to Israel. Most went directly into the Zahal. In fact the only one left was their former jailer, Captain Clark, whom the British still suspected of involvement in the Gilgil escape. On January 10, 1949, Chief Rabbi Rabinowitz, visiting Kenya for the Israeli United Appeal, drove out to Gilgil to find it stark and empty, the gate open. Inside there was only Captain Clark and his dog.

By then Begin and many of his colleagues were deeply involved in the first election campaign for the Knesset. There was naturally a long list of parties—something for everyone, ranging from Yellin-Mor's Fighters Party to parties for orthodox women, Sephardim, or Arab workers. The new Herut, with the old Revisionists not yet incorporated into it, ran their own slate and did not fare badly, collecting over 11 percent of the total and fourteen seats in the Knesset, in fourth place behind the United Religious party, Mapam of the farther left, and Ben-Gurion's Mapai. Yellin-Mor won the one seat of the Fighters Party and left jail for the Knesset. Soon the last of the LEHI prisoners, including Shmulevitz, were free, and politics was the order of the day for those so inclined. Most of the Irgun-LEHI, once the immediate Arab threat lessened after the Zahal offensives in the Negev, attempted to return to conventional lives and careers. It was no easy matter after years on the run and with no influence in the new government. One small group of LEHI attempted to maintain an underground organization, but there were few volunteers and some of those were Israeli security agents. It flickered out, and little was left of LEHI but recriminations and quarrels. Someone made an attempt to burn Shamir's flat. Some complained that Yellin-Mor was living in a LEHI flat and spending LEHI money raised by the robbery of Barclay's Bank in 1947. Eldad, still possessed of his vision, felt that if there could be such splits in LEHI then there had not really been a revolutionary organization. There was a need for an intellectual reevaluation, and so he established *Sulam* (Jacob's Ladder) as an ideological paper to explain "full redemption." Few bothered any more about "full redemption"; most were too busy living above ground. They now had names, families, and the real responsibilities of normal, everyday people in a new and uncertain state. An Israel, if an imperfect one, had been established. The underground was part of history, the terror out of Zion past.

NOTES

1. Samuel Katz, *Days of Fire* (London: W. H. Allen, 1968), p. 229.

2. Dan Kurzman, *Genesis 1948* (New York: World, 1970), p. 465.

3. Ibid., p. 473.

4. Menachem Begin, *The Revolt* (Los Angeles: Nash, 1972), p. 175.

5.   Katz, p. 248.

6.   Kurzman, p. 456.

7.   Katz, pp. 289-290.

8.   Kurzman, p. 456.

9.   Larry Collins and Dominique Lapierre, *O Jerusalem!* (New York: Simon and Schuster, 1972), p. 558.

10.   Kurzman, p. 545.

11.   Uncatalogued collection of papers, Jabotinsky Institute, Tel Aviv.

12.   Yellin-Mor would swear in court that he knew of no final decision to assinate Bernadotte, a position he maintains today. Certainly his movements were open, and he intended to leave for Czechoslovakia on Sunday.

13.   The best source for Bernadotte's movements is *Death of a Mediator* (London: Institute for Palestine Studies, 1968). Baruch Nadel published a detailed account in 1968 in Hebrew.

(above) The Irgun arms ship *Altalena*, June, 1948. *(right)* *Altalena* burning. *(below)* Last Irgun attack on Jerusalem's New Gate, July 17, 1948. *(facing page, top)* Count Folke Bernadotte, U.N. Mediator for Palestine *(left)*, conferring with General Lundstrom, Chief of U.N. Truce Observers in Palestine. *(facing page, bottom)* Begin signs the identity books for the members of Irgun Zvai Leumi.

(facing page) David
Shaltiel, commander
Jerusalem area, 1949. (left)
Count Folke Bernadotte in
Jerusalem. (below) Nathan
Friedman-Yellin,
and Matityahu
Schmuelewitz (left), face a
military court in 1948.

The Savoy Hotel in Tel Aviv after the 1975 fedayeen guerilla raid
from the sea.

Ben-Gurion with Joshua Cohen at Sde Boker, October, 1962.

Israel Government Press Office

EPILOGUE

If the old members of the Irgun and LEHI did not exactly live happily ever after (recent history is too painful and too raw for that), there were few surprises. Begin, with his ever-faithful aide, Haim Landau, has for a generation controlled the destiny of Herut, which expanded a bit to become the center of a new coalition, Gahal, and then again to become Likud, today the major opposition group in Israel. After a slow growth, and with the recruitment of dynamic figures like Arik Sharon, the hero of the Yom Kippur War, Likud is close to being a potential alternative government. This frightens much of the rest of the Israeli political spectrum. Not until the government crisis just before the June War in 1967 did Begin become "respectable." Then, with Dayan, he was brought into a coalition government to reassure the people that Israel was not going to be dismantled, as Nasser seemed to go from triumph to triumph under the disinterested eye of the United States. The vacillation of Premier Levi Eshkol—who, as Levi Shkolnik, had participated in the negotiations before the arrival of the *Altalena*—was serious enough to prompt Begin to suggest that his old enemy Ben-Gurion return to power from his political exile. There never was a real reconciliation, but Ben-Gurion after 1967 did suggest that he might have been "misinformed" about Begin's intentions.

In any case, Begin joined the new government as a minister without portfolio, but resigned a year later on a matter of principle, when the government appeared to be softening its stand on the occupied territories. Giving away pieces did not appeal to Begin and his colleagues. So he returned to his niche in the opposition, articulate and scathing in public, gentle and polite in private, formally dressed and gracious in a pioneer atmosphere. In the land of the sabra, the cactus that is prickly on the outside but tender within, Begin has always been the reverse.

Into the first Knesset with Begin went the other disciples, most of them long involved in the Revisionist movement or the underground. Esther Raziel-Noah, David Raziel's sister who had been arrested with the transmitter, and Samuel Merlin, back from the diaspora were there. Meridor, Ben-Eliezer, and Lankin from the African adventurers and the diaspora operations had seats. Jabotinsky's son Eri, Uri Zvi Greenberg, the poet of the redemption, Hillel Kook and Samuel Katz, along with three others made up Herut's first Knesset delegation. For one reason or another few stayed the course in the Knesset, retiring from the scene if not

347

from the party. Lankin left and opened a law office in Jerusalem. Katz separated from his wife, who had written of her adventures as a terrorist and later married Lankin. He opened a publishing firm in Tel Aviv. Ben-Eliezer stayed with the movement until his recent death. Most of the Irgun commanders in 1949 were in their thirties, so nearly all of them are still alive. Paglin, the youngest, married his girl friend Zippora Pearl, who had been along the night the Jewish businessman was kidnapped. He went into his father's bakery-machine business and led an exemplary and innocent life until the rise of the fedayeen after the June War in 1967. Then Israeli security discovered that he was smuggling arms out of the country in ovens. They detained him for a while in a hotel, finally releasing him. Yaacov Amrami, who had been along that same night, runs Hadar Publications, which has produced works on the underground.

Two members of the high command, Tavin and Shlomo Levami, wrote doctoral dissertations at Hebrew University, Tavin on operations in the diaspora and Levami on the revival of ancient heroes for present purposes. Meridor, Katz, and Lankin all wrote books. Avraham Tehomi, the first commander who withdrew and returned to the Haganah, has a jewelry-finishing business in Jerusalem. One of the greatest transformations has been that of Meridor, who was first elected to the Knesset with the occupation of worker, but who has since become Israel's greatest shipping tycoon, a rival to the Greeks, a man whose photograph has been in *Time,* who appears more often in Monaco than along Dizengoff Street. In a way the three commanders of LEHI have evolved according to expectations. Eldad teaches, translates, writes for his paper, and remains a center of a small group of disciples. His dreams are no less luminous, his convictions unchanged. Yellin-Mor's Fighters Party collapsed into wrangling splinters. He lost his seat in the Knesset and returned to journalism. He has found a place on the very far left, edits a political journal where he advocates a moderation on the Palestine issue unpalatable to many of his former colleagues. Shamir for years worked quietly for Israeli intelligence before returning to politics as a Knesset member for Likud. There he remains, still taciturn, still influential. With him in Likud is Geula Cohen, who, with the help of the Arabs of Abu Gosh, escaped to resume her LEHI underground broadcasts.

Some of the underground have had quite apolitical careers. Anshuel Spilman, who lived through the LEHI orange grove years, manages the swimming pool at Ramat Gan. Shmulevitz, who also wrote a book on his adventures, has a grand café in the old quarter of Jaffa. A most curious career has been that of Joshua Cohen, who returned to his Negev kibbutz and became Ben-Gurion's bodyguard. Mordechai Raanan is a publisher in Tel Aviv, Zettler a businessman, Heruti of the bomb factory and the Bevin assassination plot, has a small law office off Rothschild Boulevard in

Tel Aviv. Yehuda Lapidot, who directed the last assault on the Old City, is a professor, and Monroe Fein lives near Chicago with his wife, whom he met on the *Altalena*. Now a successful businessman, Jerachmiel Romm, who broke out of Acre, has been largely responsible for transforming the prison into a museum. Tavin, despite or because of his Ph.D., has remained in the movement, a traveling ambassador for Likud, and a successful businessman as well. He lives with his wife and family in a new high-rise development to the north of Tel Aviv, a long way from the nights chained to the cot in the dark. Some have chosen to remain anonymous: the thin man who shot Bernadotte has never surfaced. Some have not. Israel Levi, who set the detonators on the King David milk cans, appeared at a press conference in 1972 to discuss his role.

Even the dead have discovered new roles. In June 1975 the Egyptian government released the bodies of Eliahu Hakim and Eliahu Bet-Zouri, thirty years after the assassination of Lord Moyne, in return for twenty Arabs jailed in Israel as fedayeen or intelligence agents. In Jerusalem the two were given a heroes' burial in the Mount Herzl military cemetery, the resting place of Israeli premiers and presidents. Thousands of mourners passed by the coffins, including Premier Yitzhak Rabin, who had been second in command at Palmach headquarters in the Ritz Hotel during the end of the *Altalena* incident. His commander then, Yigal Allon, lost out in the leadership sweepstakes when Golda Meir retired, and settled for foreign minister. In any case, soon after the funeral, British Ambassador Sir Bernard Ledwidge made it clear to the Israeli government "that we very much regret that an act of terrorism should be honoured in this way."[1] The past was still very much alive. So much so in Israel, for example, that the demand for an investigation of the Arlosoroff affair—seemingly a matter of only academic interest, since Stavsky died on the *Altalena*—created an election issue in 1973 when *Maariv* published new evidence that appeared to clear the accused.

Some of the bit players went on to greater things. Rabbi Gorontzik, who had sheltered Shmulevitz after his Jerusalem escape, became Chief Rabbi Goren. Boris Senior became Colonel Ron Elder of the Israeli Air Force. Now a successful businessman he still manages to fly his own plane. His pilot colleague, Ezer Weizmann, rose to be commander of the Israeli Air Force, and when it became clear he would not be made chief of staff, resigned and began a political career in Likud. Moshe Dayan, who had avoided the beach at Kfar Vitkin, directed the 1956 Sinai campaign as chief of staff, and the June and Yom Kippur wars as defense minister. The latter responsibility led to his removal from the center of the political stage. Most of the Irgun's rivals in the leadership of the Haganah and Palmach went on to distinguished military careers. David Shaltiel, however, entered the diplomatic corps and spent much of his time out of Israel, which some of his old adversaries felt was just as well; for they remained convinced he never wanted to capture the Old City. The Irgun's bitter rival, Israel Galili, has served as minister of information, and Yigal Yadin has become Israel's most famous archaeologist.

Most of the bit players have led conventional lives. A few did not. Charles Bayer, who had been preparing his fruit bowls in the King David when the milk cans detonated, decided to move on to more tranquil grounds and left for Cairo, were he obtained a position at Shepheard's Hotel. After Shepheard's was stormed and burned to the ground by an inflamed Egyptian mob on January 26, 1952, Bayer moved down to Aswan where he found the quiet life, not appearing again until the droves of reporters arrived with the Kissinger party seeking human interest.

On the British side, Sir John Shaw, who escaped the King David explosion, went on to become a royal governor and is now retired with his wife Josephine in the charming Sussex village of Winchelsea. Sir Alan Cunningham and General Barker soon retired. Bevin died in 1951, still hated by many Israelis. Farran, after his brother's death when the book bomb exploded, moved to Canada. Reinhold, once he escaped from the Irgun in Brussels, disappeared with the help of the British. The mufti lived in exile in a mountain village in Lebanon, dabbling in Palestine matters, and after 1967 was involved with the fedayeen until his death. Abdullah was assassinated on July 20, 1951 as he entered the Mosque of Omar, Pasha Glubb was dismissed by King Hussein in 1955 and has written extensively on Arab matters since then. Fawzi el-Kaukji retired to Beirut.

It all seems to the observer so far away. Stern's son—unborn at the time of his death—is a sports commentator on Israeli television. Deir Yassin has become an insane asylum, Acre prison a museum, the Jewish Old City has been rebuilt. In front of the Wailing Wall, where the first scuffle in 1928 led to the Hebron massacre and Haganah-bet, a great area has been cleared for visitors, resembling nothing so much as a vast parking lot. It is rumored that Yassir Arafat, leader of Al-Fatah, lost his ancestral home as a result. Hebron, where the story began, has since 1967 been a crisis spot, as various orthodox and ultranationalist groups have sought to expand the Jewish presence in the area. Tel Aviv has been transformed from a low, vaguely Italianate city, cut by gentle boulevards, into a teeming metropolis pocked by skyscrapers and surrounded by high-rise housing developments. The old Savoy Hotel, where Begin and Ben-Eliezer planned the revolt, gradually decayed into a seedy condition with a dubious clientele, only to reach the news again when a group of fedayeen attempted to seize the building after landing on the beach in a raft.

Much of the Manshiya quarter, where Paglin drove his above-ground tunnel to the sea, has never been rebuilt, although the old city of Jaffa has been turned into a model and somewhat sterile colony of art studios and restaurants. On King George Street there is a tall glass building to house the movement—Herut, the Jabotinsky Institute, and the rest—now all very much above ground. From time to time old members drift in or out, recalling earlier days. It is a matter of history for David Niv, who spent the revolt in African detention camps, and is already four volumes into his definitive study.

Nothing about Irgun and LEHI is merely history; for there is the residue of bitterness and rancor from old quarrels; and outside that glass and concrete building on King George Street there is no consensus as to the importance and impact of the revolt. It was such a small matter, as revolts go, that up to December 1947 only twenty-seven Irgun men were killed and eight executed. Even in the real war only 322 more were killed by the end of 1949. Yet to some the revolt seemed to have had a disproportionate effect on the course of history. A generation later the judgment of history is still out, and the old quarrels continue.

For Begin, on reflection, the Irgun was a band of heroes and martyrs. "Their life was struggle; their death heroism; their sacrifice sacred; their memory eternal." Outside the underground few would agree. For most Israelis the dissidents, however bold and daring, only complicated the struggle to establish Israel, and damaged the cause. Moyne, King David, Deir Yassin, Bernadotte—all tarnished the moral posture of the state. The Irgun and LEHI for years were disowned, their political successors isolated, the benefits of the state withheld when possible. Nothing was forgiven or forgotten. For the Arabs Irgun-LEHI have remained archterrorists—brutal, ruthless men, far from being dissidents, who represented the actual essence of Zionism. The long and painful exile from Palestine began at the village of Deir Yassin. There the Arabs saw manifested the actual intentions of Zionism, and the façade of conciliation and accommodation was ripped away. Deir Yassin, more than the bombs tossed into crowds of innocent civilians, was what the Arabs remember. Stamps have been issued, memorials held, and books written about that one day in April.

Beyond the bounds of the Middle East, Begin and the others somehow never went through that strange transmutation from rebels to respected statesmen. In a few years Jomo Kenyatta has been transformed from a leader of darkness and death, evil personified, into the grand old man of East Africa, the best hope for moderation and democracy. All the old terrorists, rebels against the Crown—de Valera and Nehru, Nkrumah and Makarios—all became respectable. Begin did not. For one thing, unlike the others, he was denied political power. But this was not the entire matter. The British could excuse the outrages of the others because they were a lesser breed, outside the law. Certainly in the case of the Irish, after eight-hundred years of rebellion, the British might have become inured to murder from a ditch. Somehow, when the terrorists were Jewish, it was more difficult. After Hitler and the holocaust, British imperial oppression in Palestine was especially difficult to rationalize. The argument that a British presence kept the peace between Arab and Jew was denied by both Arab and Jew, and by the facts. Thus some, whose bitterness remained year after year, clung to the righteousness of a cause that was difficult to defend. Finally, by the time Cunningham climbed aboard the cruiser *Euralyus,* British policies and postures were universally condemned, particularly by those they left behind in Palestine, who had to struggle along in a vacuum. The British blunders were legion, and those who tried to do good were condemned along with those who did not. No one understood the British or sympathized with their incompetence when the righteous Jews of the Irgun and LEHI shot, murdered, maimed, and tortured. Very few forgot or forgave. Perhaps a Begin in power, his edges blunted by responsibilities, a man redeemed from murder, might have eased matters. But Begin remained unrepentant, on the far side of the Knesset, with neither substantive power nor parliamentary prospects. As always he and his friends remained the odd men out: no one need accommodate himself to the old terrorists. Terror should be condemned, and moral indignation exercised.

As the years passed, the consensus formed that the underground people responsible for the terror out of Zion were wicked and evil. Whenever Begin travels abroad and speaks to the press, the letter columns of the newspapers blossom with indignation. "The work of the Irgun fighters is a blot on world Jewry of which righteous thinking members should justly be ashamed."[2] Begin may not have helped greatly by maintaining the old positions—that there was no massacre of any sort at Deir Yassin, that the British refused to evacuate the King David after being warned—thus reviving "old and unhappy things, especially in such a tendentious manner." For many the Irgun-LEHI campaign was the epitome of terror, and terror has always appalled and disturbed the West. Few could understand or condone LEHI's strategy of personal terror or the rationales and explanations of the Irgun. Terror was murder, and murder was sickening. Somehow the very people who could accept fire bombing of civilian targets in the air war over Germany a few years before could find no excuse for the Irgun's smaller bombs. And in truth some of those small bombs, mindless, ineffectual, emotional retaliation against Arab irregular attacks are difficult to condone for all but the involved. The Irgun did (though LEHI did not) always give warning, not that the ninety-one dead in the ruins of the King David would be greatly comforted by that. The Irgun did attempt in a nasty, brutish war to live by the rules. Given the grisly events of the next generation, the Palestine underground was remarkably restrained, as were, for that matter, the British security forces.

For the underground, terror was an unavoidable means. Thus it must be judged on results; for the only options were acquiescence to oppression or revolt with the scanty available resources. The people of the underground had to choose for themselves, to act without uniforms, recognized institutions, or societal approval. They had to be very sure their deeds were righteous, no matter how ruthless. There was no state to protect them, no appeal to protocol or convention. One descends into the underground in more ways than one. As Shamir argued, they should not murder unless history would be changed, but they did murder—as revolutionaries, as an army without banners. Very few would not do it all again—hang the sergeants, fuse the milk cans in the basement, empty the Schmeisser through the car window; but each had hoped that the next generation would not face such choices. In this their dream has been flawed, for there have been three more Palestinian wars. If the descendants of the underground need no longer be outlaws in their own country, they must still fight their own wars.

Despite the exacting and unrelenting recollection of their Zionist rivals, their Arab opponents, their British enemies, the war of the underground has gradually receded into history. There have been too many other wars, too many more dead. Where once a revolver was priceless, used again and again, Israel now depends on billions of dollars of complex and technologically sophisticated weapons systems. A full generation later the old dream of the underground has had to be adjusted to new realities. An accommodation with the Arabs has not been reached, justice not done; now there is a new diaspora and a new Palestinian dream. There is still no Zionist state on both sides of the Jordan, and few foresee one; there is still no Third Temple, no peace in the land. Yet there is Israel, free, democratic, and relatively secure in a troubled world. The British are long gone from Palestine, from the Middle East, from the ranks of the great powers. Yet the Arabs remain, unable to win, refusing to lose, still uncompromising, dedicated to justice and their dream, willing or forced to employ the tactics of spectacular terror while citing the Zionist precedent. Perhaps, as so many of the underground believed, a way to balance the clashing destinies of both may yet be found, perhaps not. When Palestine was promised, twice promised, there was no guarantee that possession would be easy. Those of the underground believed their state could only be won by resort to force, and most assume it can only be so maintained. This they see as their legacy. For this small state, this remnant of their dream, this special land redeemed from history, for this they called for terror out of Zion and not in vain.

NOTES

1. *Irish Times*, 30 June 1975.

2. *Times* (London), 13 January 1972.

SOURCES

Any attempt to present a formal, academic bibliography of sources for the Palestine Mandate or the establishment of Israel would be a foolhardy venture; for seldom has so much, often of dubious merit, been written about so small an area. Yet Palestinian events have obviously fascinated all sorts and conditions of people, have absorbed for decades the energies of the famous and powerful, and have regularly produced new and dramatic confrontations, always postponing the definitive coda. In any case, too much has been published for any bibliography to be all inclusive—see, for example, the extensive and detailed bibliography in J. C. Hurewitz's superb *Struggle for Palestine*, reprinted by Greenwood in 1968, or my more general one in *The Long War: Israel and the Arabs Since 1946* (Englewood Cliffs, N.J.: Prentice-Hall, 1968). Even if the list is restricted to items directly relevant to the Palestine underground, there are massive primary and secondary sources ranging from the relevant British documents gradually being classified to the ragged pamphlets of the illicit presses of the time. There are memoirs, commentaries, articles in academic journals, special supplements to Hebrew newspapers, journalistic accounts, scholarly investigations—the entire range of printed sources, much of it in language usually beyond the grasp of a general audience.

Both LEHI and the Irgun have published the collected documents of the underground in Hebrew. (LEHI's volume one appeared in 1959, volume two in 1960; the Irgun's four volumes, edited by Begin, in 1959 and 1961.) Many of those in the Irgun and LEHI have also written on the underground struggle, again often in Hebrew: Eldad, Yellin-Mor, and Shmulevitz of LEHI, Lankin and Tavin of the Irgun. Fortunately, some of the most interesting or important works are in English: Begin's *The Revolt* (Los Angeles: Nash, 1972), which has become a handbook for aspiring revolutionaries—my copy was given me by a former IRA commander in Derry—Samuel Katz's *Days of Fire* (London: W. H. Allen, 1968), and his wife's recollections, *The Lady was a Terrorist* (New York: Shiloni, 1953), Meridor's *Long is the Road to Freedom* (Johannesburg: Newzo Press, 1955), Geula Cohen's *Woman of Violence: Memoirs of a Young Terrorist, 1943–1948* (London: Rupert Hart-Davis, 1966), and even a somewhat fictionalized *Memoirs of an Assassin* by "Avner" (London: Anthony Blond, 1959) which, like Cohen's book, gives the flavor of LEHI. On the other side of the hill, R. D. Wilson's *Cordon and Search*

(Aldershot: Gale and Polden, 1949) gives a British view. The basic work on the Irgun is David Niv's monumental six-volume study—four have been published—but again it is in Hebrew. Thus there is no single source in English for either LEHI or the Irgun, although there are several useful examinations, including Yehuda Bauer's impressive *From Diplomacy to Resistance: A History of Jewish Palestine, 1939–1945* (Philadelphia: Jewish Publication Society, 1970), the more emotional *Conquest of Acre Fortress* (Tel Aviv: Hardar, 1962) by Jan Gitlin, and a considerable number of scholarly articles, ranging from Y. S. Breener, "The 'Stern Gang' 1948," *Middle Eastern Studies*, October 1965, through M. J. Cohen, "British Strategy and the Palestine Question," *Journal of Contemporary History*, 7, nos. 3–4, July-October 1972.

There are a host of dissertations, theses and seminar papers, mostly in Hebrew, an exception being Daniel Levine's useful "David Raziel, the Man and His Times" (Doctorate of Hebrew letters, Yeshiva University, New York, 1969). Two excellent popular accounts are Larry Collins and Dominique Lapierre, *O Jerusalem!* (New York: Simon and Schuster, 1972) and Dan Kurzman, *Genesis 1948* (New York: World, 1970).

My primary sources for the book, however, were people rather than the printed word.

GREAT BRITAIN:

Lord Alport
Julian Amery
Lord Chandos (Oliver Lyttelton)
Lord Colyton (Henry Hopkinson)
Lord Harding
Sir Evelyn Hone
Tom Little
Lord Lloyd

Lord Radcliffe
John Reddaway
Lord Samuel
Lord Trevelyan
Sir Richard Turnbell
Sir John Shaw
Kenneth Younger

ISRAEL:

Haim Adar (Enders)
Bezalel Amizur
Yaakov Amrami
Menachem Begin
Yoel Bela
Yehuda Ben Ari
Arieh Ben-Eliezer
Yosef Chitirt
Geula Cohen
Yisrael Eldad (Scheib)
Julie Elazar-Torenberg
Yaacov Heruti
Yitshak Shamir (Izernitsky)

Yehuda Lapidot
Shlomo Levami
Eitan Livni
Yaacov Meridor
David Niv
Amihai Paglin
Jerachmiel Romm
Moshe Rosenberg
Avraham Selman
Boris Senior
Mattiyahu Shmulevitz
Anshuel Spilman
David Tahori

Meir (Marc) Kahan
Samuel Katz
Chaua Kirshenbaum (Lapidot)
Raphael Kotlovitz
Haim Landau
Eliahu Lankin

Palech Tamir
Ely Tavin
Avraham Tehomi
Moses Vegman
Ruth Winograd
Nathan Yellin-Mor (Friedman)

OTHER:

Emile el-Ghouri (Jordan)
Walid Khalidi (Lebanon)
Youseff Sayegh (Lebanon)
Khairy Hamad (Egypt)
Joseph B. Schectman (USA)

DATE DUE

12 May 77			
NOV 1 6 1979			
FE 4 '85			
GAYLORD			PRINTED IN U.S.A.